THE ROUGH GUIDE TO

CAMPING
IN BRITAIN

Publishing information

This 1st edition published March 2010 by

Rough Guides Ltd, 80 Strand, London WC2R 0RL

14 Local Shopping Centre, Panchsheel Park, New Delhi 110017, India

Distributed by the Penguin Group

Penguin Books Ltd, 80 Strand, London, WC2R 0RL

Penguin Group (USA), 375 Hudson Street, NY 10014, USA

Penguin Group (Australia) 250 Camberwell Road, Camberwell, Victoria 3124, Australia

Penguin Books Canada Ltd, 10 Alcorn Avenue, Toronto, Ontario, Canada, M4V 1E4

Penguin Group (NZ) 67 Apollo Drive, Mairangi Bay, Auckland 1310, New Zealand

Typeset in Gill Sans and Minion to an original design by Nicola Erdpresser

Printed and bound in China

© Rough Guides 2010

390pp includes index

A catalogue record for this book is available from the British Library

ISBN: 978-1-84836-214-7

The publishers and authors have done their best to ensure the accuracy and currency of all the
information in **The Rough Guide to Camping in Britain**, however, they can accept no responsibility
for any loss, injury, or inconvenience sustained by any traveller as a result of information or advice contained in the guide.

1   3   5   7   9   8   6   4   2

Credits and acknowledgements

Editor: James Smart **Managing editor**: Mani Ramaswamy **Contributing editors**: Lucy Cowie, Emma Gibbs,
James Rice, Alison Roberts, Harry Wilson **Design and layout**: Nicola Erdpresser **Picture editor**: Sarah Cummins
Cartographer: Ed Wright **Cover design**: Diana Jarvis **Proofreader**: Jennifer Speake
Production: Rebecca Short **Fact-checking**: Lisa Pettitt and Graeme Yeo

Writers

Devon and Cornwall: Hayley Spurway **The West Country**: James Stewart **Southeast England**: Ed Aves, Lucy Cowie, Keith Drew, Amanda Howard,
Rebecca Omonira-Oyekanmi, Alison Roberts and Viv Watton **East England**: Helena Smith **Midlands**: Rebecca Omonira-Oyekanmi and Helena Smith
South Wales: James Stewart with contributions from Alf Alderson **North Wales**: James Stewart **Northwest England**: Seb Bacon
Yorkshire: Alf Alderson **Cumbria and the Lakes**: Helena Smith **Northeast England**: Sarah Hone and Lucy White **Lowlands**: Ally Thompson
Highlands: Ally Thompson **Scottish Islands**: Rob Humpreys and Ally Thompson **Equipment**: Hayley Spurway **Glamping**: Amanda Howard
Adventure sports: James Stewart **Campsite cuisine**: Hayley Spurway **Festivals**: James Smart
Wild camping: Richard Hammond **Directory**: Harry Wilson

Thanks are due to our fine and indefatigable writers, to all the campsite owners and staff they visited and to all the campers they met on the way. Thanks also
to everyone at Rough Guides, especially Scott Stickland for calm problem-solving, Jo Kirby and Kathryn Lane for early planning, Nicole Newman and Mark
Thomas for additional photo help, Natasha Foges for indexing and Martin Dunford for his boundless experience and enthusiasm.

This book is printed on paper produced from environmentally sustainable sources certified by the Forest Stewardship Council (www.fsc.org).

Contents

Introduction

Camping has come of age since Rough Guides began in the 1980s. It's always been a big part of what we do, but back then camping was seen as the preserve of nerdy enthusiasts and budget holidays. It's become much more popular of late, with designer-print tents and glampsites with four-poster beds and chandeliers giving canvas a groovy image and a luxury sideline. But the essential appeal of camping – getting out into the fresh air and under the skin of a beautiful part of the country – remains unchanged.

Camping of course has its ups and downs: it's great in the summer when the sun is shining, and grim in the pounding rain when you can't see past your hands. Our writers have experienced their share of blue skies and muddy pitches while covering the length and breadth of Britain, from the Isles of Scilly to Shetland, using tent, car, foot, train, bus and campervan to separate the wheat from the chaff. We've hand-picked over three hundred sites, and visited them all.

This book contains some quirky and unique places – if you want to share your porch with a llama or stay on Britain's most remote peninsula, you've come to the right place. But we haven't neglected sites that just do their job well: well-run places that have decent facilities and enjoy great locations. We've flagged up those that are good for families, hikers, hedonists and more, noted where you can light a fire, take a dog, ride a bike or surf great breaks, grumbled when things aren't up to scratch and praised them wholeheartedly when they are. Our aim is that the *Rough Guide to Camping in Britain* will be your essential companion, discerning but wide-ranging, and full of practical detail and real enthusiasm. We hope you'll find it as useful as your tent.

James Smart
Editor

◀ Preparation is everything ▶ Getting close to nature on the Isle of Arran; a welcome sign; a campfire can enliven any trip

Britain's best campsites

We've recommended sites that are good for everything from cycling to solitude in the introduction to every regional chapter. The selection below spans the whole country, pinpointing the UK's very best campsites for the eco-conscious, campers with kids, outdoor fanatics, first-timers and more. There are scores more great sites in this book, but the ones below are a good place to start.

Bring the kids

Dan-yr-Ogof Atmospheric showcaves, fibreglass dinosaurs and real rheas in the Brecon Beacons. p.167

Fisherground Picturesque Lake District site with an adventure playground and a steam train. p.260

Lochhouses Farm Spot seabirds, explore East Lothian's countryside and head to the beach at this nostalgic glampsite. p.318

Treloan Kids can explore rock pools and collect eggs at this festive working farm in Cornwall. p.27

Welsummer Back to nature at a homely and hospitable North Downs gem. p.94

Green as the grass

Caerfai Organic Farm Anaerobic digesters, solar panels and a stunning Pembrokeshire seascape. p.152

Comrie Croft Compost toilets, low-energy lighting and more on this woodland-set Perthshire cooperative. p.328

Eco Retreats Top-end tipis with a conscience in Wales's renewable energy capital. p.182

Eweleaze Farm Splendidly simple Dorset organic farm that's one of England's most distinctive sites. p.48

South Penquite There's acres of space, the showers run on rainwater and Bodmin Moor is just round the corner. p.22

◄ Clockwise from top left: *Welsummer*; *Abbey Home Farm*; *fforestcamp*; *New House Farm*; *Caerfai Organic Farm*; *Shell Island*

Eat and be merry

Abbey Home Farm Gloucestershire's organic wonderland even has a resident cheesemaker. p.62

Dennis Cove Set on an estuary ten minutes from Padstow, with Rick Stein, a fish market and a vineyard on its doorstep. p.23

Hidden Spring Vineyard Relaxed Sussex vineyard offering their own strong cider and red and white wine. p.93

Talton Lodge Home-grown food, pasta-making courses and breakfast boxes at a tipi site near Stratford. p.132

Wapsbourne Manor Farm With excellent farm shops, on-site hog roasts and great pubs, this East Sussex beauty is fully stocked. p.82

Back of beyond

Crawshaw Farm It may be right by Britain's geographical centre, but this Lancashire site sits in glorious isolation. p.211

Kielder England's largest red squirrel colony – as well as midges – lurk in sprawling woodland near the Scottish border. p.292

Lundy Island Head through protected waters off the Devon coast to this island populated by puffins, deer and strange cabbages. p.31

Rackwick A half-deserted village and sandstone cliffs are your neighbours on the rocky Orkney island of Hoy. p.370

Sunk Island Hunker down at this simple, tranquil site, set by the dykes and mudflats of the Humber Estuary. p.240

Location, location

Beachcomber A short hop from Holy Island and a stone's throw from stunning Goswick Sands. p.299

Calgary Bay Wild camp by a stunning, Caribbean-style beach – the temperatures don't always match – on appealing Mull. p.361

Park Lodge Cool pools, crashing waterfalls and splendid Dales scenery distinguish this low-key Yorkshire base. p.230

Shell Island The largest campsite in Europe sits on a sandy hook off Cardigan Bay; it feels like another world. p.190

Southwold The static caravans may not appeal; the sandy beaches, ancient villages and lovely town of Southwold will. p.112

The great outdoors

Cwmcarn Forest World-class mountain-bike trails cut through the forest that surrounds this Welsh Valleys site. p.169

Gillside Hike up Helvellyn, cycle round tremendous Lakeland scenery or glide out onto Ullswater from this working farm. p.275

Llyn Gwynant Rock climbing, coasteering and kayaking trips run from this scenic spot, only a few miles from Snowdon. p.189

Marthrown of Mabie An impressive range of bike tracks head from the door of this sauna-boasting, activity-packed Dumfries-shire site. p.308

North Lees Mighty Stanage Edge looms above this friendly Peak District campsite, a fine base for hikers and climbers. p.146

Weird and wonderful

Barge Inn Popular with crop circlers, mystics and boaties, this pub-garden has a reputation as Wiltshire's "Hotel California". p.59

Caerlaverock Simple camping in a Lowlands nature reserve with ospreys, geese and dragonflies. p.314

New House Farm Learn weaving or blacksmithery, walk ley lines and lounge in yurts at this inspiring Derbyshire base. p.139

Orchard Camping UFOs have been spotted above these Suffolk fields; there's a registered observatory on site. p.108

Vintage Vacations Stay in one of ten classic trailers on the Isle of Wight, eat with retro crockery and groove to Fifties tunes. p.74

First-timers

Clippesby Hall Heated toilet and shower blocks, archery, mini-golf and a grass tennis court on a big, friendly Norfolk site. p.110

fforestcamp Home to a sauna, room service and tipis; canoeing, bushcraft and surfing get you out into the Welsh wilds. p.164

Highside Farm Welcoming owners, cooked breakfasts and Pennines views – and only eight pitches keeps things personal. p.286

South Breazle Pine-seated loos, flower-bordered pitches and trim lawns make this Devon site a decidedly civilized one. p.26

Woodland Tipis Yurts and tipis set in the Herefordshire woods with quirky personal touches and a great shared kitchen. p.129

Devon and Cornwall

A region crammed with wild moors and rugged sea cliffs, the western toe of the country boasts the UK's mildest climate and lures campers long beyond the summer months.

For coast fans there are few better places to enjoy life under canvas than in Devon and Cornwall. Here you can pitch a tent by pearly bays, atop staggering cliffs and in beach-view meadows, or cast off from the mainland and camp out on the Isles of Scilly or Lundy Island.

As beaches are one of the region's biggest attractions, it's no surprise that campsites nudging the wave-lashed shores get crowded in the holidays — especially when the sun shines. So to truly get away from it all, step inland to the beguiling moors, rolling countryside and wooded valleys. Here you can wake to the dawn chorus, share woodland with deer and light a campfire by a stream.

Shrugging off their dowdy image, campsites in Devon and Cornwall offer quirky, original and, at times, luxurious places to stay. Bypass the busy holiday parks and choose from yurts and tipis with all the trimmings, tent-and-breakfast by the sea or old-school camping where stereos are banned and campfires encouraged. There's also an abundance of low-impact, eco-friendly campsites.

Cyclists will enjoy the mineral trails and moors, watersports fans the waves and estuaries, and hikers the coastal paths. But it's not all about the great outdoors — you're never far from an appealing country village for locally sourced provisions and a pint of real ale, while dedicated foodies can pitch their tents close to the restaurants of chefs Jamie Oliver and Rick Stein.

Lundy Island

Ilfracombe
North Morte Farm
Little Meadow
A361
A3123
A39
Barnstap
A39
Bideford
B32
A377
A388
A386
A3124
A3072
DEVO
Hole Station
A3079
Okehampto
South Breazle
B3263
A39
B3254
A30
Belle Tents
A395
Launceston
Cornish Tipis
Bodmin Moor
DARTMOO
Padstow
B3314
A30
NATIONAL P
Tavistock
B3357
Dennis Cove
South Penquite
A389
B3276
Bedruthan Steps
A39
CORNWALL
A388
Newquay
A390
Liskeard
A38
A391
A390
Plymouth
A38
A3075
A30
A3058
St Austell
A387
A390
A379
Churchtown Farm
Truro
Broad Meadow House
St Ives
A30
Redruth
A39
A3078
Golden Lion Inn
Noongallas
B3311
B3306
Treloan
B3280
Penzance
B3297
A394
Falmouth
B3315
A394
Helston
Gear Farm
Treen Farm
B3293
A3083
St Martin's
Henry's
Troytown Farm

Cloud Farm
A39 Minehead
B3358
EXMOOR
NATIONAL PARK
A396
A39
A358
Taunton
A38
A361
B3137
Tiverton
M5
A3072
A373
A303
Honiton
A30
A35
A358
A377
Exeter
Cuckoo Down Yurts
A376
A3052
A379
Exmouth
Prattshayes Farm
Cockingford Farm
A383
Torquay
Paignton
A3122
Dartmouth
Old Cotmore Farm

Devon and Cornwall

	PAGE	🚶	🚲	⛵	🍷	🏔	👥	👨‍👩‍👧‍👦	🚐	🚌	♿
Bedruthan Steps	26	✓			✓				✓	✓	
Belle Tents	30	✓						✓			
Broad Meadow House	24	✓	✓	✓	✓						
Churchtown Farm	15				✓		✓		✓		✓
Cloud Farm	39	✓	✓								
Cockingford Farm	38		✓				✓		✓		
Cornish Tipis	19						✓	✓			
Cuckoo Down Yurts	36					✓					
Dennis Cove	23			✓	✓						
Gear Farm	19						✓		✓	✓	
Golden Lion Inn	18		✓				✓		✓		
Henry's	14						✓		✓		
Hole Station	30		✓				✓				
Little Meadow	32	✓		✓					✓	✓	
Lundy Island	31	✓		✓			✓				
Noongallas	15						✓	✓	✓		✓
North Morte Farm	34	✓					✓		✓		✓
Old Cotmore Farm	35				✓		✓		✓		✓
Prattshayes Farm	38		✓	✓			✓		✓	✓	✓
South Breazle	26			✓			✓		✓		✓
South Penquite	22	✓	✓				✓				
St Martin's	12						✓	✓	✓		
Treen Farm	20								✓		
Treloan	27	✓		✓			✓		✓	✓	
Troytown Farm	16			✓		✓		✓			

See front flap for key to symbols

St Martin's

Get sand between your toes on an Atlantic archipelago

Tempted by the barefoot lifestyle? Bag a pitch by the white-sand beach in this pristine island location: although you miss out on sea views from your tent, if you lobbed a pebble over the pittosporum hedge it would probably land in the ocean. Yes, paradise is that close to your sleeping bag. And the hedge isn't just there to block the view – it offers a good bit of shelter when the setting is less sunny-Caribbean and more stormy-Cornwall.

With its stunning location, super-friendly, safe environment and sparkly-clean facilities, it's no wonder this campsite is a family haven. Don't even bother trying to bag a spot in mid-summer – they're snapped up a year in advance. *St Martin's* is at its best outside the holidays, but even at full capacity there's enough space for the beach lovers, couples and kayakers that flock to this former flower farm.

Part of an archipelago 28 miles off the southwest tip of England, St Martin's is the third-largest of the Isles of Scilly. Just a short hop from the mainland by ferry or flight, life here is light years away from the rest of Britain, and this tiny island (just two-miles by three-quarters of a mile) offers a lot more than seaside camping. Think cliff-top walks, gourmet food and miles of sandy beaches for windsurfing, kayaking, diving, snorkelling (equipment and tuition provided) and swimming (beware, the sea isn't as balmy as it looks). Away from the beaches, you can explore ancient burial sites and meadows of wildflowers, spot rare birds or play tennis. When rain stops play most visitors head to St Mary's, the biggest of the islands and home to a museum, heritage centre and pretty boutiques, but even if it's wet on St Martin's you can still go snorkelling with seals or sample wine on the UK's most westerly vineyard.

If you don't fancy lighting a stove or barbecue, the site owners will bake jacket potatoes to order and pizza can be delivered from the bakery. Beyond base camp lies a smorgasbord of foodie gems: enjoy Michelin-starred dining at *St Martin's on the Isle* hotel's *Tean Restaurant*, pub grub at the *Sevenstones Inn*, organic fare at *Little Arthur's Café* and fish and chips from *Adam's* – one of the UK's smallest, most remote takeaways. Fill up on fresh veg from the campsite and farm stalls, or stroll ten minutes to Highertown for the post office and general store, bakery and tearooms.

Practicalities

St Martin's Campsite, Middletown, St Martin's, Isles of Scilly, TR25 0QN ☎*01720 422888,* Ⓦ*www.stmartinscampsite.co.uk*

Pitches & price 50 standard/trailer tent pitches (100 campers maximum). £8–10 per person (children under 5 half price). Booking essential at peak times. If you don't fancy sleeping under canvas, there's a 1950s self-catering chalet in the garden (£170 per week).

Facilities A chalet-style male/female shower and toilet block is decked out with hand basins, loos (rated the cleanest in Scilly), 2 decent showers for each sex, baby-changing facilities and hair dryers. As well as 2 sheltered washing-up sinks and separate water tap, there's a laundry with washing machine, dryer, iron and sinks. In the barn are power points, freezers for ice-blocks and basic camping gear (pegs, gas, disposable BBQs etc) for sale. Limited disabled access. Wi-fi on site.

Restrictions No dogs. Campfires only permitted on the beach. No noise after 10.30pm. Single-sex groups out of peak times only.

Open Mar–Oct. Arrivals here are restricted to local boat times.

Getting there Ferry or helicopter from Penzance, or fly from Land's End, Newquay, Exeter, Bristol or Southampton. Flights land on St Mary's – a 15min ferry hop to St Martin's, where the owners will pick you up in the Landrover or tractor (£7 return/£10 for camping trailers).

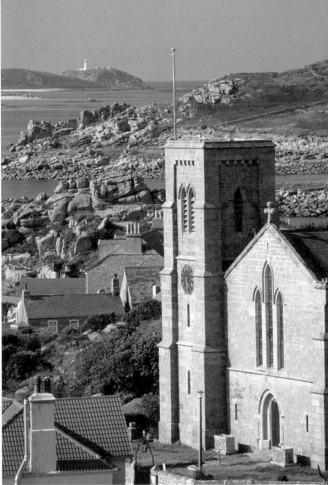

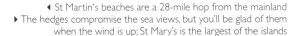

◀ St Martin's beaches are a 28-mile hop from the mainland
▶ The hedges compromise the sea views, but you'll be glad of them when the wind is up; St Mary's is the largest of the islands

Henry's
Basking sharks, sunsets and sub-tropical serenity

Switch off your mobile and leave your radio at home. Beyond the shelter belt of plants there is nothing but verdant meadows between you and the beat of the Atlantic. Pitch a tent at *Henry's* and you're in a prime spot to crack open a beer and watch the sunset away from the tourist huddle at the foot of the Lizard lighthouse.

With its level, grassy pitches bordered by sub-tropical plants, this lush garden campsite is the backyard of Jo and Ron Lyne, who took over from Ron's dad, Henry himself. For all the ramshackle charm of its farmyard setting, the quirky site is lovingly tended to: wafts of Jo's delicious scones leak from the farmhouse, art sculptures are positioned among the foliage, chickens cluck on the sidelines and colourful kites flutter in the ocean breeze.

Stray from your tent and the coast path will lead you on a scenic tour in either direction. Kynance Cove – dubbed one of Britain's most beautiful beaches – is a twenty-minute walk west along a dramatic coastline chiselled by wind and waves. A chal-

lenging hike along the eastern flank of the peninsula leads to the fishing village of Cadgwith, where you can pick up the daily catch for your barbecue. Further on, Kennack Sands is made for snorkelling and kayaking, and Coverack for windsurfing or spotting basking sharks. For a day out with a difference opt for camel trekking on the downs or just ogle these friendly beasts at Cornish Camels (Ⓦwww.cornishcamels.com).

It's rare to find a campsite this special that's so easily accessible by public transport and just minutes' walk from a village hub. With its twee cottages and gift shops trading the area's serpentine rock, Lizard has all the essentials – from a post office, café and pub to Ann's famous pasty shop. In peak season a small shop is run on the campsite (selling tea, fresh eggs and camping gas) and you can get your hands on fresh lobster and crab from the neighbours. The only downside about coming here in the holidays – if you can bag a pitch – is that it gets swamped by high-spirited kids who can somewhat alter the peace and quiet of the setting.

▾ Lizard Point, a few minutes' walk from *Henry's*

Practicalities

Henry's Caerthillian Farm, The Lizard, Cornwall, TR I 2 7NX Ⓣ*01326 290596,* Ⓦ*www.henryscampsite.co.uk*

Pitches & price 45 level, grassy pitches (20 hook-ups, 10 spaces for caravans/trailer tents). £7 per adult, £3 per child.

Facilities Unisex amenities include 7 loos and 3 showers spread across stone-and-wood farm buildings. Drinking water and a washing-up sink are outside. Washing machine and mobile phone-charging facilities. Ice-blocks can be frozen for you.

Restrictions Dogs permitted. Campfires not permitted, but braziers are available to borrow.

Open Year round.

Getting there Hop on a bus from Helston; it's a 5min walk from the stop at Lizard village. By car follow the A3083 from Helston to Lizard, take the first right across the village green, then the second right.

Churchtown Farm

When the swell's up, surfers flock to this expansive, bay-side site, which nudges a maze of "towans" (Cornish for sand dunes) and is linked to one of Cornwall's top surfing beaches by a sandy walkway. But, with generous grassy pitches looking out to Godrevy lighthouse (immortalized in Virginia Woolf's *To the Lighthouse*), the South West Coast Path on its doorstep and three miles of pearly sand a short barefoot walk away, the wave-riders aren't *Churchtown Farm*'s only fans.

In the twenty years since the site was handed down through the family to Geoffrey and Barbara James, the setting – pampas-swathed dunes on one side and the quintessential Cornish village of Gwithian on the other – has remained virtually unchanged. But the business has moved with the times, now offering sleek modern amenities. As well as an on-site shop, the milkman delivers newspapers and basic provisions, and within walking distance there's the cosy *Red River Inn* for a pint and local cuisine, and a handful of beach cafés for cakes served with a side order of surf lessons.

Practicalities

Churchtown Farm Caravan & Camping Site, Gwithian, Hayle, Cornwall, TR27 5BX ☎01736 753219, Ⓦwww.churchtownfarm.org.uk

Pitches & price 100 pitches (75 hook-ups). £9–20 for a two-person tent; £10.50–21.50 for a 6-berth tent (including 2 adults and 2 children under 10). Additional adults £4, children (under 16) £2.50.

Facilities Excellent male/female amenities block with plentiful showers, loos and basins. 2 baby-changing cubicles, disabled bathroom, wetsuit shower, laundry, indoor utility room. Shop and information point on site.

Restrictions Dogs allowed (£2–3). No campfires.

Open Easter–Oct.

Getting there Leave the A30 at Hayle and follow the B3301 to Gwithian. The campsite is past the church on the left. Western Greyhound runs a bus service from Penzance.

Noongallas

Its five sprawling meadows climbing up from a wooded valley and trickling stream, *Noongallas* feels miles from anywhere. But this well-hidden site is in fact just two miles from harbour-side Penzance, where trains arrive regularly from London Paddington. Owners John and Kay Line have stowed themselves away here for more than thirty years, so it only seems fair they share it with a few campers in the summertime.

Pitch up high for far-reaching views to Mount's Bay, or down low to shelter by the woods (the downside to the latter is the clamber back uphill to the loos). There are swings, a see-saw and crash mats for kids, and house martins nest in the rafters of an old dance hall where impromptu music sessions take place on many summer evenings. Penzance, with art galleries, antique shops and excursions to St Michael's Mount, is a short bus ride away, but many visitors are content to sit by the campfire, stargaze or join in a jamming session in this wild meadow setting. If you can't chill out at *Noongallas*, your strings are well and truly taut.

Practicalities

Noongallas Campsite, Gulval, Penzance, Cornwall, TR20 8YR ☎01736 366698, Ⓦwww.noongallas.com

Pitches & price About 100 pitches. £5 per adult (£2.50 per child). 2 holiday cottages also to let.

Facilities Simple but decent amenities with large showers, fridge/freezers and a kettle. Sheltered washing-up area.

Restrictions Dogs allowed (free). Campfires permitted.

Open July & Aug (extension applied for).

Getting there Leave the A30 at Crowlas, turning right at the crossroads just after the pub. Turn left onto the B3311, following the road towards Gulval, where you take a tiny right turning, which is signposted Rosemorran and Polkinghorne. *Noongallas* is about 1.5 miles up the lane. From Penzance station (trains run to Exeter, London Paddington and Bristol) it's about £6–7 by taxi.

Troytown Farm
Simple pleasures at the world's end

Perched on what quite literally feels like the edge of the world, *Troytown Farm* stares out to sea from Britain's most westerly outpost. Gently sloping fields meet the shores of the mile-wide island of St Agnes, from where you can open your tent to view a scattering of uninhabited islets petering out into 3000 miles of uninterrupted Atlantic – an enviable location until you're at the brunt of a storm. For all its rugged personality, the location also boasts a strip of pearly white sand that's safe for swimming and snorkelling (bring a wetsuit, the water's cold!). A working family farm, *Troytown* not only gets Brownie points for its wild paradise setting, but also for its lip-smacking ice cream, made from a small herd of Jersey and Ayrshire cows.

To fit in here you need to be self-sufficient. Entertainment comes in the form of simply getting on with the camping lifestyle: light a fire on the beach as the sun sets, take a breath of briny air and let the world go by. Those looking for a little more activity might grab a shrimp net, cast a line out to sea in search of supper or spot the rare birds – including the red-breasted flycatcher and yellow-browed warbler – that pause here during spring and autumn migrations. This is an idyllic location for kayaking and snorkelling, and divers flock here to check out the wrecks that litter the island's shores. A place of such minute pro-portions (the population is just seventy) doesn't come decked out with a water-sports shop, but kit rental and tuition are avail-able from other islands.

A circuit of St Agnes reveals cliff-top downs strewn with wild-flowers, granite stacks rising from aquamarine depths and shel-tered coves perfect for bathing and rock-pooling. When the tide ebbs you can cross the sand bar to the neighbouring Isle of Gugh. For all the drama of its landscape, the island's inner character is chocolate-box quaint, with teashops, pretty stone cottages and a decommissioned lighthouse.

The site doesn't match up to the island's flawless beauty in every arena – the amenities are a bit tired and the occasional whiff of manure reminds you this is a working farm. Still, that means you don't have to go far from your tent to sample a taste of Scilly: there's an on-site shop for ice cream, fresh milk, clotted cream and farm-reared meat. The post office and general store is ten minutes' walk, but to save you the footwork you can pre-order groceries to be delivered on arrival.

The Turk's Head is the only watering hole, serving stunning waterside views alongside decent pub grub, local ales and live music. In addition there's a couple of cream-tea cafés, including the *Coastguard's Café*, a former model boat shop that dresses up into a decent fish restaurant in the evening.

If you feel the need to escape, regular boat trips will take you island-hopping, bird-watching and out to cheer on the gig races, in which local rowing clubs challenge each other. Apart from eating and drinking there's little to do on rainy days, save hiding out in the cafés, donning waterproofs for a coastal wander or

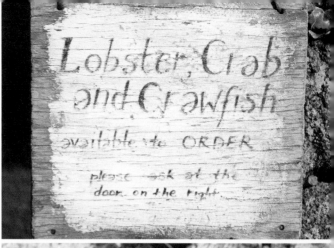

Practicalities

Troytown Farm, St Agnes, Isles of Scilly, TR22 0PL
☏ *01720 422360,* Ⓦ *www.troytown.co.uk*

Pitches & price About 50 standard pitches (100 people maximum); trailer tents welcome (large groups accommodated in a separate field). £7–8 per person (under-3s free). An additional charge of £1–7 per tent during summer holidays. 3 self-catering lets are also available.

Facilities A tired but adequate shower block with 4 unisex showers, separate male and female loos, baby-changing station and hair dryers. Water is precious here and you are asked to conserve it. Indoor washing-up area and laundry (washing machine, dryer, iron and power points). Gas cartridges, methylated spirits, barbecues and ice packs available.

Restrictions Dogs permitted (£2), although this must be pre-arranged. Campfires forbidden in the fields but allowed on the beach.

Open March–Oct. Arrival times restricted by local boat schedules.

Getting there Ferry or helicopter from Penzance, or fly from Land's End, Newquay, Exeter, Bristol or Southampton. Flights land on St Mary's – a 15min ferry ride to St Agnes, where the last leg is a 15min trot on foot (some of it on bumpy farm track), or the owners will pick up from the quay (£3 return/£14 for a camping trailer).

heading to the main island of St Mary's for a spot of shopping. Of course, this being Cornwall, most of the rain tends to fall in the six weeks of midsummer – the right time to avoid the site as it's fully booked way in advance.

◀ *Troytown Farm* stares across the Atlantic ▶ Seafood can be bought from local fishermen; the farm's cows supply milk for the on-site shop

Golden Lion Inn

Eat, drink, sleep and play Boggle by the lake

Not only is this intimate and friendly campsite on the edge of a water-sports and angling centre, but your tent is also pitched in the garden of a cosy inn serving award-winning tucker and fine local ales. So far, so good.

A family set-up, the nineteenth-century inn was once a farmers' drinking den where machinery auctions used to take place. Despite being a stone's throw from the bar, the small, level site is a peaceful spot and certainly not kitted out for rowdy groups. Instead it attracts active couples, a handful of families and more mature campers looking to relax.

Located just footsteps from the five-mile-long reservoir and Stithians Lake Watersports Centre, this is a great site for those looking to get out on the water. At the more sedate end of the spectrum there's lakeside walking, fishing, bird-watching and plenty of space to relax under the palm fronds. When you've dried out and got back to base camp, pull up a chair at the inn and fuel up on local fare washed down with Cornish ales or fine wines and perhaps accompanied by a game of Boggle or Monopoly.

A fine choice for foodies of all calibres, here the best Cornish ingredients are whipped into a range of dishes from pies to posh nosh. Whatever you order, you can choose to dine al-fresco on the heated terrace, in the garden-flanked restaurant or by the roaring fire. There's also a café and plenty of picnic spots around the lake, and if you want to pick up produce for the camping stove or barbecue, it's not far to the Four Lanes farm shop.

Although you could happily stay here without a car – it's just a couple of miles to Stithians village for supplies – the location between the north and south coasts (about 15min drive to each) makes it a good base to explore Cornwall. There are surfing beaches to the north and Falmouth to the south, with Poldark Mine and the Great Flat Lode Trail (where you can walk and cycle through some of the region's richest mining heritage) in the middle.

▼ The *Golden Lion Inn* is a tranqil spot

Practicalities

Golden Lion Inn, Stithians Lake, Menherion, Redruth, Cornwall, TR16 6NW ☎01209 860332, Ⓦ*www.golden-lion-inn.co.uk*

Pitches & price 22 pitches (10 standard, 12 hook-ups, including 2 hard-standing). £13–17 for 2 people; £2 per extra person per night.

Facilities 2 toilets and 2 showers in individual cubicles. Separate indoor washing-up/clothes-washing area. Power points and wi-fi available in the inn. Disabled access to campsite and pub.

Restrictions Dogs allowed on site and in the bar. No campfires.

Open Year round.

Getting there Turn off the B3280 at Four Lanes (towards Stithians) and follow the lane to a T-junction – the *Golden Lion Inn* is signposted. Turn right and it's 500yds on the left. The closest train station is Redruth, about 5 miles away.

Gear Farm

Above the banks of the Helford River, where wealthy waterside residents are far outnumbered by wildlife, a small piece of land has been set aside for campers. And despite being an exclusive corner of Cornwall, there are no airs and graces at this back-to-basics campsite: you get a field with a view and a barn with clean – certainly not posh – scrubbing-up facilities. A few footsteps from the handful of tents, wafts of baking summon you to the Gear Farm Shop, which offers an assortment of local food – from home-baked bread to hot pasties and fresh seafood.

Although your tent bags a four-star view of the Helford River, it takes about half-an-hour to reach the water's edge on foot. But being a simple, fair-weather site, walking is just the sort of activity most campers have in mind. At the riverside you can picnic and spot egrets and herons. Four miles from the campsite a ferry runs over the river to Helford Passage, from where it's a short stroll to Trebah or Glendurgan gardens. If it's raining, you might meet the cows and eat ice cream at Roskilly's Farm or opt for a more upmarket taste of Cornwall at the *New Yard Restaurant*, which is part of the squeaky-green Trelowarren Estate.

Practicalities

Gear Farm, St Martin, Helston, Cornwall, TR12 6DE
℡ *01326 221364*, Ⓦ *www.caravancampingsites.co.uk/ cornwall/gearfarmcamping.htm*
Pitches & price 15 tents (no hook-ups), £8 per adult, £20 per family (2 adults and 2 under-14s). There is also a Caravan Club site (5 spaces).
Facilities Toilet and sink in the field; separate barn with toilets, showers, washing-up facilities and power points.
Restrictions Dogs welcome but limited to 1 per family. No campfires.
Open Spring Bank Holiday–end Sept. Campers should arrive by dark.
Getting there Follow the A3083 from Helston. After 2 miles take the first exit at the roundabout onto the B3293. At the next roundabout, take the second exit to Mawgan. *Gear Farm* is 2 miles further on at the top of the hill (after the second bridge).

Cornish Tipis

Tipis are often associated with the luxurious end of camping, and here the canvas dens are already in situ, decked out with rugs, stove, cool-box, cooking equipment and gas lamps. But, with basic camping mats, BYO sleeping bags and no electricity or vehicles on site, this former quarry is simple enough to make its sixteen-acre setting in a wooded valley the focus of visits. The welcome booklet primes you with a guide to local wildlife and, with fire-pits outside each tipi, campfires and kicking back are a big part of life here.

There are private clearings and more sociable village fields, but the pièce de la résistance is the lake – a Swallows and Amazons setting ideal for swimming, fishing and messing around on rowing boats. The downside is that the valley can get soggy, you have to lug your kit to your site, and some of the older tipis are looking a bit fed up with the British weather. It feels remote, but you're just ten minutes' drive from the surf beaches and the fishing village of Port Isaac on the north coast, while the country pubs and wild walking terrain of Bodmin Moor are within easy reach to the south.

Practicalities

Cornish Tipi Holidays, Tregeare, Pendoggett, St Kew, Cornwall, PL30 3LW ℡ *01208 880781,*
Ⓦ *www.cornish-tipi-holidays.co.uk*
Pitches & price 40 tipis sleeping 2–12 people. Weekly: £375–745 per tipi, £35 per person. Short breaks from £275 per tipi. Minimum stay 2 nights.
Facilities Small blocks with loos and showers in both the upper and lower village fields, as well as a larger shower block and drying barn with washing facilities.
Restrictions No stag groups and no dogs allowed. Campfires permitted.
Open Mid-March to end Oct.
Getting there Coming from the north on the B3314 continue a couple of miles out of Delabole and take the second of two left turnings signposted to St Teath (at the cross-roads with Port Gaverne). After the old railway bridge take the first right.

Treen Farm

Camp on a Cornish cliff-top

During World War II *Treen Farm* was commandeered by the RAF as a radar station, where the best feature of the barracks was surely the world-class view to some of West Cornwall's most rugged coastline. Now the farm is back in the hands of the Hall family, who reclaimed it and opened it up to campers. And although the barracks are still standing as a toilet block, it's the same stunning location that is the campsite's trump card.

Picnic benches have been thoughtfully scattered to take in the view over some of the UK's most unpolluted waters. On a blue-sky day you can see as far as the Isles of Scilly. But when foul weather scuds across the Atlantic, there's little to shelter your tent from storms (which is why the owners keep a stock of spare poles and camping equipment to hand). As a place where the landscape provides the entertainment, boom boxes are not welcome, although you often hear fiddlers and banjo players strumming more mellow tunes before quiet descends at 10pm.

From the barely sloping fields perched atop staggering cliffs – terrain much favoured by climbers – a steep path leads down to the pristine Pedn Vounder beach, where sunbathers (and some naturists) enjoy the white sands. A hop further is Porthcurno beach, above which the famous Minack Theatre is carved into the rocks – a spectacular setting where unscripted dolphins have turned up in the backdrop of many plays. With easy access to the South West Coast Path, the site attracts hikers making their way between Cape Cornwall and Mousehole, while more leisurely walkers stroll the couple of miles to Land's End.

Although the site is remote and the atmosphere edging on sleepy, there's enough going on locally to ditch the car on arrival. The tiny village of Treen has a café serving breakfasts and cream teas, as well as the *Logan Rock Inn* – a proper Cornish boozer with low-beamed ceilings, local ales, a roaring fire and decent food. It's about four miles to St Buryan for a grocery store, post office and another drinking hole, but you don't even have to stray that far to get your hands on supplies: organic dairy produce can be bought from neighbouring farms and the campsite shop sells essentials – from freshly baked bread and free-range eggs to camping gas.

If the rain kicks in, take shelter at the Porthcurno Telegraph Museum and discover how this little outpost was the epicentre

Practicalities

Treen Farm, St Levan, Penzance, Cornwall, TR19 6LF
☎*01736 810273,* ⓦ*www.treenfarmcampsite.co.uk*

Pitches & price About 50 standard pitches (100 people maximum); trailer tents welcome (groups accommodated in a separate field, though see below for restrictions). £7–8 per person (under-3s free). An additional charge of £1–7 per tent in summer holidays. 3 self-catering lets are also available.

Facilities Ample, clean facilities, with 2 male/female shower blocks plus 4 unisex shower cubicles, washing machine, tumble dryer and freezers. Covered washing-up areas. Disabled access.

Restrictions Dogs allowed for no extra charge. Maximum stay 3 weeks. No campfires. No caravans. No large groups (except for climbers or walkers).

Open April–Oct.

Getting there Follow the A30 past Penzance, then turn off on the B3283 (signposted Porthcurno) and join the B3315 just past St Buryan. Turn left into Treen and past the *Logan Rock Inn*; the campsite is along a farm track opposite the village shop/café.

of Victorian communications, or head north to the Geevor Tin Mine for an underground tour and a pasty. For a change of beach scene, Sennen Cove is a good spot to try surfing.

In this popular little place, pitches can't be booked ahead and are delegated on a first-come, first-served basis (with the exception of a handful set aside for coast-path walkers), so it can be a hard task to bag a pitch in midsummer. If you insist on coming here in the holidays, arrive at 8am and be patient. It's worth it – just ask the couple who have been coming back for fifty years.

◀ Lovely Porthcurno beach, surrounded by granite cliffs ▶ Geevor Tin Mine operated until 1990 and is now a museum; the Minack Theatre

South Penquite
Farmyard camping on the Moor

"Once upon a time I owned a farm with a campsite on the side. Now I've got a campsite with a farm on the side," jokes Dominic Fairman of his family's debut on the camping scene. For first-timers they've got the ingredients spot on – a spacious, peaceful location, excellent (eco-friendly) amenities and all just a swerve off the A30. Of the two-hundred-acre organic farm nudging Bodmin Moor, four grassy acres have been designated for a maximum of 120 campers to sprawl out. "When I tell people we're fully booked in the summer, they take one look and insist there's plenty of room. But that's the way we like it."

The Fairmans have farmed *South Penquite* since 1977, but it wasn't until 1999 that they invested in basic toilets and showers and opened a camping field for the eclipse. Fast-forward a decade and the spanking-new shower block has solar panels and family-sized shower cubicles waterproofed using recycled yoghurt pots. If that isn't impressive enough, add phosphorate-free shower gel, extensive recycling facilities and showers that run on rainwater.

Yet for all its green credentials, the ethos here is all about plain and simple camping. No hook-ups. No frills. That is unless you stay in one of the four locally made yurts with wood burners, gas stoves and futons.

Aside from space and super-sized showers, there are yet more family credentials worth mentioning. Situated far off the road, it's a safe location for kids to run around, plus there are swings, a football ground, a farm education centre and a farm trail that winds through disused quarries and along the banks of the De Lank River, bringing you face-to-face with Cheviot sheep and Galloway cows en route. The nearby village of St Breward has riding stables.

If it's not the sort of weather for tramping across the moors to ancient standing stones or scaling Cornwall's highest peak (Brown Willy), take cover in the cosy teashops and pubs of Blisland and St Breward, book a massage in your tent or hop in the car and head to the Eden Project (about 30min away).

> ▼ Three stone circles known as the Hurlers stand on Bodmin Moor

Practicalities

South Penquite, Blisland, Bodmin, Cornwall, PL30 4LH
☏ 01208 850491, Ⓦ *www.southpenquite.co.uk*
Pitches & price 120 campers maximum. No hook-ups. Large groups welcome out of peak season. £6 per adult, £3 per child (5–16). Four yurts sleeping 2–6 (weekly stays £190–290). VW Camper also for rent (from £64 per day, £470 per week).
Facilities Family-sized, solar-heated showers in a wood-panelled block with sheltered washing-up area. New pine-clad loo block. Laundry and freezer. Secure lockers for charging mobile phones. Walking books, firewood, farm sausages and burgers available. Limited disabled access.
Restrictions No dogs. Campfires allowed.
Open May–Oct.
Getting there Turn off the A30 towards St Breward, winding along the road about 2 miles across open moor and ignoring any turns until you reach the *South Penquite* lane on your right.

Dennis Cove
Foodie delights and tranquil slopes

An unassuming little gem nestled alongside the Camel estuary, *Dennis Cove* is a ten-minute amble from one the country's most notable foodie havens – Padstow. Once known as "Petrock's Stow", after the saint who founded a monastery here, these days the Cornish fishing village is more often referred to as "Padstein" after Rick Stein, the chef who has launched a plethora of gastronomic havens amid its twisting lanes.

For all its proximity to the preened charm of Padstow, the campsite's offerings are low-key and tranquil. Birdsong dominates the airwaves and lush meadows slope towards a glistening estuary that yawns into the Atlantic. But as you'd expect in a place so well known for its food, the simple life comes with a side order of indulgence as filling as you care to tuck into: go fishing for mackerel, buy seafood from the harbour fish market and sizzle it on the barbecue, or eat fish and chips by the sea. Beyond a cluster of establishments bearing the famous chef's icon there's a trove of places to eat and drink – *The Shipwrights Inn* is a great spot to watch quayside life and *Number 6 Restaurant* (launched by Paul Ainsworth, one of Ramsay's protégés) rivals the offerings of the town's master chef.

The stunning backdrop by no means takes a backseat to the gourmet reputation of the location. As well as sailing and surfing, the biggest attraction is the Camel Trail – an eighteen-mile walking and cycling route between Bodmin and Padstow. Being virtually flat it's a family favourite, and a stop-off at the market town of Wadebridge or the award-winning Camel Valley vineyard adds a civilized touch to any two-wheeled adventure (bike rental is available within walking distance of the campsite). Keen walkers should also note the site is by the Saints' Way, an ancient pilgrimage route between Padstow and Fowey.

Practicalities

Dennis Cove Camping, Dennis, Padstow, Cornwall, PL28 8DR ☎*01841 532349,* Ⓦ*www.denniscove.co.uk*

Pitches & price 43 standard (5 with hook-ups). An additional meadow opens in midsummer. £13.50–18 per pitch (tent, van/car and 2 people). Additional adult/child from £4/£1.90. Hikers (no car) £6.50–8.50.

Facilities Basic amenities block with ample showers, toilets and basins (power points for mobiles and hair dryers). Separate family shower. Washing-up stall with multiple sinks; laundry facilities. Information point at reception. Limited disabled access.

Restrictions Noise restrictions 10pm–7.30am. Dogs allowed (£1.30–2 per night). No campfires.

Open Easter–end Sept. Latest arrivals 9.30pm (pre-arrange arrivals after 7pm).

Getting there Turn into Padstow on the A389 and take the first right at Tesco – there is a brown campsite sign. Down the hill, turn right at the crossroads into Dennis Lane. Keep going past a lake to the campsite.

▼ Padstow harbour, a ten-minute walk from the campsite

Broad Meadow House

Breakfast in bed and tall ships on the horizon

Any seasoned camper can admit to occasionally wishing they didn't have to rise from a snug sleeping bag and faff around with a camping stove, last night's dishes and today's breakfast. At *Broad Meadow House*, tucked into a picturesque crease in south Cornwall's undulating coastline, you can wake up to bacon, croissants and fresh coffee delivered to your tent door. With three breakfast baskets to choose from, all you have to do is pop your order through the letterbox of the owner's house – footsteps from your pitch – before you go to bed. And it's not just the novelty factor of an Aga-cooked breakfast in bed that scores well here: the tomatoes are fresh from the vine (in season), eggs are laid by hens on site, croissants are home-baked, and the rest is locally sourced where possible.

The camper firmly in search of creature comforts needn't even erect a tent. As well as room for a handful of DIY campers, there are three pre-pitched luxury tents with large airbeds, fluffy duvets and porch-set deckchairs. Alongside one double and one twin, there's a family-sized tent (the latter only available in July and Aug), which sleeps four in two spacious bedrooms. With a shower room and loo decked out with driftwood detail and seaside decor (shared by all campers), this stunning cliff-top site is almost a hotel under canvas.

Being right on the coast path – more applause for the cracking sea views – this is a popular venue with walkers. The enterprise sparked when owners Deborah and Neil Best ran *Broad Meadow House* as a B&B, and a weary hiker arrived to find no room at the inn. "He was so tired he asked if he could sleep in the greenhouse," recalls Deborah, "so I pitched our old tent for him in the meadow and cooked him breakfast." With such a unique idea they could fill the meadow ten times over, but keeping it small – to a maximum of twelve guests – keeps it special.

Just 30 yards from the cliff-edge coast path as the crow flies (about 120 yards on foot), the seaside meadow boasts views over historic Charlestown harbour, where the masts of the majestic Square Sail tall ships dominate the view. The surrounding area is the south coast of Cornwall at its best: sheltered beaches made for rock-pooling, swimming, snorkelling, fishing and kayaking, lush countryside rolling to the edge of the sea and the coast path winding along from cliffs to coves. Maps can be borrowed from the campsite and the cycle trail network winds through the lush wetland and woodland trails of Pentewan valley (bike rental nearby). On a rainy day it's a quick dash (about 100 yards from your tent) to the Shipwreck and Heritage Centre, which houses Europe's largest private collection of maritime artefacts, and the Eden Project is just four miles away.

Back on site, where picnic benches face the ocean, entertainment is all about nature. The rule is "a touch of hush after dusk", and the silence creates the perfect environment to lie back and stargaze or listen for tawny owls. By day you can spot buzzards and sparrowhawks, and look out for passing pods of dolphins or even basking sharks.

Practicalities

Broad Meadow House Camp & Breakfast, Quay Road, Charlestown, nr St Austell, Cornwall, PL25 3NX
☎*01726 76636,* ⓦ*www.broadmeadowhouse.com*

Pitches & price Tent & breakfast package in luxury tents (4-person, double or twin) £19–24 per adult (under-12s £16–21). BYO tent (small campervans welcome out of season) £8 per adult (£4 under-12s/ free under-2s). 3 hook-ups available at £3.50 per night; breakfast £6 per adult. Accommodation in the on-site Posh Shed luxury chalet is £395–645 per week.

Facilities Separate loo and shower room with hand basin in a converted stone house. Sheltered pot-wash; covered power points and free wi-fi; mini fridge/ freezer; foot pump for airbeds. Towels, walking boots and wet kit can be dried by the Aga.

Restrictions Dogs permitted. No campfires.

Open End May–late Sept in luxury tents. BYO tents/ campers year round.

Getting there Turn off the A39 north of St Austell, following signs into Charlestown. Turn left at mini-roundabout by the Shipwreck Centre, bear right until lane splits and take middle lane up the hill then turn right at the top (marked "private road"). *Broad Meadow* is the last house on the left.

Aside from the marvellous breakfasts, there's plenty of choice for food and drink, including a posh seafood restaurant, *Wreckers*, a couple of waterside pubs, a village store and a café. You can order a morning pint with the local milkman and grab the best local produce (think smoked fish, fresh crab and just-picked veg) from Richard's Fruit, Veg & Wet Fish Shop in Par (three miles) or Lobb's Farm Shop at Heligan Garden (eight miles).

◄ Roaming the fine, sheltered beaches near *Broad Meadow*
▶ The shower room, in a converted stone house; hens supply eggs for breakfast; the site is walking distance from the Eden Project

Bedruthan Steps

Overlooking a wild stretch of coastline punctuated by giant rock stacks, this simple site hogs poll position above one of the south-west's most famous beauty spots. A wild, boulder-strewn bay, where golden sand slaloms around towers of granite, Bedruthan Steps is a serious rival to Australia's dramatic Twelve Apostles. Easily accessed on the "Atlantic Highway" stretch of the A39, it's a popular sightseeing spot, yet a knee-wobbling descent down 142 steps means the beach is rarely crowded.

Pitched in the fields above, you bear the brunt of bad weather but get to wake up to a world-class view. Bordered by the coast path, National Trust land and the highway, the camping field (much of whose profits go to the Cornwall Air Ambulance is little more than a huge expanse of grass sloping seaward. A short pad over cliff-tops strewn with wild thyme and you're on the coast path. From here chic, surfy Watergate Bay – home to Jamie Oliver's *Fifteen Cornwall* – lies three miles to the west, Park Head is a popular climbing site a few minutes' walk to the east and there's wonderful snorkelling a mile and a half past that at Porthcothan.

Practicalities

Bedruthan Steps Camping, Bedruthan Steps, nr Wadebridge, Cornwall, PL27 7UW ☎01637 860943, Ⓦwww.bedruthanstepscamping.co.uk

Pitches & price No limit on tents (if the main field fills up, an overspill field opens). 5 caravan pitches – no hard-standing pitches or hook-ups. No pre-booking. £6 per person, under-10s free.

Facilities Immaculate male loo, female loo (with baby-changer and fresh flowers) and small shower. Extra portaloos and showers during Aug. Refreshment kiosk.

Restrictions Dogs allowed (£2). Campfires permitted.

Open July & Aug.

Getting there The campsite is clearly marked on the ocean side of the B3276 between Watergate Bay and Padstow. Newquay airport is 10min by taxi and Western Greyhound runs a bus service between Newquay and Padstow.

South Breazle

It may sit on a hundred-acre farm on the northern flanks of Dartmoor, but at *South Breazle* you won't be camping with the great unwashed. Indeed, with just 25 super-size pitches laid out around a trim lawn, this is a rather exclusive little canvas and caravan congregation. Each neat, flower-bordered pitch has its own placard – "The Rook", "Deer's Corner" and "Hedgehog Burrow" to name a few – echoing the site's wildlife-rich surroundings. The amenities, meanwhile, make it feel more like a private leisure club than a country campsite, with power showers, hair dryers and pine-seated loos in spotless, pastel-tiled bathrooms.

You don't have to trek the ten miles to Okehampton for decent grub: pick fresh herbs to season pork, beef, salad leaves and eggs bought fresh from the farm. You're only a couple of miles from Bratton Clovelly, where the *Clovelly Inn* serves a selection of real ales and reasonably priced food, and Roadford Lake, where you can dine at *Lakeside* and go windsurfing, sailing, angling or kayaking. The lake also has its own, much bigger campsite; but why cramp your camping style when you can bag a super-size "Hedgehog Burrow" down the lane?

Practicalities

South Breazle Holidays, Bratton Clovelly, Okehampton, Devon, EX20 4JS ☎01837 871752, Ⓦwww.southbreazleholidays.co.uk

Pitches & price 15 pitches with hook-ups (most hard-standing) and 10 tent pitches. £11.50–18 per pitch (tent/caravan and 2 adults). Backpackers (without a car) £4.50–6.50.

Facilities Home-from-home amenities block with power showers and loos, disabled bathroom and baby-changing. Indoor utility room with washing-up sinks, washing machine. Free wi-fi. Shop, information point.

Restrictions No dogs. No campfires. Quiet after 10pm.

Open March–Oct.

Getting there Leave the A30 at Stowford Cross and follow sign for Roadford Lake. Turn right to Bratton Clovelly, take the second left to Germansweek and *South Breazle* is along the first farm lane on the right.

Treloan

A family farmyard by the sea

"I've got a bit of festival fever," says Debbie Walker, her pink dress fluttering in the breeze like the bright yellow and orange flags she's hoisted. With its communal ambience and a regular huddle of storytellers and musicians around the campfire, *Treloan* does often feel like a festival – albeit a very placid one.

The Walkers were regular visitors here until they fled Hampshire to take the helm of the hillside farm that occupied this spot. Edged by rolling meadows, with sweeping views over Gerrans Bay – where dolphins, basking sharks and sailing boats come to play – it's easy to see what attracted them.

Although shire horses are no longer used to plough the land, the farm is still home to pigs, chickens, goats, ducks and fantails, and young campers can help collect eggs and feed the animals. Head through a couple of gates and you're on the coast path, with three idyllic coves for snorkelling, rock-pooling and swimming. You can explore the Roseland Peninsula on foot, or amble to Place and jump aboard a ferry to St Mawes then on to maritime Falmouth. For groceries it's just five minutes' walk to picturesque Portscatho, where you can rent sailing boats, windsurfers or kayaks, sip a pint in the *Plume of Feathers* or nose around the Spindrift Gallery.

Practicalities

Treloan Coastal Holidays, Treloan Lane, Portscatho, Cornwall, TR2 5EF ☎01872 580989, Ⓦwww.coastalfarmholidays.co.uk

Pitches & price 60 pitches (caravans & tents welcome), mostly hook-ups. £13–20.50 per pitch (with 2 adults). Hook-ups £2.25, additional adults £4.50, additional children £3.50. Campers without cars pay £5. 3 touring vans and 7 static caravans available to rent.
Facilities 2 adequate amenities blocks with showers and loos. 2 family/disabled shower rooms with baby bath. Sheltered washing-up areas. Braziers to rent (£5).
Restrictions Dogs allowed. One communal campfire.
Open Year round.
Getting there From the A390 take the A3078 towards Tregony/St Mawes. After about 7 miles turn left to Gerrans/Portscatho. Enter along Treloan Lane, next to the *Old Standard Inn* in Gerrans. Buses run from Truro to Portscatho, or take the train/bus to Falmouth, ferry hop to St Mawes and catch a bus on to Portscatho.

▼ *Treloan*'s campers can help feed the farm's animals

Equipment

The equipment you set out with can make or break a camping trip. Your tent is the most important piece of kit so take time to find one that does the job and – whatever the season – don't forget your waterproofs.

Visit any outdoors shop and you'll be confronted with a mind-boggling array of camping gear and gadgets. While you can budget here – a two-person tent from Argos could set you back as little as £12.99 – it's worth buying the best you can afford and favouring function over looks. A designer, hand-painted tipi may look cute in store but not so cute when the wind rips a hole in it on your first night. Check out our Directory section on p.376 for recommended shops.

When it comes to **tents** you'll find things have come a long way from the *Carry on Camping*-style canvas versions of the past. Today it's all about streamlined contours and high-strength, lightweight materials. Of the many options available, dome tents are the most popular. Simple to pitch – using poles that thread through sleeves in the fabric – they come in all shapes and sizes. What's more, they pack up small enough to be squirrelled away at the back of your wardrobe between trips. For those heading to wilder, windier terrain, a "geodesic" dome tent is worth considering – these have a crisscross pole design aimed to cope with mountain blizzards and gale-force winds and should stand up to the worst of the British climate. For families and larger groups there are a few more options – the tunnel (basically an extended dome tent for three or more people), the vis-a-vis (two sleeping areas facing a central, shared space) and the larger, cabin-style frame tent (lots of headroom and often very waterproof, but a pig to cart around).

If you can't be bothered working out which pole goes where, you could try a pop-up tent (see ⓦwww.gelert.com or ⓦwww.quechua.com). These erect themselves in seconds simply by being flung in the air, perfect for festival-goers. Then just stab in a few pegs and you're all set to crack open a beer, although taking them down again can be a frustrating process.

Popular amongst glampers and larger groups, Mongolian-style **yurts** and Native American **tipis** are elegant and spacious and often incorporate the luxury of an indoor stove or fire. Authentic models are expensive and impractical to lug around and erect (think reams of heavy canvas and large wooden poles); however, there are lightweight, compact versions available (see ⓦwww.tentipi.com), which are easier to pitch but still cost a lot more than the average tent.

Second to your tent, what you choose to sleep in and, perhaps more importantly *on*, will dictate the comfort of your camping experience. Many first-time campers underestimate the importance of a decent **sleeping mat**. While a simple foam roll mat is a cheap and cheerful option, it offers little padding and on a cold night you'll soon find the chill seeping into your bones. Air mattresses give lots of cushioning but are a hassle to pump up and deflate and are often surprisingly cold. For most campers the best option is a lightweight, self-inflating sleeping mat (try ⓦwww.thermarest.com); not only are they comfy but they also retain your body heat, double up as a camp chair and, when deflated, take up next to no space in your backpack.

With **sleeping bags** the main decision is whether to opt for down or synthetic stuffing. Down sleeping bags are warmer and compress better, but they are more expensive, difficult to clean and lose insulation when they get wet. Cheaper synthetic sleeping bags are quicker to dry and retain heat when wet, but they are also heavier and not quite as toasty-warm. Whatever they're made of, sleeping bags are classed by season – a two-season bag is fine for the fairest-weather British camping, but a three-season bag (with a lower comfort limit of around -5°C) will keep you snug from spring through to autumn.

With a few select **gadgets**, tent life needn't leave you pining for the creature comforts of home. Although they are something of a fashion disaster, a small LED head torch (try ⓦwww.petzl.com) will come in very useful if you need to stumble outside to fix a guy rope or make a dash to the loo. Snap lights (chemical, light-emitting sticks) are also great for tagging onto your tent so you can find it in the dark. Finally, while you can live without a solar iPod charger, don't forget a sharp knife and a corkscrew.

FIVE TIPS FOR CAMPING CONTENTMENT

 Before you head off into the wilds with a new tent, always practise erecting it in your garden or living room.

 If you're worried about the cold, treat yourself to some silk underwear and cashmere socks.

 Apart from looking pretty, citronella candles make excellent insect repellent – light up a few in jam jars around your tent.

 If you are a camping couple, try sleeping bags with compatible zips so you can join them together and snuggle under the stars.

 Keep your bedding in waterproof drybags – even if you arrive in the wet, at least your sleeping bag will be dry.

◀ Did you remember the wet wipes? Packing the right gear will keep you warm, comfortable and on speaking terms

Hole Station

Deep in the woods, in one of the least densely populated areas of the country, music and cars are banned and nature provides the soundtrack to tent life. Set on a former backwater railway line, *Hole Station* is home to 45 acres of neglected West Devon woodland, which owner Greg Brown is in the process of restoring – an endeavour funded by his back-to-basics campsite. Campfires are encouraged, there are compost loos, the amenities hut is made from recycled pallets and the shower will soon be solar-powered. The set-up might be too rustic for some, although you can hire a pre-pitched "Rent-a-Tent" (sleeping up to twelve) complete with airbeds, seating and kitchen – useful for cyclists stopping over halfway along Devon's Coast to Coast trail. Visitors are encouraged to cook on the campfire, look out for deer, rooks and woodpeckers and get involved in coppicing and clearing for the woodland project. Alternatively, you could just sink into the laid-back ambience and put your car keys away – *The Golden Inn* pub is a short walk through the woods, and Evergreen Farm shop will deliver locally sourced supplies. Should you want to stray, there's an archery centre and coarse fishery down the road.

Practicalities

Hole Station Campsite, Highampton, Beaworthy, Devon, EX21 5JH ☏*01409 231266,* Ⓦ*www.freewebs.com/ holestationcampsite*

Pitches & price 8 standard pitches, £10–12 with 2 adults. 4 Rent-a-Tents, £17–21 with 2 adults.

Facilities Basic amenities block with 2 compost loos and 2 showers. Kettle provided for washing up.

Restrictions Dogs allowed (£1). Campfires permitted – fire-kits £5. No music. No cars in camping area.

Open April–Oct.

Getting there Exit the A30 at Okehampton and follow signs to Hatherleigh. At Hatherleigh roundabout head to Highampton, go past *The Golden Inn* and turn left at the next crossroads – the turning is signposted camping, footpath and cycle track. Buses run from Exeter to Halwill Junction (4 miles away), from where transport can be arranged (no charge).

Belle Tents

After a house fire in 2004, tent-makers David and Laura Rothwell moved themselves and all their furniture into one of their beautiful tents, conceiving the idea of this campsite while their home was being rebuilt. Decked out with beds, rugs and reclaimed furniture, the stripy round-tops huddle in the Rothwells' wild, flower-littered garden, where visiting birdlife includes goldfinches, blue tits and a greater spotted woodpecker. Well-equipped kitchens rival the best self-catering accommodation and all the tents have raised wooden floors and solar lights. But what really sets the ambience of this quirky place is the communal tent, with its cherry wood and mahogany bar (self-stock and self-service), wood-burner, board games and retro table football (fed by old 10p pieces). Just outside, a defunct TV sits by the fire-pit – a favourite spot for sundowners. You don't even have to go the four miles to Camelford for your shopping – a hamper of local goodies can be delivered. A footpath runs from the campsite to Bodmin Moor, where you can scale Rough Tor and Brown Willy, or take a ten-minute drive to the north coast to tackle a challenging section of coast path between Boscastle and Crackington Haven.

Practicalities

Belle Tents, Owls Gate, Davidstow, Camelford, Cornwall, PL32 9XY ☏*01840 261556,* Ⓦ*www.belletentscamping. co.uk*

Pitches & price Total of 17 people in 3 camps (4–6 in each). From £510 per camp per week, £120 per night, including 2 bedroom tents and a kitchen tent. Individual tents (sleeping 2–3) from £420 per week, £75 per night (you may have to share a kitchen).

Facilities Simple, unisex amenities block with powerful showers, Ecover soap and hair dryer. Outdoor washing-up area.

Restrictions No dogs. Campfires permitted.

Open May–Sept.

Getting there From the A30 take the A395 (nr Launceston), then turn left opposite Davidstow church (signposted Tremail). About 600yds along the lane turn right at the red and white *Belle Tents* sign.

Lundy Island

Marooned on puffin island

Cast off for a dose of real-deal island life: on Lundy Island there's no electricity after midnight, supplies chug in by boat, and the thirty-odd residents are far outnumbered by birds and seals. The adventure begins as you slip away from the mainland on board *MS Oldenburg*. Dolphins often surf the bow waves, leading the way to the granite hulk, just three miles long and half-a-mile wide, its craggy, green-topped cliffs plummeting into the ocean.

Lundy is Norse for "Puffin Island" (puffin: *lund*, island: *ey*), and the bright-beaked birds attract hordes of twitchers, binoculars at the ready. Seals, porpoises and sea birds can be seen offshore, while Sika deer, Soay sheep and Lundy ponies roam the wild interior, among whose scrub-topped cliffs you can find the endemic Lundy cabbage, standing stones and medieval settlements.

Indeed, nature provides most of the island's activities. Lundy's waters are a Marine Nature Reserve (one of only three in the UK), and the area's rich sea life can be explored on a trip with one of the dive charter boats. A blackboard outside the village shop, meanwhile, details an exhausting itinerary of snorkel safaris, rock-pooling, guided wildlife walks and slide shows. Rock-climbers test their nerve on challenging routes such as the Devil's Slide (though many climbing routes are closed during nesting season from spring to July), while the less adrenalin-inclined can take in dizzying views from the lighthouse and follow clues round the island on a letterboxing trail.

Walking is the only means of transport, and the steep climb to the island's hub (a shop, pub, church and a few stone houses) is enough to deter folk who don't like legwork. At least you don't have to lug your baggage – it will find its own way to the site on the back of a trailer. The campsite itself offers little more than a stone-walled field and basic, clean amenities, while the village shop supplies enough for basic cooking. *The Marisco Tavern*, a traditional inn and the heart of the community, serves a decent breakfast, lunch and dinner, and has board games.

Once the boat leaves with the day-visitors the island really turns on its magic. The sun sets over the ocean leaving you utterly marooned. And with the generator switched off, stars glint more brightly than anywhere on the mainland.

Practicalities

Lundy Island, Bristol Channel, EX39 2LY. Book with The Landmark Trust ☎01628 825925, Ⓦwww.landmarktrust. org.uk. Information about the campsite and island activities on ☎01237 431831, Ⓦwww.lundyisland.co.uk
Pitches & price Space for 40 campers (no hook-ups). £8–11 per person. Ferry fare approximately £56 per adult, £28 per child.
Facilities Basic unisex amenities block with showers, loos, washing-up area and power point. Shop and information point in village shop (30 seconds' walk).
Restrictions No dogs. No campfires. No stag or hen groups.
Open Year round.
Getting there Travel from Ilfracombe or Bideford on board the *MS Oldenburg* between March and Oct. From Nov to mid-March a helicopter service runs from Hartland Point.

▼ Lundy's old lighthouse

Little Meadow

A mellow pasture with an ocean view

The sun rises on one side of the tent and sets on the other. Barbecue smoke spirals skyward from grassy pitches where rows of campers kick back, jaws dropped, eyes on green-topped cliffs that plummet into endless blue where sailing boats, porpoises, seals and basking sharks come by. It's not only the tiers of level,

flower-bordered pitches clinging to the hillside that pay blissful attention to the view: here you even get to stare out to sea from the washing-up sinks.

As a punter you might think you're on a winner just because of the location, but it takes good housekeeping to make a gem like this tick over so peacefully. "The trick is to keep it small," says owner Nick Barten who, along with his wife Sian, has been running the site for twelve years. Despite owning a hundred acres of farmland the number of pitches is limited to less than fifty, and they run a strict booking system along with a no-nonsense attitude to camping. "No politicians," they claim. "No footballers. And recycling is compulsory."

Farming is Barten's passion, and he couldn't have bagged a more scenic location for rearing his beef cattle. His grandparents set up the campsite in 1954 and its popularity snowballed. But even when midsummer madness embraces the surrounding coast, this isn't a busy place. Far enough from the big sandy beaches and pounding surf of Woolacombe and Saunton Sands, it deters the younger surfy crowds and bucket-and-spade brigades. Up here the campers are a calmer sort who meander down the steep slope to watch boats come and go in Samson's Bay, or don walking boots to explore the Hangman Hills of Exmoor, which dominate views to the east. The only twitter comes from the birds and a handful of children running amuck in the wooded play area.

While all is mellow up on the hilltop, there's plenty going on down below. The kids need only go next door to Watermouth Castle & Family Theme Park, where they can pan for gold in Gnome Land, or hop down the road to Combe Martin to visit the Wildlife and Dinosaur Park. Combe Martin's *Pack o' Cards Inn* – said to have been built by a local man who won a fortune gambling – has a decent garden to enjoy a pint in, while for food you're best served a couple of miles away in Ilfracombe, where the restaurant scene includes Damien Hirst's much-lauded *11 The Quay* and lesser-known local star *La Gendarmerie*, a modern brasserie set in an old police station.

Ilfracombe's other big draw card is Tunnels beaches, where visitors can walk through passages carved into the hillside

Practicalities

Little Meadow Campsite, Watermouth, nr Ilfracombe, Devon, EX34 9SJ ℡*01271 866862,* Ⓦ*www.littlemeadow.co.uk*

Pitches & price 46 grass pitches (10 with hook-ups). Tents and caravans welcome. £11–16 per pitch with 2 people. Hiker and tent £4–5. Booking essential. Minimum stay 1 week during summer holidays. 3 on-site caravans to rent.

Facilities Excellent amenities block with showers, loos, hair dryers in women's and a disabled toilet and shower for each sex. Utility room with washing machine and freezer. Covered washing-up area. Basic shop and information point, wi-fi.

Restrictions Dogs allowed (£1–2). No campfires. No single-sex groups.

Open April–Sept. No arrivals after 9pm.

Getting there From the M5 take the A361 to Barnstaple and turn onto the A399 (signposted Blackmoor Gate). The campsite is between Combe Martin and Ilfracombe – the entrance is a sharp right about 500yds after Watermouth Castle. Regular bus services run from Ilfracombe and Combe Martin.

during Victorian times to enable access to the beaches. As well as genning up on Victorian bathing etiquette and taking a dip in the tidal pool, you can enjoy rock-pooling and snorkelling on the sheltered blue-flag beach, hire a kayak or head to nearby Ilfracombe harbour and hop on a wildlife adventure cruise. Once you've had your fill of waterside fun, leave the seaside crowds behind, grab a fresh steak from the campsite shop, light the barbecue and chill out back at your tent with a view.

◀ *Little Meadow*'s spacious pitches overlook the sea ▶ Watermouth Castle doubles as a theme park; Tunnels beaches, Ilfracombe

North Morte Farm

A glittering cove, rolling fields and fresh crab

The star of *North Morte Farm* is secluded Rockham beach, a steep four-hundred-yard descent from the campsite. Hidden in a crease in the cliffs, it glitters beneath the tents, inviting rock-poolers and swimmers to explore amongst granite teeth and dip in sandy-bottomed shallows.

▼ *North Morte Farm* backs on to National Trust-owned coastline

Backing onto a wedge of wild, undulating coastline owned by the National Trust, *North Morte*'s fields haven't been levelled to accommodate campers, and the uneven terrain makes the site feel more intimate than its 150 pitches might suggest. Indeed, focusing seaward it's easy to forget this is part of a bigger holiday park – a setting that makes the atmosphere a little busier and less personal, but brings benefits including extensive amenities, a decent shop and a visiting fish-and-chip van.

Beyond your virtually private cove and the stunning section of coast path around Morte Point, you're within striking distance of the surf at Woolacombe (about five minutes' drive) and less than a mile from Mortehoe. Of three pubs in the village the *Chichester Arms* is a good bet for real ale and decent grub, while *Mortehoe Shellfish* serves up lobster and crab fresh from the boat.

Practicalities

North Morte Farm Caravan & Camping Park, Mortehoe, Woolacombe, North Devon, EX34 7EG ☎01271 870381, Ⓦ www.northmortefarm.co.uk

Pitches & price About 150 tent pitches (£6–8.50 per person). 24 hard-standing pitches for caravans, most with hook-ups (£12.70–18.60 per pitch for 2 adults). £2.50–3 per child. No booking for tents. Static caravans available to rent.

Facilities Spick-and-span amenities include separate male and female toilets, showers, baby-changing, disabled facilities and indoor washing-up area. Laundry, shop/off-licence and information point.

Restrictions Dogs £1.50–2. No campfires. No single-sex groups.

Open Easter–end Sept.

Getting there Take the A361 to Ilfracombe and take the first exit (signposted Mortehoe/Woolacombe) at the Mullacott Cross roundabout. In Mortehoe village turn right (signposted *North Morte Farm*) and the campsite is about 500yds on the left.

Old Cotmore Farm

A green and pleasant haven on Devon's southernmost peninsula

Old Cotmore Farm isn't the coolest or quirkiest campsite in this pretty corner of the South Hams – crammed with verdant meadows, rocky coves and pearly bays – but stands out as a faultless all-rounder. Enveloped by countryside and a short drive from the rugged coast, its green grass is beautifully manicured and the pink-and-blue themed ladies' and men's amenities say everything about the level of attention to detail.

"For decent pub grub by the sea there's *The Cricket Inn* in Beesands," explains Gwen Needham, who owns the site with her husband Matthew. "You must book – the number's in the laundry. Here's a list of dog-friendly beaches – our favourite is Lannacombe. And you must go to Mill Bay at East Portlemouth – kids just love making sand pies there."

You can forgive Needham for giving torrents of information. Visitors can pick strawberries at Stokeley Farm Shop in nearby Stokeham, skip to the nearest beach to buy freshly landed fish from *Britannia of Beesands*, or take a ten-minute drive to East Prawle to catch a rock band at *The Pigs Nose*. Many visitors board the ferry from East Portlemouth to trendy Salcombe, while food lovers head to Torcross to dine on some of the finest fish and chips in Devon at the *Start Bay Inn*, or bag a table at the cosy *Millbrook Inn* in South Pool, with live jazz on Sunday afternoons.

Walkers and cyclists can borrow one of the maps detailing all sorts of routes from coastal jaunts to challenging bike rides. One of the most exposed parts of the south coast, Prawle Point is the southernmost peninsula of Devon and a tough section of coast path takes you east to Start Point lighthouse. Carry on past the sea-ravaged remains of the village of Hallsands and end up at the fragile geological wonder of Slapton Sands – a shingle bar dividing the sea and a freshwater lake. With 22 acres of parkland, *Old Cotmore* is popular with families, who come for the beaches and enjoy the relaxed site, where there's a play area and basic playroom. There's a trio of holiday cottages, and caravans take up many pitches, but a lush corner is set aside for campers and an extra field (with bay views) opens to tents in midsummer.

Practicalities

Old Cotmore Farm, Stokenham, Kingsbridge, Devon, TQ7 2LR ☎*01548 580240,* Ⓦ*www.holiday-in-devon.com*

Pitches & price 30 pitches (all hook-ups, 24 hard-standing). 35 extra tent pitches in midsummer. £11–18 per pitch (for a caravan/tent and 2 adults), £1.50–3.50 per child.

Facilities A tidy amenities block with showers and loos. Excellent family/disabled shower room with baby-changing and baby bath. Disabled access. Laundry room. Free wi-fi. Shop and information point.

Restrictions Dogs £1–1.50. No campfires. No groups.

Open Mid-March to Oct. Arrive by 8pm.

Getting there From Kingsbridge follow the A379 towards Dartmouth. *Old Cotmore* is signposted from the mini-roundabout at Stokenham – turn right to Beesands and the farm is just over a mile on the right. Buses run to Stokenham.

▾ Slapton, home to a famous shingle bar and a nudist beach

Cuckoo Down Yurts
Designer tents and grourmet goodies

Rugs underfoot, a log-burning stove and space to stand up. Stars twinkle through the roof panel above a duvet-clad double bed. This is life under canvas, but not as you know it.

Cuckoo Down Yurts is a family-owned farm that isn't your typical campsite location: winding along narrow lanes in rural Devon you are clearly in the domain of mansion-dwellers, not hardy campers. But half a mile down a bumpy track the rest of civilization is long forgotten, leaving thirty lush acres of meadows and woodland, with just a babbling stream, birdlife and sheep for company. And spaced out along the top edge of an oak-lined paddock – a huge, car-free space where dogs and children can roam – are three Mongolian-style yurts.

OK, you've got a big field and a big "tent". So what? Well, the big deal here is the level of luxury teamed with a low-carbon footprint. Each yurt (sleeping up to six) is decked out with solar-powered fairylights, wind-up lanterns and a separate compost loo. And, on a more practical level, each has a fully equipped kitchen, plump furnishings, a picnic bench and a fire-pit.

When it comes to food and drink, you don't have to go far to get a taste of the West Country. Preorder a hamper of gourmet goodies (think just-picked salad, organic bread and home-baked cakes) or stock up in a local farm shop – Joshua's Harvest Store in Ottery St Mary, Dart's Farm at Topsham or Kenniton Farm Shop at Clyst St Mary. The West Hill village shop is ten minutes' walk away, and if you don't fancy sizzling up a DIY feast it's a two-mile walk to the award-winning *Golden Lion* pub at Tipton St John, a short hop to the *Combe House Hotel* at Gittisham and three miles to Ottery St Mary for fish and chips.

If you've got kids in tow they can play hide-and-seek in the woods or dam the stream, and there's all sorts of child-friendly extras to hand, from toy boxes to travel cots. For a family day out, head for Sidmouth Donkey Sanctuary, Escot House (with a maze, pirate ship and café in stately home parkland) or Crealy Adventure Park.

Although this is essentially a countryside location, it's only a short jaunt to the pebble beaches, ice-cream kiosks and staggering cliffy scenery of Sidmouth, Beer, Branscombe and Budleigh Salterton. You can rent a mountain bike and head to Woodbury

Practicalities

Cuckoo Down Farm Yurts, Lower Broad Oak Road, West Hill, Ottery St Mary, Devon, EX11 1UE ☎01404 811714, ⓦwww.luxurydevonyurts.co.uk

Pitches & price 4-night mid-week breaks (Mon–Thurs) £230 per yurt; 3-night weekends (Fri–Sun) £215; one week (Fri–Fri) £445. Individual nights £60 per night. Includes linen, camping gas, organic wine and logs. Hampers from £40; massages and reflexology from £30; yoga sessions from £20.

Facilities Each yurt has a compost loo, picnic table, fire-pit, wood-burning stove, camping lanterns, solar-powered lights, clothes airer and outdoor covered kitchen. There are 2 hot showers in the barn area, with a fridge, laundry facilities and sockets for mobiles.

Restrictions Well-behaved dogs allowed. Campfires permitted. No stag groups.

Open April–Sept. Campers should arrive in daylight. Checkout by 10am.

Getting there Take the B3174 exit from the A30 and turn onto the B3180. Turn left at Bendarroch Road and veer right at School Lane. Turn right at West Hill Road and left at Elsdon Lane, at the end of which cross over Lower Broad Oak Road; the farm is about 0.5 miles down a bumpy track (marked footpath). Pick-ups can be arranged from Exeter, Honiton and Whimple train stations (from £5).

Common and Halden Forest, hike along the coast path or rock-climb at Chudleigh Rocks, but there's little temptation to leave the serenity of the site – not when you can enjoy an in-tent massage (by arrangement), stargaze by the campfire and snuggle down in a cosy canvas abode which stretches camping to its luxurious limits.

◄ Mongolian yurts and English refreshments ► *Cuckoo Down* is set in thirty acres of meadows and woodland; Sidmouth Donkey Sanctuary

Prattshayes Farm

Just over a mile inland from the start of the Jurassic Heritage Coastline at Orcombe Point, *Prattshayes Farm* has an enviable countryside setting. Sat close to the rust-red cliffs of Sandy Bay, it's also just a couple of miles from the mouth of the River Exe – home to grey seals, otters and ospreys, and a water-sports Mecca attracting all sorts from fishermen and sailors to kite-surfers.

Given to the National Trust along with the fields and cliffs of Orcombe in the 1960s by one Miss Edith Helen Pratt, this small and friendly Devon site has grass pitches and a walkers' bunkhouse. Here coast-path ramblers rest weary legs, kids ride on tractors and trikes and cyclists set off along the Exe Estuary Trail or the former railway route from Littleham to Budleigh Salterton. Greenies on a car-free jaunt can arrive by bus, have rental bikes delivered from Exmouth and come back to a solar-heated shower. A fifteen-minute trot away, the road widens and green pastures are swapped for the red-brick houses of Littleham, handy for local shops and a family pub. In the other direction it's a short drive to Sandy Bay, which curves away from the Jurassic coast and towards the promenade, pubs and seafront pavilion of Exmouth.

Practicalities

Prattshayes Farm, Maer Lane, Littleham, Exmouth, Devon, EX8 5DB ☎01395 276626

Pitches & price 30 grass pitches, many with hook-ups. Tents and caravans welcome. £4–5 per person (£2 per child), plus £1.50 for a hook-up. Bunkhouse accommodation (sleeping 14) also available.

Facilities Well-tended amenities with solar showers (baby bath in women's). Disabled wet-room. Sheltered washing-up area. Small shop and information point.

Restrictions Dogs allowed. No campfires. No stag or hen groups.

Open April–Sept. Arrive before dark.

Getting there From the M5 take the A376 into Exmouth and follow signs for Littleham. Turn right at *The Clinton Arms* into Maer Lane and the campsite is about 0.5 miles on the right. Buses run to the end of the road from Exeter and Exmouth.

Cockingford Farm

If you're a self-sufficient camper who puts the lure of nature and the great outdoors before creature comforts, you'll be right at home at *Cockingford Farm*. The beauty of Dartmoor's landscape needs little explanation: it's a natural playground for walkers, mountain bikers and outdoor enthusiasts. And the rugged character of *Cockingford Farm* goes hand-in-hand with its stunning surroundings.

Simplicity sums up its charm: grassy slopes flatten out at the banks of a babbling stream where you can kick back by a campfire, launch into the water from a rope swing or wander deep into the woodland. On site there's nothing to soften the blow of bad weather, but it isn't far to Widecombe-in-the-Moor, where *The Old Inn* serves up good Devonshire ales and locally sourced pub food.

One tip for campers at *Cockingford* is to avoid peak season and really wet weather. Don't erect your tent in the first field, where caravans dominate. Sleep with your head uphill as there aren't many flat pitches.

Practicalities

Cockingford Farm Campsite, Widecombe-in-the-Moor, Devon, TQ13 7TG ☎01364 621258

Pitches & price Up to 30 caravans and no limits on tents (find a pitch and it's yours). No hook-ups. £3 per adult, £1 per child aged 11–18, 50p per child aged 5–10, under-4s free.

Facilities Not flash, but fully functional amenities – a block with toilets, showers and basins for each sex. Outdoor (cold-water) washing-up sink.

Restrictions Dogs allowed. Campfires permitted by the stream.

Open Mid-March to mid-Nov.

Getting there Turn off the A38 at Ashburton and head to Buckland-in-the-Moor. A mile further on from Buckland, turn left (signposted Widecombe-in-the-Moor). The campsite is located at the bottom of the hill on the left.

Cloud Farm

A river runs by in the valley of Doone

Nestled amidst scenery that inspired Richard Doddridge Blackmore's classic, *Lorna Doone, Cloud Farm* offers much more than a romantic landscape in a wooded valley of Exmoor. As well as watching the herons, sheep and hikers go by, here you can mount a trusty steed for a horse trek from the on-site stables, take a dip or cast a line into the bubbling stream and bike or hike the trails from the woods to the hilltops that border Devon and Somerset.

Campers have been coming to this gloriously simple place, with no creature comforts or fancy amenities, no mobile phone reception and a spring-fed water supply, since 1928. It's not perfect – the staff could be cheerier, and queuing for the limited amenities won't be the highlight of your trip – but it's tranquil enough to make you feel smug and happy. Having wound down into the depths of the valley, you might as well switch off the car engine until it's time to go home again; forget getting here without your own transport unless you're hiking across Exmoor or are prepared to walk six miles from Lynton, where the bus stops.

The camping fields stretch out alongside the stream, with most of the pitches sitting right by the water on the flattest ground. If you're armed with just a tent head into the furthest meadow, where cars and vans aren't permitted.

It's so far off the beaten track you wouldn't expect many passers-by, but visitors head along footpaths and country lanes, stopping at the entrance to *Cloud Farm*, where the riverside teashop serves loaf-sized scones piled high with jam and cream. Eggs, cakes, wine and basic groceries are all available on site, but the closest hit of busy civilization is at the twin towns of Lynmouth and Lynton (about fifteen minutes' drive away), where you'll find a cliff railway, seaside cafés and souvenir shops.

Practicalities

Doone Valley Holidays, Cloud Farm, Oare, Lynton, North Devon, EX35 6NU ☎ *01598 741234,* Ⓦ *www.doonevalleyholidays.co.uk*

Pitches & price No set number of pitches. Caravans allowed (no hook-ups or hard-standing). £5.50–7.50 per person (£4–5.50 per child).

Facilities The amenities block is far from flash, with just 2 loos and showers for each sex and a disabled loo. There are a couple of additional loos by the stables. Small, basic utility room with washing machines, dryer, fridge, freezer and washing-up sinks. On-site shop/tearoom/off-licence.

Restrictions Dogs allowed. Campfires permitted – logs from £5 per bag.

Open Year round.

Getting there From the A39 Minehead to Lynton road the small turning into Doone Valley and Oare is signposted (between Porlock and Lynmouth). Follow this road into the valley and *Cloud Farm* is signposted on the left. Access is along a farm track.

▼ *Cloud Farm* has on-site stables and a landscape ripe for exploration

The West Country

If anywhere can stake a claim to being the wellspring of quintessential rural England, it's the West Country. This chapter spans the counties of Dorset, Somerset, Gloucestershire and Wiltshire – Devon and Cornwall's campsites are covered separately (see p.8). Home to buildings of honey-hued stone, dairy herds and white-chalk horses, the West Country is full of rose-strewn villages with neat cricket greens, classic cream-tea shops and low-beamed pubs serving local beer.

In retrospect, holidays here can assume a dream-like quality to match the picture-postcard images. There's a sense of magic, and it's not just at Stonehenge. And adventure, too – it's no surprise to learn Enid Blyton based her Famous Five tales on Dorset's Isle of Purbeck.

The region's gentle fields are marvellously benign places to push in a peg. Even on Exmoor, the only national park in this chapter and the only area that approximates wild country, you'll find well-appointed campsites folded into a rolling pastoral carpet. Throw in the fossil-studded UNESCO-listed Jurassic Coast, handsome Regency towns like Bath, Cheltenham or Lyme Regis, or a mystical Wiltshire tour and you have a camping area that's as intoxicating as a pint of Somerset scrumpy.

It's not all cider and roses, though. In a region that's been a holiday favourite for centuries, you have to go an extra mile to escape the high-season crowds, especially on the Dorset coast. But if you don't mind sacrificing swish facilities to escape the holiday hordes, the West Country's true essence will reveal itself.

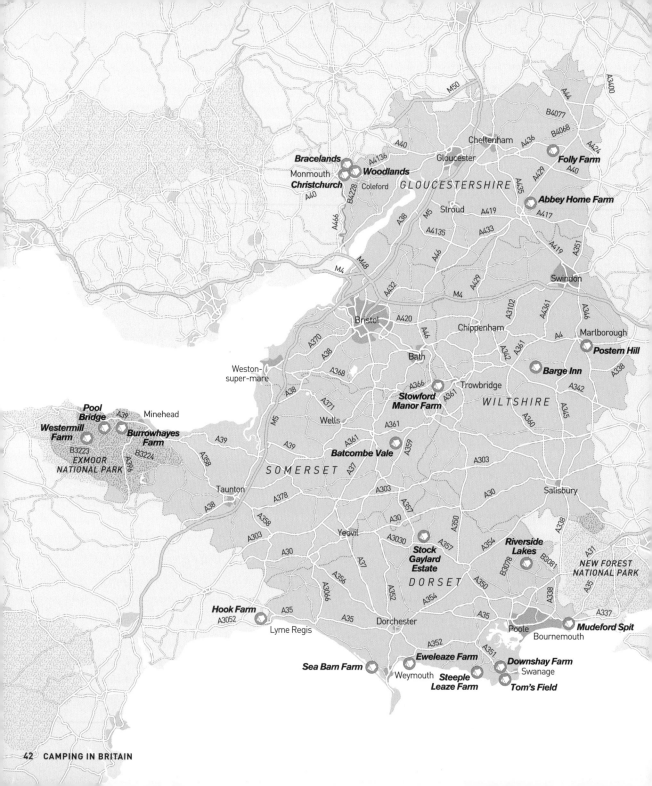

Bracelands
Woodlands
Christchurch
Monmouth
Coleford
A4136
A40
A4228
A466
A40

Cheltenham
Gloucester
Folly Farm
B4077
B4068
A424
A44
A3400
M50
A436
A429
A40
A435

GLOUCESTERSHIRE
Stroud
Abbey Home Farm
A419
A417
A419
A351
A46
A4135
A433

Swindon
A102
A361
A4
Marlborough
A346
Postern Hill
A342
A338
A345
A360

Bristol
A420
A46
Chippenham
M4
A432
M4
A370
A38
Bath
A366
A361
Trowbridge
Barge Inn
WILTSHIRE

Weston-super-mare
A38
A368
A371
Wells
Stowford Manor Farm
A359
Batcombe Vale
A37
A361

Pool Bridge
Westermill Farm
Burrowhayes Farm
Minehead
A39
B3223
B3224
A396
EXMOOR NATIONAL PARK
A39
SOMERSET
A39
M5

Taunton
A358
A38
A303
A378
A358
A30

A303
A357
A30
A350
A30
Salisbury
A338
NEW FOREST NATIONAL PARK
A37
A35

Yeovil
A3030
A357
Stock Gaylard Estate
A354
Riverside Lakes
B3078
B3081
A35

A356
A37
A352
A3066
A354
DORSET
A350

Hook Farm
A3052
A35
Lyme Regis
A35
Dorchester
A35
Poole
Bournemouth
Mudeford Spit
A337
A338

Sea Barn Farm
Weymouth
A352
Eweleaze Farm
A351
Downshay Farm
Swanage
Steeple Leaze Farm
Tom's Field

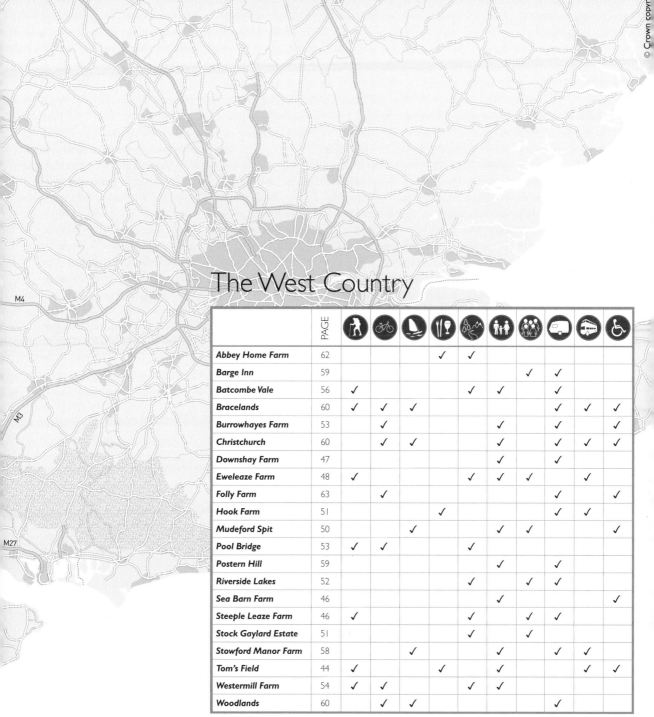

The West Country

	PAGE	walking	cycling	watersports	food/drink	nature	family (child)	family	caravan	bus	accessible
Abbey Home Farm	62				✓	✓					
Barge Inn	59							✓	✓		
Batcombe Vale	56	✓				✓	✓		✓		
Bracelands	60	✓	✓	✓					✓	✓	✓
Burrowhayes Farm	53		✓				✓		✓		✓
Christchurch	60		✓	✓			✓		✓	✓	✓
Downshay Farm	47						✓		✓		
Eweleaze Farm	48	✓				✓	✓	✓		✓	
Folly Farm	63		✓						✓		✓
Hook Farm	51				✓				✓	✓	
Mudeford Spit	50			✓			✓	✓			✓
Pool Bridge	53	✓	✓			✓					
Postern Hill	59						✓		✓		
Riverside Lakes	52						✓		✓	✓	
Sea Barn Farm	46						✓				✓
Steeple Leaze Farm	46	✓				✓	✓		✓		
Stock Gaylard Estate	51					✓		✓			
Stowford Manor Farm	58			✓			✓		✓	✓	
Tom's Field	44	✓			✓		✓			✓	✓
Westermill Farm	54	✓	✓			✓	✓				
Woodlands	60		✓	✓					✓		

See front flap for key to symbols

Tom's Field
Pure holiday magic

Ask five different campers to explain the magic of *Tom's Field* and you'll receive five different answers. Even the name imbues this intimate place with personality, thanks to charismatic smallholder Tom Bower, who opened the field as a campsite in the early 1960s, when the residential street now adjacent to the site was just a twinkle in a developer's eye. Now gone to the great haybarn in the sky, he might approve that his erstwhile sheep paddock has acquired a personality of its own.

It starts with the site's arrangement. Forget the moniker – *Tom's Field* is not one area. It is a cluster of plots; a jigsaw of fieldlets cleverly slotted together at different heights. This is a laid-back, first-come, first-served sort of site that only takes bookings for the Family Field, a lower rectangular area just big enough for child-sized cricket matches, and the smaller Nissen Field. Part of the site's charm is that you can pitch up anywhere: sharing with

four other tents on The Plateau, for example, or in The Glade, a two-tent clearing in a copse, or on the mellow Hikers Field reserved for small tents. All these are car-free, so there's no shortage of places to revel in the nature that abounds on-site. The Family Field has the only hook-ups, but who needs electronic gizmos when there are rabbits to watch and thick hedges full of flitting and furry things?

It's no wonder conservationists love *Tom's Field* as much as children do. The site has can-crushers and recycling of everything from bottles to batteries. There are barbecues for hire at bargain prices to curb the use of environmentally unsound disposables – Dorset charcoal is sold on site – and a shop that brims with local goodies such as free-range eggs, Dorset ice cream and Purbeck honey as well as the usual fresh bread and produce. It also has camping supplies, OS maps (and laminates to borrow), activities guides, secondhand books and fishing nets – the full gamut of holiday essentials except plastic bags, and bravo to that. Whether because of its feel-good factor or understated simplicity – which extends to a clean but basic amenities block – *Tom's Field* maintains a blissed-out atmosphere even when it fills in peak season (it can get very busy during school holidays, so call ahead).

Yet much of the abiding appeal is not on site at all. An undulating meadow spreads behind the stone walls. Swing through a kissing gate, hoik over a stile and you are swishing uphill through long grass. Within ten minutes you'll be standing on the brow of the Jurassic Coast, gawping at enormous seascapes. Within twenty you can be taking a dip at Dancing Ledge. Beloved by swimmers and rock climbers alike, it's a magical spot. On hot calm days, when people leap into the deep blue water and sunbathe on a ledge carved from the cliffs, you could be in northern Spain or Crete. Take to the South West Coast Path from here and you can arrive in Swanage after two miles, accessing its buckets and spades and fish and chips without paying and displaying. A mile or so in the other direction is the wonderfully eccentric *Square & Compasses* pub in Worth Matravers, a gem celebrated for its sea views, tasty homebrew ciders and delicious pasties.

And all this without venturing inland: to the Purbeck hills, Corfe Castle, cream teas, steam trains from Swanage to Corfe

Practicalities

Tom's Field Campsite, Tom's Field Road, Langton Matravers, Swanage, Dorset, BH19 3HN ☎01929 427110, ⓦwww.tomsfieldcamping.co.uk

Pitches & price 4 hard-standing pitches (all with hook-ups), 96 grass pitches (10 hook-ups). 1 person £5–6, 2 people £10–12, families (2 adults, 2 children) £12–14. Bunkhouse accommodation available, £9 per person.

Facilities Rather dated but clean amenities block with showers, toilets and basins (hair dryer in women's), disabled toilet/shower, heated laundry and drying room with babychanging facilities, dishwashing area, BBQs available to rent.

Restrictions Dogs permitted on leads. No campfires. Minimum 5 nights reservation in school holidays and bank holidays; 2 nights minimum if busy over bank holidays and high season.

Open Campsite mid–March to Oct. Bunkhouse year round (except Christmas Eve, Christmas Day, New Year's Eve).

Getting there Turn right onto the B3069 in Corfe Castle and go through Kingston to reach Langton Matravers after 2 miles. Tom's Field Road is on the right-hand side, 220yds beyond the village sign marked "Campsite & Shop". The Poole–Swanage #40 bus stops in Langton Matravers.

Castle or the powder beaches at Studland Bay. Enid Blyton based her Famous Five adventures on the Isle of Purbeck and holidays from *Tom's Field* seem imbued with the same intangible magic; the sense of having entered a parallel world where real life is suspended and anything is possible. Isn't that what camping holidays are all about?

◀ *Tom's waymarker* ▶ Dancing Ledge, a short walk from *Tom's Field*, and loved by swimmers and climbers; ovine neighbours taking it easy

Steeple Leaze Farm

There are few sites left in Dorset like *Steeple Leaze Farm*. For around 25 years this wildlife-friendly working farm has been a secret passed among campers who value hands-off management, gorgeous views and tranquillity more than tiled toilet blocks. The antithesis to the commercial enterprises elsewhere on the coast, it's a place of utter escapism set in two spacious fields that swoop up the valley side – the views get better the higher you go. Drink in the lanscape across the vale to the Purbeck Hills with your morning cuppa before relaxing under wide-open skies as butter-flies drift past. Later, indulge in the spectacular sunset, grill some sausages over the campfire and stargaze to your heart's content.

It's not all lazy days and tranquil nights, though – activity awaits should you need it. A footpath from the far left field tracks a blustery coastal ridge to Kimmeridge a mile away, home to the excellent *Clavell's Cafe & Farm Shop* (closed Mon Nov–March, and Sun–Wed evening Oct–June, ☎01929 480701) and a gem of a bay designated a marine nature reserve. The problem is leaving. And why would you? In this corner of Thomas Hardy country, *Steeple Leaze* truly is far from the madding crowd.

Practicalities

Steeple Leaze Farm, Steeple, Wareham, Dorset, BH20 5NY ☎01929 480733
Pitches & prices About 50. Adults £5, children (4–10) £2.50.
Facilities Minimal: toilets and basins by the farmhouse, and an outdoor sink in the lower field for washing-up. Depending on the owners' other activites, an unofficial massage tent and tent-café serving breakfasts may be set up in the main field in Aug.
Restrictions Dogs permitted (£1). Campfires permitted (wood sold on site). No stereos or drums.
Open Easter–Oct.
Getting there Turn off the A351 beside ruined Corfe Castle and drive through Church Knowle. The entrance to Steeple Leaze Farm is on the left, on a right-hand bend a mile further on from the turn-off to Kimmeridge.

Sea Barn Farm

When is a holiday park not a holiday park? When it's as scenic as this hill-top site above Chesil Beach. Opposite the entrance lies sister-site *West Fleet Holiday Farm*, which shares its outdoor pool, spacious play area and dated "Bar in the Barn". Who wants to stay there, however, when pitches at either end of *Sea Barn* gaze over stone walls to the shingle beach arcing into the distance before the Fleet, a brackish lagoon? A two-hour walk from the site goes down to the lagoon nature reserve, known for its birdlife.

While not the sea of static caravans elsewhere on the Jurassic Coast, *Sea Barn* isn't all cosy farm idyll. Reception staff can be offhand and some prices in the on-site shop will raise an eye-brow; stock up in nearby Weymouth, a chirpy bucket-and-spade beach resort. Don't expect privacy at peak times either, although the site's division into smaller paddocks does provide some intimacy and peace. The new amenities block is also a bonus, and has excellent facilities.

Camping purists might hate it. But what will appeal to every-one – from families to hikers on the coast path to rock climbers at Portland – is the immensity of sky and sea on this hill-top eyrie.

Practicalities

Sea Barn Farm Camping Park, Fleet, Weymouth, Dorset, DT3 4ED ☎01305 782218, ⓦwww.seabarnfarm.co.uk
Pitches & prices 250 pitches (50 hook-ups). 2 people, £11–13 low season, £19 high season, additional adult £4–5, additional child (2–15) £1–2.50.
Facilities Amenities block with showers, toilets, basins, hair dryers, 2 family rooms and disabled facilities; older block with showers, toilets and basins; dishwashing areas, on-site store, playground, off-site pool and bar-restaurant (both high season only).
Restrictions Dogs (£1–2) permitted on leads. No campfires. Last arrival by 9pm. Adult groups £20 (cash) per person noise bond.
Open 15 March–Oct.
Getting there At the roundabout in Chickerell on the B3157, turn towards Fleet. Entrance is on the left a mile further. Buses from Weymouth during school holidays.

Downshay Farm
Storybook charm in Famous Five country

Should you ever hanker for bygone charm, take your picnic hamper to *Downshay Farm*. The Isle of Purbeck hooked around Poole Harbour was the inspiration for Enid Blyton's Famous Five tales, and a stay on the dairy farm is a story of innocence and adventure in equal parts for your very own Julian, Dick, Anne or George – perhaps even Timmy the dog. A visit here is about vintage steam trains and dairy herds, powdery sand beaches, country strolls to romantic ruins and even farmers of the cheerful variety in owners Martin and Justine Pike.

With space to spare when most sites hereabouts are tripwired with guyropes, the site is a dream for children. They have room to gambol, and there are goalposts and a playground – a tangled copse with tyres for swings – as well. This leaves adults free to relax with the papers (now that is a dream) and a picturebook view over the Vale of Purbeck, which gets more gorgeous the higher uphill you go. The best pitches – in the middle, at the back or in a quieter far right corner – gaze across the valley to the toothy ruins of Corfe Castle framed in low hills – utter magic when hazed in sunset. You'll be on a slope everywhere except the flat(ish) ground at the front, where there isn't much in the way of views.

A van arrives each morning with basic stores, so campers never need leave the site. However, just downhill from *Downshay* is the historic Swanage railway, whose 1950s-vintage steam trains rattle beneath the site through the valley every hour. What better transport for a jaunt to the traditional resort of Swanage, three miles east? Otherwise, National Trust-listed Studland Bay, to Swanage's north, is a gem for connoisseurs of wild beaches, with a pub and café shack to help make a day of it. And if there is a more appealing conclusion to an evening spent soaking up the mottled-stone charm of Corfe Castle village – where locals' choice for pints is *The Fox* and for food the *Castle Inn* – than to catch a vintage train to Harmans Cross station, then stroll home up a sleepy lane, it's being kept quiet. Enid Blyton couldn't have plotted it better.

Practicalities

Downshay Farm, Haycrafts Lane, Swanage, Dorset, BH19 3EB ☎01929 480316,
Ⓦ*www.downshayfarm.co.uk*

Pitches & price 12 caravan pitches in touring park (all with hook-ups), 100 tent pitches. Caravans £10–12 for 2, additional adult £3, additional child (4–11) £2; tents £2–4, adults £4, children (11–16) £2, (4–11) £1.

Facilities Amenities block in a barn with showers, basins and toilets, basic Portakabin block with the same and dishwashing area, small separate block for caravans, ice-pack freezer.

Restrictions Dogs permitted on leads. No campfires. Caravans minimum 4 nights mid-season, 5 nights high season. No transit vans or motorbikes.

Open Caravan park: April–Nov. Campsite: Whitsun school holidays and summer holidays (mid-July to Aug).

Getting there On the A351 to Swanage go through Corfe Castle. At the central crossroads in Harmans Cross, turn right into Haycrafts Lane, passing the steam train station. The entrance is 440yds uphill on the right. Occasional buses go from Wareham, while steam trains go from Swanage or Corfe Castle.

▼ The view across the Vale of Purbeck from *Downshay Farm*

Eweleaze Farm
Going free range on the Jurassic Coast

For eleven months of the year, Dorset's exceptional *Eweleaze Farm* is quiet save for the occasional moo and bleat of organic livestock. Then in August, after a heroic two-month effort by an eight-strong team, these lush fields folded into a valley between Durdle Door and Weymouth are transformed into one of the most distinctive campsites in England.

Actually, campsite is too mean a word. Definitively non-commercial, *Eweleaze* is not a site in the traditional sense – it has too few rules and too few facilities. It is more a destination. Many campers settle in for two weeks or more, only occasionally venturing off site to places like Durdle Door and Lulworth Cove. Both can be reached from the site on the spectacular South West Coast Path, an enjoyable if long day-trip that avoids the traffic

which clogs up this part of Dorset during school holidays. For something more lively than the former's picture-postcard chalk arch or a dip in the latter's semi-circular cove, Weymouth is just around the bay; a bucket-and-spade, fish-and-chips sort of British beach resort that's as knockabout and unpretentious as its Punch and Judy show.

The problem is leaving – why would you when much of the joy of Dorset's Jurassic Coast is just outside your tent? If it's space you're after, there are eighty acres divided into seven camping fields, each with its own appeal: Flat Field and the Paddock in a central valley are the most sheltered when winds whip in off the coast; far-flung Corner Field is the quietest. Seeking views? Pastoral loveliness lies all around in Top Field, but in car-free Point Field or busier Beach Field you can wake each morning to a grandstand panorama over the coast curving past Weymouth to the knobbly hump of Portland. A steep path from the latter field scrambles downhill to the farm's private, for-campers-only half-mile shingle beach. It's ideal for swimming, fossil-hunting and fishing for supper.

Underlying the site are eco-ethics – minimal-impact camping is taken seriously on a farm whose camping fields are pasture for most of the year. Most toilets, dotted two or three to a field, are of the composting variety, while the centrally located showers are solar-powered. Consequently hot water is in short supply in the average British summer, warm morning showers out of the question and there are no basins except those for washing-up. If you're a tiled-toilet-block sort of camper, *Eweleaze* is probably not the place for you. A fabulous farm shop is stuffed with good things, some of it homegrown, nearly all organic except for the bags of marshmallows. Wood-fired pizza and Dorset pasties – organic, naturally – are also available to take away. Off site, the historic *Smugglers Inn* in Osmington Mills, a 35-minute walk along the coast path, is one of a number of good pubs in the area. It's always heaving in August, so for a quiet meal go to the *Springhead Inn* in Sutton Poyntz, near Preston.

It's a sign of how different *Eweleaze* is from the usual campsite that its character changes after dark. By early evening campfires spark up across the valley – haybales for seats and firewood can

Practicalities

Eweleaze Farm, Osmington Hill, Osmington, Dorset, DT3 6ED ☎01305 833690, Ⓦwww.eweleaze.co.uk

Pitches & price About 200. Adults Sun–Thurs £6, Fri & Sat (and bank holiday Sun) £12, children (5–14) Sun–Thurs £3, Fri & Sat (and bank holiday Sun) £6, booking fee for groups with cars/motorbikes £10, booking fee without vehicle £2. Self-contained cottage available.

Facilities 3 solar-powered shower blocks, 3 flushing toilet blocks, composting toilets in each field, cold-water showers by beach, dishwashing sinks in most fields, free brushwood for fires plus logs for sale, farm shop, takeaway hot food.

Restrictions Dogs welcome. Campfires permitted. Bookings are essential and should be made online (booking system opens in mid-Jan).

Open Aug only; exact dates posted on website.

Getting there The site is 4 miles east of Weymouth off the A353; the approach road is on the right just before the sign for Osmington village. Buses to Preston drop you just over half-a-mile from the site; #503 and #4B from Weymouth to Preston, or the #X53 Poole–Exeter. Taxis from Weymouth station cost around £10.

be delivered direct to your tent – and fields have a gentle buzz. Go for a walk at such times and the abiding impression is of a genteel festival. Not in a party sense – the atmosphere and clientele are somewhere between school holidays and Hay-on-Wye – but in its detachment from everyday life, its freedom and its friendly community spirit, whatever the weather. Beneath these enormous skies, lung-busting dawns burn brighter, kites soar higher and kids go free range. Rock on, *Eweleaze*.

◀ Sea, sky and *Eweleaze* in the distance ▶ Campfire fuel gets the chop; the *Smugglers Inn*, a fine spot to sneak a pint

Mudeford Spit
Beach holidays like they used to be

You notice the quirky seaside character even before you arrive at this half-mile of sandbank poked into Christchurch Bay. Where you embark from Mudeford quay, hoisting your bags onto a ferry that runs across a channel to your holiday home, a price list informs that "Dogs, cats and parrots go free". Welcome to the charming parallel world of *Mudeford Spit* – perhaps also the perfect beach getaway.

A big word, that "perfect", especially when foisted onto the humble beach hut. Bournemouth claims to be the resort that invented this quintessentially British obsession, yet only the 350 that jostle along *Mudeford Spit* – a jaunty parade placed back to back, so that decks open onto either silky sands or the estuary inland – have residential status for overnight stays. These are the royals of British beach huts, whose one room is designed for a family; think a kitchen/living area with settee beds and alcove bunkbeds and sometimes a bed or two in the roofspace. Decor ranges from cheerful seaside simplicity to beach-shack chic.

▼ Camping in spirit: Mudeford's famed beach huts

Forget mod cons, though. Notwithstanding the odd solar panel on the roof, you'll leave electricity on the mainland and get your water from the standpipes at five public toilet blocks. This is camping in spirit, if not canvas.

Therein lies the charm. *Mudeford Spit* is somewhere to kick off the shoes for a week. Once in the groove of its slower rhythm, you lose days simply drifting between an on-site shop for the papers and the *Beach House Café*, home to tasty food and a bar. Want more activity? Try walks beneath huge skies to Hengistbury Head nature reserve whose greenery holds Bournemouth at bay. Children, meanwhile, are free to wander, safe in this supersized adventure playground whose only traffic is the "Noddy Train" up to the head. They'll also have abundant playmates when families arrive for their six weeks in summer.

Indeed, the magic of *Mudeford Spit* is partly due to the huts being family affairs. Their owners treasure this as a place to recreate the simple beach holidays of dog-eared black-and-white photos. The spit isn't ideally suited to the PlayStation generation or particularly large, but boat trips to Christchurch or to go mackerel fishing from Mudeford quay offer good away-days.

Practicalities

Mudeford Spit, Mudeford, Christchurch, Dorset, BH23 3ND

Pitches & price All huts are privately owned; lettings online via Ⓦwww.beach-huts.com. Weekly rates for 4 from £450–475.

Facilities 5 public toilet and shower blocks; largest in the centre has disabled facilities and baby-changing.

Restrictions Dogs permitted. No campfires. No on-site parking (some owners have private spaces); Mudeford quay public parking £14 for 24 hours, £50 per week.

Open March–Nov.

Getting there A ferry runs every 12min in summer from Mudeford quay (Ⓦwww.mudefordferry.co.uk). Mudeford is off the A35/A337, east of Christchurch.

Hook Farm

Unashamedly English and enjoyably old-fashioned, once you get beyond its high street Lyme Regis is all bright Georgian facades and seascapes, with proper teashops, fish-and-chips and fossil-hunting. Everyone forgets about the parking problem in summer, though, so thank goodness for *Hook Farm*, two miles west of town. Not only can you stroll into Lyme Regis from your tent, the jaunt is a forty-minute nature-walk over fields dotted with horses and alongside a river. If you aren't up for it, don't worry – bus #31 stops by the family-friendly *Talbot Arms* three hundred yards from the site roughly every half-hour. But it's the rural views of the Lyn Valley and a relaxed air that really help make this well-planned site such a joy. Owner Adrian Morgan did everything right when he landscaped it. What could have become an overmanicured holiday park is instead a peaceful haven with spacious terraced pitches and good amenities. Top Field is the choice chill-out spot; pitches 80–99 enjoy the best views. For foodies, a visit to Hugh Fearnley–Whittingstall's *River Cottage Store & Canteen* (℡01297 631862), four miles west in Axminster, is a must; walk it off on the view-tastic South West Coast Path, which passes behind the site.

Practicalities

Hook Farm Caravan & Camping Park, Gore Lane, Uplyme, Lyme Regis, Dorset, DT7 3UU ℡*01297 442801,* Ⓦ*www.hookfarm-uplyme.co.uk*
Pitches & price 4 hard-standing pitches (with hook-ups), 96 grass pitches (53 hook-ups). 2 people, £10–12 low season, £18–22 high season. Additional adult £3, additional child (5–15) £1.50.
Facilities New block with showers, toilets and basins, older block with showers, toilets and basins; baby-changing at both. Dish-washing areas. On-site shop.
Restrictions Most dogs permitted (see website). No campfires. No stereos. Max 6-person group. Easter and bank holidays minimum 3-night stay.
Open March–Oct.
Getting there From the A35 take the B3165, passing through Uplyme. Turn right into Gore Lane opposite the *Talbot Arms*. The site is 330yds uphill on the right.

Stock Gaylard Estate

There are yurt holidays and then there is *Stock Gaylard Estate*. Its two three-yurt groups are positioned for utter privacy on a 1,800-acre Georgian estate – an English savannah, as Kenya-enthusiast owner Andy Langmead calls its centuries-old deer park. The Brickles yurts get sunrises over Dorset's undulating greens in front and a sixty-acre woodland behind, where wild deer flit through the shadows. The Withybed yurts, in a bucolic fold of fields and woods a ten-minute walk from the deer park, feel more secluded and benefit from their proximity to a shared proper shower in a barn.

With two-bedroom yurts and a living/kitchen yurt built from the estate's ash, the complexes are conceived as cottage-style accommodation for groups or sharing families. Yet Langmead's African influences shine through. Despite the carpet and tasteful linen, the bespoke furniture and the kitchens with gas stoves, a stay here is all about the great outdoors: heating water with an open fire, taking outdoor baths and using composting loos open on one side to the forest. It's about long rambles on what – for one week at least – is your very own stately estate. Magic.

Practicalities

Stock Gaylard Estate, Sturminster Newton, Dorset, DT10 2BG ℡*01963 23511,* Ⓦ*www.stockgaylard.com*
Pitches & price 2 yurt complexes for up to 8 adults (or 4 adults and 6 children) each. Single yurt (possibly sharing kitchen/living yurt) £225–450 per week, 3-yurt complex £560–850 per week.
Facilities Each group has a composting toilet, solar-heated shower and outdoor dishwashing area. There's a separate shower, basin and toilet in the barn near Withybed yurts.
Restrictions Campfires permitted in designated areas. Dogs welcome.
Open Mid-May to Sept.
Getting there The estate is around 5 miles east of Sherborne on the A3030. The entrance is at the lodge opposite the right-hand turning to King's Stag and Dorchester (B3143).

Riverside Lakes

Nature and nurture by the New Forest

Global capitalism is the last thing that comes to mind in this supremely chilled-out meadow. Eco-loveliness or tranquillity, perhaps. Maybe even convenience, given its location equidistant from the New Forest and Dorset coast, both around twenty minutes away by car. Nevertheless, it is Tony and Lisa Perkins's work for multinational corporations that has funded this subtly counter-culture site where eco-ethics and chilled vibes abound. Its non-commercial, alternative vibe only adds to the joke.

Riverside Lakes feels a long, long way from work. With a maximum of 120 people on 22 acres, it is the de-stress site par excellence. This is partly down to its space and environment – most of its widely dispersed camping areas, each under ten-pitches small, are cut from long grass in a car-free meadow. But look closer and you'll see some thoughtful touches, too. Full marks for a communal fire-pit in each area; campers can also borrow braziers and buy wood on site. Bonus points for a facility to prebook favourite pitches online; the "chill-out" area in the far corner lives up to

its name, while pitches in the "woodland" come with a shared hammock. Hire a "soulpad" and you won't need a tent at all. Positioned for privacy and provided with a bonfire camp kitchen to help tap into your inner Ray Mears, these jute-floored bell tents come with futons and are ideal for couples or small groups – the latter will love a three-tent grouping on an island in the site's fishing lakes, which are also open to those brave enough to swim. Hard-standing pitches are hidden discreetly near the entrance.

Perhaps because the site feels like a shared secret, or possibly because its minimal-impact, soul-nurturing ethos appeals to campers who are unfazed by basic amenities in a Portakabin, *Riverside Lakes* exudes a community vibe. Laid-back and endlessly helpful, the Perkinses see their site as an opportunity to reconnect to the real world. It is, they say, somewhere for children to remember how to play, a place to cook sausages on a campfire and enjoy the starlight. Amen to that.

▼ The "Soulpad" scene, complete with camp kitchen

Practicalities

Riverside Lakes, Slough Lane, Horton, Dorset, BH21 7JL
☎*01202 821212,* Ⓦ*www.riverside-lakes.co.uk*
Pitches & price 45 grass pitches, 7 bell tents for 2–6 people, 5 caravan pitches & 7 hard-standing pitches (12 hook-ups). Adults £7, children (5–14) £5; Camping & Caravan Club membership (if required) £36 annual for 6 people. Bell tents £38 for 2, £70 for 4, £90 for 6.
Facilities Basic, clean amenities block with showers, mixed toilets and basins, composting loo, dishwashing area, fishing lakes (£5–8 per day; own gear required).
Restrictions Dogs permitted. Campfires in designated areas and braziers.
Open May–Sept.
Getting there At the A31/A338 roundabout south of Ringwood, turn west and drive through the village of Three Legged Cross. After 2.5 miles look for Global Orange Groves citrus nurseries on the right. Slough Lane is 220yds further on, also on the right.

Burrowhayes Farm

A pretty packhorse bridge by the entrance hints at what's in store at this site near Exmoor's beaches. The Dascombe family's former farm is known as much for its stables as for its picturesque small campsite and touring park. With both child-sized ponies and horses in the stable, and riding programmes throughout the day (except Saturdays), there's something for all riders. Parents get to lead their aspiring cowboys and girls on thirty-minute rides, while more confident riders get one- to three-hour hacks. Can't face the yomp uphill to those wind-blown moorlands? Try the gentler ride up through the wooded Horner Valley instead.

Burrowhayes Farm is Exmoor camping for softies. Whatever the bucolic appeal of a stream that gurgles past the touring park, or the trees that break up a slightly sloping camping area, the immaculate site is well provided for: helpful staff, a laundry and an amenities block whose rustic looks belie heating and excellent hot showers. It's more convenient than the average rural site, too. The shops and restaurants of Porlock are three-quarters of a mile away via a woodland track behind the site; historic boozer *The Ship* is pick of the places for a pint.

Practicalities

Burrowhayes Farm, West Luccombe, Porlock, Minehead, Somerset, TA24 8HT ☏*01643 862463,* Ⓦ*www.burrowhayes.co.uk*

Pitches & price 54 caravan pitches (10 hard-standing, all with hook-ups), 66 tent pitches (8 hook-ups). Single tent £6–8, 2 people £10–14, additional adult £4–5, children (3–15) £2–2.50.

Facilities Amenities block with showers, basins, toilets, hair dryer and disabled facilities; second basic toilet block with basins. On-site shop, static caravans for hire.

Restrictions No campfires. Dogs permitted on leads.

Open Easter–Oct.

Getting there Turn off the A39, 5 miles west of Minehead, towards West Luccombe and Horner. Go 550yds to the mini-roundabout; the entrance is beyond it on the right. Buses go from Minehead to the West Luccombe turn-off.

Pool Bridge

For the ultimate in Exmoor escapism, visit this back-to-nature site deep in the oak woods of the Horner Valley. Just be prepared to put in some effort first: squeezing between hedgerows on narrow lanes and twisting around hairpin turns – no chance for caravans or large motor homes. The reward for your motor-gymnastics is a hideaway that feels closer to wild camping than any other site in the national park. Although not quite the secret it was a decade ago, *Pool Bridge* is sufficiently remote to make the shops of Porlock three miles away seem a memory. Mobile phone reception certainly is, but maybe that's the point.

The choice pitches are riverside, where you can light a fire – the best midge-deterrent there is. All campers benefit from largely flat ground and shelter from steep, thickly wooded slopes. With only rope swings for the kids, no on-site management – the owner pops by daily to collect fees and sell firewood – and basic amenities, this is a place to revel in the dawn chorus and watch bats dart about at dusk. Days are best spent in boots: a three-mile trail downriver to Horner village for cream teas or a day circuit to Exmoor's literal highpoint, Dunkery Beacon.

Practicalities

Pool Bridge Campsite, Porlock, Minehead, Somerset, TA24 8HQ ☏*01643 862521*

Pitches & price About 50 tent pitches. Adults £6, children (6–12) £3, under-5s £1.

Facilities Basic amenities block with male and female showers, toilets and basins, a dishwashing area and a payphone.

Restrictions Dogs permitted on leads. Campfires permitted within 3yds of stream.

Open Easter–Oct.

Getting there Turn left off the A39, about 5 miles west of Minehead, towards the villages of West Luccombe and Horner. After 550yds turn right at the sign for "Filter Station". Head uphill, take the next left turn and continue for a further 2 miles until you reach the river. The campsite entrance is on the right, just before the bridge.

Westermill Farm

Back to nature in the heart of Exmoor

Great sites generally feel right from the moment you enter their fields. Some appeal before you even arrive. And there are those gems that do both and get better the longer you stay. *Westermill Farm*, in the heart of Exmoor National Park, is one of these. It ticks all the right boxes should you wish to drop off the radar before you push in a single peg. To reach it, turn off at Exford and tunnel through tangled hedgerows on narrow lanes – rural

seclusion yet two miles from Exford's excellent *Crown Hotel*. Through the farmyard, past sheepdogs in kennels and a glossy chicken or two, you check in at a farmhouse with framed awards for its Angus cattle and conservation efforts – a working farm governed by ecology. The anticipation increases after you meet your easygoing hosts, Oliver and Jill Edwards, and discover that homegrown free-range steaks and burgers, lamb and pork-and-apple sausages are stocked in the on-site farm shop, alongside local fresh bread, ice cream, basic stores and an off-licence. Not bad for a family-owned campsite. And that's before the moment of truth – the site itself.

With a blissfully chilled-out vibe, nature-led farming that has won a David Bellamy conservation gold medal for 12 years running and a sense of deep pastoral peace, the site is tailor-made for escaping the everyday. Turn off your mobile phone – there's no reception anyway – and tune in instead to whatever drifts over these meadows cradled in the River Exe valley: wind in the trees, birdsong, the occasional delighted shriek of children from the river. The loudest noise you'll hear while tucked in your sleeping bag is a dawn chorus of pedigree livestock on slopes above. Apparently, some campers actually complain.

With fifteen acres set aside for camping, space is less of a problem than the decision over where to pitch. The first of four camping areas is a good choice for those with very young children; directly beneath the best amenities block, it's the only area fenced off from the river that runs alongside the site – a constant source of wonder and hazard for toddlers.

Everyone else should push on to Thricelet meadow, *Westermill*'s largest and most natural area at the far end of the site. Its amenities block is simple, and solar-heated hot water can run out at peak times, but the compensations are open-ended views down the valley and campfires in a limited number of firegrates-cum-barbecues – as good a reason as any to prebook. Down here the outdoors really is great at dusk. Low sunshine illuminates the valley in an orange haze and campfires crackle. By 10.30pm the whole place is asleep, silent except for the river.

At such times, it's easy to understand why the place is so special. With neither hook-ups nor fancy facilities, it's about

Practicalities

Westermill Farm, Exford, Exmoor, Minehead, Somerset, TA24 7NJ ☎01643 831238, Ⓦwww.exmoorcamping. co.uk

Pitches & price 60 tent pitches. Adults £5, children £3, cars £2.50.

Facilities 2 simple amenities blocks with showers, toilets, basins and dishwashing area. On-site farm shop, laundry facilities, payphone, B&B and self-catering cottages available.

Restrictions Dogs welcome (£2.50) but must be kept on a lead. Campfires permitted in firegrates (wood sold on site). No stereos or radios. No showers available between Nov and Easter.

Open Year round.

Getting there Head to Exford on the B3224 in the centre of the national park. Turn north towards Porlock beside Exford's village green. At a sharp right bend after 440yds take a single-track road, following signposts to the farm. The entrance is 2 miles further on the left.

underrated joys like back-to-nature simplicity, tranquillity and space. Factor in the absence of traffic and you have kiddie-heaven. Who needs a playground when there's a shallow river with rope swings and trout fry to net? What greater adventure than tractor tours, feeding the lambs or exploring the five-hundred-acre farm on waymarked paths? Ascend the valley sides and you plateau out onto the moors where red deer roam and buzzards soar. Of course, you only learn that if you stay a while. That's *Westermill* – great on first impressions, but even better on close acquaintance.

◀ Getting some farmyard facetime at *Westermill* ▶ Fields stretch away from Dunkery Beacon, Exmoor's highest point; happy campers

Batcombe Vale
The good of small things

Size matters in campsites. As a rule of thumb, small pitch-quotas equate to personal and interesting, large suggest anonymous and bland. The trouble is, small sites often fall under the tap-in-field category; great for budding Ray Mearses, back-to-basics horrors for others. Character versus facilities – the choice is yours. Unless, that is, you head to *Batcombe Vale*, a small site in a miniature vale that bucks the trend and ticks almost every box in the process.

The site feels like a secret world, one far more remote than the seven miles to Shepton Mallet suggest. Doves on the weather-vane coo, housemartins chitter as they swoop into a barn, dairy cows call in stereo on the slopes and the occasional buzzard rides a thermal. All that's left for you to do is pitch a tent, pop a cork and relax into the soporific calm of deepest rural Somerset. Bliss.

It's only on closer inspection that you realize much of the site's air of tranquillity derives from attention to detail. Those spacious pitches attractively terraced around the vale? Immaculately trimmed. The abundant trees and flowerbeds planted to screen the neighbours? Spiky semi-tropical, not suburban prissy. Similarly, the spotless central amenities block comes with fresh wildflowers as well as plentiful hot water; *Batcombe Vale*'s blend of charm and comfort in a nutshell. Every inch warrants its status as an Area of Outstanding Natural Beauty, yet order and calm reign supreme.

Features like these make reservations essential to ensure a place in summer. Each of the site's thirty pitches is allocated according to their campers' tent size and group members. Motor homes and caravans are kept apart from campers and noisy children are (usually) separated from quiet couples. If given a choice, opt for leafy pitches at the rear right that bask in the morning sun when the weather gods smile. Bespoke booking might be anathema to those used to pitch-where-you-like freedom, but it ensures *Batcombe Vale* is happy campers all round, from touring retirees in caravans to walking couples to young families. The latter will appreciate the size of the site, which is small enough to let kids off the leash safely. Children gravitate towards a tent-free central lawn to kick balls or hunt frogs in the hedgerows. By 9am, older children – and many an adult – are afloat on the lake in a free rowing boat, or trying their luck for tench and the odd

Practicalities

Batcombe Vale Campsite, Batcombe Vale, Shepton Mallet, Somerset, BA4 6BW ☎01749 831207, Ⓦwww.batcombevale.co.uk

Pitches & price 30 grass pitches (17 hook-ups). Pitch (2 people) £15.75, additional adult £4.75, child (4–15) £2.75.

Facilities Small, clean amenities block with showers, toilets, basins and dishwashing area. BBQs available. Fishing lake (no equipment rental) daily permit: adults £5, children £2.50.

Restrictions Dogs permitted (£1) on leads, but no pitbull terriers, dobermanns or rottweilers. No campfires. Minimum 2 nights for pitch reservations. All arrivals before dusk. No groups larger than 4 families.

Open Easter–Sept, reservations essential in summer.

Getting there Follow the brown signs either from Bruton, north of Wincanton, or from the A36/A371 roundabout south of Shepton Mallet. Taxis from Bruton station cost around £5.

monster twenty-pound carp.

A location in central Somerset puts crowd-pleaser day-trips within reach: Longleat Safari Park, Bath, Glastonbury, Cheddar Gorge and Wookey Hole in the Mendip Hills, even Exmoor at push. Yet with free rein over 120 surrounding acres of lush Somerset meadows, there's enough to occupy you for a few days at least. And therein is the beauty of *Batcombe*. With its walks, ducks, rowing boats and fishing and balance between comforts and tranquillity, the site squares the circular arguments over wild site versus holiday park. It is a miniature holiday of its own: small, certainly, but perfectly formed.

◀ *Batcombe's rowing boats at the ready* ▶ View of the tranquil, wildlife packed vale; meet the residents at Longleat Safari Park

Stowford Manor Farm

Take a dip in Wiltshire's cool waters

Like the cream teas served in its garden, *Stowford Manor Farm* is a site best savoured slowly. There's little to provide that wow-factor hit – indeed, first-timers may wonder what all the fuss is about. Wind down, settle in, and little by little you realize why this gem has a devoted following. As understated as its owners, the Bryant family, who have owned the farm for three generations, the site has a wonderful old-fashioned appeal that hasn't changed much in the forty years since it took its first tent.

Setting plays an important part. Pitches – all twenty of them on a field small enough to keep an eye on roaming kids – are behind a pretty, medieval manor complex the colour of clotted cream. There are appealing retro touches, too: facilities in the old stables – nippy on cold days but how pleasingly tactile to stand on smooth cobbles for your shower; fresh unpasteurized milk from the farm's Jersey cows for sale in the fridge; or those cream

▼ Bursting bubbles and loving it at *Stowford Manor Farm*

teas – as good a pastime as any for a wet afternoon.

All are charming, of course. Yet the real delight of *Stowford* is the Frome River. Although a shallow ford by the site's old mill is fine for kiddies to cool off in, a half-mile downriver are the cool depths of Farleigh Weir, where bathers of the only river-swimming club in the country have congregated since 1933 (bring shoes for the dip). There's a changing room, too, so make a day of it by going a field further to explore the ruins of Farleigh Castle. Start investigating and other day-trips abound: Longleat Safari Park, picture-postcard Bradford-on-Avon or Bath, whose aquatic pleasures are more sophisticated than ever thanks to the rooftop Thermae Baths spa. All that without a mention of the Trowbridge Village Pump Folk Festival (Ⓦwww.trowbridgefestival.co.uk) held at the farm over the last weekend in July.

Stowford Manor Farm is more than just a tranquil riverside campsite with a handy choice of pubs (the *Hungerford Arms* near the weir for a pint, *The New Inn* or *The Poplars* 1.5 miles away for food). It takes time to sift through its multi-layered appeal. You've heard of slow food and slow travel. Perhaps it's time for slow camping – you read it here first.

Practicalities

Stowford Manor Farm, Wingfield, Trowbridge, Wiltshire, BA14 9LH ☎*01225 752253,* Ⓦ*www.stowfordmanorfarm.co.uk*

Pitches & price 20 grass pitches (16 hook-ups). Tents £8–15, caravans and campervans £13.

Facilities Simple but sweet: 2 showers and basins in old stables, toilets with basins in separate block, dishwashing area, B&B available in manor house.

Restrictions Dogs permitted on leads. No campfires. Young groups by prior arrangement.

Open Easter–Oct.

Getting there From Trowbridge on the A366, the site is on the left just under a mile from the crossroads in Wingfield. Taxis from Trowbridge station cost £5.

Barge Inn

Set aside the scepticism, dig out the divining rod and push a peg into the ley lines of mystic England at this pub-garden site. Not far south is Stonehenge. Just over the chalk hills of the Pewsey Downs in the other direction are the sacred sites of occultist Albion – Silbury Hill, Avebury's stone circle, West Kennet Long Barrow. It's no surprise to see a white horse carved in the hills opposite the site, or even to discover the engagingly eccentric pub on the Kennet and Avon canal is the unofficial rallying point of the crop-circle set. A disparate bunch of boozers, boaties and believers gather in crop-circle season (April–Sept) to discuss the latest sightings of stellar visitors: aliens in the wheat fields (marked on a map in the games room) and celebrities in the pub.

The willow-fringed field beneath the canal embankment appeals less for comfort – facilities are rudimentary – than the convenience of a pub being just steps away and an atmosphere of chilled escapism. Some campers check in for a night and stay for a week – "Hotel California" locals call it. Who can blame them? Sit by the canal with a pint, watching the white horse vanish into the dusk, and you can almost feel the magic in the air.

Practicalities

Barge Inn, Honeystreet, Pewsey, Wiltshire, SN9 5PS
☎*01672 851705,* Ⓦ*www.the-barge-inn.com*
Pitches & price 10 small caravan pitches, about 35 tent pitches. Adults £5, children (4–12) £2.50.
Facilities Basic: male and female toilet area with shower, toilet and basin, outdoor sink for dishwashing. Live music on Sat nights in the pub.
Restrictions Dogs (£1) permitted on leads. No campfires. No reservations (arrival by early evening recommended on Fri in summer; busy either side of Glastonbury Festival weekend).
Open Year round.
Getting there A couple of miles north of Devizes on the A36, turn right towards Horton. Continue to Alton Barnes, turn right to Honeystreet, and once over the canal bridge, turn right towards the pub at the sawmill.

Postern Hill

For proof that caravans and conservation are not mutually exclusive come to this woodland site near Marlborough. Owned by Forest Holidays, the vacation arm of the Forestry Commission, the clearing in the Savernake Forest features flat ground and eco-credentials to appeal to caravanners and camping families alike. The freedom to pick your pitch helps – from well-drained grassy areas with hook-ups to the left of the entrance, to spots beneath oak and ash trees in the centre, to cosy corners everywhere in the woods. But as important is that *Postern Hill* is a site where nature rules; kids can follow wildlife trails or join walks with forest rangers, and early risers may see grazing deer. Small wonder it has a wallful of green tourism awards to its name.

The caveats to this simple charm are a lack of showers – campers can use those in a leisure centre a mile away for a small charge – and an evening curfew. Yet Marlborough's handsome high-street pubs and restaurants are only a 35-minute walk away, and even closer if you rent the on-site bikes. By the time you return from a bite and a pint or three, the only thing that will keep you awake is the sound of the owls in the woods.

Practicalities

Postern Hill, Postern Hill, Marlborough, Wiltshire, SN8 4ND ☎*01672 515195,* Ⓦ*www.forestholidays.co.uk*
Pitches & price 170 grass pitches (35 hook-ups). Pitches for 2 £7–13, £3.50 supplement for non-members of the Caravan & Camping Club, £1–3.50 supplement for Fri & Sat.
Facilities Simple amenities block with toilets (summer months only), basins and dishwashing area. Milk, fresh bread and croissants are available at reception if pre-ordered. Bike rental. Recycling facilities.
Restrictions Dogs permitted (£1). No campfires. No toilet facilities in winter months. Site curfew in effect from 10pm Sun–Thurs, 10.30pm Fri–Sat.
Open Year round.
Getting there The entrance to *Postern Hill* campsite is signposted off the A346, approximately a mile south of Marlborough.

Christchurch, Bracelands & Woodlands

A woodland playground where three sites fit all

From the one-time hunting ground of kings – Saxon, Norman and Tudor alike – to its designation as England's first national forest park in 1938, the Forest of Dean, sandwiched between the Severn and Wye rivers, has long been revered as one of Britain's most magical woodlands. Everyone should wander through its ancient oak forests at least once. Visit in spring, and bluebells carpet the floor between twenty million trees and villages are frothy with apple blossom. Autumn is mellow and golden. Year round the forest represents a fourty-two-square-mile adventure playground for walkers, cyclists and canoeists. Despite the space, it does get crowded – but the surprise is that it's easy to escape the happy hordes if you hit the trails; there are numerous ones for walkers, while mountain bikers can use the rooty red-grade Fodca Trail.

You could say the same of this trio of campsites managed by Forestry Holidays, the vacation arm of the Forestry Commission. Come late Friday afternoon in summer, every weekender from Bristol to the Midlands seems to arrive for a getaway – get there before 4pm to avoid queues. That all vanish onto 890 pitches says as much about the sizes and distinctive characters of the three sites as the forest's cross-camper appeal. Take *Christchurch*. The first of the sites is the most family-friendly due to its outdoor playground and proximity to an on-site shop. Many campers say its slightly sloping field wrapped up within beech trees is the prettiest of the three sites. It's also the busiest – at weekends and school holidays calm camping this is not.

Fortunately, mellow *Bracelands* lies a half-mile beyond the shared reception block. Poised at the lip of the Wye valley, pitches here receive views and sunsets, both at their best from the furthest campers-only field. You'll almost certainly be on a slope – lower pitches on the first field are flatter but boggy after heavy rain – yet the reward is broad, open skies that contribute to a wonderful sense of space. Owls hoot in the woods nudging the site, while wild boar root beyond the fence. Lift a head from your pillow at dawn and you may see fallow deer. To cater to eight hundred pitches combined, both sites scatter modest but adequate facilities blocks throughout their areas. Unusually, carvanners have the option of going wilder – the *Woodlands* site behind *Christchurch* has ninety caravan-only pitches in the forest itself. Shops and pubs are a ten-minute walk away from *Christchurch* in Berry Hill; with a car, the *Dog & Muffler* (closed Mondays) five minutes away is the pick for food and views.

Whatever the appeal for parents of loafing around the tent while the kids join forest rangers on free nature walks, you're here to experience the forest. How you do so is up to you. A forty-five-minute woodland walk from *Bracelands* emerges at Symonds Yat viewpoint, where peregrine falcons nest among the cliffs each summer. A ferryman pulls a passenger ferry across the Wye from the riverside *Saracens Head Inn* below, not nearly as much fun as hiring canoes here; Symonds Yat Adventure Centre (☎01600 890129, ⓦwww.wyedean.co.uk) provides collection for one-way paddlers. Closer to the site, the Sculpture

Practicalities

Christchurch, Bracelands and Woodlands Caravan and Campsite, Bracelands Drive, Christchurch, Coleford, Gloucestershire, GL16 7NN ☏*01594 837258,* Ⓦ*www.forestholidays.co.uk*

Pitches & price *Christchurch:* 280 pitches (90 hook-ups); *Bracelands:* 520 pitches (92 hook-ups); *Woodlands:* 90 caravan pitches (27 hook-ups). Pitches £8–14, £2 surcharge for 1-night stay, £3.50 discount for Camping and Caravanning Club members. £10 cash deposit required for electronic car barrier.

Facilities *Christchurch* and *Bracelands:* main amenities block with showers, toilets, basins, hair dryers, baby-changing facilities, disabled access, launderette and dishwashing area; smaller blocks with toilets and basins (plus showers at *Bracelands*) and dishwashing area. Well-stocked shop at reception.

Restrictions Dogs permitted (£1) on leads. No campfires. Last arrival at dusk, site barrier closed 10.30pm–7am.

Open *Christchurch:* year round; *Bracelands* and *Woodlands:* Easter–Sept.

Getting there The site entrance is signposted off the A4136, 6 miles northeast of Monmouth. Buses #30 and #31 from Gloucester stop in central Berry Hill, 440yds from the entrance.

Trail is a three-and-a-half mile woodland route lined with work by international artists. By car, the twenty-mile Royal Forest Route circuits through the best of the forest via Puzzle Wood. Some say its extraordinary maze of gulleys, bridges, dead ends and fantastically twisted roots inspired Mirkwood and Lothlorien in J.R.R. Tolkein's *Lord of the Rings*. As we said, magic.

◀ Peregrine falcons nest at Symonds Yat ▶ Pretty, family-friendly and sometimes-busy *Christchurch*; play spot the ents in Puzzle Wood

Abbey Home Farm
Pure camping in a foodie heaven

Some campsites create a feeling of genuine inspiration. Others instil a sense of escapism as soon as you've hammered in that last peg. Somehow *Abbey Home Farm* manages to do both, even though neither its facilities (minimal) nor its location (within earshot of an A-road in westerly winds) really impress.

But on this Cotswold farm, just east of Cirencester, the inspiration comes in the form of green ethics and integrity, and the escapism from being surrounded by nothing but fields. Oh, and the food helps, too. The 1800-acre farm, one of the country's leading organic food producers, has a multi-award-winning shop (Tues–Sat 9am–5pm, Sun 11am–4pm) selling its wonderland of succulent meats, gorgeous greens, juicy fruits and deliciously crumbly cheeses – try the Dancy's Fancy. Food miles don't come lower than this. In fact, there's no need to cook at all. A licensed café (same hours as shop) produces farm-grown veggie meals and the finest Sunday roast for miles around – reservations are a must.

If the food is one reason to come, the purity of the pitches is another. The environmental awareness of Hilary and Will Chester-Master's farming practices also shapes the camping areas. Whether on the principal site, with lovely views across the wheat fields, or nestled into a four-pitch glade near a composting loo and a groups-only green field, this is minimal-impact, natural camping where lighting at night is of the stellar variety. Even a four-yurt eco-camp in a woodland clearing, or a single yurt and magical shack by a pond, the latter pair in a quiet corner near the farmstead, are laudably simple; foam mattresses, wood burners, composting loos and peace.

Most campers spend their days on long farm rambles to meet the locals – roe deer, foxes, badgers, hares, buzzards and the domestic livestock. Others sign up to workshops run several times a month (check the website): from basket-weaving to bushcraft, and cookery to cheese-making with the farm's master cheesemaker. Extra features like these make *Abbey Home* not just a campsite, but a destination in its own right. Warmed by campfires and a feel-good glow, everything is on hand to simply, utterly chill out. You couldn't ask for much more of a campsite than that.

Practicalities

Abbey Home Farm, Burford Road, Cirencester, Gloucestershire, GL7 5HF ☎01285 640441, Ⓦwww.theorganicfarmshop.co.uk

Pitches & price 35 pitches (15 in groups-only field), adults £4, children £1. Yurts for 4 or 5, £40–75 (min 2 nights), shack for 2, £45 (min 2 nights, adults only).

Facilities Showers, composting toilets at main camping area, composting toilets in other areas; 4-yurt camp has composting loos and fire water-heater; single yurt and shack have gas stove, shared shower, toilet and basin.

Restrictions No dogs. Campfires permitted in braziers (£5 hire) and designated areas. No large motor homes or caravans; campervans permitted. Arrive during shop hours unless by prior arrangement. All rubbish must be removed.

Open Easter–Oct, shack year round.

Getting there From the A417–A429 junction two miles east of Cirencester, take the B4425 and turn left following the "organic shop" signs.

▼ *Abbey Home Farm*'s award-winning shop and cafe

Folly Farm
Back to basics in Gloucestershire

Come peak season, Cotswold tourism magnets like Bourton on the Water and Lower Slaughter are besieged as day-trippers dawdle through centres the colour of the shortbread in the local tearooms. A map will tell you both are just three miles from *Folly Farm*, yet this relaxed site seems a world away from the tourist trail.

Sited in an area of outstanding natural beauty near the Gloucestershire Way footpath, this low-key place feels less a campsite than a stay in the garden of the Kenwright family – especially for caravanners, who get first call on pretty pitches on a sycamore-canopied front lawn; tents are only allowed here if there's space. Those under canvas should pitch in the Rally Field, where you can drink in pastoral views and an exhilarating space with your morning cuppa. The back-to-basics vibe, which extends to simple amenities, is a deliberate ploy to attract die-hard campers. Sure you'll need a torch at night, but who wants artificial light when they can stargaze?

A mile or so across the fields is *The Plough* in Cold Aston village, another Cotswold classic of creamy stone. Luckily the tour groups haven't caught on yet – being away from the action seems to have its advantages.

▼ A vintage car drives through Lower Slaughter

Practicalities

Folly Farm, Bourton on the Water, Cheltenham, Gloucestershire, GL54 3BY ☏*01451 820285,* Ⓦ*www.cotswoldcamping.net*

Pitches & price 15 caravan pitches and 45 tent pitches (12 hook-ups). Pitches £6–10, adults £2.50, children (3–12) £1.50.

Facilities Simple amenities block with 2 showers, 5 toilets, basins and washing-up area, disabled toilet. Also has a basic second toilet block with basins.

Restrictions Dogs (£1) permitted on leads. No campfires. Reservations essential for bank holidays.

Open Mid-March to mid-Oct.

Getting there The site entrance is on the left, 2.5 miles west of Bourton on the Water on the A436 to Cheltenham. The #801 bus from Cheltenham stops outside on request.

Southeast England

Camping in the southeast, England's most populous region, is about getting away from it all and finding your own patch of peace and quiet, be it in a shady glen in Hampshire or on a cliff-top clearing in Kent.

Though extending as far north as Banbury and as far east as Folkestone, many of the campsites in this chapter are dotted across the bucolic landscape of the Sussex Weald, within easy reach of the dramatic rolling chalklands of the South Downs, England's newest National Park, and the excellent hiking along its eponymous national trail. More woodland awaits to the west, where the sprawling New Forest offers miles of dedicated cycle routes and camping comes with the added novelty of wild ponies grazing just outside your tent. And for a holiday with a hint of overseas travel,

there's always the genteel Isle of Wight, a short ferry ride from Southampton or Portsmouth.

Escaping to the country doesn't have to mean kissing goodbye to your creature comforts, though. Appealing to the weekending Londoner who'd rather experience the countryside from under soft linen sheets than on a hard canvas floor, the Southeast, perhaps more than any other region, has embraced the concept of glamping (see p.84), and for every back-to-basics campsite there is seemingly another offering wood-floored tipis or luxurious Mongolian yurts.

Indeed, this close proximity to the capital is something of a mixed blessing: standards are uniformly high, but prices can be equally so – and you certainly won't be the only one looking for that little bit of tranquillity.

Southeast England

	PAGE	🥾	🚲	⛵	🍷	⛰	👪	👫	🚐	🚍	♿
Ashwood Farm	79		✓				✓			✓	
Billycan Camping	78				✓		✓			✓	
Blackberry Wood	90					✓	✓	✓			
Britchcombe Farm	68	✓	✓				✓	✓			
Cheney Manor House	69	✓	✓				✓	✓			
Cobbs Hill Farm	96						✓		✓	✓	✓
Dernwood Farm	92	✓			✓	✓					
Grange Farm	72					✓					
Hidden Spring Vineyard	93				✓		✓		✓	✓	
Manor Court Farm	89						✓			✓	
Matley Wood	72		✓			✓					
Neals Place Farm	98	✓	✓			✓				✓	
Normans Bay	92						✓	✓	✓	✓	
Palace Farm	97	✓	✓				✓	✓			
Roundhill	70		✓				✓			✓	
Safari Britain	80					✓	✓	✓			
Shadow Woods	76	✓				✓				✓	
Southdown Farm	89								✓	✓	✓
Spring Barn Farm Park	88						✓			✓	
St Ives Farm	86	✓			✓	✓		✓	✓		
Stoats Farm	73	✓									✓
Swiss Farm International	69	✓	✓	✓					✓		✓
Vintage Vacations	74						✓				
Wapsbourne Manor Farm	82	✓	✓		✓	✓	✓				
The Warren	100	✓	✓					✓		✓	✓
Welsummer	94					✓	✓				
Woodland Farm	97					✓		✓			

See front flap for key to symbols

Milton
Keynes
A421
A509 A422
A5
Aylesbury
A4129
BUCKINGHAM-
SHIRE
Amersham
High
Wycombe Beaconsfield
A40
wiss Farm
ernational
A4155
A4130
Harrow
Enfield
enley-
Thames Maidenhead
Slough Uxbridge
Windsor
LONDON
Romford
Bracknell
Bromley
Gravesend
Sheerness
A2
M25
Herne Bay
Margate
Camberley
Croydon
Gillingham
Whitstable
A299
Broadstairs
Farnborough
Sutton
Rochester A227
Sittingbourne
M2
A2 Faversham
A290
Ramsgate
A257
Woking
A269
A20
Palace Farm
A28
Fleet
A233
A227
Maidstone
A2070
Neals Place
Farm
Canterbury
A256
Aldershot
Guildford
Dorking
Reigate
Sevenoaks
A25
A26
A20 Lenham
A251
A252 A28
B2068
A2
B2046
A258
Deal
Farnham
SURREY
A24
A22
A21
Tonbridge A228
Welsummer
A274
Woodland Farm
A260 A20
Dover
004
Haslemere
A281
B2133
Crawley
B2110
East
Grinstead
St Ives
Farm
B2026
B2188
A264
Royal
Tunbridge
Wells
K E N T
Ashford
A20
Folkestone
The Warren
Shadow
Woods
Horsham
Ashwood
Farm
B2110
Manor
Court Farm
A262
A229
A28
Petworth
ersfield
A272
Midhurst
A283
A29
A272
Hayward
Heath
A22
A275
Crowborough
E A S T S U S S E X
A265
A268
A259
Rye
Dungeness
SOUTH DOWNS
NATIONAL PARK
W E S T S U S S E X
B2139
Burgess Hill
A23
B2112
Wapsbourne Manor Farm
Dernwood
Farm
A272 Uckfield
Horam
Hidden
Spring
Vineyard
Battle
A21
A259
Southdown Farm
B2116
Blackberry
Wood
A26
A27
Lewes
A22
A267
Hailsham
A271
Cobbs Hill Farm
Hastings
Bexhill
t
A27 A286
A29
Arundel
Billycan
Camping
Littlehampton
A259
Brighton
Spring Barn
Farm Park
Newhaven
Safari Britain
A26
A259
Normans Bay
Eastbourne
Chichester
West
Vittering
Bognor
Regis
Worthing
Seaford
East
ittering
Selsey
Beachy Head
A27

Britchcombe Farm
Cream tea and chalk walks

Tucked away in the stunning, unspoilt Oxfordshire countryside, *Britchcombe Farm* sprawls across five lush meadows strewn with buttercups, hedgerows and lazily grazing cows and sheep. Aside from the dawn chorus of chirruping birds overhead and the crow of the farm's cockerel, this is a wonderfully peaceful setting. The energetic, no-nonsense and somewhat eccentric owner, Marcella Seymour, makes daily rounds in an old 4X4, booming greetings, dishing out advice on local walks and warning campers to picnic away from her cows. Don't miss her delicious home-made cream teas at the on-site tearoom every Sunday, 3–6pm. Despite the categorized pitches (families, adults only, caravanners, motorcyclists), there are no hard and fast rules about where people stay. Britchcombe's fifth field – the overflow site – sits on a hill with great views across the rest of the campsite; it's quiet here and feels more like wild camping. People are free to wander the farm

and there's even a designated area for dogs to run about without a lead. Forking off the campsite, through lolloping countryside, chalk hills and forests, are winding routes, bridle paths and the 87-mile Ridgeway trail, Britain's oldest road – especially pretty in spring, when wildflowers bloom alongside the inviting green and yellow meadows.

A steep half-hour walk leads to the Iron Age hillfort of Uffington Castle on the summit of White Horse Hill, Oxfordshire's highest point at 786ft. Carved into the upper slope, the magnificent outline of the famous 374-foot-long White Horse – one of Britain's oldest chalk-cut hill figures – can be seen for miles and is worth visiting for its stunning views across the Berkshire downlands. Stop off at the nearby *Fox and Hounds* in Uffington for a refreshing real ale and satisfying home-made pub food such as steak and ale pie or beer-battered fish and chips. The village shop in Uffington sells essentials or drive to Wantage (five miles) for larger supermarkets.

▾ Oxforshire's unmissable chalk White Horse

Practicalities

Britchcombe Farm, Uffington, Faringdon, Oxfordshire, SN7 7QJ ☎*01367 820667*

Pitches & price 5 large fields for tents, 8 hard-standing pitches for caravans. £3–6 per adult, under-5s free, £6 extra per gazebo, hook-ups £6.

Facilities 5 unisex showers with changing rooms, portable toilets on each field. 2 fridges and sinks for washing up. Disabled toilets.

Restrictions Dogs allowed but must be kept on a lead. No noise after 11pm. Campfires permitted.

Open Year round.

Getting there *Britchcombe Farm* is located off the B4507 between Wantage and Uffington. Nearest train station is Didcot (trains from London, Oxford, Banbury), 11 miles away. Bus #32 runs from Didcot to Wantage and it's a 20-minute taxi ride (around £18) or 5-mile walk from Wantage to the campsite.

Cheney Manor House

Hidden deep in Oxfordshire, on the edge of the small, picturesque village of Barford St Michael, *Cheney Manor House* overlooks deep green meadows dotted with cattle and wild hedgerows – the perfect starting point for rural exploration. Though settled on a spacious, slightly sloped hill, have a wander and you're likely to find a flat patch to pitch on. Facilities here are basic but the simplicity and peace are refreshing, and it's the perfect setting for a quiet day's fishing – five sizeable fishing lakes on site house carp, tench, rudd, rainbow trout and perch. Kids and dogs will be happy running about in the huge fields, while walkers and cyclists weave their way along the many surrounding nature trails. Every few miles, the generally flat landscape slopes into steep hills with panoramic views across gorgeous meadows and farmland. The village itself is small, with one friendly village pub, the *George Inn*, which is great for a pint of ale but unfortunately doesn't serve food. The campsite has its own shop for basics, and Banbury (five miles away) has a good choice of pubs, bistros and restaurants.

Practicalities

Cheney Manor House, Barford St Michael, Oxfordshire, OX15 0RJ ☎01869 338207

Pitches & price 46 tent pitches; 23 hard-standing pitches with hook-ups: £1–6 plus £2.50–3.50 for hook-ups. Fishing £2–4 per person (includes rod).

Facilities Basic unisex shower and toilet block. Outdoor sink for washing up. The on-site shop (also the village post office) sells essentials such as bread and milk, and serves hot pies, tea and coffee.

Restrictions No noise after 11pm. No campfires. Dogs allowed.

Open Year round.

Getting there Exit the M40 from Junction 10, and take the A43 towards Brackley, then the B4100 to Aynho. From Aynho follow the B4301 to Hempton and turn right to Barford St Michael. The site is past the church. The nearest train station is Banbury (£10 by taxi).

Swiss Farm International

Immaculately maintained and in a beautiful location in Oxfordshire's picturesque Henley-on-Thames, *Swiss Farm* is a sizeable campsite which manages to retain an intimate feel, in great part down to the friendly and laid-back approach of owner Joseph Borlase and his staff. Campers have a choice of where to pitch in the large, relatively flat field and a number of communal facilities encourage interaction. The adventure playground, outdoor pool and clubhouse with TV room and pool table make this place popular with families who need not venture far for entertainment, and children's theme park Legoland is only a twenty-minute drive.

Those in search of more sedate activities can while away several lazy hours at the well-stocked fishing lake, hoping to catch carp, tench or roach (from £3). Alternatively, get out on the Thames and hire a boat from Hobbs of Henley (☎01491 572035) or try out one of their public cruises. Ramblers also frequently rest up at *Swiss Farm* at the end of the challenging 67-mile Oxfordshire Way Trail, which finishes in Henley where there are plenty of options for dining out. There's a large *Waitrose* supermarket ten minutes' walk from the site.

Practicalities

Swiss Farm International Touring and Camping Park, Marlow Road, Henley-on-Thames, Oxfordshire, RG9 2HY ☎01491 573419, ⓦwww.swissfarmcamping.co.uk

Pitches & price Approx. 280 tent pitches: £11–15, £13–18 with hook-ups. 56 hard-standing pitches: £15–18. Up to £5 per extra adult, £2.50 per extra child (5–15) and £2 per extra car.

Facilities 2 large shower blocks with separate male/female facilities. Disabled toilets. Laundry. Basic shop.

Restrictions No noise after 10pm. No campfires and no radios. Dogs only allowed during low season (£2).

Open March–Oct.

Getting there Leave the M4 at junction 8/9, to the A404, following signs to Henley-on-Thames. Go down Hart Street, right onto Bell Street and right again onto Marlow Road. *Swiss Farm* is 200m on the left. The nearest train station is Henley-on-Thames (1.5 miles).

Roundhill

Horsing about in the New Forest

Covering a large swathe of southwest Hampshire, the New Forest – despite its name – is almost a thousand years old. Requisitioned as a hunting ground by William the Conqueror, its 220 square miles of thick woodland and open heath provide a glorious backdrop for the perfect UK break of short walks and long lunches.

At the heart of all this woodland, sprawling across acres of soft ground on the northwestern edge of Beaulieu Heath, is

Roundhill, the pick of the Forestry Commission's National Park campsites. It's a large site – there's even a separate field reserved for rallies – and it's usually teeming with families, but it rarely feels crowded here, despite the absence of designated pitches that results in an appealingly haphazard jigsaw of tents strewn across the grass or tucked behind pine trees on the fringes.

Perhaps its biggest attraction are the wild New Forest ponies that wander around the campsite at will, grazing under awnings and tiptoeing between the guy ropes. They're easily spotted throughout the forest, but nowhere else do they seem quite so oblivious to humans, and they lend a huge charm to a stay at *Roundhill* – you can often hear them neighing in the night. They're very much wild animals, though, and can sometimes get a little too close for comfort – don't leave any food in your tent or you'll almost certainly receive some uninvited guests.

There are none of the climbing frames, slides or swings that you might expect at a child-friendly campsite of this size, but it's not a problem when the place is one big natural playground: there's a small pond near the entrance for what brochures describe as "junior fishing" (ie pond-dipping with a little net), but otherwise kids seem perfectly happy to whizz amongst the bushes on their bikes (which are available to rent from Cyclexperience in nearby Brockenhurst if you haven't got your own; ☏01590 623407), stopping only to join in one of the spontaneous games of cricket and volleyball that get going each afternoon. At the far southeastern corner of the campsite, tracks loop out into tranquil Beaulieu Heath itself, an open area of gorse and heather that's speckled with ponies, while just to the north you can follow a dozen of the forest's beautiful cycle routes across Ramnor, Frame Heath and Pondhead inclosures.

The site's organized activities are equally focused on its natural environment. Twice a week, *Roundhill*'s forest rangers run a variety of events in the surrounding woods and heathland, from hour-long natural craft sessions to half-day guided walks on the lookout for wildlife such as roe deer and honey buzzards. Dusk Watch sessions are particularly novel – three-quarters of

Practicalities

Roundhill, Beaulieu Road, Brockenhurst, Hampshire, SO42 7QL ☎01590 624344, ⓦwww.forestholidays.co.uk

Pitches & price 500 standard pitches £9–23.50. Additional person (3 or more) £7.25 per night, children £3.75. Pre-pitched, fully equipped 6-person tents available (run in conjunction with Eurocamp, ☎0844 406 0439, ⓦwww.eurocamp.co.uk/uk-camping-breaks.html; midweek from £90, weekends from £100, week-long from £160). Minimum 2-night stay (3 nights for pre-pitched tents) when booked in advance.

Facilities 3 modern shower blocks (refurbished in 2008) with toilets (including disabled toilets), and 6-sink washing-up rooms – central blocks can get a bit too busy in high season. Nearest shops (and pubs) are in Brockenhurst. Ranger-led activities (Wed & Sun; additional charges apply, 50 percent discount if booked 2 weeks in advance).

Restrictions Up to 3 "well-behaved" dogs per pitch (£1 per dog per night). No campfires. BBQs allowed. Entrance gate open 7am–10.30pm.

Open Late March–late Nov.

Getting there From junction 1 of the M27, take the A31 towards Cadnam, turning right at the first roundabout onto the A337 for Lyndhurst and then Brockenhurst. Just before Brockenhurst, turn left on to the B3055 (signposted Beaulieu); after about 1.5 miles, you'll see the entrance to *Roundhill* campsite on your right.

the UK's native bat species are found in the New Forest, and, armed with an ultra-sonic bat detector, there's no excuse for not spotting them.

◀ Pitching under pines at *Roundhill* ▶ New Forest ponies are one of the site's most attractive features; a cycle route on Beaulieu Heath

Matley Wood

If you like things the way nature intended, you'll love *Matley Wood*, one of the smallest – and certainly the simplest – campsites in the New Forest. Part of the Forestry Commission's network of national park sites, it lies in a cluster of oak and beech trees, just off the B3056 but a world away from civilization. Due to the lack of facilities (there are no toilets or showers), it tends to attract small motor homes or adventurous campers happy to cart around their own chemical loos – the site is dotted with toilet tardises. The payoff is the beautiful location, in the middle of thick woodland, and the peace that comes with the absence of creature comforts.

There are some lovely walking and cycling tracks leading into the forest, with sun-dappled clearings providing perfect spots for a picnic. You can cycle to the attractive town of Brockenhurst or, at the end of summer or early autumn, head to the pony sales yard a mile or so down the road, where New Forest ponies are bought and sold by commoners exercising their traditional rights to graze livestock on the open forest.

Practicalities

Matley Wood Caravan Park & Campsite, Beaulieu Road, Lyndhurst, Hampshire, SO43 7FZ
☎02380 293144, Ⓦ*www.forestholidays.co.uk*
Pitches & price 70 standard pitches. £7–15 for a 2-person tent. Additional adult £4.25 per night, child £2.25.
Facilities No toilets or showers: bring a chemical toilet. There are recycling bins.
Restrictions Up to 3 "well-behaved" dogs per pitch (£1 per dog). No campfires.
Open Late March–late Sept.
Getting there From the M27, take the A31 towards Cadnam, turning right at the first roundabout onto the A337 for Lyndhurst. At Lyndhurst, take the B3056; after a mile, you'll see the entrance to *Matley Wood* on your left. *Denny Wood,* where you need to report for a camping permit first, is 100yds further along the road.

Grange Farm

Grange Farm is the sort of campsite that got you under canvas in the first place: a simple plot of land in a superb setting, surrounded by an area of outstanding natural beauty and clinging to the cliffs on the Isle of Wight's exposed south coast. The site has been left pretty much the way that nature intended, its three pancake-flat fields stretching away from the coastal road towards the sea, where the wind whips off the Channel and buffets the flysheets of anyone brave enough to pitch their tent down here. If you do, though – and you'll need a strong tent and even stronger pegs – you'll feel like you're camping on the very edge of Britain.

Aside from testing the mettle of your tent, entertainment comes in the form of fossicking on the beach, pottering around Brighstone village (try *The Countryman* pub for hearty home-cooked grub) or admiring the assortment of animals, including a couple of alpacas, dotted amongst the farm buildings or grazing in the chine that runs alongside – the most obvious sign to visitors that this is still very much a working farm.

Practicalities

Grange Farm, Military Road, Brighstone Bay, Isle of Wight, PO30 4DA ☎01983 740296, Ⓦ*www.brighstonebay.fsnet. co.uk*
Pitches & price 100 pitches £8–20, hook-ups £14–23. There are also 6- and 8-berth static caravans on a plateau below the campsite, and converted barns.
Facilities Heated shower block with wash basins, toilets and shaver points; separate family washroom. Small laundrette. Well-equipped play area and on-site shop.
Restrictions Dogs (£1.50 per night) must be kept on a lead at all times. No campfires, no loud music.
Open March–Nov. Arrive by 9pm, leave by noon.
Getting there Follow signs for Newport and pick up the B3323 to Carisbrooke and then Shorwell. At Shorwell, take the B3399 to Brighstone. Just before the village, turn left by the church down New Road and follow it to the end. *Grange Farm* is directly opposite.

Stoats Farm

Countryside camping at the foot of the Tennyson Downs

Tucked away in a beautiful patch of rural England at the western tip of the Isle of Wight, *Stoats Farm* is a relaxed and intimate little spot. The farm originally bred stoats to help protect haystacks from the local rat population – you can still sometimes catch flashes of brown fur darting through the grass around here – but the present owners have fashioned it into a friendly base from which to enjoy some of the island's finest scenery.

The campsite, set in a field up behind the farm and framed by trees on three sides, has idyllic views down over the pretty farmhouse and across the rolling hills that tumble along the horizon. These are the Tennyson Downs, and the principal reason that

Stoats Farm fills with canvas each summer. From the site, it's just a few minutes' walk to the start of hiking trails that trace the coast east towards Freshwater or west to the serrated, chalky tips of the Needles at the very end of the island.

There's a row of brick BBQs down one side of the site, but if you don't fancy cooking you can always let the local take the strain: the excellent *Highdown Inn* is directly opposite the campsite's entrance, and does a good line in local seafood (especially crab and lobster) and game, plus an interesting variety of vegetarian options – needless to say, its selection of real ales is all the tastier at the end of a day on the Downs.

▼ The farmhouse at *Stoats Farm*

Practicalities

Stoats Farm Camping, Weston Lane, Totland, Isle of Wight, PO39 0HE ☎01983 755258, ⓦ*www.stoats-farm.co.uk*

Pitches & price 100 pitches. £5–11.50 for a 2-person tent, campervans and motor homes £10.50–13.50. Additional adult £3, under-5s free. Hook-ups £3.50 extra. There's also a self-catering "Shepherds Cottage", sleeping up to 6 (£200–400 per week).

Facilities Smart, insulated shower block with toilets (including disabled toilets), shaver points and an open washing-up area. BBQ area. Utility room (service laundry). The small shop stocks the basics and, in season, produce from the farm's vegetable patch.

Restrictions Dogs must be kept on a lead at all times. Campfires on slabs in lower field only.

Open March–Nov.

Getting there From Newport, follow the B3041, signposted Freshwater Bay and West Wight. Just before Freshwater, take the left turning for Freshwater Bay, and at the next T-junction turn right for Alum Bay and the Needles. This road passes *Farringford Hotel*, a mile after which – on the brow of a hill – you'll be able to see *Stoats Farm*, on the right-hand side of the road.

Vintage Vacations
Mid-century Americana on the Isle of Wight

eBay is an addictive thing. No sooner have you won one auction for an old bedside table or the like, then you're back online bidding for something else you could probably easily live without. For Helen Carey, co-owner of *Vintage Vacations*, a single Airstream trailer was never going to be enough. After picking up a 1965 Tradewind from Missouri, a '71 Safari shortly followed. A hobby became a livelihood, and the corner of a small field near Newport on the Isle of Wight suddenly found itself home to a

burgeoning fleet of sparkling land yachts.

Until they're united in a permanent place big enough to hold them all, the trailers (now ten of them) currently rotate between three pretty smallholdings dotted around Newport – simple fields with a few free-range chickens or ducks for company, and where the peace is broken only by the odd rambler quizzically peering over the farm gate. It's undeniably charming to swing the trailer door open on a sunny morning to find a hen pecking about the steps beneath you, but in reality the sites play second fiddle to the streamline structures. Here, the medium is very much the message.

It's difficult to look beyond the iconic Tradewind, the caravan of connoisseurs, sleek in the centre and domed at the ends – and most first-time guests don't, despite competition from a variety of other Airstreams, from a '54 Overlander to a '62 Safari. But many book the squat Spartanette for their second stay, the dowdier cousin with the more spacious interior. Truth be told, it's hard to keep your eyes off either, and you could easily spend the best part of a lazy morning slumped in a deckchair out front, weighing up their aesthetic plus-points, and flicking suggestive glances at both.

The trailers' beauty – and these girls are certainly showstoppers, all soft curves and gleaming side panels – also lies within. From the original wet rooms to the shiny red General Motors Frigidaires, everything has been lovingly restored; but it's the little touches and the attention to detail that elevate the interiors: retro crockery in the kitchen drawers, crocheted blankets draped across the day-bed, Babycham in the fridge. Even the entertainment – Fifties CDs to play on the Studebaker radio, Fuzzy Felt and Pick Up Sticks to pass the evenings – is a nod to a different decade.

The toilets are equally retro, which is why you have to nip outside to use one of the "beach hut" bogs instead. Indeed, the only thing that's really up to date is the list of recommended activities, excursions, restaurants and pubs in each trailer's "manual", which, at the site in Bembridge, ranged from the excellent café at the nearby Garlic Farm to where to get the best crab pasties in picturesque Steephill Cove. Alternatively,

Practicalities

Vintage Vacations, Newport, Isle of Wight ☎07802 758113, ⓦwww.vintagevacations.co.uk

Pitches & price 10 trailers, 5 at each site (8 sleeping 4, 2 sleeping 2). Midweek (2–4 nights; £145–360 per trailer), weekend (2–3 nights; £160–340) or week-long (7 nights; £360–495) stays.

Facilities Trailers are kitted out with cooker, fridge, toaster, well-stocked kitchen, bath or shower, radio/CD player and hair dryer; toilets are in the neighbouring farmhouse or in external "beach huts" (Elson disposal). Bed linen and towels are provided, as is a small collection of old-school board games (Coppit, Tiddlywinks and the like). Welcome cream tea, and enough tea, coffee and milk to tide you over. Spartanettes are big enough for a cot (available free). Depending on the site, home-grown seasonal fruit and veg may be available to buy, as well as eggs. Substantial facilities, including an allotment, a shop and a retro shower block, are planned for the new site, due to open in 2010.

Restrictions No pets. No smoking. No campfires. The owners don't live on site; you need to arrive after 3.30pm and leave before 11am.

Open April–Nov.

Getting there The trailers currently rotate between 3 smallholdings around Newport; detailed directions given at the time of booking.

you can arrange to have local produce delivered direct to your trailer, ideal if you can't quite face breaking out of your bohemian bubble just yet.

◀ 1954 Spartanette ▶ The Garlic Farm in nearby Newchurch; the '54 Spartanette includes an original Fifties General Motors Frigidaire

Shadow Woods
Woodland skills and comfy frills

Learn to survive in the wild, Ray Mears-style, and then retreat to a cosy yurt at this enchantingly hidden pocket of wild woodland. The track from the road wends its way through ancient hawthorn and oak woods, complete with skittish deer and fighting pheasants. Then, in true fairytale-fashion, you stumble upon a clearing with a barn and five perfect red, white and blue Mongolian yurts. Even though it's near Gatwick Airport, it feels suitably remote.

Shadow Woods was originally set up as a woodland skills centre and now offers holistic massages and comfy yurts: a slightly odd mix, but a happy one. Courses in everything from making a shelter and building a fire to pot-making and basket-weaving are available, as are discovery walks through the woods to identify the medicinal uses of different plants, dig up pig nuts and burdock roots to eat and pick wild herbs for dinner. The courses are accessible to all, even urbanites who need help opening a ready meal. After all that shelter-building and herb-picking take a short walk through the woods to the healing hands of Amanda Joanne at her holistic massage room on the edge of the flower meadow.

The site's ambience is created by the trees and the natural sculptures positioned haphazardly within the woods, and the friendly welcome cannot be faulted. Whilst not everyone will get on with the composting loos, they're surprisingly fragrant, and if you don't fancy the alfresco showers, there's a hot shower inside. Although the site is eco-friendly, it's lacking any brown-rice worthiness and austerity. In fact, it's quite comfortable – all yurts have mattress beds, carpets, wardrobes and cooking boxes containing everything you might need to whip up a gourmet meal.

Shadow Woods provides the perfect tonic for those with busy lives and you can do as little or as much as you want here. Bushcraft tools (knives, axes, chisels, saws) will impress most men, while the holistic massages and restorative atmosphere will suit anyone looking to dial down a notch.

There's little to do at night apart from sit next to your fire bowl listening to hooting owls and rustling wildlife, but that's part of the charm of staying at *Shadow Woods*. During wet

Practicalities

Shadow Woods, Keeper's Cottage Barn, Tittlesfold,
The Haven, Billingshurst, West Sussex, RH14 9BG
☎ *01403 824057,* Ⓦ *www.woodlandyurting.com*

Pitches & price 4 double-occupancy yurts and 1 family
yurt (sleeps 4): Tues–Thurs £40/£60 per night; Fri–Sun,
£100/£140; Fri–Fri £240/£360.

Facilities 2 composting loos, 2 alfresco showers
(solar-heated water bags available). The barn has a
fully equipped kitchen, shower, composting loo, power
points and wi-fi. Extras: bedding £15 per yurt; massages
£40 (1hr); bushcraft sessions £15 per person (3hrs).

Restrictions Minimum stay 2 nights. Check in from
3pm; check out by 10am. No dogs allowed. No noise.
Each yurt has a fire bowl for cooking on.

Open Mid-April to mid-Oct.

Getting there Take the Haven road off the A281. As
you enter the village, the first house on your right has
a lamppost in the garden; turn left opposite down
the drive signposted Tittlesfold. Turn right at the end
of the field (signposted Keeper's Cottage). When the
track forks, head left and follow it up to the barn. The
nearest train station is Billingshurst, a 10min drive away,
and *Shadow Woods* can supply a list of local taxi firms
to whisk you to the site.

weather, the fully equipped barn with its woodburning stove
is a welcome retreat, but the woodland skills courses continue
outside under tarpaulin, and there are plenty of attractions
nearby, including Arundel Castle, Goodwood racecourse and
Bignor Roman Villa.

◀ Step into a comfy Mongolian yurt ▶ The enchanting *Shadow Woods*;
a bright spark makes fire with fungi on one of the on-site courses

Billycan Camping
Warm cockles near Arundel's soaring spires

Nestled amongst quiet, golden meadows by the meandering River Arun, *Billycan Camping* is a peaceful spot with stunning views of the rolling South Downs and the scenic skyline of nearby Arundel. Each of the six vintage-style canvas bell tents is carpeted and simply, but stylishly, furnished so you can roll into bed every night and feel snug. Communal areas are well equipped, and bunting and fresh flowers give a nostalgic nod to jolly 1950s-style camping. The comfort factor is perfect for first-timers and you can still retain some camping kudos as there's no electricity. Chic tent silhouettes and shadows bounce atmospherically off the scattered lanterns and tealights at night, adding to the site's charm.

On Fridays a cockle-warming stew is served to all and the small number of campers makes for a sociable gathering around the communal fire – everyone happily toasting marshmallows. Each tent also receives a hamper of local produce, so you can rustle up a delicious breakfast on your barbecue. Junior campers can

plunder the toy tent or visit George, the unnervingly affectionate bull who lives in the adjacent field. Art classes, face-painting and horseriding can also be pre-booked, or make for the Flying Fortress – a giant indoor play area near Ford, a short drive away. Bring your bike to explore the idyllic surrounding countryside.

Fifteen minutes by foot along the River Arun towpath will bring you directly to the heart of historic Arundel, with antique shops to potter around and a lido for outdoor dips when it's sunny. The castle and lofty, Gothic cathedral are both well worth a visit and behind them lies the town's world-famous cricket pitch and Arundel Wetland Centre, a haven for birds – great crested grebes, kingfishers and herons can occasionally be spotted gliding above *Billycan*. For tasty fresh seafood, head to *The Bay Tree* or *The Eagle Inn*, while *The Black Rabbit* is best for a riverside tipple. And don't forget the seaside; Littlehampton's *East Beach Café* features outstanding fish dishes and award-winning architecture, and pristine sands are thirty minutes by car in West Wittering.

▼ Swapping tall tales around the campfire

Practicalities

Billycan Camping, Manor Farm, Arundel, West Sussex, BN18 0BG ☎*01903 882103* or *07919 252757,* Ⓦ*www.billycancamping.co.uk*

Pitches & price 4 tents (12ft): 2 nights £185, increasing to £399 for a week (Fri–Fri). 2 tents (15ft): 2 nights £225, £425 for a week. All tents sleep 4.

Facilities Toilet block and wash-tent (solar shower bags available). Kitchen tent. Charcoal and logs £5. Tepee: sheepskin rugs, board games. Fully stocked "toy tent".

Restrictions Quiet after 11pm. No hen or stag parties. Dogs and campfires (in communal fire-pit) permitted.

Open June–Sept.

Getting there Take the A27 towards Arundel and at the first roundabout past the river, turn left onto Ford Road. After a mile, you'll see a small sign "B.C.C." on your left, just before the concealed entrance. Nearest train stations are Arundel and Ford, both £5 by taxi.

Ashwood Farm

Bluebells and archery on the Greenwich Meridian

Part organic farm, part Montessori school and part campsite, *Ashwood Farm* is a calming nook in West Sussex's leafy north-east corner. Sitting in a snug valley with a babbling stream, the tall canopy of ash, sycamore and sweet chestnut trees overhead lends privacy and shelter to the pitches and each spot has its own brick fire-pit for cosy campfires. The place looks like a hidden fairy dell, with a giant flag and maypole at its centre, and at Easter the woods come alive with a thick carpet of bluebells. The site is popular with families seeking simplicity; plenty of dads can be spotted passing their fire-making skills down the generations, and kids are free to go wild in the woods. Outdoor types will also be happy here; archery sessions are available at

£40 per session and nearby Deers Leap Park and Weir Wood Reservoir offer extensive mountain biking, canoeing, fishing and birdwatching.

Unusual goings-on are not uncommon around Ashwood; the Church of Scientology has its UK headquarters next door, and the Rosicrucians and Mormons are just a few of the many religious organizations nearby. It's not clear why they've congregated here, but it may be related to the Greenwich Meridian (or 0° longitude), which runs through the pastures of the farm, separating the eastern and western hemispheres.

The historic market town of East Grinstead, a ten-minute walk away, is full of attractive timbered buildings and has a leisure centre, cinema and theatre for rainy days. Alternatively, you could puff your way through the Sussex countryside on a the nostalgic steam locomotives of the Bluebell Railway, pop into local National Trust property Standen to admire the notable William Morris textiles or visit Ashdown Forest – home of A.A. Milne's Winnie-the-Pooh – which is just down the road (see p.86). A short stroll across the fields, *The Old Mill* offers excellent pub grub and a warm hearth.

Practicalities

Ashwood Farm Woodland Campsite, Ashwood Farm, West Hoathly Road, East Grinstead, West Sussex, RH19 4ND ☎01342 316129, ⬤www.woodlandcampingeco.wordpress.com

Pitches & price 12 tent pitches. £12 per adult, £6 per child (under 14). Campers without car £8, £4 per child.
Facilities 2 pine-fresh compost toilets. Water delivered as no tap near pitches. Toilet, shower and sink at farm. Recycling bins. A tractor-taxi runs from the car park to the campsite on request £5. Wheelbarrows also available to transport gear. Luxurious shepherd's huts planned – call for update.
Restrictions No stereos, drums, dogs or DofE groups. Quiet after 11pm. Teenagers must be accompanied by an adult. Campfires permitted.
Open April–Sept.
Getting there From the B2110 turn onto Hurst Farm Road and then right at the T-junction with Dunning's Road. This becomes West Hoathly Road and the farm is on the left, past the Tobias Art & Therapy Centre. East Grinstead mainline station is 2 miles from the campsite (£5 by taxi).

▼ The handsome Bluebell Railway – not just for train buffs

Safari Britain

Luxury and wildlife in the Sussex wilderness

Set up with a view to recreating the adventure of an African safari camp, the *Safari Britain* experience is deliciously luxurious and a far cry from your average camping trip. For a start you needn't bring a tent or sleeping bag, and you don't have to cook huddled over a tiny stove or share a shower with other campers. You can choose from several "wild" adventures (included in the price of your stay) such as hunting game, exploring the countryside, foraging and learning how to start fires and read maps. Groups are encouraged to book for a maximum of sixteen people, or to share with one or two other families, so it's likely you'll have the place to yourselves. Near Lewes, the site boasts two large deluxe yurts and several spacious bell tents, surrounded by the spectacular lush green valleys and streams of the undulating South Downs.

The safari experience kicks off with a bumpy ride from the car park up to the main campsite on a rickety mud track in owner Dan Renton's red and white pick-up. A regular car probably wouldn't make the journey without getting stuck, hence the necessity of leaving your vehicle behind, loading your stuff into Dan's truck and belting tight for the ride. Though just a few miles from the nearest town, the site has a hint of the wilderness about it, with wild horses roaming freely and nothing but fields and trees for miles. The idea while you're here is to get close to nature by immersing yourself in an English-style safari. You can learn how to identify different species of bats, insects and birds or how to hunt and skin a rabbit before cooking it over an open fire for dinner. If rabbits aren't to your taste, try preparing a stew from foraged goodies such as wild plants, squirrels, berries and mushrooms. A safari expert runs through the basics in a few hours and then off you go. Most activities are outdoor-based, offer the chance to get a bit dirty and to fling yourself outside your comfort zone in a thrilling, safari-like way.

In the evening, campers gather around the fire and trade tales of the day's adventures before heading to their comfy foam mattress. One yurt is a dedicated lounge area, decorated with thick Moroccan rugs, sofas, pouffes, candles and a wood-burning stove – perfect for whiling away time reading, chatting or just relaxing. Yurt number two is an impressively well-stocked

Practicalities

Safari Britain, nr Firle Site, Old Shepherd's Cottage, Lewes, East Sussex, BN8 6LL ℡01273 474134/07780 871996, Ⓦwww.safari britain.com

Pitches & price £30/£140 per adult, £20/£70 per child (Mon–Thu, arrange guided activities separately/ weekend booking, guided activities included). Exclusive group bookings for maximum 16 people: £800/ £1400 (Mon–Thu inclusive, arrange guided activities separately/weekend booking, guided activities included).
Facilities Outdoor shower (hot water) and toilet. Well-stocked kitchen. Local food hampers can be ordered in advance.
Restrictions No dogs. Campfires allowed.
Open May–Sept.
Getting there From Brighton, follow the A27 7 miles beyond Lewes to the village of Selmeston. Turn right at the *Barley Mow* pub onto Bo Peep Lane, signposted "By Way". Turn right again opposite *Bo Peep B&B*, and Old Shepherd's Cottage is a quarter of a mile further on the right. The campsite is a 15min walk from the car park or arrange for a pick-up. The nearest train stations are Lewes and Glynde. Buses #125 and #25 towards Alfriston stop in Selmeston, within walking distance of the *Safari Britain* site.

kitchen area with a cooker and large selection of utensils – if the weather's good, cook up a feast outdoors on the open fire. Dan offers a hamper service of delicious locally sourced food and wine, if ordered in advance. Or venture out to Middle Farm shop, on the A27 between Firle and Selmeston, for a good selection of vegetables, meat, cheeses and freshly baked bread.

◀ *Safari Britain* is surrounded by the lush South Downs ▶ Foraging for blackberries; some kids, conspicuously failing to leave that hay alone

Wapsbourne Manor Farm

Steam trains and fragrant flames

Paul Cragg is apt to venture into Eastern cosmology when he attempts to define what brings campers by their tentloads to *Wapsbourne Manor Farm*, the idyllic site he runs with his wife and daughter on a former strawberry farm in Sussex's Ouse valley. "Of the five elements, the one that modern urban man is most deprived of is fire", he theorizes, offloading another crate of fragrant conifer wood from the tractor trailer. A glance across the damp Lower Moat field at a huddled group of campers, staring hypnotized on a chilly May evening into the dancing flames of their fire-pit, underlines his point.

Opened in 2007, *Wapsbourne – Wowo* to its friends – hasn't taken long to become an essential summer refuge amongst savvy campers down from the capital or up from Brighton. Aside from the primeval draw of an open fire (an uncommon liberty in the rule-prone southeast), its back-to-basics simplic-ity, with no hook-ups and no laid-on entertainment, will appeal to anyone who appreciates the essence of camping. It's ideal for young families – with generous plots, acres of green space and rope swings aplenty, kids can roam free – yet retains an alternative, bohemian edge neatly illustrated by the fact that musicians (except bongo players) stay for free on Friday nights. Yet the modern glamper needn't suffer either: if you're not the guy ropes and air pump type, bed down in one of the cosy yurts, secluded in the woodland Tipi Trail at the far end of the site, particularly romantic in late spring when the bluebells are out. Unlike the rest of the site, which can get damp and feel a tad exposed out of season, the ten woodland pitches here are cosy and sheltered, making *Wowo* a destination for year-round campers.

Unmissable amongst activities nearby is a nostalgic ride on the vintage Bluebell Railway – its Sheffield Park terminus is

Practicalities

Wapsbourne Manor Farm, Sheffield Park, Uckfield, East Sussex, TN22 3QT ☎*01825 723414,* ⊛*www.wowo.co.uk*

Pitches & price 48 pitches. Adults £10/children £5 (minimum 2 nights at weekends). Likely to adopt a membership scheme in 2010. Yurts from around £70–160. Discount for cyclists (20 percent).

Facilities Separate, fairly basic shower/lavatory blocks, plus a pair of compost loos. Tennis court and ping-pong table; washing-up area; laundry room, plus well-stocked information point at reception, with free OS maps for hire (deposit required).

Restrictions Certain dog breeds (including Alsatians) not allowed. Campfires and barbecues permitted.

Open Year round.

Getting there Turn off the A22 onto the A275 at Wych Cross; *Wowo* is the second right (look for the faded strawberry sign) after Sheffield Park station. Haywards Heath is the nearest mainline station (£20 by taxi).

less than a mile away – from which cheery steam whistles pipe across the fields at regular intervals, while for foodies the local area is an attraction in itself. Stock up on free-range meat and seasonal veg for the barbecue at The Old Dairy (Thurs–Sat only) a couple of miles down the road, one of several excellent local farm shops, tuck into *Wowo*'s Saturday night hog roast or make for the superb *Griffin Inn*, three miles away in picturesque Fletching – with a long list of locally sourced specials, summer barbecues and magnificent views over endless countryside from its sloping garden, this is one of Sussex's loveliest pubs.

◀ Take refuge at *Wapsbourne Manor Farm* ▶ Local favourite the *Griffin Inn,* in nearby Fletching; *Wowo*'s sheltered Tipi Trail

Glamping it up...

If you recoil at the thought of getting mud on your Hunter wellies and can't bear to be without your creature comforts, the new breed of stylish campsites may be for you.

We've listed over sixty sites offering pre-erected accommodation in this guide; about half of them don't even let you pitch your own tent. These glamorous places (while it's not popular among all site owners, the term "glamping" is here to stay) give you the opportunity to get back to nature minus the earthworms and muddy sleeping bags. There's still that wilderness feel – you are sleeping under canvas – but you might be dozing in a bed with a duvet, warming yourself by a wood-burning stoves and delighting in your very own flushing loo.

Once the preserve of extortionate African safaris, this level of luxury first hit these shores as part of the UK's festival circuit, and now the middle-class cognoscenti are snapping up upmarket camping breaks as fast as you can say Cath Kidston.

Sites with high-thread-count sheets, four-poster beds and wooden floors are not uncommon. Featherdown Farms (℡01420 80804, Ⓦwww.featherdownfarm.co.uk, see pp.214 & 318), based on around thirty working farms across the UK, seek to evoke a 1920s rural idyll with rustic tents, wood-burning stoves and vintage flushing loos, while kids will enjoy coming nose-to-nose with the farm animals. Places tapping into a similar nostalgia include *Billycan Camping* (see p.78), whose immaculate Sussex bell tents have a real community feel, serving up a shared camp stew on Friday nights, and *Jollydays Luxury Camping* (℡01759 371776, Ⓦwww.jollydaysluxurycamping.co.uk), which boasts chandeliers, four-posters, hot water and proper floors in a patch of enchanting Yorkshire woodland. The site manages to indulge childhood camping memories while providing adult-friendly boutique-hotel-style accommodation, some of it in lodges bigger than a hotel suite.

Indeed, the real draw of these posh sites is their hassle-free nature. Pre-erected tents, beds and crockery boxes mean all you need to bring is some wellies, bunting and a copy of the Famous Five for inspiration.

If you want to feel like you've left the country without increasing your carbon footprint, opt for a North American tipi or its warmer cousin the Mongolian yurt. You can also stay in a 1950s Airstream trailer on the Isle of Wight (see p.74), a cosy Roma caravan in Yorkshire (see p.242) and a replica Iron Age roundhouse complete with a thatched roof in the bike-friendly Mabie Forest in the Scottish Lowlands (see p.308). Some sites trade on their exclusivity: at *Barefoot Yurts* in Sussex (℡01424 883057, Ⓦwww.barefoot-yurts.co.uk) the two beautifully appointed yurts, rented as one accommodation space, make this place the perfect romantic getaway, while almost everything is made using recycled materials.

Indeed, as glampers get more savvy, it's no longer enough to provide some flash yurts or tipis. Many sites have adopted an eco-slant as a means of differentiating themselves, and recycling stations, composting loos and tents that don't damage the earth are popping up everywhere, giving campers a guilt-free stay.

Come sundown there's often little to do except star gaze or tell campfire stories, glass of organic wine in hand, but getting away from modern life – if not modern amenities – is the whole idea. Some sites build on this by offering activities with a focus on traditional skills. You can learn to bake bread at *Jollydays* and Featherdown Farms, bag yourself a trout on a fly-fishing course at *Meon Springs* (℡01730 823870, Ⓦwww.meonsprings.co.uk), take a Bruce Parry-style bushcraft course and a basket-weaving lesson at *Shadow Woods* (see p.76) or go on a marshland safari at *fforestcamp* (see p.164).

Needless to say, all this comes at a price, and a weekend at the plusher operations can easily cost you £300. Many of these sites, with their elegant accommodation and quirky activities, offer what is effectively a branded experience for campers with cash to spare. Hardened campers might argue that this is camping for cheats, and there is some truth in that, but why should holidays be uncomfortable? Space is the ultimate camping luxury, especially with the uncertain British weather, and the new styles of accommodation have oodles of it. Yurts, bell tents and tipis with room to do a cartwheel are most definitely in; tents that leave you with a permanent hunchback are out.

Camping in style is having your cake and eating it. You get fresh air and that close-to-nature experience without the bother of erecting the bloody tent – and those Egyptian-cotton sheets and duck-down pillows do make for a blissful night's shuteye.

◀ The handmade bed in one of *Barefoot Yurts*'s Mongolian yurts

St Ives Farm

Shady pitches and Poohsticks

There's something enchantingly old-fashioned about *St Ives Farm*, set amidst the rolling hills, scattered farmsteads and sunken lanes of Sussex's High Weald. For a start, you'll probably arrive via the picturesque village of Hartfield, home to A.A. Milne – Winnie-the-Pooh, his most famous creation, wandered

the ancient woodlands of nearby Ashdown Forest, and the village is a paean to all things Pooh. By the time you get here you'll probably have forgotten the shocking traffic on the A22 and started grinning like a carefree eight-year-old.

Once on site, the illusion of a bygone era continues. There are no modern trappings at *St Ives* – just four shady and secluded camping fields set around a peaceful fishing lake (stuffed full of perch, carp and tench) and surrounded by endless vistas of gently undulating countryside. You're three miles from the nearest main road here, and if you can come midweek, when the place is usually deserted (it tends to be full at other times), you'll likely hear little – bar the occasional rumble of an overhead plane – but the mellow chirruping of birdsong.

Like much else hereabouts, *St Ives* grew organically. "It was never intended to be a campsite," explains David Chapman, the genial owner, as he reaches into his shed for a sack of firewood (£4 – two should see you through the evening) for a new arrival, "but people came to fish and wanted to stay for the weekend – or longer." David has run the site for over twenty years but retains the enthusiasm of someone in their first season: he gets to know all his campers, two-thirds of whom are regulars.

There aren't really any rules at *St Ives* – it's a laid-back sort of place where everyone mucks in and gets along, and the diverse, good-humoured crowd creates something of a low-key festival feel. With the tents packed in on a busy weekend, noise levels might rise during the daytime – kids love it and tend to run gleefully amok (though you might need to watch them close to the lake) – so for a bit more peace and quiet try to make for the compact Top Field, the choicest and cosiest spot, which tapers round to the six-pitch, car-free "Peninsula".

Once you're settled, there are dozens of scenic trails across the surrounding fields to explore, including the pretty walk down to Pooh Bridge for a spot of Poohsticks. And if the Sussex weather lets you down, Groombridge Place, a fine moated Elizabethan manor on the Kent border, or Hever Castle, Anne Boleyn's childhood home, will keep you occupied for a few hours.

As befits an area famed for its produce – Emerson College, a great focus for enthusiasts of biodynamic agriculture, is just

Practicalities

St Ives Farm, Butcherfield Lane, Hartfield, East Sussex, TN7 4JX ☎*01892 770213,* Ⓦ*www.stives-farm.co.uk*

Pitches & price Around 50 pitches (unmarked). £12–18 per tent; campervans £14.

Facilities Single fairly basic loo/shower block, plus portaloos. No hook-ups. No disabled facilities.

Restrictions Dogs and campfires permitted.

Open April–Oct.

Getting there Turn left off the A22 at Forest Row, south of East Grinstead, onto the B2210. Past Hartfield village, take the left-hand fork (B2026 towards Edenbridge) and after three-quarters of a mile turn left again onto Butcher Field Lane, following the signs for *St Ives Tea Gardens*. East Grinstead is the nearest mainline station, a £10 taxi ride from the site, or take a bus (hourly Mon–Sat) to Hartfield and walk.

down the road – good food is high on the agenda, with plenty of attractive, historic pubs nearby, plus a wisteria-clad tearoom just five minutes' walk away. The standout for foodies is the exceptional *Hatch Inn* at Coleman's Hatch, an hour by foot, where the emphasis is on local, seasonal produce lovingly prepared and fairly priced, though either of the pubs in Hartfield will serve a pint of local Larkins or Harveys and a filling meal. If an evening around the fire beckons, it's only a twenty-minute walk across the fields to Perryhill Orchards, where the trees (when not sheltering hunny-loving bears) are set to work producing cider apples: at the farm shop here, you can sample up to two-dozen of the potent concoctions – mainly from Kent and Sussex, including three of the orchard's own – from casks helpfully labelled with tasting notes, before staggering back to the site with an armful of barbecue essentials.

◀ Poohsticks in Ashdown Forest ▶ Lakeside pitches at *St Ives*; historic Groombridge Place, home to gardens and a bird sanctuary

Spring Barn Farm Park
Quacking great fun on the South Downs

Whichever way you pitch your tent on *Spring Barn's* one gently sloping field, you're guaranteed a delightfully bucolic view, with the South Downs on one side and happily grazing animals on the other. Little ones won't believe their luck – not only do they get to go camping, but, joy of joys, there are sheep, chickens, slides and sandpits right next door at the farm park (reduced admission for campers). Parents can sit back while children enjoy themselves

▼ Feeding time at the farm park

chasing ducks, feeding lambs or getting lost in the summertime Giant Maize Maze. You'll feel like you're miles from anywhere, yet quirky Lewes is just a twenty-minute walk up the hill, and Brighton, with its bustling shops and restaurants, is fifteen minutes from Lewes by train.

Opened in 2008, amenities at *Spring Barn* are currently pretty basic, with just two portaloos and a standpipe. But the staff are friendly and unfazed by small-child chaos and, if you're happy to rough it a little, the ideal setting more than makes up for the modest facilities. Family-friendly food, including a tasty breakfast of fresh eggs and sausages, is on offer at the on-site *Farmhouse Kitchen* throughout the day – useful if camp cooking isn't your thing. They also sell their own meat and sausages if you fancy a barbecue. Alternatively stock up on quiches, cakes and pies from an amazing array of fresh and organic produce at acclaimed *Bill's* in Lewes.

Practicalities

Spring Barn Farm Park, Kingston Rd, Lewes, East Sussex, BN7 3ND ☏01273 488450, ⓦwww.springbarnfarm park.co.uk

Pitches & price 32 pitches: adults £7, children (2–16 years) £3.50.

Facilities 2 well-kept portaloos, standpipe. On-site café and shop selling farm produce. Reduced farm park admission (adults £6.50, children £5.50, under-2s free).

Restrictions No caravans. No dogs. Campfires only in hired fire-pits (£15). Phone if arriving after 5pm.

Open April–Oct. Check in at *Spring Barn's* main farm park entrance.

Getting there Take the A27 and exit for Kingston village. Drive through the village to the T-junction (opposite Wyevale garden centre) and turn left. The farm park is 500yds further on the left. Lewes train station is a 20min walk; the #123 bus from Lewes bus station stops just outside the farm.

Southdown Farm

Situated at the foot of the South Downs, just fifteen minutes by train from the bright lights of Brighton, *Southdown Farm* attracts a wide range of campers. You might encounter children playing football, morris dancers en route to Lewes or even men in giant inflatable Sumo suits – stag groups are not uncommon due to the proximity to Brighton, though this is not primarily a "party" site.

The main field is flat and airy with pitches scattered around the edges, leaving plenty of room in the middle for campers to do their own thing. There are panoramic views across the South Downs from here and walkers need only cross the road to access the Sussex countryside footpaths; families are within thirty minutes of Brighton beach and the Bluebell Railway; and nearby postcard-pretty Ditchling will satisfy foodies and craft-lovers. Disabled campers are also welcome at *Southdown Farm* and the site's owners have plans to put in a number of "supertents" (pre-erected tents with wooden floors and hoists) in the near future.

Practicalities

Keymer Caravan & Camping Park, Southdown Farm, Lodge Lane, Keymer, Hassocks, West Sussex, BN6 8LX ℡*01273 843278,* 🅦*www.southdown-farm.co.uk*
Pitches & price 50 tent pitches, 8 hard pitches with hook-ups. £9–20 per tent with 2 adults. £15–20 per caravan with 2 adults. Extra adults £5, children £2–3.
Facilities Excellent male and female shower blocks, disabled toilet and shower room, laundry room.
Restrictions No noise after 11pm and before 7am, dogs on leads, no campfires.
Open Fields: Easter–Oct; hard-standing: year round.
Getting there Exit the A23 at Hassocks/Pycombe onto the A273. At the bottom of the steep hill, turn right onto the B2112 towards Ditchling. Turn left after about a mile, signposted Keymer. The campsite is immediately on your left. Hassocks train station is a 15–20min walk.

Manor Court Farm

In the Kentish hamlet of Stone Cross, just five miles from the gentrified spa-town of Tunbridge Wells, *Manor Court Farm* has a pleasant sense of space and seclusion, with wonderful views towards Ashdown Forest and the Medway Valley. Its large, self-contained pitches, informally arranged around an attractive Georgian farmhouse, particularly appeal to groups and families. Sarah Goodwill, the thoughtful manageress, tries to place campers in areas best suited to their needs, whether they are couples seeking romantic privacy or families keen to camp close to the farmhouse. Those who'd prefer the comfort of a mattress can be accommodated in one of the three B&B rooms.

The surrounding area has many attractions – from rock-climbing in Groombridge to Vita Sackville-West's celebrated garden at Sissinghurst. But young families should have no trouble finding enough entertainment on site; children love the roaming chickens, and a football goal and wooden swing offer further distraction. A short walk away, the *Chafford Arms* serves real ale and local food, which can be savoured alongside stunning views of the High Weald.

Practicalities

Manor Court Farm, Ashurst, Tunbridge Wells, Kent, TN3 9TB ℡*01892 740279,* 🅦*www.manorcourtfarm.co.uk*
Pitches & price 20 pitches, £8 per adult, children £4.50 or less depending on age. Hook-ups £2.50.
Facilities A renovated cowshed has been converted into a decent shower and loo block. There's also a microwave, a washing-up and laundry area with coin-operated washing machine and dryer, recycling, and firewood (£4.50) and eggs for sale at the farmhouse.
Restrictions Dogs allowed (free) but must be tied up. No radios or stereos. Campfires allowed.
Open March–Oct.
Getting there On the A264 towards Langton Green, *Manor Court* is located approximately 600yds beyond the village of Ashurst. Trains from London Bridge to Ashurst station run every hour; if you call ahead, a pick-up from the station can be arranged.

Blackberry Wood
Old-fashioned camping in cosy hideaways

Quirky and dedicated to the basic joys of camping – being outside, close to nature and free of the trappings of modern life – *Blackberry Wood* oozes charm and character. Owners Tim Johnson and Eva Olsson wanted to keep the site simple but to offer more than just a field of tents. A testament to their success is that campers come here for a down-to-earth, back-to-basics experience, preferring to escape to the secluded clearings in the woods and nestle up to nature than to use the site as a base to explore nearby attractions.

Bordering the lush fields and chalk hills of the South Downs, the site's twenty pitches are concealed by thick woodland, fragrant mint plants and abundant blackberries. It's impossible not to get distracted by the dark and peaceful forest, where the towering trees look magnificent beside vast golden cornfields. On arrival, you're given a hand-drawn map with directions to the various signposted pitches, which have been named to reflect their individual characters – Minty has mint growing around it, Mecca

faces east and Humpty Dumpty is large. Apart from a murmuring stream, the distant chatter of other campers and the occasional flash of colour through the trees, you'll feel snugly cordoned off and find yourself quickly growing attached to and taking pride in your secret little woodland home. Complete with log chairs and a pit for open fires, the cosy atmosphere at night is enhanced by the cackle of open fires, the wafting smell of barbecued meat and the starry sky above.

Those who want some creature comforts can opt to stay in the eye-catching classic caravan area, in a bright red double-decker Routemaster bus, a romantic 1960s retro caravan, an original 1930s gypsy wagon or an old static caravan. The owners scoured ebay to furnish their stylish fleet of mini homes with random bits and bobs and even if you're camping in the woods, it's worth having a wander down to admire this unique part of the site.

Get the most out of the area by following part of the South Downs Way, a hundred-mile trail through the woodlands,

Practicalities

Blackberry Wood, Streat Lane, nr Ditchling, East Sussex, BN6 8RS ☎01273 890035, ⓦwww.blackberrywood.com

Pitches & price 20 pitches, 3 caravans and a holiday bus. £5–7 per person, half-price for children under 12, plus £5 (tent), £15 (static caravan), £20 (retro caravan), £35 (gypsy caravan) or £50 (Routemaster bus).

Facilities 2 shower/toilet blocks with separate male/female facilities.

Restrictions Dogs allowed but must be kept on a lead. No loud noise or music after 11pm. Children must be supervised in the woodlands. Children and dogs can't camp in the caravan area but are free to play outside.

Open Year round.

Getting there Driving south on the A23, turn left at the A273 for one mile, heading towards Clayton. Go right onto the B2112 to Ditchling and right onto the B2116 (Lewes Road). Continue for 2 miles and turn left onto Streat Lane, past Sandpit Cottages. The nearest station is Plumpton (trains run from London, Brighton, and Lewes), about 1.5 miles from the campsite. Take the bridleway from outside the station towards Plumpton Racecourse and follow the path past some houses and across a field, which backs the campsite.

which runs from Winchester to Eastbourne by the sea. For food, try *The Jolly Sportsman* in nearby East Chiltington – a cosy, gourmet pub with a daily changing menu of pricey but good-quality food, including cucumber soup with home-smoked salmon, or pork chops and black pudding mash – or Plumpton's child-friendly *Half Moon*, which offers campers a ten percent discount.

◀ Views across the South Downs ▶ Stay in a converted Routemaster bus; snuggle down in one of *Blackberry Wood*'s secluded clearings

Dernwood Farm

Since opening in 2008, *Dernwood Farm* has gained a loyal clientele who enjoy its family-friendly seclusion, pristine Weald forest and campfire-friendly attitude – all a hop and a skip from the south coast. The site is popular with ex-festival-goers and their offspring, who relish the challenges of spartan facilities and don't mind the odd splash of mud. The large, grassy camping field is surrounded by ancient coppiced woodland – traversed at one end by a sizeable pylon – and in April and May the forest trails are awash with sleepy-looking bluebells, anemones and orchids. You will also spot small craters in the forest floor, remnants of the Tudor iron industry that once flourished here. Access is via a ten-minute woodland walk, and wheelbarrows are available for transporting gear: bring strong arms.

Wild dining needn't mean boil-in-a-bag, as a selection of meat reared on the family-run farm is for sale to campers, including tender sirloin steaks, best seared to perfection over an open fire. The *Six Bells* in nearby Chiddingly also serves tasty pub grub, and Brighton and Eastbourne are just forty minutes away by car.

Practicalities

Dernwood Farm Wild Campsite, Little Derwood Farm, Dern Lane, Waldron, Heathfield, East Sussex, TN21 0PN ☎01435 812726, Ⓦwww.dernwoodfarm.co.uk
Pitches & price 30 pitches, £6.50 per adult, £4.50 per child (over 5), family (2 adults, 2 children) £17.50 per night. No hook-ups.
Facilities Outside tap and well-maintained shed-cum-toilet: BYO toilet roll. Logs £5. Milk, bread and newspapers can be pre-ordered.
Restrictions No noise after midnight and no loud stereos. No caravans. Campfires permitted. Dogs must be kept under control.
Open April–Sept.
Getting there From the A267 in Horam, turn left onto Furnace Lane, just as you leave the village. After a mile, turn left onto Dern Lane, and *Dernwood* is another mile away, on the right – opposite Copford Farm.

Normans Bay

Occupying a strip of green parallel to the pebble beach where William the Conqueror landed in 1066 and camped in preparation for battle, *Normans Bay* is steeped in history. Commanding uninterrupted views across the English Channel, and with an empty private beach literally a stone's throw from the actual site, this scenic location will delight campers. Large groups have plenty of space to spread out, and the neat, trim grass is easy to pitch tents on, though it can get quite windy here so don't forget windbreaks and steel pegs. The secluded, empty beach is perfect for a stroll and kids will be kept occupied for hours running about and collecting shells.

Welcoming, well-organized, and particularly popular with caravanning families, *Normans Bay* also caters to first-timers, with cheerful staff always on hand to help and frequently chatty fellow campers creating a friendly communal feel. The town's only pub, The *Star Inn*, serves basic pub food with a midweek discount on the carvery for campers. Or stock up on local produce at one of the farm shops in Pevensey Bay, about a mile away.

Practicalities

Normans Bay Camping and Caravanning Club Site, Normans Bay, Pevensey, East Sussex, BN24 6PR ☎01323 761190, Ⓦwww.siteseeker.co.uk
Pitches & price 200 hard-standing pitches and room for 28 tents. Prices range from £2.50 to around £9.50 per person including discounts for club members.
Facilities Clean shower blocks with separate male and female facilities, disabled toilets and changing room for mums and tots. Well-stocked on-site shop.
Restrictions Dogs allowed on leads. No campfires.
Open April–Oct.
Getting there Take the A259 and follow the signs to Pevensey Bay; turn left at the second set of traffic lights into Coast Road leading to Beach Road. The campsite is on the left after about 1.5 miles. The nearest train station is Normans Bay, with links to Brighton and Hastings, a 5min walk from the site.

Hidden Spring Vineyard

Grapes on the Weald

Since setting up home at *Hidden Spring* in 2007, welcoming own- ers Tamzin and David Whittingham have established an attractive family campsite on this 23-acre working vineyard and smallhold- ing. They offer an impressive range of sleeping options – from straightforward pitches to pre-erected geodome tents and yurts beautifully furnished with double beds, rugs and stoves. Three separate, spacious sites for tents, caravans and yurts are situated alongside orchards and a field of grazing Jacob sheep. Popular with families escaping nearby London and Brighton at weekends, the site, located in the East Sussex countryside a short walk from the village of Horam, has a relaxed and quiet atmosphere which unwinds adults, while Jake the Shetland pony and the resident chickens entertain the little ones.

Informal tasting sessions (£2.50) offer the chance to sample generous glasses of *Hidden Spring*'s white and red wines, as well as to indulge in some strong homemade cider. Much of the deli- cious farm produce, including wine, cider, apple juice, eggs and honey, is sold at the on-site shop, but if the effort of campsite cooking seems too strenuous, the *Brewers Arms* in Vine's Cross, a ten-minute walk through fields of wildflowers, is a very pleasant option for locally sourced food or an early evening pint.

Beyond the orchards, the Cuckoo Trail, a thirteen-mile cycling and walking route that follows a disused railway track, passes through Horam; with 24 hours' notice, bikes can be hired from M's Cycle Hire (☎07852986165). Wilderness Wood, five miles away in the Sussex High Weald, is another local highlight.

Practicalities

Hidden Spring Vineyard, Vines Cross Road, Horam, East Sussex, TN21 0HG ☎01435 812640, Ⓦ www.hiddenspring.co.uk

Pitches & price 10–15 pitches for tents. £12 for 1- to 4-person tents (2 adults & 2 children). £5 per extra adult. £2 per extra child under 5; 5–15 years £3. Additional charges for larger tents. 10 pitches with hook-ups for caravans and motor homes £12 (2 adults & 2 children). 2 yurts, £100 each per weekend. Bell and geodome tents also available (call ahead).
Facilities Good male and female amenities. Useful on- site shop and information area.
Restrictions Well-behaved dogs on leads allowed (call ahead). No drumming or amplified music. Minimal noise and vehicle movement after 10pm. Only prior bookings accepted. Campfires allowed on tent field. Tents for more than 6 people by arrangement only.
Open March–Oct.
Getting there Leave the A267 at Horam and turn left onto the B2203; shortly afterwards turn right down Vines Cross Road. The campsite is well signposted. Bus #52 runs from Tunbridge Wells (the nearest mainline train station) to Horam, a short walk away.

▼ Tending the vines at *Hidden Spring*

Welsummer

Weald wildflowers, yews and nut orchards

The homely atmosphere and warm welcome at *Welsummer* make it feel a bit like you're camping in someone's back garden – which is exactly what you're doing. Owners Laura and Med Benaggoune created this back-to-basics campsite on the grounds of Laura's parents' home in the picturesque Weald of Kent. Scattered with fruit trees, grasses and wildflowers, this small and intimate spot has two adjoining fields plus a woodland area for wilder camping, with five secluded pitches in their own little clearing. Children will love getting back to nature here and exploring the woods, orchards and an enchanting circle of yew trees. Evenings are relaxed with families rustling up dinner together around campfires. The 10.30pm noise curfew means this isn't really a place for groups who want to stay up late and party.

Sincere hospitality and personal touches really set *Welsummer* apart: flowers in an old perfume bottle above the sink; pots of geraniums dotted around; a bag of tennis racquets hanging in a tree; hot cinnamon muffins fresh from the oven for breakfast; and most especially the chance to cook on a campfire and spend the evening chatting and gazing into the embers. The owners really care about your experience and can often be seen wandering around and sharing a cup of tea or glass of wine with campers.

Local footpath networks are directly accessible from the site and hikers will enjoy exploring the surrounding slopes of the North Downs – pick up handy laminated maps at the campsite office. Nearby family-friendly attractions include historic Leeds Castle and Bedgebury National Pinetum and Forest, with its extensive trails, adventure playground and Go Ape high-wire challenge. Those in search of more sedate pleasures should take a tasting tour at Biddenden Vineyards and bring a bottle back to toast the night sky around a warming campfire.

A lovely forty-minute walk south, through woods, fields and apple orchards, will bring you to Grafty Green. Stop for a drink at the *King's Head* – they don't serve food, except on a Friday evening when you can have excellent fish and chips. For legendary Sunday roasts, try The *Pepper-*

Practicalities

Welsummer Camping, Chalk House, Lenham Road, Kent, ME17 1NQ ☎01622 844048, ⓦwww.welsummer. moonfruit.co.uk

Pitches & price 20 pitches: £12 per pitch plus £3 per adult and £1 per child (3–13 years).

Facilities 2 showers heated by a woodburner and 2 toilets (shared male and female), standpipe, outdoor washing-up area, composting and recycling, washing machine. Small on-site shop selling home-grown produce, basics and sustainably harvested wood for campfires. Home-cooked breakfast available.

Restrictions No campervans or caravans. 10.30pm noise curfew. No loud music. Dogs allowed on leads. Fires only in fire-pits.

Open April–Sept.

Getting there Exit the M20 at junction 8 and follow signs to Lenham on the A20. Turn onto Fairbourne Lane towards Ulcombe and left at the crossroads with Lenham road towards Platts Heath. Go past Greenhill Lane, and *Welsummer* is on your right, before Elmstone Hole Lane. Trains run from London Victoria to Harrietsham, 2 miles from the campsite. From there it's either a 40min uphill hike or an £8 taxi ride (pre-booking essential, no rank).

box Inn, half an hour southwest through nut orchards near Ulcombe, with superb views over the rolling Wealden hills. Further afield, the scenic villages of Lenham and Headcorn have teashops, delis, pubs and a few browsable shops. Sainsbury's in Headcorn is useful for stocking up and has a cash machine.

◀ Wilder camping in *Welsummer*'s woodland area ▶ Relax among the fruit trees; a woodburner heats showers in the rustic toilet block

Cobbs Hill Farm
Cuddly animals and seasoned statics

Wholesome, orderly and pleasantly uncommercial, *Cobbs Hill Farm* is a peaceful family site in rolling Sussex countryside, just three miles inland from the sleepy seaside resort of Bexhill, home to the modernist masterpiece of the De La Warr Pavilion. Though surrounded by open space, the site feels nicely sheltered, its four neat and level camping fields separated by well-trimmed hedges and screened by a fine row of firs – perhaps why too it feels a little cramped on a busy weekend. Run with brisk efficiency, seasoned family caravanners, some in statics, make up most of the regulars. Youngsters love the farm's menagerie of cuddlesome animals, including a pair of adorable Shetland ponies, while safety-conscious parents will appreciate the well-constructed playing area at the heart of the site. Further afield, there's plenty more to keep the little ones amused, with Drusillas and Knockhatch Adventure Park a short drive away, while the atmospheric lanes and nautical attractions of unpretentious Hastings make for a fascinating day-trip.

▼ Bexhill's rejuvenated De La Warr Pavilion

Practicalities

Cobbs Hill Farm, Watermill Lane, Bexhill-on-Sea, East Sussex, TN39 5JA ☎*01424 213460,* Ⓦ*www.cobbshillfarm.co.uk*

Pitches & price 55 pitches with hook-ups, plus 2 rental caravans and seasonal tent-only field. £9–15 per pitch, including 2 adults; extra adult £2, children under 5 £1; gazebos £3. Caravans from £140.

Facilities Spartan but spotless separate toilet/coin-operated shower blocks, plus separate disabled/baby change block. Large laundry and washing-up area. Shop and information point (open 8am–9pm) on site.

Restrictions No campfires (bricks provided for barbecues). Dogs permitted (50p).

Open April–Oct.

Getting there Take the A269 (towards Battle) out of Bexhill, and turn right onto Watermill Lane at Sidley; the site is a mile along on the left. Bexhill is the nearest train station, 2.5 miles away (around £6.50 by taxi).

Palace Farm

Buried deep in the Kent Downs, *Palace Farm* attracts walkers, cyclists and wildlife lovers intent on exploring the surrounding landscape of orchards, poppy fields and wooded hilltops. Sprawled over a large field with only 25 pitches (and two tipis), it rarely feels crowded here and there's plenty of space for lively communal ball games and barbecues, and for children to run about. This designated Area of Outstanding Natural Beauty includes the long-distance North Downs Way, a 150-mile trail from Farnham to Canterbury; for shorter hikes (less than six miles) head to the market towns of Sittingbourne and Faversham. Those with plenty of time and energy should take to the country lanes, past sweeping farmland and cider orchards, to Whitstable (ten miles) for tasty fish and chips at a local chip-pie or the day's fresh catch at renowned *Wheelers Oyster Bar*. Tired campers may decide the perfect end to their long day is to hire a fire pit (£2) and cook up a feast on site. Get to know the locals at the popular *Chequers* pub, but remember to take a torch as there aren't any streetlights late at night.

Practicalities

Palace Farm Camping, Down Court Road, Doddington, Kent, ME9 0AU ☎01795 886200, Ⓦwww.palacefarm.com

Pitches & price 25 tent pitches, £2.50–8 per person; two tipis, £50 per night/£250 per week.

Facilities Unisex shower block. Disabled toilets and shower. Ordnance Survey maps available with local routes marked. Six bikes to rent (£5 per day).

Restrictions Dogs allowed but must be kept on leads. No noise after 11pm. Campfires permitted.

Open April–Oct.

Getting there Leave the M20 at junction 8 and take the A20 to Lenham. Continue to Doddington, turn left at *Chequers* pub, and left again onto Down Court Road. Nearest train stations are Faversham and Sittingbourne. Catch bus #344 (Mon–Sat) from Sittingbourne to *Chequers* pub or a £12 taxi from Faversham.

Woodland Farm

Dwarfed by the surrounding 25 acres of tall dark woodlands, *Woodland Farm* is a tiny campsite hidden deep in the Kent countryside, overlooking the meadows and chalk downlands of Elham Valley in the North Downs. Peace reigns here, with only ten pitches allowed on the flat patch of green and occasional birdsong breaking the silence. Campers can pitch anywhere – the level ground is comfy to sleep on but can be difficult to knock a peg into. Several paths lead through the trees and heading south, there's a shelter with a bench and two tables – a perfect little dining spot – and communal areas for barbecues and open fires.

For a good selection of restaurants, pubs and shops, head to Canterbury city centre, which is twenty minutes by car (see p.99), or take a stroll to the nearby village of Kingston (two miles) and tuck into a wholesome steak and kidney pudding in the *Black Robin*'s spacious beer garden. At the small shop next door (☎01227 830230), you can order fresh meat, fish and poultry to smoke on the barbecue.

Practicalities

Woodland Farm, Walderchain, Barham, Canterbury, Kent, CT4 6NS ☎01227 831892

Pitches & price 10 tent pitches, maximum 2 caravans but no hook-ups: £5 per adult, £2.50 per child.

Facilities Shower and toilet block with a separate sink for washing up. Bags of firewood £3.50.

Restrictions Campfires allowed. Dogs allowed (50p) on leads.

Open March–Oct.

Getting there Take the A2 from Canterbury and follow signs to Barham. After the village take the first left signposted to Lodge Lees, and you'll reach Walderchain. The farm is 200yds past the first sharp bend on the right. The nearest train station is in Canterbury. Bus #17 runs every hour from Canterbury to Barham; get off at Barham post office. Or get a taxi from Canterbury for about £20.

Neals Place Farm

Cider and strawberries under the apple tree

Perched on a hill overlooking the picturesque skyline of Canterbury, *Neals Place* is a small working farm with a scenic apple orchard and lots of juicy homemade produce. Tucked between grand manor houses and a large field (Dukes Meadow) bordered by tall trees and shrubs, a narrow path winds up from the main road to the entrance, where you'll be greeted by friendly owner Ken Jordan.

Part of the charm of this site is being able to camp on soft, neatly cut grass in the middle of an orchard, surrounded by rows of apple trees, nestled among swathes of lush green countryside. It's a truly stunning location, with the farm fenced off from the spacious and self-contained pitches by stubby hedgerows, and strawberry shrubs and cattle fields scattered behind the orchards. While most campers tend to use the site as a resting place mid-hike or -cycle trip, others stop to pick some of the farm's delicious strawberries. Other treats for sale in the on-site shop include delicious homemade cider, apple juice and jam, and if the site's busy, Ken bakes fresh bread. Alternatively, you can pick up essentials half a mile down the road in Rough Common. For relaxation, grab some fresh cider and venture out into the neighbouring fields for a picnic, with unspoilt views of Canterbury Cathedral, which towers grandly over the city in the distance.

As it's just off the national cycle route network, cyclists and

Practicalities

Neals Place Farm Caravan and Campsite, Neals Place Road, Canterbury, Kent, CT2 8HX ☎01227 765632 or 07802 211434, ✉kenrol@orbitalnetwork.net

Pitches & price 18 pitches for caravans and tents: £10 per pitch (for 2 people, £2 per extra person), hook-ups £5.

Facilities Portable toilet block with separate male and female facilities. No showers.

Restrictions Dogs allowed but must be kept on a lead. No campfires.

Open April–Sept.

Getting there Take the A290 from the centre of Canterbury towards Whitstable. Turn into Neals Place Road 2 miles later when you reach the white water tower. The road sweeps right leading to *Neals Farm*. Nearest stations are Canterbury West and Canterbury East (with connections to several London stations in just under two hours). Buses #4a and #4b stop on the main road outside the campsite.

hikers stay at *Neals Place* to explore the area's scenic trails. The Chalk and Channel Way is dotted with art installations and takes in the dramatic chalk ridges and cliffs that form part of the Kent Downs. Canterbury city centre, a twenty-minute walk away, is perfect for lazy relaxation. Its charming streets lined with cafés, bistros, bars and independent shops are great for pottering about – stop off for freshly ground coffee and cake at *Karl's* on St Peter's Street. Those in search of historical interest shouldn't miss the magnificent cathedral, and just outside the city walls the impressive ruins of St Augustine's Abbey and St Martin's Church (one of England's oldest churches) are also worth a visit.

◀ A sweeping panorama of Canterbury from *Neals Place Farm* ▶ The dramatic chalk cliffs of the Kent Downs; St Augustine's Abbey

The Warren

Cosy beachside hideaways beneath the white cliffs

Few campsites in England can boast as dramatic a coastal setting as *The Warren*, the Camping and Caravanning Club's Folkestone outpost, perched precariously on a narrow strip of undercliff beneath towering chalky cliffs above the crashing waves of the Dover Strait. You're halfway to France here – even Calais, its twinkling lights just visible on a clear night, can seem romantic from the site's prettily garlanded viewing deck – and, with both ferry port and the Channel Tunnel just a hop away, it's an ideal stop-off en route to the Continent. But there are plenty of reasons to linger.

Despite its exposed position, the site itself, shielded from the sea winds by a screen of thicket, is surprisingly sheltered. Pitches are pancake-flat, and with five-star facilities, the camping is easy (though bring a stout tent-peg mallet to hammer through that stubborn chalk). Families and groups are well catered for – they're usually placed in the Frying Pan, a sociable ring of pitches (at least until 11pm, when it's strictly lights out) away from the road at the far end of the site. But *The Warren*'s peachiest

spots are its series of cosy hideaways – a sequence of dips and plateaus (mostly) overlooking the ocean, each with space for just a handful of dinkier-sized tents, concealed amongst the bushes off the main field. They're first come, first served, so arrive early – and leave the eight-manner at home.

It's just a couple of minutes' walk down to the beach, a curved sweep of groyned pebbly bay lent added curiosity by the presence of a monumental concrete apron, designed to prevent further landslip. Picturesque it is not, but there's good fishing – sea bass, mackerel, sole – from its flat platform. Further afield, popular day-trips include the vertiginous six-mile walk along the cliffs to Dover, and the tranquil nature reserve at Samphire Hoe, constructed from the spoils of the Channel Tunnel excavation. But the coolest customers these days make for reanimated Folkestone, whose attractive fishing port sits a mile or so along the coast. From the harbour, where you can tuck into fresh seafood from the irrepressible *Chummy's*, it's only a few paces up to

Practicalities

Folkestone Camping and Caravanning Club Site, The Warren, Folkestone, Kent, CT19 6NQ ☎01303 255093, Ⓦwww.campingandcaravanningclub.co.uk

Pitches & price 80 pitches, including 16 hard and 21 grass pitches with hook-ups. Adults around £7–9.50 (kids £2.50), plus non-member pitch fee of £6.50.

Facilities Pair of immaculately maintained utility blocks with toilet, hot showers, separate disabled and parent/child rooms (£10 deposit), laundry/ironing room and washing-up area. Small shop selling basics, plus information kiosk. Wi-fi available (not free).

Restrictions No caravans or campfires. Dogs permitted.

Open Week before Easter to early Nov.

Getting there Turn off the M20 at junction 13 onto the A20, cross the motorway and take the first left at the roundabout towards Folkestone Harbour. Follow the brown "Country Park" road signs at three further roundabouts, then cross Dover Road onto Wear Bay Road. Take the first left after the sea comes into view, a few hundred yards along; it's then another half-mile down to the site. Folkestone Central is the nearest station (3 miles); bus #72 drops half a mile away.

the town's fledgling Creative Quarter, an eclectic band of galleries and café-bars and a good springboard for a tour of the permanent artworks – by luminaries such as Mark Wallinger and Tracey Emin – commissioned for 2008's inaugural Folkestone Triennial (next scheduled for summer 2011). And if you've kids in tow, don't miss the revamped Lower Leas Coastal Park, where the southeast's largest adventure playground is home to a spiral helter-skelter, huge sandpits for toddlers and a half-buried ship for budding pirates.

◀ Seaside camping overlooking chalk cliffs at *The Warren* ▶ Boats at low tide in Folkestone harbour; Folkestone's buzzy Creative Quarter

East England

Dry, flat and blessed by a long, arching coastline, East England has an obvious appeal to campers, so it's a shame that Cambridgeshire and Essex are low on good sites. There are some exceptions in these counties – we've included one on Ely's watery flatlands and another that's accessible by tube but bordered by the deceptive bulk of Epping Forest – but Norfolk and Suffolk are home to the region's best campsites, boasting cliff-top views, quiet villages, bird-watching and some fine beaches.

Suffolk is perhaps the most enticing, with the handsome and prosperous little coastal towns of Aldeburgh and Southwold providing bucket-and-spade fun, fine Georgian architecture and good pubs, cafés and boutiques. Further north, Norfolk's capital, Norwich, has a wonderful Norman cathedral and a cutting-edge art gallery, the Sainsbury Centre.

But the little-known star of the region is the north Norfolk coast, where a string of resort towns and villages offer crab-catching, seal trips and intriguing marsh landscapes. The North Norfolk Coastal Path runs all along the shoreline, and is a great way for walkers to immerse themselves in the watery charms of the area – the string of campsites listed in the chapter provides handy stopping-off points.

Most of the region is criss-crossed by cycle paths which take advantage of the flat landscape, so bringing or renting a bike is a good option. If you want sandy beaches, head either for Southwold or, further north into Norfolk, go for the lower-key charms of the long strands at Waxham.

East England

See front flap for key to symbols

	PAGE	🚶	🚲	⛵	🍷	⛰	👨‍👧	👪	🚐	🚌	♿
Beeston Regis	116	✓							✓	✓	
Cliff House Park	107								✓		
Clippesby Hall	110		✓	✓			✓				
Debden House	106							✓	✓	✓	
Deepdale Farm	122	✓		✓					✓		✓
Deer's Glade	115						✓		✓		✓
Diglea	120	✓		✓					✓		
Foxhills	116	✓							✓	✓	
Galley Hill Farm	117						✓		✓		
High Sand Creek	118	✓							✓		
Kelling Heath	120						✓		✓	✓	✓
Manor Farm	114	✓							✓	✓	✓
Orchard Camping	108						✓	✓	✓		
Pinewoods	121	✓					✓		✓	✓	
Riverside	107		✓							✓	
Southwold	112	✓				✓	✓				
Waxham Sands	111						✓				
Woodside Farm	114		✓	✓					✓		

© Crown copyright

Hunstanton

Deepdale Farm
Pinewoods
High Sand Creek
Galley Hill Farm
Kelling Heath
Foxhills
Sheringham
Manor Farm
Cromer
Beeston Regis
Deer's Glade

Diglea

A149
B1454
B1153
B1355
B1105
B1148
A148
A1149
B1354
A140
A149
B1159
A1151
A1062
A149
B1147
A1067

Waxham Sands

Woodside Farm
Clippesby Hall
A1064

A17
King's Lynn
A47
A10
A1122
A134
A47

N O R F O L K

Norwich
A47
A146

THE BROADS
Great Yarmouth

Wisbech

Peterborough
A47
A605
A141
A142

C A M B R I D G E S H I R E

A1(M)

A1101
Riverside
Ely
A1065
A1075
A11
B1113
B1332

A1145
Lowestoft

Thetford

A1066
A140
A143
A144
A145
B1127
Southwold

Southwold

A14

Huntingdon
A14
A428
A10
A14
A1088
B1123
B1117

Newmarket

Bury St Edmunds

A1120
B1119
A12
B1122
Cliff House Park
Aldeburgh

Cambridge
A11
A1198

Orchard Camping
B1078
A1094

Bedford
A421
A1307
A1092
A143
A134
A1141
A1071
Ipswich

S U F F O L K
Woodbridge

B E D F O R D S H I R E
M1
A507
A6
A505

A1017
A131
A1124
A12
Felixstowe

Leighton Buzzard

Letchworth
Hitchin
Stevenage

Luton
Dunstable
A5
A6

B184
B1053

Colchester

Clacton-on-Sea

H E R T F O R D S H I R E
Harpenden
Welwyn Garden City
Hertford
Hatfield
Harlow
A10
M11
A130
A1060
A12

E S S E X

Chelmsford

Hemel Hempstead
St Albans
Cheshunt
M25
A414

Watford
A104

A113
A128
Debden House
Brentwood

A127
Basildon
Southend-on-Sea

LONDON

Grays

Debden House

A capital camping getaway in Epping Forest

Starting in the northeast fringes of London, the ancient deciduous woodland of Epping Forest stretches along a high gravel ridge for almost twelve miles into the Essex countryside. Covering some six thousand acres, the forest is the capital's largest public open space, and its sheer scale and beauty come as a surprise to the first-time visitor, not least because of its proximity to the urban sprawl.

The campsite is on the southern edge of the forest, providing an escapist retreat for Londoners in need of green space, or a pitch within striking distance of the capital for those out of town. It's split into seven separate areas: field 5 is the "fire field", with a communal campfire feel, and you can also light fires on 6 and 7. Field 1 is recommended if you're after peace and quiet, which can otherwise be a little hard to find at this lively place. There's a café on site, but otherwise you're best off cooking by the campfire.

From the site itself you can make a ten-minute walk to a deer park, which should keep the kids happy. Head to the visitor centre at High Beech for information on longer walks; you can follow forest tracks south from here for a couple of miles to Queen Elizabeth's hunting lodge. Built for Henry VIII in 1543, and renovated for Elizabeth I in 1589, the timber-framed lodge served as a grandstand from which hunts on the plain below could be watched – it would originally have been open to the elements, though its timber frame was later enclosed with plaster. The lodge has been used variously as a law court, tearooms and a family home. It now houses a small museum (March–Sept Wed–Sun 12.30–5.30pm; Oct–Feb Fri–Sun 11am–4pm; free), with low-key exhibits on the history of the building; as you'd expect, there are great views from the gallery across the plain, where hunts would have taken place.

▼ Forest-bordered *Debden House* is within reach of the tube

Practicalities

Debden House Camping, Debden Green, Loughton, Essex, IG10 2NZ ☎*0208 5083008,* Ⓦ*www.debdenhouse.com*
Pitches & price 800 pitches, with 50 for caravans. Hook-ups available. Adult £7, child £3.50.
Facilities Café, small basic shop and 2 playgrounds. Token-operated laundry. Logs supplied for fires.
Restrictions Dogs on leads (£1). On the fire field you can use the pits to light campfires.
Open May–Sept.
Getting there From the M25, exit at junction 26, take the A121 to Loughton (2 miles), and turn left at the double mini roundabout. Take the A1168 (Rectory Lane) and then the second left (Pyrles Lane). Turn right into England's Lane; *Debden House* is down the second turning on the left. From the M11 (from London), exit junction 5 and turn left to A1168 Rectory Lane, then follow the instructions above. You can take the Central Line on the Underground to Theydon Bois station, then a taxi or bus #167 or #20.

Riverside

The rich arable land of the fens, scored by ditches and rivers and dotted with windmills, is like nowhere else in the country. Huge skies and vast, perfectly flat fields stretch out to the horizon around well-kept *Riverside*, a site dotted with apple trees, willows and birches on the edge of the village of Littleport. Kids are banned, keeping noise levels down, though you may be bothered by traffic from the adjacent road. Beyond the road is the Great Ouse River – you can buy tickets (£5/day) at the riverbank and try your luck with perch, pike, tench, bream, roach and carp.

The main draw here is Ely, whose romantic cathedral dominates the surrounding farmland from its modest hill-top perch. It's only ten minutes from Littleport by train; Cambridge is around half an hour away.

For more outdoorsy activities, head to the intriguing nature reserve at Wicken Fen, just south of Ely, for watery walks (Ⓦwww.wicken.org.uk). *The Blackhorse Inn* is just down the road, though you'll do better in Ely, where the riverside *Cutter Inn* (Ⓣ01353 662713), serves great food – fishcakes, pies, burgers and so on – in its attached restaurant.

Practicalities

Riverside Caravan & Camping Park, 21 New River Bank, Littleport, Ely, Cambridgeshire, CB7 4TA Ⓣ*01353 860255,* Ⓦ*www.riversideccp.co.uk*

Pitches & prices 49 pitches, mostly with hook-ups. Tents from £7.50 per person, 2-person caravan from £10.

Facilities Old-fashioned but clean toilet block. Wi-fi.

Restrictions No children. Dogs (free) must be kept on leads. No campfires.

Open Year round.

Getting there Heading north on the A10, pass Ely and ignore signs for Littleport. Go round the Littleport bypass, over the railway crossing and the Great Ouse. Turn right at the roundabout signposted Queen Adelaide; *Riverside* is a mile down on the left. There are trains from London, Ely and Cambridge to Littleport; the site is a 15min walk south from the station.

Cliff House Park

Cliff House Park is rather bizarrely located within a stone's throw of the Sizewell nuclear power station, with its distinctive white dome and massed power cables. If you can ignore this, or if you're interested in visiting Sizewell, you'll find this a rather lovely location.

To the north is the alluring little town of Southwold (see p.112) and to the south is Aldeburgh (see p.109), with its brightly painted Victorian villas and smart cafés. In between the towns, and right on the edge of *Cliff House Park* campsite itself, are long pebble-and-sand strands – the beaches are so extensive that you can easily find a solitary spot, even during high summer.

The site itself is well equipped, with a café and decent bar (serving Adnams) that share a sea-view terrace. In terms of punters it's very family-orientated, with lots of static caravans and a more domesticated than outdoor vibe; not a place for a wild weekend. But if you're in search of a beach and a couple of nice towns to potter in, it's ideal.

Practicalities

Cliff House Caravan Park, Sizewell Common, Leiston, Suffolk, IP16 4TU Ⓣ*01728 830724,* Ⓦ*www.cliffhousepark.co.uk*

Pitches & prices 62 serviced caravan pitches; separate area with 60 touring pitches. Pitch (caravan or tent, 1 car & 2 adults with free hook-up) £16–24; additional adult £4–4.50, child £2–2.50.

Facilities Games room with table tennis, table football, pool and arcade games; bar and café with wi-fi. Access to a private beach.

Restrictions Dogs (£1.30) welcome but must be kept on a lead. No campfires.

Open March–Nov.

Getting there Leave the A12 at Saxmundham, taking the B1119 to Leiston. From Leiston, follow the sign for Sizewell Beach; for the campsite, turn right off the road just before you reach the beach.

Orchard Camping
Campfires, wild men and alien invasions

Family-run *Orchard Camping* has a lot going for it. There's a jolly welcome at the pretty camping field, which gently slopes towards the River Deben and a plantation of willow trees (for the production of cricket bats). But the major draw is that this is a site with its eye on the sky – it is perhaps the world's only campsite with a registered observatory. This is run by site warden Barry, who built the deceptively shed-like structure, with retractable roof, in which the telescope is housed. Inside is the state-of-the-art telescope, alongside computer monitors and a flat-screen TV on which the observations are broadcast. Barry is a true enthusiast, and will point out celestial features such as ring nebulae thousands of light years away. Unusually for a campsite, winter is a good time to visit, as the extra hours of darkness make for easier star-gazing.

As well as identifiable objects in the sky, keep your eyes peeled for unidentifiable ones. Since a supposed spotting of a "triangular metallic object" in 1980 on the US air base near Rendlesham Forest, there have been reports of alien activity in these parts. The campsite is in on the act with its wacky Alien Encounter Weekends (see website for details). There are also plans for star parties where you can bring your own telescope. A quirky edge pervades – take a look at the literature outside the loos about UFOs, the Wild Man of Orford (a supposed merman captured in 1167) and a plethora of local ghosts.

If you're inspired to tell a few ghost stories yourself, you can do so round the campfire – the staff sell seasoned logs and will help you develop your fire-lighting skills. A pretty pond lies at the bottom of the site, and if you fancy fishing you can rent rods (£5 per day) and buy bait on site. The camp shop sells some tinned food, chocolate and camping essentials – otherwise you can buy food at the Co-op in Wickham Market, reached from the site via a footpath.

Practicalities

Orchard Camping, 28 Spring Lane, Wickham Market, Suffolk, IP13 0SJ ☎01728 746170, ⓦwww.orchardcampsite.co.uk

Pitches & price 60 pitches, 20 hook-ups. £20 per caravan/tent with hook-up; £15 without.

Facilities Good toilet/washing and laundry facilities. Freezer, microwave, kettle, washing machine, BBQ area. Bike rental, table tennis and small play area.

Restrictions Campfires permitted. No music speakers allowed after 11pm.

Open Year round.

Getting there From Ipswich, take the A12 north towards Lowestoft. Take the second exit to Wickham Market into the village, then the third left onto Spring Lane. The site is about 500yds up the lane on the left-hand side. From Lowestoft, take the A12 south towards Ipswich. Take the first exit to Wickham Market and proceed as above. From the west, leave the A14 and turn onto the A140 towards Norwich. Pick up the B1078 to Wickham Market. Turn left and first right into Spring Lane.

Just to the east, the village of Orford – of Wild Man fame – has a well-preserved early medieval castle. North up the coast is Aldeburgh, one of the most handsome towns in the area, with brightly coloured villas and terraces, two excellent chip shops, good boutiques and miles of shingle beach, from where you can have a bracing dip in the North Sea. Benjamin Britten lived in Aldeburgh, and the area maintains strong musical traditions; five miles inland at Snape, there's a cutting edge concert hall that hosts year-round events (ⓦwww.aldeburgh.co.uk).

◀ Tents among the trees at *Orchard Camping* ▶ The pebble beach at nearby Aldeburgh; site warden Barry and his beloved telescope

Clippesby Hall
Laid-back leisure on the Norfolk Broads

This large site in the Norfolk Broads National Park is cleverly divided into separate sections so it doesn't feel too overwhelming: there's spacious Cedar Lawn, for tents and caravans; Rabbit's Grove, surrounded by mature trees and more tucked away; Pine Woods, dog-free and with larger pitches; and the Dell, a quiet area with large pitches in the woods. It's a site that offers umpteen ways of entertaining potentially bored children – think solar-heated pool, mini-golf, archery lessons, an adventure play area, a tree house, grass tennis courts, table tennis and a volleyball net. Yet the site manages to avoid a Butlins-type feel in favour of something more personal and laid-back. Friendly staff do their best to find you the best pitch, whether you'd prefer to be surrounded by woodland or in the thick of things.

There's a cute café – *Susie's Coffee Shop* – next to the reception, which serves good coffee and home-made cakes, and the site shop is a cut above the average, offering local produce, bottled ales and newspapers as well as the usual tinned food. Further into the site, near the hall itself where the site owner lives, the *Muskett Arms* pub has decent pub grub, farm ciders and Norfolk ale, and hosts an autumn beer festival each September, celebrating brews such as Nelson's Revenge and Old Stoatwobbler. Adjoining the pub is a kids' room with arcade games and a pool table.

Clippesby Hall is just a short drive from Norwich, with its Norman cathedral and the outstanding Sainsbury Centre for Visual Arts on the university campus, with its beautifully displayed collection of ethnographic objects alongside pieces by Giacometti, Epstein and Henry Moore.

But outdoorsy types will find plenty to occupy them in and around the site. Pancake-flat Norfolk is of course prime cycling country, and the site rents out bikes (from £12 per day for adults, £8 for children). The reception has a wealth of leaflets, including one on the Wherryman's Way, a 35-mile route that takes its name from the black-sailed barges that used to be common here. Otherwise, grab a copy of the site's own (free) *Discover the Broads* publication, which has info on bird-watching, canoeing, fishing, cycling, horse-riding, walking and sailing in the area.

▼ The grassy expanse of Cedar Lawn

Practicalities

Clippesby Hall, Hall Lane, Clippesby, Norfolk, NR29 3BL
ⓣ*01493 367800,* ⓦ*www.clippesby.com*

Pitches & price 130 pitches. Camping/touring pitches (tent or caravan, 2 people plus infants under 3) from £10 per night. Extra adult £5, child £2.50.

Facilities Very good toilet and shower facilities with a family bathroom and central heating. Café, shop, pub, table tennis, swimming pool, mini-golf and cycle rental. Tree house and play area.

Restrictions Dogs (£3.50) must be kept on a lead at all times; 1 dog per pitch. Maximum 5 people per pitch. No campfires.

Open Easter–Oct.

Getting there From the A47, between Norwich and Great Yarmouth, take the A1064 at Acle (Caister-on-Sea road), and after a mile or so turn first left at Clippesby on the B1152.

Waxham Sands
Seals, sand and fish and chips

The eastern coast of Norfolk is blessed with gorgeous long golden beaches but doesn't have the campsites to match. The only other options in the area are a site that's only open for a month in the summer and a caravan-dominated park. So this is the best of the bunch, a large, friendly site with a slightly raffish edge to it: there's a heavily tattooed (though extremely friendly) receptionist, a fish-and-chip van hovering outside, and a rather run-down air.

The location is superb, behind a high dune that conceals the open sea. The miles of open and undeveloped beach are regularly visited by seals, making it a brilliant place to take kids, who might also enjoy the campsite's mini-golf course. There's a good grocery on site, and the chip van, but if you want a decent café you need to head a mile or so north to the quirky mini-resort of Sea Palling where there's a pub, cafés, a farm shop, a fish stall and another great stretch of open sandy beach.

Sadly, despite the pancake qualities of the surrounding countryside, this is not a good area for cycling as there aren't any designated routes, just roads which can be busy. But it's a fine location for exploring the flatlands of the Broads, dotted with old windmills such as the imposing National Trust-owned windpump at Horsey, a ten-minute drive away. Heading the same distance inland you come to the village of Hickling where you can fish or sail on the River Thurne; for information head to the Hickling Broad Visitor Centre (☎01692 598276). Some fifteen miles south down the coast is the fishing port of Great Yarmouth, a central location in *David Copperfield*; it's very much a resort town, with amusement arcades and a pleasure beach.

▼ Lovely beaches sweep just behind *Waxham Sands*

Practicalities

Waxham Sands Holiday Park, Warren Farm, Horsey, nr Great Yarmouth, Norfolk, NR29 4EJ ☎*01692 598325,* Ⓦ*www.waxhamsandsholidaypark.co.uk*

Pitches & price 200 pitches, 100 with hook-ups. From £12 per pitch. £1 per extra person, £2 per hook-up.

Facilities Reasonable shower blocks with coin-operated showers. Good shop, mini-golf, play area with swings, laundry.

Restrictions Dogs must be kept on leads except in the dog recreation area (no charge for 1 dog, extra animals 50p per night). No campfires; raised BBQs allowed.

Open May–Oct.

Getting there From Norwich, take the A1151 to the junction with the A149. Turn right here, then left towards Sea Palling. From Sea Palling continue on the B1159 coastal road for a couple of miles until you reach the signed left-hand turn-off for the site.

Southwold

Crabs and cream teas on the Suffolk coast

Set in a dip behind sand dunes and surrounded by cornfields, this likeable site doesn't initially show its prettiest face – at the entrance you're faced with a barrage of static caravans. But follow the lane round to the right and you come to the attractive tent field, ringed with shrubs and tall grasses, and with appealing views of the civilized seaside town of Southwold. It's flat, and ideal for badminton and football, but such are the charms of the surrounding area that the site itself is pretty empty for much of the day.

This is a great place to spend a couple of days, and longer if you've got good weather and can swim from the sandy beaches. From the campsite it's a lovely fifteen-minute stroll to the town's promenade, lined with brightly painted beach huts, the long golden strand parcelled up by wooden groynes and the view framed by the long lines of the pier.

The rest of the town, with a gleaming white lighthouse rising over the rooftops, has a wonderful mixture of Victorian terraces and Georgian villas. There was a fire here in 1659 which destroyed most of the town, and many plots were left open and evolved into open greens. It's an unexpected place for a fashion splurge, with very classy independent boutiques, as well as an organic grocery, good cafés and small galleries selling pottery and seasidey sculptures.

Southwold is the home of Adnams ales – their brewery is right in the centre of the town, and you can sample their renowned regular and seasonal ales at either the *Swan* or the *Crown Hotel* pubs on the High Street. Another lovely and quirky refreshment stop is *Tilly's* 1920s-style café, also on the High Street, which offers a fantastic "layered tea" – tiers of scones, cucumber sandwiches and cakes. Otherwise, there are plenty of options for good fish and chips, including a stall just round the corner from the campsite. In the evenings, campers fire up their barbecues and kids play as the sun sets.

Lovely walks criss-cross the unspoilt countryside around. A three-hour route heads south from the site across the River Blythe (via a little ferry) into the ancient village of Walberswick, where you can have a pint at the six-hundred-year-old *Bell Inn*. In August the village hosts the British Open Crabbing Competi-

Practicalities

Southwold Harbour Camping & Caravan Site, Ferry Road, Southwold, Suffolk, IP18 6ND ☎01502 722486

Pitches & price 165 pitches for tents and caravans, but no hook-ups; 160 statics. £15 per pitch, including 2 people; £2.20 per extra adult, £1.10 per extra child.

Facilities Simple loo and shower block. Washing-up area, laundry, fridge-freezer.

Restrictions Dogs (free) must be kept on a lead at all times. No campfires, but BBQs allowed.

Open April–Oct.

Getting there From the A12 between Ipswich and Great Yarmouth, follow signs to Southwold on the A1095 for 3 miles. Then follow signs for the campsite, which is on the southern edge of the town. By public transport, take the train to Lowestoft, then buses #99, #99b or #601 to Southwold.

tion, with a prize for the heaviest specimen.

Another intriguing settlement on this coast is Dunwich, to the south of Walberswick; once a major port, it was battered by the sea to the point of near-abandonment – it was a famous rotten borough in the eighteenth century, with voters apparently taking boats out to the point of the submerged former town hall to cast their ballots.

The only blot on the landscape – quite literally – is the hulking presence of the Sizewell nuclear power station on the coast to the south. If you find yourself strangely drawn to it, head down the coast and camp over the road from the power station at *Cliff House Park* (see p.107). Otherwise, take a kite and head out onto the dunes for a truly refreshing blast of salty sea air.

◀ Beach huts at Southwold, with the lighthouse rising above ▶ Wide skies at the campsite; Adnams ales are brewed in Southwold

Woodside Farm

This little farm site in classic Broads country has quiet appeal – it's green and verging on manicured, but with large clumps of lavender, willow trees and a small lake thick with reeds. Just up the lane is Thurne, which straddles the River Thurne and is home to picturesque Thurne Dyke windmill, once used for drainage, and the *Lion Inn*, with several real ales, reasonable pub grub and pool tables.

The best and most relaxing way to see the Broads is by boat, most easily achieved by heading four miles north to Potter Heigham, where several companies offer rental and cruises – try Ⓦwww.blakes.co.uk. If you do want to stay on dry land, *Woodside Farm* is on the route of the Weavers' Way, an inland walk which connects Cromer with Great Yarmouth.

The site itself is located at the end of a dead-end road, so is very peaceful, with plenty of space for games and running around. The portable toilets are decent but simple, and the second field has a wooden shed with washing-up facilities (bring provisions if you want to cook).

Practicalities

Woodside Farm Camping Site, Common Lane, Thurne, Norfolk, NR29 3BX Ⓣ*01692 670367,* Ⓦ*www.woodside-farm.co.uk*

Pitches & prices 10 pitches, 6 of which have hook-ups. Car and up to 4 people £17. £3 per hook-up.
Facilities Shower, loos and separate washing-up area.
Restrictions Dogs (free) must be kept on a lead. No campfires.
Open Year round.
Getting there From Acle on the A47, follow signs for Caister (on the A1064) and continue for 0.5 miles. Turn left, following the sign for Clippesby/Oby. Continue 0.5 miles to the crossroads, and take a left turn signposted Oby/Thurne. Head straight down this road for 2 miles to Thurne, and continue down the road until you see a dead-end sign immediately in front of you. Follow the lane to the right to the farm.

Manor Farm

Spacious and undulating, *Manor Farm* is a handy option if the coastal sites are full. It has sea views and good access to beaches and the Victorian resort town of Cromer but, despite being attractive and well run, lacks the charm of the seaside sites. The camping fields are some distance from the brick and flint buildings of the working farm, where you'll be given a map and directed to one of three distinct areas in the campsite. Gurney's Plantation is for caravans and motor homes, and features level pitches and a play area for kids. The other two fields are for tent campers: Marl Pit is ringed by hedges and woodland, while Moll's Meadow has some high pitches with magnificent sea views.

Cromer has all the requisite attractions: a sandy beach, a pier, fish-and-chip shops and a carnival (held in August). The neighbouring village of East Runton, just to the west, is picture-postcard pretty with a duck pond, village green and a beach with rock pools. There are two venerable recommended pubs in the village: the *Fishing Boat* and the *White Horse Inn*. Just inland from the campsite is Felbrigg Hall, a seventeenth-century manor house with an orangery and walled gardens.

Practicalities

Manor Farm Caravan and Camping Site, East Runton, Cromer, Norfolk, NR27 9PR Ⓣ*01263 512858,* Ⓦ*www.manorfarmcaravansite.co.uk*

Pitches & prices 147 pitches from £12.50 per night, including 2 adults. Additional adult £5, child £1.
Facilities 6 excellent shower blocks with hair dryer and shaver points. Disabled toilets. 2 laundry rooms.
Restrictions Dogs on leads (£1) are confined to the Moll's Meadow area.
Open Easter–Sept.
Getting there Leave the A148 at the Sheringham turn-off. Turn right at the roundabout in Sheringham towards West and East Runton. After a few miles turn right at the *Manor Farm Camping* sign in East Runton. Go under a railway bridge, past the pond and turn left to Manor Farm. For public transport, just take the train to Cromer; the station is a 5min walk from the site.

Deer's Glade
Marshmallows and muntjacs

A lane off the A140 north of Norwich takes you to this verdant site, via an area of dense oak and pine woodland where the eponymous deer hang out – if you're lucky you'll spot red deer and muntjacs. The site itself is a wide, open space, efficiently run by a welcoming family. Apart from the reception, which has a simple shop and some tourist bumf, it comprises the spacious field, with a log-cabin-style loo block to either side. At the far end there's a tranquil fishing pond, stocked with carp, roach and bream; you can rent rods for £4.50 per day (children £2.50). Bike rental is also available (£10 per day; £5.50 for kids).

There's a small playground, and the site has an eco-friendly water-treatment plant which has won it a David Bellamy Award.

The owners also operate Muntjac Meadow, a site on a nearby field (August only) where there's no electricity and they have a nightly campfire. If you're staying at the main site you can stroll by and toast a few marshmallows, and if you're on the meadow then you can visit the main one for the shop and play area.

While you're here, make sure you have a stroll through Hamworth itself, on the other side of the A140. Accessed via a single-track lane, it's a beautifully preserved little place with a common complete with duck pond and cows ambling down the lanes. Otherwise, you're well located between Norwich and the attractive little run of settlements on the north Norfolk coast, including Cromer and Blakeney (see p.117). The site reception can advise on cycling, walking and horse-riding in the area.

▼ The seafront and pier at Cromer

Practicalities

Deer's Glade Caravan and Camping Park, White Post Road, Hanworth, Norfolk, NR11 7HN ☎01263 768633, Ⓦwww.deersglade.co.uk

Pitches & price 100 deluxe pitches, with electricity and hook-up; 25 standard pitches. Prices per person: from £5.75 for adults, from £3.50 for children. See website for family deals.

Facilities 2 amenities blocks with showers, loos, basins, disabled/family rooms, laundry and washing-up facilities; small shop; play area; dog walk; wi-fi.

Restrictions Dogs (£1) allowed on leads. No campfires on main site.

Open Year round.

Getting there From Norwich, take the A140 towards Cromer. 5 miles beyond Aylsham, turn right towards Suffield Green, signed White Post Road. The site is 0.5 miles on the right. From King's Lynn, take the A148 towards Cromer. Turn right onto the B1436 towards Roughton, then join the A140 towards Norwich. 2 miles beyond Roughton, turn left towards Suffield Green, signed White Post Road. The site is 0.5 miles on the right.

Beeston Regis

This site isn't an instant winner – it's got rather a commercial feel as they sell caravans and lodges, and the first thing you'll see as you enter are rows and rows of uninspiring static caravans. But the welcome is warm, and the tucked-away area designated for campers is quite special: you turn right on entering the site, past a dramatically sited flint church, and the field is on the cliff edge with high sea views. It's a good spot for walkers, kite-flyers and anyone hardy enough to swim: you're right on the route of the Norfolk Coastal Path, and the campsite has its own little stretch of sand beach, reached via a steep staircase.

From the site you'll see the path wind east up the golden cliff towards the resort town of Sheringham. While it hasn't got the charm of the smaller settlements further west, Sheringham is a distinctive and interesting place, a railway town which until a hundred years ago enjoyed a boom in crab and lobster fishing. The resulting wealth was poured into the town's varied and grand flint buildings. The town also has a range of individual book, antique and fishing shops, and a popular market on Wednesdays and Saturdays.

Practicalities

Beeston Regis Caravan & Camping Park, Cromer Road, West Runton, Cromer, Norfolk, NR27 9QZ ☎01263 823614, Ⓦwww.beestonregis.co.uk

Pitches & prices 41 pitches. From £16 per pitch including 2 adults and hook-up. Additional adult £3.50, child from £1.70.

Facilities Decent if old-fashioned portable toilets and laundry.

Restrictions Dogs (£1.50) welcome but must be kept on a lead. No campfires.

Open March–Oct.

Getting there The site is located on the A149 coast road between Sheringham and West Runton at Beeston Regis. It's on the coast side of the road opposite Beeston Hall School. For public transport, just take the train to Sheringham and walk the mile to the site.

Foxhills

Hikers on the North Norfolk Coastal Path may find this a useful staging post – although it's a small site, they promise never to turn walkers away. It's an endearing campsite, not much more than a field enclosed by trees and hedges and a rather worn shower block, but the owner is a huge plant enthusiast and the place is piled high with tubs of bright geraniums, hydrangeas and fuchsias. It tends to be quiet, with the only entertainment provided by games of badminton. Right next door you'll find the Muckleburgh Collection, which proudly announces itself as having the UK's largest privately owned military acquisition. With sixteen tanks among the miscellanea, they may well have a case: tank demos and rides are available, a sure winner with kids.

This innocuous-seeming stretch of coast has been of huge military significance since the repulse of the Spanish Armada in 1588. Nearby Weybourne has a deep shoreline that makes landing easy, and in both World Wars it was a military encampment. There's no good swimming from the site – for this you need to take to the coastal path and head a little further east to the resort of Sheringham (see above).

Practicalities

Foxhills Camping, Weybourne, Holt, Norfolk, NR25 7EH ☎01263 588253

Pitches & prices 22 pitches, 5 hook-ups. £10 per pitch plus £1 for each additional adult.

Facilities Minimal facilities; old but clean toilet blocks.

Restrictions Dogs on leads. No campfires but raised BBQs. Caravan Club members only for caravans.

Open Year round.

Getting There The site is on the A149 coast road, just west of Sheringham. Approaching from Sheringham, you turn right off the road to the site, immediately before the (signed) Muckleburgh Collection. For public transport, take the Coast Hopper bus service (Ⓦwww.norfolkgreen.co.uk), which runs along the coast. Or take the train to Sheringham and then the North Norfolk Railway (Ⓦwww.nnrailway.co.uk) to Weybourne, from where it's a mile walk to the site.

Galley Hill Farm

Peace and quiet by the buzzing sea shore

A quiet hillside site on a small farm, *Galley Hill* is pretty but undramatic – you get a wide grassy field, some portable toilets and not a lot else. The owners are friendly and knowledgeable about the local area, and can organize bike rental for you, but the big draw is that the field is only a mile-long stroll down the hill to the delightful resort town of Blakeney. The quay here is a scene of family fun in summer, with canoeing, seal trips, dinghies in the water and highly competitive crab-catching competitions.

Boat trips to view the common and grey seals are great fun – you'll see at least part of the colony of five hundred seals lolling on the sandbanks at the end of Blakeney Point, which is also a breeding place for migrant birds including terns, oyster-catchers, plovers and (in winter) ducks and geese. For peace and quiet, take one of the raised paths, lined with tall reeds, that lead through the marshes. A good route leads you from the National Trust car park, via the Cley Windmill, to Cley-next-the-Sea. Make sure that your route takes in the excellent tearooms at Wiveton Hall (Ⓦwww.wivetonhall.co.uk); these are housed in a beautiful and brightly painted wooden building with outdoor seating, local art on the walls and PYO raspberries and strawberries in season.

Back in the town, the *King's Arms* near the quay on Westgate Street is a fine pub serving good bar meals, or there's the more upmarket *White Horse* on the High Street; both do excellent seafood. In summer you can have a side order of samphire, which is also known as sea asparagus and grows in great quantities here.

Practicalities

Galley Hill Farm Camping, Langham Road, Blakeney, Holt, Norfolk, NR25 7PR ☎01263 741201, Ⓦ*www.glavenvalley.co.uk/galleyhillcamping*

Pitches & price 20 pitches, no hook-ups. £6 per adult, £3 per child, under-3s free.

Facilities Simple but decent portable toilets and shower facilities.

Restrictions No dogs allowed. No campfires; but raised BBQs permitted.

Open End May to mid-Sept.

Getting there Blakeney is on the main cost road west of Cromer, the A149. Once in Blakeney, follow the sign to Langham on the B1156, up the hill to the campsite (1 mile). On public transport, take the Coast Hopper bus service (Ⓦwww.norfolkgreen.co.uk), which runs along the coast. Get off at Blakeney; it's then a mile up the road to the site. The bus service runs from Hunstanton to Sheringham, often from King's Lynn and Cromer too, which links up with the trains from Norwich to Sheringham and also the trains from London to King's Lynn.

▼ Crab fishing at Blakeney

High Sand Creek

Salt marshes, cockles and kites

Sitting above the Stiffkey salt marshes, *High Sand Creek* is a relaxed site geared to tent campers. Pitches are scattered on a gentle hill with a bird's-eye view out over the marsh, which is dotted with sea lavender and yellow-horned poppies, and provides wonderful walking and bird-watching opportunities. Campers need to be aware of the tides here though, which can leave you stranded, and wellies are essential for exploring.

The North Norfolk Coastal Path is located between the campsite and the vast expanses of the salt marsh, one of the oldest in Norfolk. Keep your eyes peeled for long-beaked curlews and redshanks, with their long gawky red legs, and ask the campsite owners about the walk along the coastal path and then over wooden platforms, from where you can often spot seals. Otherwise, walkers should turn left on the coastal path facing the marsh to arrive at Wells four miles to the west (see p.121), or right for two miles to reach quiet Morston or the quirky little resort of Blakeney (3.5 miles; see p.117).

The spacious slanting field of the campsite is bordered by a tall hedge to one side (this provides handy shelter in windy weather) and a strip of trees on the other, with a cluster of farm buildings nearby. Atmosphere-wise things are low-key: the reception is comprised of a shed, where you'll meet the welcoming owners, who give good advice on walks, the tides and places to visit nearby. They also provide maps, ice-pack rental and camping gas. Amenities at the site are fairly basic and caravans are not allowed, so expect lots of tents, vintage campervans, mountain bikes, outdoorsy punters and kite-flying kids. It gets a little crowded during school and bank holidays, but the atmosphere is good, with communal footie, frisbee-throwing and badminton taking place in the gaps between the tents.

As well as the marshes, the village of Stiffkey is well worth exploring: it's a gorgeous little place with red-brick and flint houses, narrow streets, appealing antique shops and the *Red Lion*, which serves Norfolk ales and seafood. Stiffkey Stores sells good bread, cheeses and cakes; otherwise shop at the excellent deli in Wells. The medieval church is worth a look, and adjoins the tower of an earlier church and the fairy-tale buildings of sixteenth-century Stiffkey Hall, imposing but partially ruined.

Practicalities

High Sand Creek Campsite, Greenway, Stiffkey, Norfolk, NR23 1QF ☎*01328 830235*

Pitches & price 80 pitches. Tent with 2 adults from £10, families from £12.

Facilities Decent toilet block, washing-up area, laundry.

Restrictions Dogs on a lead. No caravans but campervans allowed. No campfires, though raised BBQs permitted. No loud music.

Open March–Oct.

Getting there The site is off the North Norfolk coastal road – the A149 – just west of the village of Stiffkey (follow signs for the site). For public transport, take the Coast Hopper bus service (Ⓦwww.norfolkgreen.co.uk), which runs along the coast. Stop at Stiffkey; the site is signed just to the west of the village. The bus service runs from Hunstanton to Sheringham, often from King's Lynn and Cromer too, which links up with the trains from Norwich to Sheringham and the trains from London to King's Lynn.

The village is famous for cockles, known as "Stewkey Blues" for their grey-blue shells, and for Harold Davidson, who was rector here in the 1930s. Rather than hang around in Stiffkey he had a penchant for nipping off to Soho to minister to fallen women; his motives were deemed to be less than altruistic, and he was eventually defrocked.

The proximity of the site to the attractions of the village – and the pub – is a big plus, and combined with the adjoining marshland makes *High Sand Creek* pretty special. If you want an unassuming natural getaway, this could be just the place.

◀ Common sea lavender on the salt marshes ▶ A sign welcomes visitors to historic Stiffkey; tents at spacious *High Sand Creek*

Kelling Heath

You'll find *Kelling Heath* is very much in holiday-camp mode, with a bricked "village" centre (somewhat resembling a supermarket forecourt) and the various facilities arrayed around it. Definitely not a get-away-from-it-all option, then, but if you have a gaggle of kids to entertain it's a winner, with a nice outdoor pool, archery, clown shows and craft lessons. Nature trails radiate out from the site and onto the heath's pine woodland, open marshes, pebble beaches and dunes.

Also nearby is the cute North Norfolk Railway (Ⓦwww.nnrailway.co.uk), whose steam train runs between Holt and Sheringham. The site has its own request stop, but because of the very steep gradient, trains don't stop here on the journey to Holt, although they will make a request stop on the return trip from Holt to Sheringham.

Sheringham Park (open all year, dawn to dusk), a National Trust garden landscaped by Humphry Repton in the early nineteenth century, is an easy walk away. It's best in May and June when the rhododendrons and azaleas are in bloom.

Practicalities

Kelling Heath, Weybourne, Holt, Norfolk, NR25 7HW
Ⓣ*01263 588181,* Ⓦ*www.kellingheath.co.uk*
Pitches & prices Tent and car from £16.75 per pitch per night. During high season, bookings of a week minimum apply.
Facilities Individual washing cubicles and shaver points. Disabled and baby-changing facilities plus dishwashing and laundry sinks. Café, pub, shop, swimming pool.
Restrictions Dogs (from £3) on a lead.
Open Year round.
Getting there On the A148 from Holt, turn left into Sandy Lane just before Bodham and you'll see a sign for "The Forge Kelling Heath" pointing left. From Cromer, travel through Bodham, pass a plant-hire firm on the right and then take the first right into Sandy Lane. You'll see the same sign pointing right. Continue down Sandy Lane. The entrance is on the left.

Diglea

Diglea is located on the Wash, the angular estuary that separates East Anglia from Lincolnshire. It's not the most beautiful part of the region – the coast further north is dotted with attractive small towns, and the east coast features lovely golden beaches. But Snettisham is perfect for twitchers, as its lagoons and salt marshes attract large numbers of wading birds including ducks, geese, plovers, lapwings and redshanks. Conveniently, *Diglea* is sited on the very edge of the reserve. There's a sand-and-stone beach a ten-minute walk away, and the sandy beach at Hunstanton is just to the north, with distinctive striped sandstone-and-chalk cliffs and fossil-finding opportunities.

The campsite is friendly, though not worth making a beeline for in itself. You're greeted by ranks of static caravans, and the fields are flat and featureless. The on-site bar and club provide live music, and this can mean it's noisy: there's no get-away-from-it-all feel until you reach the lakes, grassy banks and marshland of the reserve. One big plus point is that, because this coast faces west, you should enjoy some glorious sunsets.

Practicalities

Diglea Caravan and Camping Park, 34 Beach Road, Snettisham, King's Lynn, Norfolk, PE31 7RA
Ⓣ*01485 541367*
Pitches & prices 132 pitches approx. £15 per tent per night.
Facilities Dishwashing, clean though old-fashioned toilet blocks, children's playground, bar, laundry, games room, club house with entertainment.
Restrictions Dogs are allowed but they must be kept on leads; there's a dog-walking track at the far end of the site.
Open April–Oct.
Getting there From King's Lynn, take the A149 Hunstanton road past Babingley and Dersingham to Snettisham. Turn left at the sign marked Snettisham Beach. *Diglea* is 1.5 miles on the left, a few hundred yards from the beach.

Pinewoods

Ride the narrow-gauge railway to a buzzing resort

Located near the north Norfolk town of Wells-next-the-Sea, *Pinewoods* is a huge site with rather a commercial feel. But it does have some real charms: kids will love the dinky narrow-gauge Wells Harbour Railway that chugs back and forth between the town and the site every fifteen minutes in high season. And a short walk away, beyond the strip of pine woods, is a spacious sandy beach, edged by traditional beach huts. These lovely structures are painted in shades of lemon-yellow, sky-blue and rust-red, and feature tall steps up to a tiny terrace and front door; they come with two deck chairs and a windbreak, and can be rented from the site either for the day or for the duration of your holiday (from £10 per day).

On site, you're greeted by ranks of caravans, beyond which there's a boating lake where you pitch, though in high season a larger overflow field is opened for tents. This can become waterlogged in bad weather, so check in advance before booking if there has been heavy rain.

Wells is a bigger and slightly brasher version of Blakeney (see p.117), with the same attractions in the form of crab fishing, a lively quay area, individual shops and a scattering of pubs – try the *Bowling Green Inn* or *The Crown*. Burger bars, betting shops and kitsch seaside trinkets give it a slightly downmarket air, though an excellent deli (🅦www.wellsdeli.co.uk) makes up for this a little. Look out for the imposing granary building on the quay built in 1904, and St Nicholas' church: local boy John Fryer, the sailing master on *HMS Bounty*, is buried here. The site is on the route of the Norfolk Coastal Path, and just to the west is the decidedly upmarket village of Holkham, which has a magnificent Palladian villa, Holkham Hall (🅦www.holkham.co.uk), one of the locations where Keira Knightley strode around in various large hats in the film *The Duchess*.

Practicalities

Pinewoods, Beach Road, Wells-next-the-Sea, Norfolk, NR23 1DR ☎*01328 710439,* 🅦*www.pinewoods.co.uk*
Pitches & price 800 pitches, many with hook-ups. From £10 per night for tents or £15 for tourers.
Facilities Portable toilets, mini-market, bakery and coffee shop.
Restrictions Dogs on leads (£3). Minimum 2-night advance booking.
Open March–Oct.
Getting there Blakeney is on the main coast road west of Cromer, the A149. For public transport, take the Coast Hopper bus service (🅦www.norfolkgreen.co.uk), which runs along the coast. Stop at Wells, then hop onto the Wells Harbour Railway for the final stretch to the campsite. The Coast Hopper service runs from Hunstanton to Sheringham, often from King's Lynn and Cromer too, which links up with trains from Norwich to Sheringham and trains from London to King's Lynn.

▼ Traditional beach huts near *Pinewoods*

Deepdale Farm

Eco-friendly fun on the north Norfolk coast

Wonderfully located at the western part of the north Norfolk Coast, *Deepdale Farm* is close to the beaches and channels where the infant Nelson is said to have learnt to sail. Just down the hill from the site, which is in the elongated village of Burnham Deepdale, you'll come to the shore, which at low tide is dotted with fishing boats and yachts perched on clumps of moss and samphire. The unusual semi-watery landscape is a draw at any time of year, and providing you're wrapped up, a winter visit with some bracing walks can have just as much appeal as a summer one – plus there's a café on hand to provide warming soup and hot meals.

The site adjoins the flint buildings of a working arable farm and a backpackers' hostel, and is split into five paddocks bounded by stone walls. Caravans aren't allowed, and the vibe here is gently hippyish and family-friendly. It's not a good place for groups as late-night noise is frowned upon – there's a curfew after 10pm, which may be too restrictive for some campers, but it makes it a good option if you're trying to get kids to sleep. If you don't want to bring your own tent, book in advance for one of the handsome tipis or the Mongolian yurt. The tipis are decked out attractively with a sleeping mat, cast-iron chimenea and barbecue, while the spacious yurt can easily accommodate a family, with two double futons, two mattresses, a barbecue and a wood-burning stove.

The cheery *Deepdale Café*, part of a cluster of buildings on the farm, has local art for sale on the walls. Self-caterers can buy all the supplies they need at the supermarket. For eating out, turn left out of the site and walk for around five minutes to *The White Horse*, which sits in the neighbouring village of Brancaster Staithe – it has a lovely sea-facing terrace at the back and the food is excellent, albeit with rather small portions.

Outdoor options are plentiful. The route of the Norfolk Coastal Path, which is designated for walkers rather than cyclists and runs from Hunstanton in the west to Cromer in the east, is only a few yards from where you camp. It's a terrific way to visit some of the nearby villages, such as Brancaster and Wells-next-the-Sea (see p.121). This is also a big area for kitesurfing (Ⓦwww.kitesurfhunstanton.com) and windsurfing

Practicalities

Deepdale Backpackers and Camping, Deepdale Farm, Burnham Deepdale, Norfolk, PE31 8DD ☎01485 210256, ⓦwww.deepdalebackpackers.co.uk

Pitches & price 82 pitches. Prices for camping and campervans: adult £4.50–9, child £2.50–5. Tipis from £40 for 2, yurts from £50 for 2.

Facilities Visitor information, laundry, café, shop, disabled facilities, internet access.

Restrictions Campervans allowed but no caravans. Dogs on a lead.

Open Year round.

Getting there From London, take the A11, turning off to Swaffham. From the Midlands head to King's Lynn and either take the A149 coast road or the A148 and turn off at Hillington to Bircham. On public transport, take the Coast Hopper bus service (ⓦwww.norfolkgreen.co.uk), which runs along the coast and stops right outside the front door. It runs from Hunstanton to Sheringham, often from King's Lynn and Cromer too, and links up with trains from Norwich to Sheringham and trains from London to King's Lynn.

(ⓦwww.windsurfhunstanton.co.uk), sailing and yachting – the campsite information centre is extremely helpful and has an abundance of leaflets on things to do in the area, from bird-watching to cycling to seal cruises.

In keeping with the environmental credentials of the site there are plenty of attractions within walking distance – a mile inland is Burnham Market, with its fine Georgian houses, independent shops and strikingly wide main street. Whatever you end up doing during the day, an on-site barbecue is a perfect way to round off an evening here.

◀ A boat stranded on the marsh ▶ Campervans at *Deepdale Farm*; beach huts gaze into the North Sea from nearby Wells-next-the-Sea

The Midlands

A rural idyll isn't the first thing that springs to mind when you think of the Midlands. This is a heavily populated area, with some very big cities – Birmingham, Leicester and Coventry – which are not exactly renowned for their beauty. But the countryside of Derbyshire, Staffordshire, Shropshire, Herefordshire and Warwickshire is surprisingly unspoilt and outstandingly beautiful. Much of it is reminiscent of picture-book England, with honey-coloured cottages, long hills rising above dense hedgerows and wildflower meadows fringing lazy rivers.

We've focused our reviews on the lushest and most enticing part of the region, namely the western counties bordering Wales and the Peak District, whose awesome gritstone ridges and limestone crags are interspersed with valleys and market towns.

There are some engagingly eccentric campsites here, including a back-to-basics farm with compost loos and alternative craft courses, a groovy lodge where you can sleep in a yurt and go on camel treks with an ex-lion-tamer and a chicken-pecked hill-top site set around a 1930s mansion.

Most offer great views, and all give you a stepping stone to outdoor action, whether it's mountain biking or rambling in the Peak District, canoeing down the River Wye or pony trekking across Herefordshire's hills. Alongside the gritty cities, the region has some lovely settlements: hippyish Bishop's Castle with its eclectic historic buildings; handsome Cotswolds towns such as Moreton-in-Marsh; and of course Shakespeare's own Stratford-upon-Avon.

Manchester

PEAK DISTRICT
NATIONAL PARK

A628

A57

Upper Booth Farm
Fieldhead
A57 Sheffield

North Lees

A6
A6187

Pindale Farm
A623
Worksop

Macclesfield
Buxton A6
Park House
Chesterfield
A60
A614

Shallow Grange
A619

DERBYSHIRE
A632

A53
A515
Matlock
A6
Mansfield

Leek
A5102
NOTTINGH
SHIRE

Rivendale
A6
A6097

Newcastle-
under-Lyme
A520
The Royal Oak
New House Farm
Heanor
Hucknall

Stoke-
on-Trent
A52
Ashbourne
A517
Nottingham
A46

A51
A50
A522
Uttoxeter
A52
Derby

A495
A53
STAFFORDSHIRE
A50
A42

Oswestry
A528
A519
Forestside
Farm
Burton-
upon-Trent
Loughborough

A5
A529
A518
Stafford
A515
A444
LEICESTERSHIRE

A458
A442
M6
A513
A38

Shrewsbury
A49
A41
A449
Cannock
Lichfield
A513
Leicester

Telford
A464
M51
Wolverhampton
Tamworth
A5
M42
A447
M69

SHROPSHIRE
A442
Walsall
Hinckley
M1

A488
A458
A454
Dudley
Nuneaton

Small Batch
A458
BIRMINGHAM
M6

Foxholes Castle
A489
B4368
A442
Stourbridge
Coventry

Middle
Woodbatch Farm
A488
Bishop's
Castle
B4364
Kidderminster
A448
M40
Rugby
M45

B4368
A4113
A456
Redditch
Warwick
Royal
Leamington
Spa
A45
A425

A4110
A443
A442
Daventry

A44
WORCESTERSHIRE
A422
WARWICKSHIRE
A361

Leominster
A44
Worcester
Stratford-
upon-Avon
A422

A4112
A4103
Great
Malvern
A46
Talton Lodge
A429
A422

HEREFORDSHIRE
A4104
Evesham
A3400

Hay-on-Wye
A4111
A438
A480
A465
M5

Hollybush Inn
B4348
B4352
Hereford
A4138
M50
A438

A438
A49
Woodland Tipis

Burhope
Farm
A465
Tresseck

A466
A4137
Ross-
on-Wye
A40

Monmouth
Doward Park

The Midlands

	PAGE	walking	cycling	watersports	food & drink	hill walking	adults	family	caravan	motorhome	accessible
Burhope Farm	133			✓		✓	✓		✓		✓
Doward Park	133			✓			✓				
Fieldhead	142	✓					✓			✓	✓
Forestside Farm	138						✓		✓		
Foxholes Castle	136	✓			✓				✓	✓	
Hollybush Inn	128	✓		✓			✓	✓	✓		
Middle Woodbatch Farm	134				✓	✓					
New House Farm	139						✓				
North Lees	146	✓					✓			✓	
Park House	144	✓	✓				✓				
Pindale Farm	145	✓						✓	✓	✓	
Rivendale	135	✓	✓							✓	
The Royal Oak	144	✓	✓		✓	✓					
Shallow Grange	138						✓		✓		
Small Batch	134	✓	✓				✓		✓		
Talton Lodge	132				✓				✓	✓	✓
Tresseck	130			✓			✓			✓	
Upper Booth Farm	145	✓					✓			✓	
Wing Hall	140		✓						✓		
Woodland Tipis	129				✓	✓	✓	✓			

See front flap for key to symbols

Hollybush Inn
Folk music, wild camping and canoeing on the Welsh border

Whether swimming down the neighbouring River Wye, waving excitedly to passers-by or teaching seventy bankers how to cook over an open fire, Barbara Lewthwaite is a decidedly relaxed campsite owner. Her flamboyant nature is in evidence across this ramshackle establishment, sprawled across 22 acres of field and woodland. There are no marked pitches, and you're free to choose any of the clearings in the forest. Children can explore woods dotted with trails, swings and a wildlife pond. Campers wheel about stacks of wood (£5 for a wheelbarrowful) for open fires and rest on log benches watching the river flow silently by.

Several spacious pre-erected tipis with stoves and coconut-wood floors sit in the woodland, while caravan pitches are at the trees' edge, close to the site entrance. Sleeping in the forest is a treat, and feels like wild camping. From the woods you can see the foreboding Black Mountains, clustering in the southeast of Wales.

For outdoor activities, the edge of the Brecon Beacons National Park is less than a mile away, and a half-hour drive down the A470 opens up the dramatic ridges of Pen-Y-Fan (2970ft) and Corn Du (2863ft), popular hikes that are worth taking seriously, especially in winter. Walkers and cyclists will find plenty of set trails though Herefordshire and Wales to choose from.

The River Wye backs onto the site and is mostly slow-moving, making it a popular spot for inexperienced kayakers or canoers.

▼ Pen-Y-Fan, in the Brecon Beacons

Hollybush Inn rents boats out at £20 for half a day and £30 for a full day. Lewthwaite even offers a pick-up service, so that wherever you happen to get tired along the Wye, a Land Rover to take you and the canoe back to the site is just a phone call away.

Musicians often play at the *Hollybush Inn*, the on-site pub, a lively place in the evenings; its food has received mixed reports. The campsite's makeshift shop sells sausage sandwiches, breakfast treats and snacks, while many campers bring their own supplies and cook over an open fire or venture to Hay-on-Wye, just two miles down the road. The book-besotted Hay Festival is held at the end of May in a village of tents between the campsite and Hay-on-Wye, while the town itself has cafés, restaurants, a battered castle and – most importantly – scores of bookshops, packing in well over a million old and new tomes.

Practicalities

Hollybush Inn and Campsite, Old Brecon Road, Glasbury-on-Wye, Herefordshire, HR3 5PS ☎*01497 847371,* Ⓦ*www.hollybushcamping.co.uk*

Pitches & price Plenty of standard pitches, 28 hard-standing pitches with hook-ups, 4 tipis (a 2-person, a 4-person, an 8-person and a 12-person). Tents & caravans £6 per adult, £3 per child, additional £2 for hook-ups. Tipis £12.50 per person.
Facilities 3 basic shower and toilet blocks – which can get grubby – with separate male and female facilities.
Restrictions Dogs must be kept on a lead. No loud noise or music after 11pm, although pub noise sometimes continues till late. Campfires permitted.
Open Year round.
Getting there The site is on the Old Brecon Road (the B4350) between Hay-on-Wye and Glasbury-on-Wye. The nearest train station is Hereford: buses #X15 and #445 run from the station to Brecon 3 times a day, stopping at the site on request. *Hollybush* runs a taxi service, charging 50p a mile – the minimum fare is £5.

Woodland Tipis
Hot-water bottles in the woods

Luxury campsites may have their detractors, but they can certainly help you relax. Turn up at this site, buried deep in the hills of Hereford's countryside, and you'll see your name on a blackboard at the entrance. Follow the footpath through the woodlands to your tipi and you'll find a mattress with blankets, cushions, a stove, a kettle, a vase of flowers, candles, incense and a wood-burning stove.

Woodlands Tipis' owner Julia Sanders originally planned an ecolodge on the site. However, when the council refused her planning application, she decided to put the knowledge she'd gained on a tipi-making course some years before to good use. Her personal touch adds a quirkiness to the site that is pleasantly at odds with the luxury theme. Framed pictures of traditional yurts and tipis dot the walls of the communal areas, and half-a-dozen hot-water bottles hang up in the shower block for campers' use.

Each tipi sits on a raised platform within its own section of quiet woodlands, separated from other campers by a neat footpath that leads towards the communal areas. The "back gardens", with benches, tables, outdoor lanterns, barbecues and hammocks, are perfect for groups and families, while the forest frames the site and obscures other tents, giving a real sense of wild camping and seclusion.

The shared kitchen, equipped with giant wooden chopping boards and everything you need to bake, boil, grill and fry, would make your granny envious: there are two ovens, a fridge for every tent, cafetières, pots, pans, wine glasses, mugs, plates and salad bowls, while the bakehouse boasts an outdoor clay oven. When more than one group is cooking, the lively atmosphere offers a nice break from the isolation that can characterize camping, and you may be drawn to the long wooden table in the kitchen around meal times.

Hereford itself is about six miles away, but there are plenty of places to eat and buy good food in the surrounding villages. The *Cottage of Content* pub and restaurant, in the village of Carey, a two-and-a-half-mile walk, serves home-made, locally sourced food, including beef, game, lamb and poultry. A butcher's van visits the site on Mondays and Fridays around 6pm, and the campsite itself sells frozen milk and bread.

▼ *Woodland Tipis*: personal touches, luxury furnishings

Tresseck
Back to basics in a Herefordshire meadow

Empirical evidence suggests that this site is one for the boys, which might have something to do with the fact that you're allowed to light open fires, and that the washing facilities are extremely minimal. The portaloos are totally basic – and there are no showers and no hot water – but you can stand at the tap brushing your teeth in the morning and enjoy a gorgeous view, across a buttercup-flecked meadow to the Italianate church on the hillside in Hoarwithy. The site is backed by woodland, which some people use as a source of firewood, though for environmental reasons it's better to leave deadwood where it falls (instead you can buy a bag of wood from the owner).

The owner started *Tresseck* after a canoeist asked her if he could put up a tent in one of her fields, and the whole enterprise still has a pleasingly simple and organic quality. To preserve this, and keep nearby villagers happy, the owner asks campers not to play music and to keep noise to a minimum in the evenings.

Campers and villagers meet at the *New Harp Inn*, a stroll away down the lane – it enjoyed *Good Pub Guide* listing till recently but has changed hands: while it's a great location for a pint, the food isn't particularly recommended. Instead, head for the *New Inn* in the neighbouring village of Pembridge – not in fact new, but located in a rambling half-timbered building. The grub is hearty, and meat and veg are locally sourced.

During the day, there's plenty to keep active campers entertained. Sitting on the banks of the River Wye, between Hereford and the market town of Ross-on-Wye, the site is a perfect location for canoeists and kayakers – it has its own landing spot, and you can get to Ross-on-Wye in around four hours. There are no rapids to negotiate on this stretch of the river, making it good for learners and kids. *Tresseck*'s website lists places where you can rent canoes and has links to campsites on the river in case you want to paddle from one to another.

As far as other activities go, anglers can fish in the river on site, and the owners will happily talk campers through the network of walking routes in this green and luxuriant corner of Herefordshire.

Close by, a section of the 136-mile Wye Valley Walk connects Ross-on-Wye with Hereford – the route is signed with a leaping

Practicalities

Tresseck Campsite, Hoarwithy, Hereford, HR2 6QJ
☎*01432 840235,* ⓦ*www.tresseckcampsite.co.uk*

Pitches & price Campers are free to pitch where they like in the field. Adults £4.25 per night, children £2 per night, £1 per car for length of stay. There is no reception: payments are collected in the morning.

Facilities Portaloos and water on site. No showers or washing-up facilities. There's no shop in the village, so bring supplies.

Restrictions Campfires can be lit but only in the obvious places provided. Dogs must be kept under control. No stereos.

Open Easter–Sept.

Getting there From Hereford, follow the A49 south through Much Birch, take the next left signposted Hoarwithy (turning down Laskett Lane) and follow it for 2 miles; the *New Harp Inn* is opposite the T-junction, with the campsite just to the left of the Inn. From Ross, take the A49 north and then take the second right (signposted Hoarwithy). Follow this for 4 miles to the *New Harp Inn*; the campsite is just past the pub on the right. The #37 bus from Ross or Hereford will drop you off right outside the *New Harp Inn*.

salmon logo and incorporates ravine woodland as well as gentle pastures. The market town of Ross-on-Wye is four miles away and is held to be the birthplace of the English tourist industry – in the eighteenth century, lovers of the Picturesque were taken on trips from here down the Wye to admire its steep sylvan slopes, abbeys and castles.

◀ The view from *Tresseck* stretches across a meadow to Hoarwithy
▶ Ross-on-Wye, the market town where British tourism began; the River Wye is a fine spot if you want to learn to kayak or canoe

Talton Lodge

Yurts, tipis and home-cooked food in Shakespeare country

This excellent family-run enterprise combines *Elle Decoration*-style tent accommodation with gourmet grub and a relaxed and friendly atmosphere. The setting is a smallholding, ringed around with kitchen gardens, orchards and a piggery. There's a slightly hippyish look and feel to the place – the handsome yurt and tipis are decked out with furry throws and woven cushions, and their incongruous appearance in an otherwise very English garden is very appealing. This is a real rural haven in what is a surprisingly populated area – Stratford-on-Avon is just ten minutes' drive away, and close by are the honey-stone Cotswolds towns of Moreton-in-Marsh and Bourton-on-the-Water.

The owner was a successful chef in London before moving back to her family farm, and she provides excellent home-grown and home-cooked food such as lamb tagine, pork loin and veg kebabs, and puds which could include pavlova or elderflower and gooseberry ice cream. You can buy excellent provisions at the farm shop just down the lane, or purchase the *Talton Lodge* breakfast box, with their very own sausages, bacon, eggs, bread and jam, plus local milk and butter.

The best and most sociable way to enjoy this beautiful site is in a group – the owners can accommodate up to sixteen people under canvas. *Talton Lodge* is a popular choice for alternative hen weekends – you can alternate activities with leisure time lying on the lawns or in and around the yurt. It's also perfect for groups with children – there's a rope swing, they can help feed the pigs and chickens, and there's a lovely enclosed space to play in. The owners have a creative approach to entertaining guests – as well as archery, cycle trips, canoeing, fishing, pasta-making and wine-tasting, you can do camel treks with an ex-lion-tamer who lives nearby. They also run sausage-making courses on site (though the extremely cute farm pigs might make this a challenge for some).

▼ The hippyish haven of *Talton Lodge* is great for groups

Practicalities

Talton Lodge, Newbold-on-Stour, Stratford-upon-Avon, Warwickshire, CV37 8UB ☎*07962 273417,* Ⓦ*www.taltonlodge.co.uk*

Pitches & price North American Indian tipi (1 double and 2 single beds), Mongolian yurt (1 double and 4 singles), Nordic tipi (3–4 single beds). £35–45 per person, including linen, towels, firewood, breakfast and activities. Children 4–14 half price, under-4s free. Parties of 12 or more get the kitchen garden to themselves. The barn (min price £100) has space for 5. Food £10 for a main course, £5 starter or pudding.

Facilities Tipi with running water and gas stoves. Pavilion on site with 3 loos and hot showers (wheelchair-accessible).

Restrictions Dogs permitted but must be kept on leads. Campfires allowed.

Open Yurt and tipi: April–Oct; barn: year round.

Getting there *Talton Lodge* is in Newbold-on-Stour, south of Stratford on the A3400 – follow the signs past the farm shop, then bear sharp right. Local buses run regularly from Stratford; the stop is at the turning to Talton Mill farm shop on the A3400. The owners offer 2 days' free bike hire if you arrive by public transport.

Burhope Farm

Set just a few miles from the Welsh border, this secluded site sits at the heart of Hereford's picturesque Wye valley, a few miles from the Welsh border. With nothing for miles but hills, farms and winding country lanes, its lush fields and quiet surroundings make it a fine place to relax.

Kids have plenty of space for ball games, walkers can access the 150-mile Herefordshire Trail (Ⓦwww.herefordshiretrail.com) and the River Wye is a short drive away. There's a substantial canoe and kayak shop and a demo lake on site, while a number of companies hire out equipment around Hereford, including Hereford Canoe Hire (Ⓣ01432 873020) in Lucksall Park, about seven miles from *Burhope Farm*.

Owners Philippa and Paul Hale are eager to make campers feel at home and sell firewood and free-range eggs, while an extended shower block and small shop are planned. The nearest shops and pubs are three and half miles away in the village of Ewyas Harold, including a butcher's and a fish-and-chip shop. There's no noise after 10.30pm.

Practicalities

Burhope Farm, Orcop, Herefordshire, HR2 8EU Ⓣ*01981 580275,* Ⓦ*www.burhopefarmcampsite.co.uk*

Pitches & price 30 standard pitches, 12 hard-standing pitches with hook-ups. £10–12 per 3-person tent (plus £2.50 for hook-up), £15 per caravan.

Facilities Very clean amenities block with great showers and separate male and female loos. Disabled toilet with wash basin. 2 portaloos on field.

Restrictions Dogs allowed on leads. Fires permitted.

Open Year round.

Getting there Take the A449 from the M50. After 0.5 miles take the third exit onto the A40 towards Ross-on-Wye; at the next roundabout take the fourth exit onto the A49. Follow the A49 for 4 miles, turn left and follow road for 5 miles. The nearest train station is Hereford, about 7 miles away. Bus #412 runs from Hereford to Garway, a 10–15min walk from the site.

Doward Park

Tucked away in woodland above the Wye valley, *Doward Park* is a welcoming place with an orderly Alpine feel. It's very much geared to families, and things are pretty quiet here from about 10.30pm. There's plenty to keep kids happy, including den-building in the surrounding bluebell woods, and there are great canoeing opportunities on a wide stretch of the Wye – try the Wyedean Canoe Centre (Ⓣ01594 833238) in nearby Symonds Yat East.

Woodland paths lead from the campsite to the river cliffs of the Seven Sisters Rocks and to King Arthur's Cave, a large double-chambered cavern where a giant skeleton was supposedly found in the seventeenth century, and attributed (somewhat randomly) to King Arthur. More footpaths dip down to riverside Symonds Yat, where rope ferries take you across the river to the *Olde Ferrie Inn* and the *Saracen's Head* – they're no great shakes, but both have wonderful riverside locations. Otherwise, you can barbecue food by your tent, and the site's shop provides basic provisions, ice creams and snacks.

Practicalities

Doward Park Campsite, Great Doward, Symonds Yat, Ross-on-Wye, Herefordshire, HR9 6BP Ⓣ*01600 890438,* Ⓦ*www.dowardpark.co.uk*

Pitches & price 27 pitches. £14.50 per pitch for 2 adults (£2 per child). Hook-ups available.

Facilities Good facilities including showers, toilets, washing-up room, tumble dryer.

Restrictions No campfires. Dogs allowed (£1).

Open Year round.

Getting there Travelling from Ross, turn off the A40 at exit for Symonds Yat West (not East), then second exit at small roundabout and follow brown signs for *Doward Park*. Travelling from Monmouth, turn off the A40 about 2 miles after Monmouth at exit signposted Crockers Ash. Turn left at the T-junction then take the first right (next to a few houses; it's easy to miss) after about 0.5 miles. Follow signs uphill.

Small Batch

It's a wonderful sylvan setting – the camping field is ringed by Shropshire hills, a stream runs along its bottom, and the owners, who have been running *Small Batch* for forty years, live in a picture-book seventeenth-century cottage on its edge.

A stile at the far end leads straight into great walking country; there are three main footpaths, one to Church Stretton, one to the Carding Mill Valley and one to the heather-covered Long Mynd. The name means "long hill" – it stretches for ten miles, and from your moorland vantage point you can see the jagged tors of the Stiperstones, and all the way to the peaks and ridges of Snowdonia when it's clear.

Naturally enclosed by tall trees and the stream, the site is a serene spot, perfect for a long day's walk and an early night. Unspoilt Little Stretton is a short stroll away, with the *Ragleth Inn* and the *Green Dragon* offering good grub and real ale; Ludlow, Shrewsbury and Ironbridge are all within around twelve miles; and just to the south is Stokesay Castle (☎01588 672544), a glorious timber-framed fortified manor house dating from the late thirteenth century.

Practicalities

Small Batch Camping, Ashes Valley, Little Stretton, Church Stretton, Shropshire, SY6 6PW ☎*01694 723358,* Ⓦ*www.smallbatch-camping.webeden.co.uk*

Pitches & price 18 tent pitches, 12 are for caravans. 14 hook-up points. 1-person tent £10, 2-person tent £12, larger tents £14, tent with hook-up £16. Caravans £14, £16 with hook-up.

Facilities Simple but clean shower block and toilets, washing-up area.

Restrictions No campfires; raised BBQs permitted. Dogs must be on leads at all times.

Open April–Sept.

Getting there Take the B5477 to Little Stretton, just south of Church Stretton. Turn into the lane beside the *Ragleth Inn*. Take the next right on the sharp left-hand bend; the site is straight ahead through the ford. Buses to Little Stretton runs from Ludlow and Shrewsbury.

Middle Woodbatch Farm

The single-track winding lane leading to *Middle Woodbatch Farm*, edged by tall hedgerows, gives some indication of the seclusion you'll enjoy when you get there. You can pitch your tent pretty much where you like – the welcoming owners are happy for you to set up on the hill above the farm, away from the meadows with the other campers. The sense of privacy is carefully nurtured, and the spacious fields only ever accommodate up to ten tents at a time.

From your vantage point in the Shropshire Hills you look over to the high heathland of the Long Mynd, across patchwork arable land. There's a network of paths and bridleways round about, some of which adjoin the farmland – you can use the Shropshire Way to reach the gorgeous little town of Bishop's Castle (see p.136), and riders can stable horses on the farm (see Ⓦwww.bridleways.co.uk for help on planning a riding trip). Calving and lambing time is the first two weeks in April – you're welcome to watch or to help out. Fortify yourself for a day's walking – or lambing – with a home-cooked farm breakfast for a fiver. All this plus the biggest pet pig you'll ever see.

Practicalities

Middle Woodbatch Farm Bed & Breakfast and Campsite, Woodbatch Road, Bishop's Castle, Shropshire, SY9 5JT ☎*07989 496875,* Ⓦ*www.middlewoodbatchfarm.co.uk*

Pitches & price 10 pitches. £5 per adult, £2.50 per child, under-5s free.

Facilities Excellent private bathrooms.

Restrictions Raised fires permitted. on campsite. Dogs welcome.

Open Year round.

Getting there From Shrewsbury and the A5, take the A488 Bishop's Castle road and follow it for 22 miles. On reaching the second town sign, turn right, past the school and just after the church keep to the left, rather than heading up into the town. After about 250yds, turn left onto Woodbatch Road, go straight on, then follow the road round to the right to its end.

Rivendale

Camp in a quarry and walk through the Peaks

An on-site pub, games room and restaurant give *Rivendale* a holiday-camp feel that isn't for everyone, though the setting – the site is enclosed within the high rock amphitheatre of a former hill quarry – is superb. Caravanners have the best pitches here, right under the spectacular cliffs, while tents are confined to two areas, one with electric hook-ups and one open meadow. Facilities are excellent, and toilet blocks and other buildings are made with local stone, giving the site a very harmonious and attractive look. There's a play area for kids, and this is a great location for exploring the Peak District: the thirteen-mile Tissington Trail runs past the site and, being mainly flat, is good for cyclists – both cyclists and hikers can use the route to link up with the High Peak Trail, which follows a disused railway. Plus there's Chatsworth House, with its varied art collection and famous gardens, the lush Wye valley and the limestone ravine of Dovedale – you can walk to the north end of the dale from the campsite.

▼ *Rivendale* campsite: more attractive than your average quarry

Practicalities

Rivendale Caravan & Leisure Park, Buxton Road, Alsop-en-le-Dale, Ashbourne, Derbyshire ℡*01335 310441,* Ⓦ*www.rivendalecaravanpark.co.uk*

Pitches & prices 100 pitches for caravans and motor homes; 50 pitches for tents. Caravans £19 with hook up, £14.50 without. 2-person tent in open field (with basic portacabin loos) £10, £2.50 per additional adult. Tent in caravan area (with 16-amp hook-up and access to posher loos) £19. Bring rock pegs and a hammer.

Facilities Under-floor heated shower building, laundrette and children's play area. Shop, pub and restaurant on site.

Restrictions Raised fires and BBQs permitted on camping meadow only. Dogs allowed.

Open Feb to mid-Dec.

Getting there In Ashbourne follow signs for Buxton on the A515; don't take the Alsop-en-le-Dale turn-off – simply stay on the A515 for another 0.5 miles and you'll find *Rivendale* on the right-hand side.

Foxholes Castle

Footpaths and panoramas by a quirky market town

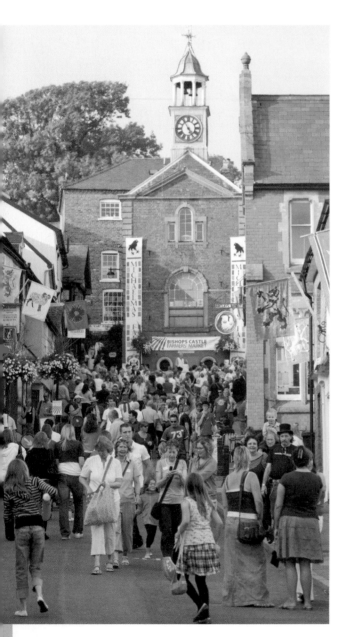

Perched just above the hillside Shropshire town of Bishop's Castle, *Foxholes Castle* offers almost 360-degree views of the green hills of southwest Shropshire, an official Area of Outstanding Natural Beauty. The camping fields encircle an eccentric crenellated 1930s mansion where the owners live, with chickens pecking around the front door and an abundant cottage garden. The proximity of the campsite to Bishop's Castle is a major draw: a tiny market town on a steep hill with half-timbered and brightly painted houses, it has an appealingly alternative air and is home to a lively community of artists, craftspeople and musicians.

While the owners ensure that noise doesn't get out of hand, there are no prescriptive rules here – the welcome is informal and friendly. There's a range of camping options, from an open field for tents (this has the best views) to a touring field, an area for motor caravans, two static caravans (one eight-berth and one five-berth) and a neat bunkhouse. Campers can light fires at the owner's discretion – they must be raised so they don't affect the grass – and there are some nice innovations such as a shower block with solar-heated water, as well as good recycling facilities.

If you're self-catering, you can stroll into Bishop's Castle to shop at the excellent farmer's market, held on the third Saturday of every month, or at the produce market held in the town hall each Friday. There are plenty of individual shops including the very classy Art & Artisan Books on the High Street, and a remarkable six pubs, two of which – the *Six Bells* and the *Three Tuns* – have their own real-ale microbreweries. For something more upmarket, go to the *Castle Hotel*, where you can eat in the gorgeous garden.

Despite the town's small size, there's a great programme of events, many of which revolve around alcohol – the Bishop's Castle Real Ale Festival, for example, is held in mid-July. The big annual event in the town's calendar is the fairly riotous two-day Michaelmas Fair in September, with parades, stalls and vintage vehicles, from pennyfarthings to steam cars. The hippyish Clun Green Man Festival is held in nearby Clun at the beginning of May – this features a craft fair, live music and a masked green man parading with local maidens.

The circular 136-mile Shropshire Way clips the edge of the site,

Practicalities

Foxholes Castle Camping, Montgomery Road, Bishop's Castle, Shropshire, SY9 5HA ☎01588 638924, Ⓦwww.foxholes-castle.co.uk

Pitches & price Around 130 well-spaced pitches. Tents, caravans and motor homes £6 per person for over 13s, £2 for under 13s. Bunkhouse £10 per bed, £40 for the whole thing (it sleeps 6).

Facilities Good, clean shower block. Chemical toilet disposal points. No hook-ups at present and no shop, though the site owners sell their own fruit and veg when it's available.

Restrictions Campfires at owners' discretion. Dogs allowed (£1).

Open Year round.

Getting there Bishop's Castle is on the A488 20 miles south of Shrewsbury and 35 miles from the M54. *Foxholes* is on the B4385 Montgomery road just north of the town. Look for the Montgomery sign to the left as you begin to drive uphill out of Bishop's Castle, and then follow the driveway for 200yds.

meaning you can step out of your tent and be in unspoilt walking country within minutes. The trail takes in the rock outcrops of the Stiperstones and the limestone escarpment of Wenlock Edge, and incorporates Bronze Age ways, Roman roads and drovers' paths. Just to the west of Bishop's Castle is the long-distance Offa's Dyke National Trail, which runs along the eighth-century earthwork built by the king of Mercia and roughly follows the border with Wales. Other outdoor options are provided by the riding stable at Lydbury North (Ⓦwww.walcotstables.co.uk), and there's good fishing at the Onny Vale Trout and Coarse Fishery, between Bishop's Castle and Minsterley.

◀ Bishop's Castle's Michaelmas Fair ▶ *Foxholes* boasts near 360-degree views of the Shropshire countryside; plus the odd chicken

Shallow Grange

Approaching *Shallow Grange*, whether from the motorway or via picturesque Buxton, the landscape becomes greener and soon the only sounds you hear are birds singing and lambs bleating. Bar the occasional shudder of a lorry passing by the road about half a mile from the site, a weekend here is a weekend away from the white noise of modern living – a feeling reinforced by the "no stereos" policy.

Set against a backdrop of rolling dales, its only neighbours lush, inviting fields, the site is also home to a B&B and a farm, but feels surprisingly small and contained, its neat, pretty pitches framed by daffodils in the spring.

Nearby footpaths lead to plenty of scenic walks in the Derbyshire Dales and the Wye valley, taking in acres of meadows framed by exquisite stone walls. Maps and books on the area can be bought at Brierlow Bar Bookshop, about a mile from the site, which claims to be the biggest bargain bookshop in the UK. Among the usual discount clutter, it sells a good range of bestsellers, cookbooks, classics and children's books.

Practicalities

Shallow Grange Farm, Old Coalpit Lane, Chelmorton, Buxton, Derbyshire, SK17 9SG ☎01298 23578, Ⓦwww.shallowgrange.com

Pitches & prices 40 standard pitches, 18 hard-standing with hook-ups. £10 for a 2-person tent, £15 for a 2-person caravan.

Facilities Clean shower and loo block. Mums and tots shower room. Coin-operated laundry facilities.

Restrictions Dogs allowed but must be kept on leads. No campfires permitted.

Open March–Oct.

Getting there From Buxton, follow A515 southbound towards Ashbourne. At Brierlow Bar, turn left onto the A5270. The campsite is signposted and on the left after just under a mile. Buses runs about 6 times a day from Buxton, the nearest train station, to outside the campsite gates on Old Coalpit Lane.

Forestside Farm

This immaculate campsite is on a dairy farm, just to the south of the Peak District National Park and with views across to Dovedale and the Weaver Hills – you'll see at least part of the herd of ninety Friesian cows ambling in the pasture below the tents. It's a small operation, occupying the top corner of a sloping field, and the owners limit numbers to put an emphasis on peace and quiet – the atmosphere is relaxed and most people are slumbering in their tents or caravans by around 10.30pm. There's a safe, fenced area for children to play or families to picnic or barbecue, and a small pool for coarse fishing (£5).

The surrounding countryside is attractive rather than spectacular, but you can use footpaths to walk in the nearby woodland, and it's a good base for the market towns of Uttoxeter, famous for horse-racing, and Ashbourne, where one half of the town plays the other in the two-day Royal Shrovetide Football Match, with the town as the pitch and three miles lying between the two goals. Also nearby is historic Lichfield, birthplace of Dr Johnson, and – should anyone fancy it – Alton Towers.

Practicalities

Forestside Farm Caravaning & Camping, Marchington, nr Uttoxeter, Staffordshire, ST14 8NA ☎01283 820353, Ⓦwww.forestsidefarm.co.uk

Pitches & prices 12 tents (not in marked-out pitches), hard-standings with hook-ups for 5 caravans. Tents £12 for 2 people, caravans £15 for 2 people. Additional adults & children £2.50 per night, no charge for under-5s.

Facilities Good, clean washrooms. Kitchen with kettle, fridge and microwave, plus local information.

Restrictions Raised fires and BBQs permitted. Pets are welcome.

Open Year round.

Getting there From Uttoxeter, take the B5017 east to Marchington. In Marchington, follow signs for the industrial estate to the east of the village. Opposite you'll see signs for *Forestside Farm*.

New House Farm

Compost loos, yurt-making and organic flower meadows

If you don't mind your camping a little on the rough side, you'll love this bucolic spot. Located on the edge of the Peak District National Park and on the outskirts of Kniveton village, it's a fully organic livestock and vegetable farm. You pitch on the sloping field overlooking the farm, backed by a wildflower meadow scattered with orchids, cowslips and saxifrage. The beautifully designed compost loos are behind the farm buildings; indeed, craftsmanship defines *New House*, from on-site willow-working to the home-built ecopod, which is also available to rent. With a shower, its own compost toilet and solar-powered electricity, the shed-like ecopod provides relative comfort and sleeps four.

Another terrific feature is the courses run by resourceful owner Mary Smail on weaving, spinning, carpentry, blacksmithing and yurt-making. If you're interested in learning a particular craft, she'll match you with a local expert. Smail also leads walks in the area, focusing on leylines and dousing, wildflowers or identifying and exploring the nearby archeological sites – there are bowl barrows, a lead mine and medieval ridge-and-furrow fields in the vicinity.

The owners emphasize respect for the site: fires are allowed only if they are raised to avoid damaging the grass, and you're discouraged from collecting fallen wood which nurtures beetles and other insects; instead you can buy firewood for £4. Campers can also buy farm produce in the form of eggs – free-range of course – and organic meat. It's a good place for walkers, with the Peak District National Park and Dovedale a short drive away, and there are water sports on Carsington Water, two miles from the site. You can make the twenty-minute walk to the *Red Lion* in Kniveton – or just crack open a beer, lie on the slope and take in the bucolic views down to the farm and the hills beyond.

▼ *New House Farm* offers craft courses and organic food

Practicalities

New House Farm, Kniveton, Ashbourne, Derbyshire, DE6 1JL ☎01335 342429, ⓦwww.newhousefarm.co.uk. Ecopod ☎07929 616282, ⓦwww.ecopodholidays.co.uk

Pitches & price Approximately 15 pitches in 3 fields; you are free to pitch where you like. Hard-standings available in the farmyard. £2 per person; ecopod £30 per person for a couple, £45 for families. Caravans £5, plus £1 per car.

Facilities No showers; compost loos and a tap for washing. Shower and compost loo in the ecopod. Laundry available.

Restrictions Dogs and raised campfires allowed. There are no shops in Knivetown, so bring supplies.

Open Year round.

Getting there Leave Ashbourne on the B5035 heading towards Wirksworth and Matlock; after 3 miles turn left in Kniveton village (opposite the church). After 400yds on a left-hand bend turn right. Go uphill for 400yds. *New House Farm* is on the right through a green gate.

Wing Hall

Free-range chickens and a great farm shop in England's smallest county

The setting here is more Gothic novel than get-away-from-it-all – a long avenue of lime trees leads to imposing *Wing Hall*, built by a velvet manufacturer in the late nineteenth century. Screened from the villa-like construction by tall trees and dense rhododendrons, tents and caravans pitch up in the nearby fields – the only interruption to the peace and quiet in this well-maintained and friendly site is from the hundred free-range chickens that peck the grass around the house. You can buy their eggs if you fancy a breakfast fry-up, and other provisions are on hand at the excellent on-site farm shop, which sells gourmet items

including Hambledon Bakery bread and great rhubarb crumble ice cream and daily papers as well as the basics. If cooking seems too much like hard work, the pretty café is a good option for breakfast and lunch, and also provides burgers in the evening in summer. Outdoor seating on the terrace overlooking the lawns makes it an idyllic spot on warm days.

While the farm shop and café add a dash of class, the toilet facilities are fairly basic – fine for most, but if you like your camping luxurious then look elsewhere. Otherwise, it's a good option for campers who like to fish – there's coarse fishing on

Practicalities

Wing Hall Camping, Wing, Oakham, Rutland, LE15 8RY
☎*01572 737090,* ⓦ*www.winghall.co.uk*
Pitches & price Spacious fields for tents and caravans. Camping £6.50 per person, £3 for children, £1 for babies. 2-person caravans with electric hook-up £18.50, £22.50 on bank holidays.
Facilities 14 toilets and 5 showers, plus washing-up units. On-site farm shop and café with indoor and outdoor seating.
Restrictions No noise between 10pm and 7am and no stereos. No campfires; raised BBQs only. Dogs to be kept on a lead at all times.
Open Year round. Last check-in is 8pm.
Getting there The village of Wing lies just north of the A47 between Leicester and Peterborough. From the A47, take the A6003 to Oakham. At the village of Preston, take a right-hand turn after the village pub, signposted to Wing. Follow the road down and then uphill to Wing, turning right into *Wing Hall* at the top of the hill.

site in two pools stocked with carp, bream and tench, and fly-fishing is available at Rutland Water. Located just a mile away, Rutland Water is also good for sailing and birdwatching, and it is encircled by a 25-mile cycle and walking track (the campsite owners will give you details of bike-rental places).

History buffs can head for Rockingham Castle, near Corby, built by William the Conqueror, or Belvoir (pronounced "beaver") Castle, the ancient seat of the dukes of Rutland, in the market town of Grantham.

◀ *Wing Hall*'s café offers breakfast, lunch and summer burgers
▶ Cycling around Rutland Water; Belvoir Castle, Grantham

Fieldhead
Rambling through time in the Peaks

There are two pubs, one shop, one school and an astonishing five campsites in Edale. It's not always enough – such is the village's popularity that in some years enterprising farmers have opened their fields to campers unable to get into its jam-packed sites.

That's not as surprising as it seems. Edale sits a stone's throw from some of the Peak District's loveliest countryside. Huge mounds of mill and moor pattern the skyline, their tips poking through the clouds. A walk up to the hilltops, looking down to the valley and streams below, reveals breathtaking views and a landscape that manages to be both pretty and grand.

Among all the campsites, *Fieldhead* shines because of its professionalism, its well-kept site and the on-site tourist centre, a helpful resource for first-timers wanting to learn a bit about the history of the area. It sits below the Edale hills, and is itself part of the Peak District National Park. That means the owners, who rent the land from the park authorities, must stick to certain rules, making sure part of the grass is neatly managed and the rest left wild. The effect is that of a well-cut garden framed by wild tufts of grass.

Yet despite this prim appearance, the atmosphere is lively and bustling. Walkers, families and school activity groups come and go, boots muddy from various countryside expeditions. The owners, Mark and Samantha Reeves, are always on hand chatting with campers and giving advice on the area. Their site's layout, spread over six small fields, includes several distinct areas, giving campers a sense of their own private space. The field furthest away across the stream is for hikers and backpackers, with no cars, children or dogs allowed. Hidden beneath tall shady trees and with a stream running through it, it's a particularly atmospheric and a peaceful retreat from the hubbub of the main site. The field nearest the car park, which is limited to twenty spaces, is for families and school groups – handy for groups with luggage or a need for quick trips to the nearby toilet and shower blocks.

Edale's Moorland Information Centre (🌐www.moorsforthe-future.org.uk) is both a decent wet-weather option – you might also want to check out the nearby limestone show caves, such as Peak Cavern, a few miles away at Castleton – and a good guide to the many nearby hikes. The centre sells maps and guidebooks, has an exhibition on the history of the Peak District National Park and a downloadable (via Bluetooth) audio guide to walks in the area, including the Pennine Way, whose 270-mile length starts in Edale, takes in some of England's most scenic and isolated countryside, and ends up in the Scottish border village of Kirk Yetholm.

The first part of the Pennine Way, accessible via a circular day-hike from Edale, takes in both fine walking country and a piece of history. The sweeping upland plateau of Kinder Scout (2088ft) is Derbyshire's highest point, scaled by thousands of walkers

Practicalities

Fieldhead Campsite, Edale, Hope Valley, Derbyshire, S33 7ZA ☎*01433 670386,* Ⓦ*www.fieldhead-campsite.co.uk*

Pitches & price 50 standard pitches. £4–5.50 per adult, £2–4 per child, £2.50 per car.

Facilities Very clean, spacious shower block with separate male and female showers and toilets. Laundry room (includes washing machine, tumble dryer, electric socket). Washing-up room. Disabled toilets.

Restrictions Dogs allowed but must be kept on a lead. No campfires. No disposable BBQs.

Open Year round.

Getting There Leave the A6187 at Hope, turning onto Edale Road, which you follow to the Vale of Edale. Turn right at Edale train station; the site is a few hundred yards down the road on the right. Edale station is a 5min walk from the site.

every year. But in the early twentieth century, in common with many wilderness areas across England and Wales, access was forbidden by its landowner, the Duke of Devonshire. In April 1932, a group of around four hundred ramblers went on a mass trespass across Kinder Scout, clashing with gamekeepers on the way – some were arrested on the way back down. The resulting public outrage encouraged the creation of National Parks (the Peak District was the UK's first), while restrictions on freedom to roam were relaxed through the twentieth century, culminating in the Countryside and Rights of Way Act 2000, which gave walkers access to most of the uncultivated land in England and Wales.

In Edale, the *Rambler* and the *Old Nag's Head* offer food and drink, while the local baker delivers fresh bread and croissants to the site on Sunday morning. The owners also sell a few chocolate and energy bars (with walkers in mind) in their on-site office.

◀ Titan, the largest cave shaft in the UK, Castleton ▶ Edale Head and Kinder Scout, where rambling history was made; The *Old Nag's Head*

The Royal Oak

The Royal Oak pub's campsite sits atop a steep hill overlooking the lush green landscape of Derbyshire, about three miles from Bakewell. It's a good resting place for walkers and cyclists taking on the many scenic paths through the southern Peak District, including the Tissington Trail (see p.135), which passes behind the camping field.

For dinner, book a table at the handsome pub (it gets busy and is a regular for both locals and tourists) – a deserving finalist of Derbyshire Pub of the Year 2008. The typical dishes here – such as beer-battered fish and chips or salmon and salad – come in jumbo-sized portions which, combined with the extensive wine list and a choice of three local beers, means you will probably be too full to notice the slope in the field as you doze off in your tent.

The Royal Oak attracts a varied bunch, and its relative isolation (pub aside, there's a distinct lack of nearby shops and facilities) encourages friendly note-swapping camaraderie amongst campers.

Practicalities

The Royal Oak, Hurdlow, nr Buxton, Derbyshire, SK17 9QJ
℡*01298 83288,* Ⓦ*www.peakpub.co.uk/camping*
Pitches & prices 40–50 standard pitches. £12 per tent with car, £7 per tent with no car. Accommodation in bunk barns £12 per person.
Facilities Brand-new shower block with separate male and female loos and showers. Outdoor sinks for washing up.
Restrictions Dogs must be kept on a lead. No campfires. No noise after 11pm.
Open Year round.
Getting there Leave the A515 at Hurdlow; *The Royal Oak* is a few hundred yards down the road on the right. The nearest train station is Buxton, about 6 miles away. Bowers runs a once-a-day bus (#442) from Buxton to Earl Sterndale, which is about 2.5 miles from the site.

Park House

Park House is a simple and pleasant place, its pitches spread out across a flat, clean-cut field. What sets it apart is its location, just a short walk from one of the Peak District's loveliest sights. Monsal Head Valley, a panorama of hills, a river and an old railway, sends shivers down the spine, and looking down over Monsal's imposing viaduct, which towers over the Monsal Dales and the River Wye, is a heady feeling.

Even better than the spectacular view over the valley from the roadside is the Monsal Trail, eight miles of disused rail track that crosses the viaduct and has been converted for walkers and cyclists.

Handily, the owners live on site, though they run a farm too, and are harder to reach during the lambing season in spring. Pitch up towards the back of the field and you won't hear a peep from the road that runs along the front of the site. The *Monsal Head Hotel*, a popular if pricey pub serving food and real ale, is just down the road, while Chatsworth House and Bakewell are less than twenty minutes' drive away.

Practicalities

Park House Campsite, Ashford Lane, Monsal Head, Bakewell, Derbyshire, DE45 1NJ ℡*01629 640463*
Pitches & prices 25 standard pitches. £4–5 per person depending on tent, £2 per gazebo.
Facilities Shower block with separate male and female loos and wash basins. 2 toilets, 1 of which is locked at night. Cold outdoor tap for washing up.
Restrictions No noise after 10pm and no large groups, excluding supervised youth groups. Dogs allowed (£1).
Open Year round.
Getting there Take the A6 from Derby or Buxton, turning on to the A6020 at Ashford in the Water. Follow the signs from here towards Monsal Head, continuing onto the B6465 (Ashford Lane). The nearest train station to *Park House* is Buxton, nearly 10 miles away.

Pindale Farm

Walking up towards *Pindale Farm*, the sprawling green loveliness of Hope Valley will put a bounce in your step. But, nearing the site, to your left stands a sprawling cement works, a concrete blot on the landscape. And beyond that is the campsite. Both blessed and cursed by its setting, *Pindale Farm* is a favourite with large activity groups, who take advantage of the site's Peak District surroundings and add to its lively atmosphere.

The rulebook proclaims that there is "zero tolerance of non-compliance with the rules. Digital pictures will be taken and you will be asked to leave." Thankfully, the owner is more genial than this warning might suggest and, set just a few miles from Edale, the site is perfectly located for walking, climbing and generally pottering about in Hope Valley. Castleton, another charming Peak District town, is also just two miles down the road. The small site also has a small, bright barn house, and those staying in it get an array of home comforts, including a microwave, cooker, fridge and showers.

Practicalities

Pindale Farm Outdoor Centre, Pindale Road, Hope, Derbyshire, S33 6RN ☎*01433 620111*

Pitches & price 80 standard. £5 per person, £8 per gazebo. Barn house £10 per person.

Facilities 2 recently renovated shower blocks, ample space and separate male and female amenities. Disabled toilet in male shower block. Good washing-up area with token-operated washing machine.

Restrictions 1-night stays have to check out by 10am. Noise kept to a minimum after 9pm. Dogs allowed but must be kept on leads.

Open March–Oct.

Getting there Take the A6187 towards Hope Valley. From here, follow the signs to *Pindale Farm* campsite from the main street, taking the turning by the church. The nearest train station is Hope, a 20min walk from the site.

Upper Booth Farm

Hikers and nature-lovers have been visiting this charming place for over fifty years, and owners Robert and Sarah Helliwell claim children who camped here decades ago now return with their families. It's one of five campsites in Edale valley and while, with only one shower, it may be more basic than some of its neighbours (see p.142), *Upper Booth* offers a calm, welcoming base in a dramatically beautiful region. Spread over a large field, sandwiched between farms of grazing cows and sheep, it's popular but never feels crowded, thanks to limits placed on the number of tents.

And what it lacks in facilities, *Upper Booth* makes up for with hospitality. From 8–9am on bank holidays and at weekends, the Helliwells take breakfast orders. They also offer a "hampers for campers" service, which sources local food, including their own free-range eggs, Swaledale lamb and Belted Galloway Beef. On Sunday mornings, the local baker delivers fresh bread and croissants to the site.

Practicalities

Upper Booth Farm & Campsite, Edale, Hope Valley, Derbyshire, S33 7ZJ ☎*01433 670250,* ⓦ*www.upperboothcamping.co.uk*

Pitches & price 40 standard. £4–5 per person, £2 per vehicle, charges for gazebos at the owners' discretion.

Facilities Amenities block with 1 shower, separate male and female toilets, basins and sinks for washing up.

Restrictions Dogs welcome, under strict control. No noise after 10.30pm. No campfires. No unaccompanied under-18s.

Open March–Nov.

Getting there Take the A6187 Hope Valley road. Follow the signs to Edale and Barber Booth. The campsite (not to be confused with nearby *Highfield*) is in the hamlet of Upper Booth, which is signposted. The nearest station is Edale, just over a mile's walk (follow the signs for the Pennine Way) from the campsite.

North Lees
Majestic moorland and a Brontë connection

North Lees was born out of an effort to accommodate hikers and climbers prone to wild camping in the area. You can't blame them for wanting to get in amongst the landscape. Set amongst the moors and woodlands of Hathersage, *North Lees* sits beneath Stanage Edge, an awe-inspiring, near-four-mile-long gritstone escarpment and a premier rock-climbing spot.

It's hard to believe you're just a few miles from Ripon, a cathedral city (albeit one of the smallest in the UK). The compact site slopes over one large and two smaller fields and campers can pitch pretty much anywhere, although those with larger tents or gazebos will find it hard to find enough flat ground for an even pitch. The site's facilities are basic but functional – there are showers, toilets and a laundry room for drying off wet clothes for those caught in the rain. That seems sufficient for the outdoor types who thrive on the region's attractions, and after a morning waking up beneath towering trees to the sharpened sounds of nature, the location's quiet and simplicity feel particularly appealing.

If that's not entertainment enough, nearby Hathersage (about a mile's walk) boasts a heated open-air pool, the David Mellor Design Museum and a range of pubs and cafés. Most campers wander into Hathersage of an evening for a hearty pub meal – there are plenty of places to choose from.

Staff at *North Lees* are friendly and full of information about the area, although it's easy enough to access under your own steam. Paths on all sides of the site lead to a countryside setting of meandering trails and picturesque woods. Up past the woodlands to the north is White Path Moss, a nesting place for birds such as the endangered ring ouzel, the red grouse, the golden plover and the long-legged curlew. Parts of White Path Moss have up to four metres of peat, formed by slow-sprouting sphagnum moss – the result of around four thousand years of growth.

The centuries-old Pack Horse Route, a paved path once used to transport goods over the moorlands to Sheffield, passes by the site on its way from Hathersage to Stanage Edge. This magnet for climbers is a mere fifteen-minute walk from *North Lees*: turn left as you leave by the main entrance and follow the path upwards. As you near the top of the hill, the campsite is down

Practicalities

North Lees Campsite, Birley Lane, Hathersage, Derbyshire, S32 1BR ☎01433 650838

Pitches & price 60 standard pitches. £5–6 per person (students £4–5, children £3–4), £1–2 per car, 50p per motorbike. Discount of 50p for campers who arrive with a valid public transport ticket.

Facilities Basic, clean shower block with male and female toilets and showers. 2 sinks for washing up, tumble dryers.

Restrictions Dogs must be kept on the lead. No campfires, no stereos and no noise after 10–11pm.

Open Year round.

Getting there Take the A625 from Sheffield on Ecclesall Road, leave the A625 at Ecclesall, turn right into Ringinglow Road. Follow the road to Cam Height, turn right, drive for about a mile, then turn right and drive past the car park towards the campsite. The nearest train station is Hathersage – the site is about 1.5 miles from the station.

below to your left, and Stanage Edge begins to peep over the horizon. It is a spectacular sight, especially if you spot climbers clinging to its expansive rock face.

Given the splendid setting, it's not surprising that several period dramas have been filmed in the area (including recent adaptations of *Pride and Prejudice* and *The Other Boleyn Girl*). The literary links are more than just cosmetic: Charlotte Brontë stayed in stately North Lees Hall in 1845, and some claim this was where she wrote *Jane Eyre*. The impressive house is not far off her descriptions of Mr Rochester's home, Thornfield Hall. It's now a luxury holiday let, open to the public just one day a year in September – unlike the gorgeous scenery around it.

◀ Watching the sun set over Stanage Edge, an escarpment popular with climbers ▶ Walking in the Peak District; grand North Lees Hall

South Wales

If ragged coastlines and big seascapes are your thing, South Wales is your place. It's largely low-lying compared to its northern counterpart, and campers will find a destination with rippling cliffs, mellow coves and stunning surf beaches. Almost all the Pembrokeshire coast is a National Park – starting near cheerful, seaside Tenby, then looping around wild St David's Head to include the less-visited north coast – and the Gower was Britain's first Area of Outstanding Natural Beauty. That has helped preserve a gorgeous stretch of the country, and makes coastal camping easy: with a spare fortnight and a rucksack full of stamina you could stay at many of the sites in this chapter while hiking the 186-mile Pembrokeshire Coast Path.

Yet the region isn't all sand dunes and salty air. That most people rush to the beach is good reason to head inland, where the scenery is lush enough to make any camper rhapsodize. There's magic in the Upper Tywi Valley (the reputed birthplace of Merlin), good walks and marvellous little market towns in the Brecon Beacons and solitude in the overlooked Vale of Ewyas. Wherever you go, natural beauty is guaranteed – the draw today as it has been for generations of visitors.

While the landscapes are ancient, the ethics aren't. An influx of city refugees over the last few decades has encouraged progressive attitudes and ideas in a region that has experienced a cultural renaissance since devolution. The buzzwords are "organic" and "sustainable", making South Wales a place for escapism with a feel-good glow – camping in a nutshell.

Aberystwyth

Tyllwyd

A44

CEREDIGION

POWY

A487

A485

A487

A44

A470

A483

Llandrindod
Wells

Builth Wells

Tipi West

PEMBROKESHIRE COAST
NATIONAL PARK

Cardigan

Lampeter

Tycanol Farm

A487

fforestcamp

A484

A498

A475

Gellifechan
Rhandirmyn

A483

Priory Mill Farm

**Trellyn
Woodland**

Fishguard

A478

Larkhill Tipis

A485

Llandovery

A482

Brecon

Whitesands
**Pencarnan
Farm**

PEMBROKESHIRE

St David's

A40

**Tir Bach
Farm**

CARMARTHENSHIRE

A40

**Pencelli
Castle**

**Caerfai
Organic Farm**

Newgale

A487

Haverfordwest

A40

Carmarthen

A48

A474

A4069

A4067

BRECON BEACONS NATIONAL PAR

Dan-yr-Ogof

A4058

A470

**West Hook
Farm**

A4076

A4075

A478

A4066

A484

A109

A445

A470

Merthyr
Tydfil

A4059

Milford
Haven

A477

Meadow Farm

Pembroke

Tenby

Llanelli

Glyn y Mul Farm

Neath

A4063

Pontyprid

PEMBROKESHIRE COAST
NATIONAL PARK

Trefalen Farm

Swansea

Port
Talbot

M4

Bridgend

Hillend

A4118

A48

Three Cliffs Bay

Bar

South Wales

	PAGE	🚶	🚲	⛵	🍴	⛰️	👪	👨‍👩‍👧‍👦	🚐	🚌	♿
Caerfai Organic Farm	152	✓		✓	✓		✓				
Court Farm	173	✓				✓					
Cwmcarn Forest	169	✓	✓						✓		
Dan-yr-Ogof	167	✓			✓		✓		✓	✓	✓
fforestcamp	164	✓		✓			✓				
Gellifechan	162					✓		✓			
Glyn Y Mul Farm	166		✓				✓	✓			
Hillend	163			✓	✓			✓			✓
Larkhill Tipis	159					✓				✓	
Lower Porthamel	172						✓	✓			
Meadow Farm	158						✓		✓		
Newgale	155	✓		✓							✓
Pencarnan Farm	154			✓			✓		✓		
Pencelli Castle	174	✓	✓			✓	✓		✓	✓	✓
Priory Mill Farm	168	✓			✓					✓	
Rhandirmyn	162								✓		
Three Cliffs Bay	170	✓		✓	✓		✓		✓		
Tipi West	162					✓		✓			
Tir Bach Farm	157					✓	✓				
Trefalen Farm	156	✓		✓		✓	✓		✓		
Trellyn Woodland	160					✓	✓			✓	
Tycanol Farm	158	✓					✓	✓	✓		
Tyllwyd	172	✓	✓			✓			✓		
West Hook Farm	156	✓			✓				✓	✓	
Whitesands	155	✓		✓							

See front flap for key to symbols

Caerfai Organic Farm
Quite simply inspirational

It wasn't so long ago that Wyn Evans was mocked by his peers as an "eccentric nutter". No one's laughing anymore. The soft-spoken dairy farmer has gone from crank to crusader as the zeitgeist has caught up with the eco-friendly organic farming he tinkered with over thirty years ago. For all the forward-thinking of his farming, however, it's the simplicity and understatement that make this site one of the most appealing in Wales – without fuss or fanfare, *Caerfai Organic Farm*, a mile from pocket-sized St David's at Wales's western tip, just gets everything right.

It's the views and relaxed atmosphere that draw people back time and again. Whether in the two main fields or popular smaller Cliff Field at the front, which backs onto the Pembrokeshire Coast Path, all pitches share a shimmering seascape of St Bride's Bay. Beneath you is Caerfai Bay, one of the nicest notches of sand in the area, whose small car park prevents it from ever becoming over-run by the typical moto sapiens. Access is no problem from the campsite – a track to the golden sands descends from Cliff Field, which explains why the site is virtually empty by day. It's only in early evening that the place resumes a gentle hum of activity.

That the farm's environmental credentials are second to none adds to the feel-good factor. Catch Evans as he pedals around the site on his bike and he'll spout statistics for the anaerobic digester that converts cow slurry to power his milk sterilization unit, or talk about the kilowatt hours of two ground-source heat pumps and the solar panels that heat water for the amenities block (backed up by a traditional oil boiler).

With stupendous views, a beach in the backyard and space galore thanks to a policy of perimeter pitching, the farm is a firm favourite with young families, but don't worry – the site never riots into kindergarten chaos. Families also appreciate the sort of details that make or break a camping trip: a well-maintained amenities block with ample showers and two family rooms; and a store that sells the farm's delicious organic cheeses – the Caerphilly with leek and garlic is delicious – alongside croissants fresh-baked every morning, tasty local cakes and organic veggies.

Neat without being manicured, the site sits as comfortably into the glorious countryside as its tangled hedgerows. And unlike

Practicalities

Caerfai Farm, St David's, Haverfordwest, Pembrokeshire, SA62 6QT ☎01437 720548, Ⓦwww.cawscaerfai.co.uk

Pitches & price 64 tent pitches over 3 fields (6 with hook-ups), 25 extra pitches in rear field for bank holidays, £6.50 per adult (£4 without car), £3 per child.

Facilities Amenities block with showers, toilets and basins (hair dryer in women's), 2 family rooms with baby-changing facilities, washing-up area.

Restrictions No caravans. Minimum 7-day stay during school holidays. Dogs allowed on leads. No campfires. No gazebos during school holidays.

Open Whitsun (second bank holiday in May) to Sept.

Getting there Follow the sign to Caerfai beach as you enter St David's from the east on the A487. The campsite is a mile down the road on the left. Buses run to St David's from Fishguard and Milford Haven.

many sites, it does not over-egg its green credentials. You would never know how eco-friendly *Caerfai* is unless you spotted the solar panels on its shower-block roof, and "organic" only appears in small print on the farm sign. To nitpick, you could point out that Cliff Field is no place for large or weak tents in a gale – Plot Field offers some shelter behind an arboreal windbreak – or that the site's popularity enforces reservations during school holidays. You could even lament that the site isn't open earlier; *Caerfai Bay Caravan & Tent Park* opposite (☎01437 720274, Ⓦwww. caerfaibay.co.uk) offers similar views in a fairly prim setting from early March. But these are minor quibbles.

Evans says he often wonders why people come back year after year; why don't they go somewhere else, he asks. What, and leave behind a site that ticks all boxes? Makes you wonder if there isn't something eccentric about him after all.

◀ Cows at *Caerfai Farm* ▶ The campsite has splendid views over the Irish Sea; nearby Caerfai beach can be blissfully quiet during the day

Pencarnan Farm

Stunning views, mystical energy and space to spare

Camping purists, brace yourselves: at *Pencarnan Farm* you learn to like static caravans. In the 1990s up to two hundred tents were shoehorned into Allan and Sian Richardson's site west of St David's. The devoted campers decided to reduce their capacity to give individual tents more room, opening up two back fields to statics to offset the lost revenue. Now campers here have space when everywhere else has vanished under groundsheets and get to enjoy the most inspirational panorama on Wales's western tip.

The mesmerizing view beyond the tents is why generations of families migrate to this relaxed site every summer. Across Whitesands Bay is St David's Head, one of the most mystical spots in Wales. Ancient civilizations revered Carn Llidi, a wild headland that tumbles from a ridge and looks eerily like a sleeping dragon; modern mystics divine it as a focus of energy lines. It's a magical place to go walking – the Pembrokeshire Coast Path passes beneath the site – and an inspiring backdrop for canoeing and

surfing at Whitesands beach. Unless you're after a wave, however, there's little reason to take the cliff path there from the site. Whitesands in summer is Blackpool beach compared to Porthsele, a sweet cove of sand directly beneath the camping fields that reveals caves as the tide recedes.

With the freedom of daisy-sprayed acres between perimeter pitches and what amounts to a private beach in the backyard, kids will vanish until meals or excursions. Reliable choices for the latter are RSPB Ramsey Island, reached by a ferry from nearby St Justinian's and joyful with puffins in spring, or the adrenalized water sports organized by operators such as TYF (see p.197) in St David's, home to a boisterous après-surf scene and good eating.

The site's uncomplicated charm extends to a campers-only amenities block behind the caravans where "Buoys" and "Gulls" signs and buntings add a chirpy air. Also here is a cluttered playroom for rainy days and a store selling everything from food and camping gear to buckets and spades.

▼ *Pencarnan Farm*: statics not pictured

Practicalities

Pencarnan Farm, St David's, Haverfordwest, Pembrokeshire, SA62 6PY ℡ *01437 720580,* Ⓦ *www.pembrokeshire-camping.co.uk*

Pitches & price 60 grass pitches (8 hook-ups in 2 rear fields). Start of July to end summer hols £15 per adult, £6 per child; other times £8 per adult, £4 per child.

Facilities Amenities block with showers, toilets, basins and hair dryers, family shower room and toilet with disabled access, washing-up area.

Restrictions Dogs allowed (£2). No campfires. No large young groups. Minimum 1-week booking in school holidays.

Open March–first week in Jan.

Getting there Follow signs to St Justinian's from St David's and drive about a mile beyond the cathedral. The site is via a track on the right opposite farmhouses. Bus #403 shuttles from St David's early April–late Sept.

Whitesands

When the swell's up, surfers head to the southwestern tip of Wales and this informal site, which is so close to the top surfing beach in west Pembrokeshire they don't even have to get out of bed to check the waves. Even when there are no breakers, this place is rarely empty. With the prettiest – and, yes, whitest – sand beach in the area just a toddler's crawl away, young families settle in for a fortnight in July and August, while walkers come for wild St David's Head and Carn Llidi ridge (worth the yomp up for its superb views) that juts above the green slopes behind the site. Consequently, space in the narrow strip is as limited as the facilities – a glorified public toilet with an outdoor shower for wetsuits. That no one really seems to mind sums up the easygoing vibe *Whitesands* is imbued with.

A beach café offers breakfasts and lunches in season, and nearby St David's is choc-a-block with stylish bistros and has the boisterous *Farmers Arms* for a pint. Whether you make it is another matter. After a hard day's coasteering on our last visit, we reckoned the surfers had it right – a beach barbecue as the sun sizzled into the sea.

Practicalities

Whitesands Campsite, Tan-y-Bryn, Whitesands Beach, St David's, Pembrokeshire, SA62 6PS ☏01437 721472

Pitches & price 30 tent pitches (4 hook-ups). Adults £5, children £2.50 but free if facilities shut in winter.

Facilities Small, basic amenities block with shower, basin and toilet in men's and women's sections, outdoor shower.

Restrictions Dogs permitted (on leads). No campfires. No vehicles bigger than a campervan (site entrance too narrow).

Open Year round.

Getting there Follow signs to Fishguard (A487) through St David's, then take the left-turn signposted to *Whitesands* just outside the town by the rugby club. The campsite entrance is unmarked, opposite the last house before the beach car park, 100yds from the beach itself.

Newgale

If you want to be close to the sea, *Newgale* is the place. You can be out of your tent and in the water in less than a minute, and while you may have to cross a main road to get there, it's rarely busy. Newgale beach is ideal for novice surfers and kayakers – gently rolling waves break onto a two-mile stretch of golden sands backed by an impressive pebble bank. The local surf shop and school (Ⓦwww.newsurf.co.uk) is next to the campsite and also offers kite-surfing and stand-up paddle surfing. Heading away from the shore, the appealing city of St David's is only ten minutes' drive away, while the Pembrokeshire Coast Path runs right by the site – the steep five-minute hike up the hill at the north end of the beach will give you sea views to die for.

The grassy, mostly flat campsite itself is fine for any size of tent but can become waterlogged in heavy rain. The *Duke of Edinburgh* pub, tucked in beside the site, and *Sands Café*, 200 yards further up the coast, are bolt holes if the weather turns foul, though a better bet is the friendly *Ship Inn*, five minutes' drive away in Solva. But if the surf is up and the sun is shining *Newgale* is hard to beat.

Practicalities

Newgale Camping Site, Newgale, Haverfordwest, Pembrokeshire, SA62 6AR ☏01437 710253, Ⓦ*www.newgalecampingsite.co.uk*

Pitches & price 70 pitches for tents and motor homes. No caravans. No hook-ups. £5 per person, under-3s free.

Facilities Basic, well-maintained facilities. Male and female shower and toilet blocks as well as a disabled toilet and washing-up area. Newsurf shop next door has a selection of surf equipment to rent and offers instruction courses.

Restrictions No dogs. No groups. No campfires.

Open March–Sept.

Getting there Take the A487 from Haverfordwest to Newgale; the campsite is located above Newgale beach. Trains run to Haverfordwest from where there are regular buses to Newgale.

West Hook Farm

You don't have to be the Bill Oddie type to love Skomer. A tussocked island off the tip of St Bride's Bay, the nature reserve here provides an invigorating romp for anyone keen on seeing the world's largest colony of Manx sheerwaters, plus storm petrels, puffins, guillemots, grey seals and the occasional passing dolphin. Camping is not permitted on the island, but nearby *West Hook Farm* is the next best thing. Just uphill from the dock for the island ferry (Apr–Oct) at Martin's Haven, it enjoys the same seascapes and space and has similar wildlife and walks. With blustery headland Deer Park nearby, and the Pembrokeshire Coast Path behind the hedgerow, the farm will suit walkers, while families will also appreciate generous pitches and the fifteen-minute walk to Musselwick Sands beach. If you need to stock up on supplies, Marloes, two miles away, has a store and local cuisine. Better still is the lovely *Griffin Inn* at Dale, a short drive south. Once you're done exploring, simply sit back at *West Hook* and gaze out at the silver, slate-greys, jade and blues that shift through St Bride's Bay, spread from horizon to horizon at the end of the site, or watch ravens tumble overhead.

Practicalities

West Hook Farm, Marloes, Haverfordwest, Pembrokeshire, SA62 3BJ ☎01646 636424

Pitches & price 30 grass pitches. Adults: £4, children (3–12) £2, cars £1. £9 for 2 people and caravan (though there are no hook-ups).

Facilities Mixed amenities block with basins and toilets, showers, washing-up area, barn with tables, chairs and washing-up area for wet weather.

Restrictions No campfires. Reservations minimum 1 week. Arrivals by 10pm (late arrivals field available). Dogs permitted.

Open Easter–Sept.

Getting there Take the B4327 towards Dale from Haverfordwest and follow signs for Marloes. The farm is on the left, 2 miles beyond the village. The "Puffin Shuttle" bus (May–Sept) between St David's and Milford Haven stops outside 3 times daily on request.

Trefalen Farm

There's something secretive about this understated site set behind the cliffs and surf beaches of south Pembrokeshire. With Broad Haven beach a hundred yards away, *Country Life* magazine's top picnicking spot, Barafundle Bay beach, around a headland and the Pembrokeshire Coast Path just beyond a hedge, it's one whose idyll is guarded by families and walkers as well as climbers and surfers. The rich and famous have tried to horn in and grab some of the peace and quiet on offer here – actor Russell Crowe apparently enquired about hiring the place in 2009 while filming in the area. Like all treasured family secrets, *Trefalen Farm* gets passed on through generations of campers. Owner Lawrence Giardelli loved the place as a boy and fulfilled a dream when he bought the site before developers pounced. Thankfully, he's preserved the natural setting and simple layout. Pitches in an large upper field are cut from long meadow grass in summer, while most of those beyond, in a lovely small dell scooped from the hills, come with sea views. Some campers even pay with their fresh-caught mackerel, which is sometimes served up later in the Giardelli-owned *St Govan's Country Inn*, a mile back in Bosherton.

Practicalities

Trefalen Farm, Bosherton, Pembrokeshire, SA71 5DR ☎01646 661643, ✉trefalen@trefalen.force9.co.uk

Pitches & price About 60 tent pitches (40 in top field, 20 in lower field). £4 per child, £2, per child, minimum £10 charge for campervans and caravans.

Facilities Small block with separate men's and women's toilets and basins, outdoor dishwashing areas.

Restrictions No campfires. Arrival by 10.30pm. Dogs permitted.

Open Year round.

Getting there Take the B4319 (towards St Petrox, Stackpole and Castlemartin) off the A4319 as you enter Pembroke from the east and follow this for 3 miles to the left turn to Bosherton. Past *St Govan's Country Inn*, turn left to Broad Haven and continue for a mile to the white farmhouse on a corner just before the road ends.

Tir Bach Farm

Mongolian yurts and pygmy goats in Pembrokeshire

Come to this relaxed farmstead to unwind into the bucolic bliss of inland Pembrokeshire – just be prepared to share it with the residents: Charlie the dog, Daisy the Andorran goat, pigs Boris and Mabel, the geese in the pond and a few pygmy goats. Tucked off a B-road to Fishguard, twenty minutes' drive from the county's north coast and fifteen from a pint in the *Tafarn Sinc* in Rosebush, Ashley Anstey and Roze Duggleby's small-holding seems tailor-made to charm kids. As well as the friendly livestock, there's an aura of storybook magic to the place, thanks to the miniature slate-roofed duckhouses with real windows built by furniture-maker Roze. There's also a barn with games for rainy days and a bluebell woodland with swimming ponds beneath the site. With all that to busy the youngsters, parents looking to decompress can simply drink in views across the hills that roll back to the Preseli Mountains.

The relaxation continues in the evening, when guests gather around the communal campfire under starry skies. Enjoying the same grandstand panorama in the privacy of a second field are two yurts. Imported from Mongolia, they have been kitted with woodburners and modern furnishings, including Roze's stylish island kitchens.

▼ *Tir Bach Farm's yurts are equipped with woodburners and kitchens*

Practicalities

Tir Bach Farm, Llanycefn, Clunderwen, Pembrokeshire, SA66 7XT ☎*01437 532362,* Ⓦ*www.tirbachfarm.co.uk*

Pitches & price 20 grass pitches, 2 yurts (for 4 and 6 people). Adults: £8 (£7 with reservation), children £4. Yurts £90–110 2 days, £110–165 4 days, £190–290 7 days.

Facilities Amenities block with great showers, toilets and basins, laundry, communal fridge-freezer and toaster, covered barn with table tennis and pool table.

Restrictions No campfires. Dogs permitted (on leads) and allowed in yurts with advance notice.

Open Easter–Sept.

Getting there Driving north of Narbeth on the A478, go through Llandissilo then take the first left 0.5 miles after the *Bush Inn* (on the right) heading towards Llanycefn. At the 5-road junction, turn right to leave the yellow house on your right and drive as far as the white thatched cottage on your left. *Tir Bach Farm* is opposite.

Meadow Farm

As British as buckets and spades, Tenby is everything a seaside town should be. It's got crab lines in the harbour, sandcastles on beaches, lanes full of fishing nets, plus frisbees, galleries, giftshops and pubs. It is, sadly, besieged by soul-sapping resort campsites – which is where *Meadow Farm* comes in.

If this establishment were anywhere else there would be little special about its sheltered hilltop fields. Admittedly, the view of the pastel harbourfront and Caldey Island is the best in town and the location just five minutes from North Beach is second to none. But what really impresses about *Meadow Farm* campsite is its simplicity. Goodbye piped muzak, farewell amusement arcades – this is a site of birdsong, Welsh horses and rabbits that lollop at dusk.

The price to pay for simple charm is simple facilities – at least until the national park authorities approve a new amenities block. Yet this is nothing you might baulk at if camping in the country. And if you want the razzmatazz that usually accompanies the larger resort sites, you're not short of options.

Practicalities

Meadow Farm, Northcliffe, Tenby, Pembrokeshire, SA70 8AU ☎*01834 844829,* ✉*meadowfarmtenby@ live.com*

Pitches & price 30 tent pitches and 3 caravan pitches (10 hook-ups). Tents: £7 per adult, £4 per child; £10 surcharge for tents over 6ft x 9ft. Caravans: £14 minimum (for 2 people).

Facilities Small toilet block with showers.

Restrictions 1 week minimum booking July–Aug. No dogs. No campfires. No young groups.

Open March–Oct.

Getting there Arriving in Tenby on the A478, follow the brown signs as far as North Beach and then turn left onto the road uphill behind it, The Croft. Where the road turns sharply to the right, continue straight ahead on a lane; the entrance to *Meadow Farm* is the second on the left.

Tycanol Farm

Dazzled by the charms of St David's, few people stray to north Pembrokeshire. Yet there are good reasons to hit the road and visit: historic little Newport town is stuffed with restaurants and pubs, while the less-tramped trails along a muscular coastline, not to mention the nearby Preseli Mountains, are a walker's paradise.

Tycanol Farm, just half a mile away from Newport, is situated to get the best of both these worlds. That it has acres of space in several fields and the best views in the area only helps make it one of the most enjoyable stays in the region. From its well-trimmed main field you can sip on your morning cuppa while gazing at cliffs that buck and rear beyond Newport beach, a compelling come-on to hit the Pembrokeshire Coast Path, which passes the end of the site. In the evening, turn around and you'll see the sunset's glow spotlighting the ridge of Carn Ingli, where St Brynach is said to have spent his days chatting to angels.

The facilities may be too basic for some, but that can be an advantage: simple, out-of-the-way *Tycanol* never really suffers the numbers that can often swamp St David's. Being overlooked isn't always a bad thing.

Practicalities

Tycanol Farm, Fishguard Road, Newport, Pembrokeshire, SA42 0ST ☎*01239 820264*

Pitches & price 60 grass pitches (12 hook-ups), 4 hard-standing pitches (with hook-ups). £7.50 per person, £20 per caravan or motor home.

Facilities Basic amenities block with 2 showers, toilets with basins, and a dishwashing area.

Restrictions Dogs permitted. Campfires permitted in braziers.

Open Year round.

Getting there From Newport, take the Fishguard Road and the entrance to *Tycanol Farm* is found beside a pale grey house on the coast side of the A487, 300yds south of the town. The campsite is accessible by public transport as Newport is on major bus routes; check ⓦwww.newporttransport.co.uk for further information.

Larkhill Tipis
Prayer flags and solar power in Merlin's birthplace

Quite why inland Carmarthenshire is so overlooked is a mystery. Its remote hills and tiny valleys are a world away from the bustle of the coast. Merlin is said to have been born here and, driving into the magical, soft green hills of the Tywi Valley, you can believe it, too. It was to this bucolic backwater that Bristolians Fran and Tony Wintle fled in the early 1990s, swapping the city for a smallholding with sweeping views over a valley. On their twenty acres, they installed wind and solar power, planted thousands of trees, farmed rare-breed sheep and nurtured wild orchid meadows by age-old methods. They now share their retreat as *Larkhill Tipis*.

Forget the joss sticks, though – this is camping chic for city refugees, the outdoors for those who like their creature comforts. The three tipis – two four- and one six-sleeper, all refabricked annually – are cosy, with sheepskins and rugs draped over futons. Lighting from hurricane lanterns is romantic, while pot-bellied braziers keep things warm and let you cook inside; try the delicious, fresh-laid hen and duck eggs Fran provides. More secluded – and luxurious – are the two woodland yurts: larch flooring, woven rugs on an ash lattice and fat cushions on daybeds around the wood-burner. Pick the Kazakh *oba* over the smaller Mongolian *ger* if you like space in your yurt.

With serene corners to discover in the garden, Buddhist prayer flags and quiet footpaths leading to meditation circles, a sense of peace and good vibes reign by day. The place only really comes alive at dusk, when guests drift towards a communal campfire for a chat. Meanwhile, the beaches and cliffs in north Pembrokeshire or chirpy family favourite Tenby are a half-hour by car – just don't be surprised if you heave a sigh of relief on your return to *Larkhill*.

▼ *Larkhill Tipis* offers camping in comfort

Practicalities

Larkhill Tipis, Cwmduad, Carmarthenshire, SA33 6AT
☎ *01559 371581,* Ⓦ *www.larkhilltipis.co.uk*

Pitches & price 3 tipis (4 or 6 people), 2 yurts (4 people). Tipis for 4 and yurts £60 per night, £360 per week, tipi for 6 £80 per night, £480 per week.

Facilities Cooking facilities in all units plus communal kitchen, showers and washing area, composting toilet.

Restrictions Minimum 1 week stay in summer holidays, other times minimum 2 nights. No dogs. No groups over 6 people. Campfires permitted in designated areas.

Open Tipis Easter–Oct, yurts March–Dec.

Getting there Take the A484 off the A40 at Carmarthen and drive north to Cwmduad. A mile north of the village, turn left (signposted to the National Wool Museum) and continue for a mile to a drive on your right with a yellow milk churn. Free pick-ups from regional train and bus stations, including Carmarthen.

Trellyn Woodland

Sustainable camping at the ultimate chill-out site

Inspirational campsites are often personal affairs, born of their owners' love of life under canvas rather than a desire to pocket an easy quid. There's no better example of this in Wales than *Trellyn Woodland* in north Pembrokeshire. Wherever you stay on its sixteen acres – whether on one of six tent pitches or in its two yurts and tipis – you are not a client on a campsite so much as a guest in the back garden of the Bird family: Kevin, Claire and son Matthew. Surplus veggies from the family patch and fresh-laid eggs are yours for the taking, while friendly messages occasionally appear to inform you about lobster landed that morning. You don't get that in your average campsite – but nor do many proprietors occasionally pop by to check you have all you need.

If the impression of staying with friends is in part down to low numbers – a limit of 35 campers ensures space and minimal environmental impact – equally important is that the Birds, who both

work off-site during the day, actually enjoy sharing the place with like-minded souls. Having relocated from Gloucestershire, they took in hand a bramble-choked woodland and replanted over a thousand native trees – sweet chestnut, ash, hawthorn, field maple, oak and willow. In its clearings are now two tipis, each with a double mattress and two futons on raised hardwood floors. Tipi rain caps help to ensure dry camping. More private – and luxurious – are the site's two eighteen-foot yurts built, from local ash. Woven rugs and sheepskins on raised wood floors, feather duvets on real beds and wood stoves keep things romantic and snug.

This is all very cosy, yet the focus of the site remains strongly on the outdoors and keeping things green. Both tipis and one yurt have well-supplied outdoor canopied kitchens with picnic tables and gas stoves to reassure reluctant camp-cooks. (Yurt 1 has an interior kitchen if they remain unconvinced.) There are also campfire circles with chunky benches and canopies, so you can chat beside a fire whatever the weather. The standard tent pitches – two in the woods, four in small fields – have a similar fire space and the same limitless supply of logs; the pick of the pitches are those in a private meadow at the back of the site. Sustainability is king here: there's solar-heated water in an immaculate amenities block and on-site sewage treatment.

No matter where you're hidden, the place feels like a secret retreat. It's the ultimate chill-out site – the loudest sound you'll hear all week is the dawn chorus. It's no wonder lives have changed here; marriage proposals have been accepted, honeymoons indulged in and career paths rerouted after campers have slowed down to *Trellyn Woodland*'s soporific pace and tuned in to its eco-ethics.

Pembrokeshire's uncommercial north coast awaits those who manage to leave the site. There's a rather muddy beach at the fishing hamlet of Abercastle, hooked around a hairpin bend a few hundred yards from the site, or within three miles are inspiring wild strands like Traeth Llyfn; the splendid *Sloop Inn* on Porthgain harbour is en route. If you're after ice creams and organized activities, St David's is only a twenty-minute drive away.

There is one big problem – getting in. You'll need to reserve at the beginning of the year to guarantee your spot for school holi-

Practicalities

Trellyn Woodland Camping, Abercastle, Haverfordwest, Pembrokeshire, SA62 5HJ ☏*01348 837762,* Ⓦ*www.trellyn.co.uk*

Pitches & price 4 tent pitches, 2 hard-standing pitches (with hook-ups), 2 tipis for up to 6 (bedding required), 2 yurts for up to 6. Camping (weekly) £170 (plus £32 Camping & Caravanning Club membership if required). Tipis £200 weekend, £365 weekly or £510 school holidays; yurts (weekly) £475 or £640 school holidays.

Facilities Amenities block with 2 family rooms (shower, toilet and basin), separate toilet, fridge and freezer, dishwashing area.

Restrictions Minimum 7 days booking (though limited Sat–Mon bookings for tipis. No dogs. Campfires permitted in designated areas.

Open Whitsun (second bank holiday in May) to Sept.

Getting there Halfway from St David's to Fishguard on the A487, turn left into Mathry and go up past the *Farmers Arms* pub to follow signs to Abercastle. The campsite entrance is on the left, 1.5 miles beyond the house with the bright pink roof; if you get to the Abercastle village sign, you have gone 100yds too far. The St David's–Fishguard bus stops outside *Trellyn Woodland* on request.

days. You might also gripe at the week-minimum stay or a mobile phone black hole, yet both are opportunities to unwind and meet other campers. And that's the point. The Birds understand camping is about more than a tent and a field. With its natural beauty, air of relaxed escapism, campfires, green ethics and personal charm by the bucketload, *Trellyn Woodland* encapsulates the best of what camping can offer. Praise doesn't come much higher.

◀ The campsite is set in lush replanted woodland ▶ Tipis sleep up to six; the rugged coast at Traeth Llyfn, three miles from *Trellyn Woodland*

Tipi West

For proof that authentic tipi living has not been smothered under silk cushions, come to Brychan Jones's defiantly non-commercial site on the north Pembrokeshire coast. There's no glamping glitz to the four tipis on this family farm. Instead, *Tipi West* is a proper campers' retreat that's all about tuning in to a chilled community vibe and dropping out from everyday pressures – think sleeping on cosy sheepskins and rugs around the tipi's charcoal ember stove and playing guitars around the glowing campfire.

If the latter is a legacy of Jones's past with Eighties Welsh rock band Jess, his enthusiasm for guests to connect with the gorgeous coastal scenery and strong Welsh culture hereabouts comes from his father, Dic Jones, one of the country's most distinguished poets; some of his verse features on an hour-long poetry trail around the 85-acre property.

For a trip further afield – and a good way to work up a thirst – take the twenty-minute walk via the beach to *The Ship*, in nearby Aberporth.

Practicalities

Tipi West, Hendre Farm, Blaenannerch, Cardigan, SA43 2AN ☎07813 672336
Pitches & prices 4 tipis for 4 to 8 people; yurt promised for 2010. £20 per adult, £15 per child (3–16).
Facilities Amenities shed with toilet and shower (straw-built toilet block planned for 2010), dishwashing area, fridges.
Restrictions No dogs. No stereos (guitars OK). Campfires permitted in designated areas.
Open Easter–Sept.
Getting there Take the first left north of Blaenannerch off the A487 into residential Fford Llwyncoed (before a perspex bus shelter). Follow this road around a sharp left then right, and continue up to the *Tipi West* entrance which is 300yds further on the right. Buses from Aberystwyth, Bangor, Cardigan and Cardiff stop on the A487.

Rhandirmyn & Gellifechan

It's not just birds and their watchers who flock north of Llandovery. Any nature-lover will appreciate the magical upper Tywi River valley as it curves and darts around wooded hummocks to the Cambrian Mountains and beautiful RSPB Dinas nature reserve. Buzzards soar over crags, woodpeckers peck, and the odd red kite wobbles overhead, saved from extinction in this forgotten corner. It's a siren call to sleep under the stars.

The decision is over where exactly to pitch your tent. *Rhandirmyn*, a Camping & Caravanning Club site, spreads alongside the river beneath pretty Rhandirmyn village, with its excellent *Royal Oak Inn* and store. This is comfy camping for caravanners and families who like facilities – the toilets won Loo of the Year in 2007. It also feels a mite prim among this eco-loveliness. There are no signs for *Gellifechan* campsite upriver, wedged into a wooded valley like an amphitheatre, and definitely no home comforts. The reward for roughing it is raw nature: a beautiful position, a pitch just above the river and campfires at night. Magic.

Practicalities

Rhandirmyn Camping and Caravanning Club, Rhandirmyn, Carmarthenshire, SA20 0NT ☎01550 760257, ⓦwww.campingandcaravanningclub.co.uk
Pitches & prices 90 pitches. Adults from £5.50–8.50.
Facilities Immaculate amenities block.
Open Week before Easter–Oct.
Gellifechan Campsite, Rhandirmyn, Carmarthenshire, SA20 0NT ☎01550 760397
Pitches & prices Grass pitches only, £6–7.50 per pitch.
Facilities Portaloo, standpipe.
Open April–Oct.
Getting there Rhandirmyn is signposted off the A40 through Llandovery. Turn left opposite the village store and go 400yds downhill to reach the *Rhandirmyn* site. *Gellifechan* campsite is 2 miles north of the village, through an unmarked gate on the left just before the signpost left to Troedyrhiw.

Hillend

Waves to surf, views to inspire poetry

Pick any weekend to visit this beach-side site and the chances are you'll find yourself among a convoy of surf-buses. Spread along the tip of the Gower peninsula is Llangennith beach, three miles of pale, broad sand which offers good waves when everywhere else in Wales's best surfing area is as flat as a mill pond. The best peaks are at the north end of its exhilarating sweep and it's here, behind a windbreak of dunes, that you'll find *Hillend*.

With the breakers just a short, barefoot walk away, this four-field site exudes a surfie, laid-back vibe, especially on summer weekends when it can feel more miniature festival than campsite. Arrive by Friday lunchtime to bag a pitch – the site does not take reservations – and earlier still for the August bank holiday, when there's themed, fancy-dress camping. Yet if hardly tranquil, *Hillend* is by no means rowdy. No-nonsense management are on site 24 hours a day to enforce peace at dusk, and families get two far fields to themselves and an excellent fenced-off playground area. Another plus is a well-maintained modern amenities block, with outdoor hot showers for wetsuits.

Just uphill from the entrance is an on-site store and *Eddy's* café-restaurant, which provides bumper breakfasts till noon. In Llangennith village the *King's Head* is the first choice for homemade pies, curries and a lively pint at weekends, and PJ's Surf Shop (☎01792 386669), run by a legend of Gower surfing, provides surf lessons and board rental.

Surfers aren't the only tribe that migrates to one of Wales's most spectacular strands, though. Walkers such as Dylan Thomas have long visited Rhossili for a stroll onto the Worm's Head, an island that appears from the waves at low tide like a recumbent Welsh dragon, or a spectacular cliff walk that follows around to Port Eynon. And now the paragliders have arrived – Fly West Wales (☎0292 125 1006) will take you airborne. Who needs waves?

▼ Surfers will relish the waves at Llangennith beach

Practicalities

Hillend Camping Park, Llangennith, Gower, Swansea, SA3 1JD ☎*01792 386204,* Ⓦ*www.hillendcamping.co.uk*
Pitches & price 270 tent pitches. Apr & Oct £12 per pitch weekdays, £15 weekends; May–Sept £17/£20.
Facilities Excellent modern block with plentiful toilets and handbasins, plus hair dryers and disabled access. 6 outdoor showers for wetsuits, 2 washing-up areas.
Restrictions No dogs. No campfires. Groups over 10 and single-sex groups only by prior arrangement.
Open Easter–Oct.
Getting there Follow signs off the A4118 or B4271 to Llangennith, then to the beach (past the *King's Head* pub then left at the mini-roundabout). The campsite is downhill on the right at the end of the road. Buses from Swansea go direct to Rhossili from where it's a 20min hike up the beach to the site.

fforestcamp
Is it a campsite? A hotel? No, it's fforestcamp

You can understand why camping in Britain has a bad name. There's the fickle weather, the sites that take style tips from anonymous commuter suburbs, and don't even get us started on the packing, unpacking and arguing over who forgot the stove. So raise your chipped enamel mug to *fforestcamp*, spread out three miles south of Cardigan in the gorgeous Teifi valley. Launched in 2008, it takes the best bits of hotels – comfy beds, interior design, real breakfasts, treats like a sauna and bar, faultless staff – and adapts them to the outdoors. The result is camping for softies: a two-hundred-acre hotel with canvas rooms, woodland corridors and – yes – room service. Purists who frown on the glamping

trend may choke on their Kendal Mint Cake, but the superb range of outdoor activities on offer here should help assuage any doubts.

Most importantly, for all its "outdoors hotel" ethos, *fforestcamp* is founded upon a love of getting under canvas. You first realize this when you select from the repertoire of tents that are ready-pitched in spacious meadows. Traditionalists can opt for the Nomad tunnel-tents, which accommodate up to four adults (or six intimate friends). If you want to up the style ante, go for the Swedish *kåtas*, whose appeal lies in their tipi-like design, jute matting, reindeer skins, wood-burners and proximity to the amenities block. Neither tents nor tipis will prepare you for the geodesic domes, the true stars of the accommodation options here. You could define these futuristic structures as tents because of their canvas skins, but really they are camping's penthouse suites; nearly twelve feet high and eighteen across, they are flooded with natural light and cleverly sited to ensure maximum privacy for their occupants. Inside are polished wood floors, rustic-chic beds with featherdown duvets and traditional Welsh embroidered blankets, the odd retro furnishing and a recycled wood-stove. All styles of tent are erected on raised decks that provide outdoor space for your giant weatherproof beanbag and an attached alfresco kitchen-"dining pod" built of local timber.

You don't have to cook, of course. As well as being a stylish spot to lounge with a book or hook up with other guests, a communal lodge provides fresh seasonal meals a couple of times a week and a venue for the breakfast included in the price: graze from muesli, toast, local jams and cheeses and eggs cooked to order, all washed down with freshly squeezed juice. Alternatively, order "tent service" and get a hamper and cafetière delivered to your tentflap. Other facilities include a cool, Scandinavian-styled amenities block, a barrel sauna and an artfully shabby bar, *Y Bwthyn*.

A stylish adult retreat as much as a family playground, the whole establishment has something of a New World feel about its embrace of the outdoors. The concept is expanding, too: from 2010, those who prefer four walls and a roof will have the stone crog lofts, four hip, retro-modern mezzanine apartments with kitchens (outdoors, naturally); and a former holiday park behind National Trust-listed Penbryn beach will have received a make-

Practicalities

fforestcamp, Cilgerran, Cardigan, SA43 2TB. ☎*01239 623633 (info only, book online),* Ⓦ*www.coldatnight.co.uk*

Pitches & price 8 nomads, 10 *kâtas,* 8 domes, 4 crog lofts (bedding required for all but domes and crog lofts). Prices based on 2 people, price range is from 4 nights midweek in spring to 1 week in school summer holidays: nomads £175–£405, *kâtas* £230–£520, domes £315–£690, crog lofts £330–£800. All prices include breakfast. Extra adult £10 per night, children £7 per night.

Facilities Stylish amenities block with showers, toilets and basins, dishwashing area, communal lodge and firepit, sauna, bar, activities centre.

Restrictions School summer holidays minimum 1 week. Dogs permitted. Campfires permitted in grates.

Open Camping April–Oct, crog lofts year round.

Getting there Go to Pen-y-Bryn on the A478 south of Cardigan, turn left to Cilgerran village and follow brown signs for the wildlife centre.

over to create *Manorafon* camp, with chalets, tents and domes.

You could call *fforest* inspiring. You can certainly call it cool. Just don't call it "glamping". For all its style, the site is all about the outdoors. That's why you have to leave your car and walk to the spacious tent pitches set in wildflower meadows; why numbers are limited to a hundred guests despite the two hundred acres. It's also why *fforest* provides a programme of on-site activities (not included in the price) – from canoeing trips through Teifi Gorge to mountain biking, bushcraft sessions to wildlife safaris in the adjacent Teifi Marshes Nature Reserve – and organizes off-site adventures to go sea kayaking, surfing or coasteering. The buzz phrase is "relaxed activity"; do as much as you like – or as little.

◀ The geodesic dome is camping's penthouse suite ▶ Hitting the beach at Penbryn; relaxing on the deck of a nomad tent

Glyn Y Mul Farm

Camp in the woods and get on yer bike

For many of us camping is about going wild. You can't just pitch up anywhere in the great outdoors of England and Wales – our feature on p.340 has more details – but you can unleash your inner Bear Grylls by setting a compass course to *Glyn Y Mul Farm*, nine miles north of Swansea, where you'll find eighteen acres of oak and silver birch wedged into the Neath Valley. There are a few

▼ Four campers go wild at *Glyn Y Mul*

anonymous camping fields by the farmstead, but you're better off heading into the trees, where cars are forbidden and you can put your tent where you like – a clearing in the oaks at the far end appeals. Chatter comes from birdsong and the River Dulais burbling past your doorway. Nightlife is a campfire of foraged wood while foxes slink through the shadows.

It's little wonder *Glyn Y Mul* attracts outdoorsy types each weekend, especially mountain bikers, who come for the trails at Afan Forest Park (Ⓦwww.afanforestpark.co.uk details routes and hire), fifteen minutes' drive away. Even they might think twice about staying in the mud-fest after a downpour – survivalists just take this is as a cue to sling up a hammock. Head here when it's dry and you'll have a taste of wilderness without the hardship – you'd never guess you were just ten minutes from the M4, never mind half an hour from central Swansea or the Gower peninsula.

Practicalities

Glyn Y Mul Farm (aka "Lone Wolf Campsite"), Cefn Yr Allt, Aberdulais, Neath, West Glamorgan, SA10 8HF ☎*01639 643204,* Ⓦ*www.glynymulfarm.co.uk*
Pitches & price About 20 pitches in the woodland, £5 per person.
Facilities Basic: 2 flush toilets, 2 portaloos, 2 showers, rudimentary washing-up area with microwave (all at the farmhouse), mountain-bike wash area.
Restrictions Reservations required. Dogs and campfires allowed.
Open April–Oct, other months on request. Last entry by 7pm.
Getting there Head towards Neath then follow signs to the Aberdulais Waterfalls on the A4109. Take the second left (with speed bumps) beyond the visitor centre and continue on the single-track road beyond the residential street for a mile – *Glyn Y Mul Farm* is through a stone gateway on the left. Taxis from Neath train station cost about £10.

Dan-yr-Ogof
Camping with dinosaurs

Don't be put off that *Dan-yr-Ogof* touts itself as a theme park and not a campsite. This relaxed, well-maintained establishment in the central Brecon Beacons might just be the most child-friendly site in south Wales. Campers are scattered around several levels beside a toy farm and playbarn on the other side of the park, a respectable distance from its premier attractions. When the last daytripper heads home, having explored three impressive show caves and a park chockful of fibreglass dinosaurs, you'll have a minor safari park all to yourself. Not even the PlayStation generation can resist the sight of a rhea strutting past their tent at breakfast.

But, framed by peaks and linked by a path to the Black Mountain, *Dan-yr-Ogof* is as much a destination for trail-junkies as families. On-site facilities include boot racks and drying rooms alongside baby-changing facilities, and pitches range from motor home "super-pitches" to a tiny riverside clearing in a copse. Local eating and drinking options include the solid *Gwyn Arms* boozer over the road, and, three miles south in Pen-y-Cae, classy pub-restaurant *Pen Y Cae Inn* and family local *The Ancient Briton*.

▼ Rheas share the farm with llamas, donkeys and Shetland ponies

Practicalities

Dan-yr-Ogof, nr Abercraf, Upper Swansea Valley, SA19 1GJ
☏ *01639 730284,* Ⓦ *www.showcaves.co.uk*

Pitches & price 30 tent pitches (5 with hook-ups) 30 hard-standing pitches (all with hook-ups). Adults £6, children £4, caravans/motor homes minimum £15.

Facilities Heated amenities block with toilets, basins, showers (including sit-down shower) and baby-changing facilities in both male and female loos, disabled toilet and shower, heated washing-up and drying room.

Restrictions No campfires. No young single-sex groups. Dogs permitted (on leads).

Open Easter–Oct.

Getting there As a major tourist attraction, *Dan-yr-Ogof* is well signposted on major routes. On the A4067 from Swansea, go through Abercraf then Craig-y-Nos – the park is a mile north on the left, and the campsite is on the right at the end of the drive. The Neath–Brecon bus stops outside.

Priory Mill Farm
Camping as it used to be

Arriving at this idyllic small site, you'd be forgiven for thinking you'd stumbled into a backwater of rural France. With its historic stone buildings, pretty cottage garden, glossy chickens and pink-cobbled yard, the farmstead feels a thousand miles not five minutes' walk from the reassuringly solid market town of Brecon.

▼ *Priory Mill Farm* is full of innoccent charm

The restoration of the Grade 2-listed complex has been a labour of love for owners Noel and Susie Gaskell, a furniture-maker and silversmith respectively, and their personalities shape the *Priory Mill Farm* camping experience. Forget flashy facilities and say goodbye to hook-ups: this is a return to camping as it used to be, full of innocent charm, where the kids can pop to the farmhouse to buy eggs for breakfast. You pitch in a beautiful small meadow behind the farmhouse; a tiny field at the far end provides privacy for small groups. The chilled vibe sees Noel put out the "Full" sign rather than compromise space. Even his cedar amenities block, designed like a railway carriage, has charm, so long as you don't mind taking a torch after 10.30pm.

Days on site can be spent fishing for salmon and trout, or spotting kingfishers and otters in a shallow river that burbles over waterfalls around the side of the meadow. Evenings are spent stargazing around a campfire. And with the decent pubs and restaurants in Brecon nearby, and the Beacons and Hay-on-Wye on its doorstep, *Priory Mill Farm* is as convenient as it is enchanting. All in all, a gem.

Practicalities

Priory Mill Farm, Hay Road, Brecon, Powys, LD3 7SR
☎*01874 611609*, ⊛*www.priorymillfarm.co.uk*
Pitches & price About 40 tent pitches. £5 per adult, £3 per child.
Facilities Amenities cabin with toilets, showers and male and female handbasins, outdoor washing-up area.
Restrictions No large groups. Lights out by 10.30pm (to benefit the starlight). Dogs permitted (£1). Campfires allowed in firegrates.
Open Year round.
Getting there In central Brecon, pass by the castle on your left and at the crossroads with traffic lights turn left up Streut. *Priory Mill Farm* is just under a mile away on the left. Buses run to Brecon from Cardiff, Hereford and other major towns.

Cwmcarn Forest

World-class mountain biking and scenery in the Valleys

No account of Wales is complete without the Valleys. As Welsh as dragons, these former coal-mining heartlands radiate north from Cardiff and Newport, and it's near the latter that you'll find this surprisingly pastoral campsite, in the Nantcarn Valley's Cwmcarn Forest (Apr–Oct daily, Nov–Mar weekends only; cars £5). It's a place full of stunning vistas, but the big draw here is the view you get from behind the handlebars of a mountain bike while juddering down some of the UK's best trails.

The Twrch Trail around the valley is a name any self-respecting mountain-biker should tick off. Rooty and rocky, its world-class nine-mile route is pure single-track riding. The Y Mynydda downhill track is harder still: complete its huge jumps and insane flat-out bottom section and you'll be rewarded with a firework display of fizzing endorphins. Ryder's Bikeshop in Cwmcarn village (☎01495 270623, Ⓦwww.rydersmtb.co.uk) rents out bikes.

There's more on offer here than just a two-wheeled adrenalin fix, though. The Cwmcarn Forest Drive is a deservedly popular scenic loop that winds slowly up around the valley to crest the upper slopes at 1275ft. Not that you'll spend much time in the car. En route are monuments to the Celts who battled Roman invaders aeons before local miners fought pit-closures – they say the ghost of a green warrior still roams hereabouts – and upland walks to an Iron Age hillfort. There are playgrounds and forest picnic spots (bring charcoal for a barbecue) with carved wooden wizards and gnomes, and views galore from windy ridges.

The campsite itself makes a perfect base for exploring either the bike trails or the forest drive, the start of which is about half a mile away uphill. Wedged onto the valley floor behind the reception centre, moments from the start of the Twrch Trail, its three intimate fields are prettily sited in front of a stream, sheltered at their backs by a wooded hillside. Everyone wants a spot in the furthest field – the most natural of the trio, with a flower-speckled lawn and just a few hook-ups – but it's worth making a reservation regardless of your pitch such is the site's popularity, especially at weekends when a visitor centre hosts child-friendly workshops and walks. The hot showers and laundry are more likely to interest bikers. The centre has a daytime café; otherwise *The Castle* pulls pints near the forest drive entrance and *The Crosskeys* in Crosskeys village rustles up post-trail pub-grub.

▼ Mountain biking in Cwmcarn Forest

Practicalities

Cwmcarn Forest Campsite, Crosskeys, Newport, NP11 7FA ☎*01495 272001,* Ⓦ*www.cwmcarnforest.co.uk*

Pitches & price 27 grass pitches and 6 hard-standing (23 hook-ups). July–Aug tents £8.50–16, campervans £11; other months, tents £7–13, campervans £9.50.

Facilities Block with showers, toilets and basins and disabled access, basic kitchen with laundry.

Restrictions No campfires. No unconverted campervans. Dogs permitted (on leads).

Open Year round. Last arrival 5pm.

Getting there Take the M4 then the A467 to Crosskeys, then follow brown signs for the Cwmcarn Forest Drive; it's on the left on the bend as you enter Cmwcarn. There are buses from Newport and Cardiff – note the stop by the drive entrance is a mile from the site itself. The nearest train station is a mile south in Crosskeys.

Three Cliffs Bay

A priceless panorama for less than a tenner

"We're a family site run by a family. Oh, and with a nice view." So says David Beynon to explain why campers have visited his sheep farm on the Gower peninsula since the late Fifties. Go down a lane channelled by hedgerows and you soon realize this is no average view. Spread out before a site that swoops along a cliff is Wales's most iconic beach, Three Cliffs Bay, a fixture in every glossy tourist board brochure and a finalist in ITV's 2007 series *Britain's Favourite View*. That it's all yours for under a tenner a night should tweak any camper's guy ropes.

What makes Three Cliffs Bay so improbably perfect is that it seems pieced together from a picturebook of Wales. The beach itself is a deep half-moon of squeaky-clean sand that is large (and remote) enough to offer space in high summer but still feels cosy thanks to a headland that wraps a protecting arm around the front. Climbers scale the headland's three triangular rocks and kids play pirates in its natural arch. The gallery of splendid Welsh clichés is completed by black cliffs full of nooks, a river that snakes through the pale sand into the sea and a green valley where a ruined castle stands on a bluff.

Benyon calls his site a holiday park, but don't worry. What you get for that tag is an orderly place that is well maintained by on-site wardens. Motor homes and touring caravans claim the flattest area of the small field, leaving perimeter pitches in the upper half to campers. Unless you snag one of the few flat pitches, reconcile yourself to a slope if you want to peg-out cliffside. Actually, the pitches at the field's summit may be the pick of the bunch – they're flatter and more sheltered when storms whip west, and most catch a glimpse of both the sea and a pastoral carpet unrolled over the peninsula inland. A flatter overspill field has similar bucolic views, but lacks that gorgeous beach seemingly within touching distance.

Both areas are busy in peak season – reservations are essential for bank holidays and summer – although an alternate car-tent pitching rule guarantees some privacy. And while the spotless toilet block can struggle with numbers, what's the hurry with a view like this to pass the time?

A farm shop sells basics plus fresh bread and Welsh cakes. For other foodstuffs there's a general store a ten-minute walk away in

Practicalities

Three Cliffs Bay Holiday Park, North Hills Farm, Penmaen, Gower, Swansea, SA3 2HB ☎01792 371218, ⓦ*www.threecliffsbay.com*

Pitches & price 75 tent pitches (12 with hook-ups), 20 caravan pitches (all with hook-ups). Caravan/tent with hook-up £20, tents £10–18 according to size.

Facilities Tidy amenities block with basins, loos and showers, disabled toilet and shower, family room with baby-changing facilities, washing-up area, laundry room.

Restrictions No campfires. No large young groups. Dogs allowed on leads.

Open April–Oct. Last entry 10.30pm.

Getting there Follow signs to Gower through Swansea then the A4118 towards Port Eynon. The site is a sharp turn left as you enter Penmaen. Buses go from Swansea – the stop is opposite the lane to the farm.

Parkmill, where you'll also find fine-food restaurant *Maes-Yr-Haf* and the *Gower Inn*, which is uninspiring but passable for a pint. For a lazy pub lunch it's hard to top *The King Arthur*, an upmarket rustic place in Reynoldston which serves good bar meals on the green and posh nosh in a smart restaurant. Walk the three miles inland to get there and you'll realize why they chose the Gower as Britain's first Area of Outstanding Natural Beauty; this is a world in miniature where tiny villages huddle on upland moors and hikers eulogize a gorgeous east coast. A bus back from Reynoldston drops you off just outside the site (ask at reception for times and details).

Of course, you could just walk down to Three Cliffs Beach via a path that clambers downhill directly from the site. Or with a grandstand view of such mesmerizing beauty, you could lose entire mornings simply watching the tide inch out.

◀ The glorious expanse of Three Cliffs Bay at low tide ▶ The site panorama – a runner-up for ITV, a winner for campers; *The King Arthur*

Tyllwyd

Waking in a remote valley beside a rushing stream is one pleasure of this tidy site cupped by the Vale of Ystwyth. Another is that the mid-Cambrian Mountains humped up around it are the forgotten uplands of Wales. While the Brecon Beacons and Snowdonia are crawling with the Kendal Mint Cake crowd, these slopes are rarely trodden. Even those who come for the area's highlights – the romantic, watercolour landscape of the Elan Valley, renowned for trout fishing, biking and horseriding, and the sublimely landscaped Hafod estate near Cwmystwyth – rarely push on the extra few miles into the valley where *Tyllwyd* sits. If you're looking for peace and quiet, this is the place for you. In the four decades that the site has been handed through the family to sheep farmer James Raw, its rugged beauty and isolation have remained un-changed. The facilities have – there are now hook-ups, swings and a slide for the kids, picnic tables and barbecues to grill your catch (snagged from a pond downstream, where you can also swim in summer). The twenty-minute drive to the pubs and restaurants in Devil's Bridge or Rhayader might deter some campers. For others, though, such isolation is the best reason seek this place out.

Practicalities

Tyllwyd, Cwmystwyth, Aberystwyth, Ceredigon, SY23 4AG
☎01974 282216
Pitches & price 50 grass pitches (20 hook-ups). Adults: £6, children (5–15) £3.
Facilities Men's and women's toilet with basin, shower, dishwashing area.
Restrictions No campfires. Dogs welcome by prior arrangement only.
Open Year round.
Getting there At Devil's Bridge on the A4120 east of Aberystwyth, turn onto the B4574 by the *Hafod Hotel* towards Cwmystwth. Continue ahead at the turn for Pont-Rhyd-y-Groes and you'll arrive at *Tyllwyd* 2 miles beyond the cattle grid; the campsite is on the right past the barn. From Rhayader, take the Cwmystwyth road right-turn south of town en route to the Elan Valley.

Lower Porthamel

There's an Enid Blytonesque innocence to this organic farm in the upper Wye Valley. It's nothing to do with the bookshops just down the road in Hay-on-Wye, rather the memories of childhood holidays cherished by its owner, Joel Durrell. "I wanted what I had as a kid, not fruit machines," he says. Expect neither arcades nor a long list of dos and don'ts at *Lower Porthamel*. Durrell doesn't do rules. He does freedom and nature.

Increasing numbers of families and young groups pitch in the orchard beside the farmhouse and duckpond, or in a larger overspill sheep field where you'll enjoy views of rolling green hills, but the site's simple pleasure of tuning in to nature remains unchanged. There's a new tots' playground behind a living willow fence, but children still disappear onto a nature trail around the farm each morning. Nearby Black Mountain Adventures (Ⓦwww.blackmountain.co.uk) rents out canoes should the kids tire of building dams or spotting otters along the banks of the River Llynfi. The nearest pub, the *Old Barn Inn*, is two miles away in Three Cocks, so all the more reason to rustle up a picnic from the Small Farms collective, four miles away in Hay-on-Wye.

Practicalities

Lower Porthamel Farm, Talgarth, Powys, LD3 0DL
☎01874 712125, Ⓔjoeldurrell@yahoo.com
Pitches & price About 50 pitches approximately. £6.50 per adult, £2.50 per child over 9 years.
Facilities Simple amenities block with toilets, basins, showers and a washing-up area. Small children's play area on site.
Restrictions Entry by dusk preferred. Dogs welcome. Campfires permitted.
Open Easter to mid-Oct (or when guests thin out).
Getting there *Lower Porthamel Farm* is located off the A4078 midway between Talgarth and Three Cocks. The campsite is signposted on the left if you're coming from the direction of Talgarth and on the right if you're driving from Three Cocks. A bus service (#39) runs between Hereford and Brecon and stops in Talgarth.

Court Farm

The great escape

People have sought solitude in the folds of the Vale of Ewyas for well over a thousand years. In the sixth century, hermits shacked up in a cell dedicated to St David. From the 1100s to the dissolution of the monasteries, Augustinian monks sang hymns in the open air at Llanthony Priory. Today, the area is beloved of escapists and walkers alike. The valley, which snakes along the English border, from broad, pastoral farmland north of Abervagenny on to the Black Mountains further north, offers some much-sought-after peace. When the central Brecon Beacons is crawling with Gore-Tex-clad walkers, the Vale of Ewyas is cocooned in hush. This sense of retreat is what makes the *Court Farm* campsite, where the river valley begins to narrow, so special. The farm, home to one of South Wales's finest riding centres (Easter–Oct), sits next to the weathered stone ruins of Llanthony Priory itself.

The field campsite here seems to have been created as an afterthought, so anyone partial to creature comforts should look elsewhere. This is true back-to-basics camping: one standpipe, an old rail wagon for rubbish and recyling, a rope swing for the kids and that's it. Unless you're in the Wain House, a rustic bunkhouse (and former cart stable) that sleeps sixteen people, toilets are in an intermittently squalid public block in the priory car park a few hundred metres away. Showers are non-existent – worth bearing in mind as the bottom of the field gets boggy after rain. Aside from the Passmores' farm-produced barbecue packs, the nearest stores are a twenty-minute drive south in Abergavenny.

Despite these shortcomings, *Court Farm* lodges itself in the memory. In the evenings, after a day on the rooftop of the Black Mountains or striding along the long-distance path of Offa's Dyke, which tracks a windy ridge directly above, the moon sails over bare hills that rise behind your tent. Dine in the quirky *Llanthony Priory Hotel* (℡01873 890487) and you can step from the cellar-bar into the haunting ruins of the priory itself – a magical experience on those wild Welsh nights when clouds scud low over the valley. *The Half Moon* pub nearby is as close as the real world gets.

▼ The ruins of Llanthony Priory

Practicalities

Court Farm, Llanthony, Abergavenny, Monmouthshire, NP7 7NN ℡*01873 890359,* Ⓦ*www.llanthony.co.uk*

Pitches & price About 40. Adults £3, children £1.50. Wain House rental £120 1 night, £200 2 nights, weekends minimum £240.

Facilities Public toilet with basins and disabled access 300yds away.

Restrictions No campfires. No music. Dogs permitted.

Open Year round.

Getting there From the A465, take the turn-off to Stanton and Llanthony at Llantilio Pertholey and drive around 5 miles north to Llanthony; the priory is on the right. From Hay-on-Wye follow signposts to Capel-y-ffin at the south end of the town centre and continue on the spectacular single road over the Black Mountains.

Pencelli Castle
Flowerbeds, countryside and awards aplenty

There was a castle in the village of Pencelli, just outside Brecon, until the 1500s. During its four-hundred-year history, the massive medieval fortification was home to assorted Welsh royalty as well as English nobles such as Sir Roger de Mortimer, a confidant of Henry III who sent his wife the head of a foe as a love troth. Bloody battles were waged outside the moat. Fast-forward several centuries and the current kings of *Pencelli Castle*, Gerwyn and Liz Rees are still besieged – only now it's families and walkers who set up camp on the historic battlegrounds.

It has to be said, first impressions can deter like castellated walls. Above an arrivals car park is a noticeboard that ticks off site rules: no dogs, no music, no shouting, no open fires, no non-breathable awning groundsheets. No fun? And rather fussy flowerbeds by the reception jar against gorgeous countryside that rolls away to mountain peaks. Purists in search of raw nature may be disappointed. Look beyond the caravans, however, and *Pencelli Castle* earns the wallfull of award plaques mounted in its barn, from Campsite of the Year to conservation gold medals via Loo of the Year. Wherever you look you'll see careful thought about visitors' needs.

Take the three fields tailored to tents. Campers are best to pass through the motor home-friendly "The Orchard" (bordered by the old moat) and "The Oaks" (neat but manicured) and to push their pegs instead into "The Meadow". A well-trimmed field at the back of the site, this natural area is pitch-where-you-like relaxed and has space galore for children – a nature trail and lovely playground beside a deer park are backups in case of boredom. The drawback is this puts you furthest from the first-class amenities block, its award-winning toilets so clean you could eat from the floor if you didn't mind weird looks.

Extra brownie points are scored for simple things done well. Current bus timetables and useful local contacts are pinned on a noticeboard, bike rental is available, including children's cycles and a collection service, and an information room is stuffed with books, maps and leaflets. There are also large communal fridges and freezers, while the store stocks camping and hiking supplies plus local produce as well as the usual foods and newspapers. It's fair to say the Reeses are good on detail.

Practicalities

Pencelli Castle, Pencelli, Brecon, Powys, LD3 7LX ☏01874 665451, Ⓦwww.pencelli-castle.com

Pitches & price 40 tent pitches, 15 grass pitches with hook-ups, 25 hard-standing caravan pitches with hook-ups. Tents £8–10 per adult, £4.50–6 per child. Caravans & motor homes £16–20 for 2 adults, plus £4.50–6.50 per child.

Facilities Outstanding. Immaculate heated amenities block with showers, basins, loos, hair dryers and soft classical muzak, plus 2 large family/disabled rooms. Dishwashing room, laundry. Information room with internet and wi-fi.

Restrictions No dogs. No stereos. No campfires. Latest arrival by 10pm.

Open Year round (closed 3–30 Dec).

Getting there A mile east from Brecon on the A40, turn right onto the B4558 to Pencelli and follow brown tent signs to the village; the site is signposted on your left. Bus #X43 (Mon–Sat) from Brecon to Cardiff stops at Pencelli.

With a location at the heart of the Brecon Beacons National Park, *Pencelli Castle* gets oversubscribed in summer and even has a loyal following over New Year. The highest peak in the park, slab-like Pen-y-Fan (2656ft), is a three-hour yomp west of the site. There are gentler pleasures, too; fishing in the Brecon Canal beneath "The Meadow" for example, or a four-mile cycle along the canal towpath to Brecon, a proper little market town yet to succumb to the la-di-da of neighbour Hay-on-Wye. Closer to home, the pleasant *Royal Oak* is literally just down the road and *The White Swan* (restaurant open Tues–Sun) at Llanfrynach is a quintessential country pub with the finest chef in the area.

◄ *Pencelli Castle's most peg-friendly field, "The Meadow"* ► *Pen-y-Fan from Corn Du; narrow boats on the Monmouthshire & Brecon Canal*

North Wales

Just as the coast defines the south, mountains are the icons of North Wales. Snowdonia is not just the country's literal crowning glory; the 840-square-mile National Park at the region's heart affects the culture as much as the scenery – the former fostered in isolated old mining or quarry villages, the latter all massive ice-sculpted crags, waterfalls and scree-strewn slopes that tumble into deep valleys. Natural drama is guaranteed, though the weather is predictably unpredictable.

The mountainous north has always attracted walkers, from the warrior-giants of Celtic legend to the first successful Everest team, and whether you opt to go around a Rhinog, over Cadair Idris or up Snowdon itself, there are enough tracks to keep trail junkies happy for months.

Thanks to these visitors, North Wales is no stranger to tourism, and some popular resorts can seem stuck in a rut compared to the south's feel-good groove: too much chintz in the decor, too many chicken Kievs on the menu. Uncommercialized south Snowdonia around Dolgellau and Machynlleth, long a magnet for well-heeled hippies, now leads the way, pioneering zeitgeist concepts such as eco-awareness and quality local food.

Less is usually more in camping – less concrete, fewer people – and North Wales is best at its wildest. Go back to basics and you come closer to an outdoors that is truly great. For camping purists, North Wales is about spending misty mornings beneath peaks and star-filled nights around campfires, and we've focused our gaze on sites where you can do just that.

Holyhead

ISLE OF ANGLESEY

A5025

A55

A5

A5025

Outdoor Alternative

A5

A4080

Bangor

Caernarfon

A4085

A4086

A499

A487

B354

B4417

B4415

A497

B4413

Mynydd Mawr

Porthmadog

A498

A498

A497

Snowdon ▲

Hafod y Llan

Cae Du (Beddgelert)

Gwern Gôf Uchaf

Gwern Gôf Isaf

Llyn Gwynant

A4086

A5

A470

A496

A496

A470

Llandudno

Conwy

A55

Conwy

Colwyn Bay

A55

B5381

Betws-y-Coed

B5106

B4406

B4407

C O N W Y

A548

A544

A543

B5113

Blaenau Ffestiniog

SNOWDONIA NATIONAL PARK

G W Y N E D D

Bala

Dolgellau

A494

A4212

B4401

Rhyl

A547

A458

A55

A541

B4501

A5

A494

B5105

A525

A5104

A470

A458

A459

Ruthin

D E N B I G H S H I R E

Llangolle

A55

A548

A5151

A494

Cwm Bychan Farm

Cae Gwyn

Bwch yn Uchaf

A470

B4403

B4391

B4393

B4396

B4395

B4392

B4389

B4580

Retreat Campsite

Welshpo

P O W Y S

Newtown

Shell Island

Nantcol Waterfalls

A496

Owen Tyddyn Farm

Graig Wen

A493

Dôl Einion

B4405

Cadair Idris ▲

A470

A487

Eco Retreats

A489

Machynlleth

A470

A44

A470

A483

A495

B4518

Cae Du (Tywyn)

A493

A550
A541
A534
Wrexham
A525

North Wales

	PAGE	🥾	🚲	⛵	🍷	🏔	👫	👨‍👩‍👧	🚐	🚌	♿
Bwych yn Uchaf	192			✓			✓		✓		
Cae Du (Beddgelert)	194	✓					✓		✓	✓	✓
Cae Du (Tywyn)	180					✓	✓		✓		
Cae Gwyn	192	✓	✓						✓	✓	
Conwy	199						✓		✓		✓
Cwm Bychan Farm	185	✓				✓					
Dôl Einion	181	✓					✓	✓	✓		
Eco Retreats	182					✓					
Graig Wen	186		✓		✓	✓	✓		✓	✓	
Gwern Gôf Isaf	198	✓									
Gwern Gôf Uchaf	198	✓									
Hafod y Llan	188	✓				✓					
Llyn Gwynant	189	✓		✓			✓	✓	✓		
Mynydd Mawr	185					✓					
Nantcol Waterfalls	181						✓		✓		✓
Outdoor Alternative	199	✓		✓		✓	✓		✓		
Owen Tyddyn Farm	184	✓				✓			✓		
Retreat Campsite	193	✓				✓			✓		
Shell Island	190						✓	✓			

See front flap for key to symbols

Cae Du (Tywyn)
Coast and campfires in the best-kept secret in Snowdonia

Pressed to the coast by the low mountains that close the magical Dysynni Valley in south Snowdonia – a particularly diverse region that has yet to succumb to the spirit-sapping commercialism further north – lies this gem of a site on a working farm. Partly through its isolation, part through fortuitous geography, *Cae Du* is the best little campsite you'll never want to share in north Wales.

The view strikes you first. Spread across the horizon beyond its low cliffs is the most astounding seascape in the region; a shimmering skin of silver, slate-grey, jade and blue that shifts beyond every pitch. The flattest are to the left of a surprisingly good amenities block – stock up on £1 coins for showers – so are often occupied by a scattering of caravans. Campers have free reign over the gently undulating right-hand side, where a top terrace saves you sleeping on a slope. Between the two areas the

site dips down onto a private shingle-and-sand beach with the odd rockpool in which to poke your shrimp net.

Days are lovely but dusk is when *Cae Du* comes into its own. Whatever the lure of a pint in the *Garthangharad*, a proper country local four miles away in Llwyngwril, you'll spend most nights on site. Some hardship. As the sun drags the sky into the sea, the site twinkles with orange campfires; scavenge for driftwood on the beach or order logs to your tent. After those cinematic sunsets, you can settle into barbecued lamb burgers bought on-site and stargazing – no light pollution here. Wake up early and you may see dolphins dip across the bay from your sleeping bag. It's at such times that *Cae Du* feels so special. Away from resorts, though close to handsome little market towns like Dolgellau and Machynlleth, it feels like dropping off the radar compared to celebrated sites like *Shell Island* forty-five minutes north (see p.190). Of course, there are quibbles: this is no place for a weak tent in a storm and the nearest shops are five miles south in Tywyn. Two things to highlight should anyone ever ask about a secret that's too good to share.

▼ Cinematic sea views come as standard at *Cae Du*

Practicalities

Cae Du Campsite, Rhoslefain, Tywyn, Gwynedd, LL36 9ND
☎01654 711234

Pitches & price Around 80 grass pitches. Single tent pitches £6–10, double & family pitches £12–20, caravans £15.

Facilities Amenities block with showers, toilets and basins, dishwashing and laundry room, communal covered area with tatty sofas and large fireplace.

Restrictions Dogs welcome but must be kept on a lead. Campfires allowed.

Open Easter–Oct.

Getting there The site entrance is signposted on the left on a sharp bend of the A493 a mile west of Rhoslefain, around 5 miles north of Tywyn. Tofanau rail station is 2 miles south.

Dôl Einion

No ascent of Cadair Idris ticks boxes like the Minffordd Path. From the hour-long grunt up through woodland to a knockout tarn – a superb destination for a summer picnic, which requires just enough effort to justify a big spread – to a ridge walk that teeters along a glaciated amphitheatre towards the summit (2830ft), it condenses some of the most breathtaking mountain scenery in Wales into a six-hour circuit. Not bad for a mountain which often takes second billing to Snowdon.

That the trail starts behind the rhododendron bushes makes this relaxed site a perennially popular choice with walkers. Yet it is just as appealing a base camp for fishermen and touring holidaymakers, too – trout snap in Tal-y-llyn lake less than a mile away and its pretty meadow has space to spare even in high summer. A convenient one, too, given that the lakeside *Tenycornel* pub, reached via a track from the site, or the *Minffordd Hotel* put sustenance within walking distance. Those who like to camp in comfort will baulk at facilities as simple as an outdoor butler's sink for the dishes. But who needs glitzy camping with Cadair's crags heaving above? Sometimes simplicity is no bad thing.

Practicalities

Dôl Einion, Tal-y-llyn, Tywyn, Gwynedd, LL36 9AJ ☎01654 761312, ✉marianrees@tiscali.co.uk

Pitches & price 20 tent pitches, 5 caravan pitches (4 hard-standing with hook-ups). £7–12 per tent, £12 per caravan.

Facilities 2 toilets, 2 showers, outdoor sink for washing-up.

Restrictions Dogs permitted. Campfires allowed in low season if grass sod replaced afterwards.

Open Year round.

Getting there The entrance to *Dôl Einion* campsite is on the right-hand side on the B4405, 330yds from the junction with the A487, which is midway between Dolgellau and Machynlleth. The campsite is accessible by public transport as the A487 is on major bus routes from Aberystwyth, Machynlleth and Dolgellau among others.

Nantcol Waterfalls

Hidden in woodland between the Rhinog mountains and the Cambrian coastline, *Nantcol Waterfalls* has always been postcard-pretty. A shallow river still elbows around its well-drained field tucked into the hills, just as it always has throughout the decades of ownership by the Jones family. There are the same pitches among bracken ferns where you can light a campfire and revel in a pure camping experience; owner Aled (not the famous one) sells logs on site. And kids still swim in the shallows, or launch themselves off a miniature island on a rope swing. But the addition of an amenities block in 2009 means getting back to nature no longer entails portable toilets and a cold-water wash.

A downside to this idyll is that the site is busy on summer weekends – it doubles as a picnic spot for the waterfalls that tumble through a gorge behind. Fortunately Harlech, a highlight of the Cambrian coast, or the Rhinog Mountains are twenty minutes' drive away, the same time it takes to walk for an evening pint in Llanbedr. By the time you return, there won't be a day-tripper in sight.

Practicalities

Nantcol Waterfalls, Cefn Uchaf, Llanbedr, Gwynedd, LL45 2PL ☎01341 241209, ⊛www.nantcolwaterfalls.co.uk

Pitches & price 62 tent pitches, 23 caravan pitches with hook-ups. Adults £7, children (4–16) £3.

Facilities Amenities block with showers, toilets, basins and dishwashing area, disabled facilities. Portable toilets on site in peak season.

Restrictions No young groups. No large groups except by permission. Dogs welcome but must be kept on a lead. Campfires permitted.

Open March–Sept.

Getting there If you're heading south on the A496 from Harlech, turn left beside the *Victoria Inn* at Llanbedr (or right if you're travelling north from Barmouth) and follow signs for Cwm Nantcol. Through Pentre Gwynfryn, turn left over a cattle grid and loop up to a green "parking" sign on your right.

Eco Retreats

As green as it gets at the ultimate escape

They're not kidding about a retreat. The further you go along a bumpy forest track towards this site, the further the real world seems to slip into the rear-view mirror. Don't believe the mileometer that suggests you're four miles from Esgairgeiliog village. The mental distance is immeasurable.

The concept of *Eco Retreats* as a world apart is a tenet of this inspirational site on an organic sheep farm near Machynlleth.

The handsome market town has been a wellspring of Wales's alternative scene for decades – its unspoilt valleys proved irresistible to city refugees even before the establishment hereabouts of the Centre for Alternative Technology (CAT) in the late 1970s, a unique community project whose model of sustainable living is more relevant than ever. *Eco Retreats* gave a nod to its hippy neighbours when it was conceived as a tipi tourism venture over a drunken game of Scrabble.

So far, so adventure break. It is since 2005 that *Eco Retreats* has evolved into the ultimate holistic chill-out with a side-order of feel-good. Under ownership of ChaNan and Michael Bonser, a well-travelled couple whose backgrounds are in high-end hospitality and tipi communities respectively, the site now provides alternative therapies, ethically sources all products and has an environmental message as authentic as the 1300 acres of organic farmland draped over the surrounding hills. Small wonder they now include tickets to CAT with every stay.

For all the laudable ethics of *Eco Retreats*, no one will condemn you for simply loafing around your tipi with a good thriller. Each is placed to enjoy plenty of space – among the best are the Waterfall tipi and Woodland tipi, the latter in a mossy forest – and has a simple cosiness inside: think wood floors, a tubby chimenea, quirky recycled furnishings and a bed with high-quality linen (Fairtrade, naturally) and sheepskins. For more comfort you can book an airy yurt, which is beautifully sited beside a river.

Lighting is of the flame variety and washing in a covered wood unit with solar-heated shower and a composting loo. The latter is what distinguishes the site from more glitzy tipi outfits. What *Eco Retreats* is emphatically not is glamping, however comfy or aspirational it may be. A site that oozes integrity, it is, like the best campsites, about a love of the outdoors. It's about slowing down and immersing yourself in the purity around you; about dawn choruses, campfires crackling outside the tipi and stargazing with a nip of whisky.

It's also about space and relaxation. With a maximum of 25 guests on site at a time, you're unlikely to see much of the neighbours except for the (optional) twilight meditations,

Practicalities

Eco Retreats, Plas Einion, Furnace, Machynlleth, Powys, SY20 8PG ☎01654 781375, Ⓦwww.ecoretreats.co.uk

Pitches & price 5 tipis and 1 yurt for up to 4 adults each. Prices by season for 2 guests for 2 nights (includes reiki session, meditations, tickets for CAT and organic welcome hamper): tipis £305–339, yurt £315–359; extra nights £65 off-peak, £75 peak. Additional adult (per night) £15, child (5–15) £7.50.

Facilities Private wash-unit with solar-powered shower, basin and toilet. Bedding and cooking/barbecue equipment provided, plus private log supply (and axe).

Restrictions No dogs. Campfires permitted.

Open Easter to mid-Nov.

Getting there Around 2 miles north of Machynlleth on the A487, turn right to Esgairgeilog and follow the road 100yds to a left turn marked by a green triangular sign with a yellow sun. The tarmac road goes downhill then becomes a forest track – continue straight along this, following the green triangles for 4 miles to the marked entrance on the left, off a sharp right bend.

which are offered for free alongside unwinding reiki sessions and massages.

Despite what time here suggests, the real world isn't so far away. Pub and art gallery *Tafarn Dwynant* (closed Mon) is in Esgairgeiliog, and a mix of well-heeled city escapees and Welsh farmers make Machynlleth one of north Wales's most engaging market towns – the Wednesday farmers' market is a regional institution. CAT, five minutes' north, is as inspiring as a day out as Cadair Idris mountain or the ClimachX mountain-bike trails in the Dyfi Forest, both twenty minutes away by car.

◀ This way to the tipis ▶ Each tipi has a chimenea for maximum snugness, as well as wood floors and sheepskin covers on the beds

Owen Tyddyn Farm
Cadair Idris at its best

Celtic mythology swirls around Cadair Idris like mountain mists. The five-peaked massif was, they say, the ancient realm of Idris Gawr, a poet-warlord of Welsh myths. Anyone who braves a night beneath his throne – an amphitheatre of thousand-foot cliffs known as Cwm Gadair – will either become a poet, go mad or die, doubtless to be dragged away by Gwyn ap Nudd, the Celtic king of the underworld who is said to roam the summit with spectral hounds in search of souls. While Cadair's isolated bulk dominates the surroundings as much as superstition hereabouts, the mountain is most awe-inspiring on the northwest face, where it thrusts suddenly from the hills into a ridge sculpted by aeons of ice. Forget Snowdonia. Here, Cadair looks more like the Pyrenees.

The grandstand view of that ridge clawing the sky is what

▼ *Owen Tyddyn Farm*, with Cadair Idris behind

distinguishes *Owen Tyddyn Farm* from two other sites nearby. You can lose hours simply watching the sun pick out detail in its crags and the clouds boil and spin into wisps from its ridges – longer, actually, if the caravan that has been parked in the field for forty years is any guide. If you feel inspired, the nine-mile "Pony Path" track to the summit (2925ft), one of the easiest ascents of the mountain, starts from a bridge nearby. Yet a big part of the appeal of this sheep and veal-suckling farm is that once the day-trippers have packed up their boots in the National Trust car park next door, it has a sense of remoteness that belies the three miles by road to good restaurants like *Dylanwad Da* in Dolgellau; *Gwernan* pub (closed Mon & Sun eve) a mile away has so-so food (until 8pm) and a decent pint.

Sure, this site is as basic as they come. A farmer's field site that you'll share with sheep, it has no toilets (there is a public loo in the car park five hundred yards away) while the nearest thing to a shower is a stream. But any hardened camper will love the purity of this mountain environment, from campfires to stargazing by a dry-stone wall, or morning cuppas in front of an awesome panorama. The big outdoors doesn't feel much bigger in Wales.

Practicalities

Owen Tyddyn Farm, Islawrdref, Dolgellau, Gwynedd, LL40 1TL ☎*01341 422472*

Pitches & price 60 tent pitches, 2 caravan pitches. £5 per pitch.

Facilities 2 standpipes. Public toilet (no shower) in car park by road.

Restrictions No dogs. Campfires permitted.

Open Year round.

Getting there Take Porth Canol Street (beside a hairdresser's) off the main square in Dolgellau and turn left at a sign to Cadair Idris diagonally opposite a Texaco garage. 3 miles on, turn right onto a track beside a National Trust car park and go through its gate – the site entrance is on the left past a cattle grid.

Mynydd Mawr

There's an end-of-the-world feel to this magical site, sheltered behind a headland of cliffs with panoramic seascapes. Perhaps because of its location just behind the tumbling cliffs at the very tip of the Llŷn peninsula, the Land's End of Wales, or because for over a millennium pilgrims stopped here en route to Bardsey Island two miles offshore – the former "Isle of Twenty Thousand Saints" is nowadays a island populated by twenty thousand or so seabirds, which makes it a great day-trip in summer – this small, uncommercial site where the road ends has an exhilaratingly escapist vibe to suit the views of sea and fields from its upper pitches.

The same is true of Aberdaron, one and a half miles away. While flashy Abersoch near Port Neigwl surf beach is thronged, this former fishing hamlet behind a long strip of pale sand has charm and space in beach-bucket loads. It's a place to build sandcastles, to idle over lunch on the beach terrace of the *Ship Hotel*, and then to return to the tent after dinner at a nearby seafood restaurant for quiet nights of stargazing. Bliss.

Practicalities

Mynydd Mawr Caravan and Camping Site, Llanllawen Fawr Farm, Aberdaron, Pwllheli, Gwynedd, LL53 8BY ☎01758 760223, Ⓦ*www.aberdaroncaravanand campingsite.co.uk*

Pitches & price 25 grass pitches (18 hook-ups). Single tents from £8; 2-person tents from £10.

Facilities 2 tin shacks with a spotless shower, toilet and basin.

Restrictions No campfires. Dogs welcome but must be kept on a lead.

Open March–Sept.

Getting there Head to Aberdaron on the B4413, and from here follow signs to Uwchmynydd. Keep going until you see a white house on the left – *Mynydd Mawr* campsite is 150yds beyond this, just before a cattle grid.

Cwm Bychan Farm

For many of us wild camping is the original and still the best. It strips camping back to its essence: the great outdoors. That it's also restricted by law in Wales and England (see p.340) is what makes *Cwm Bychan Farm* special; camping here feels as close to the wild as you can get whilst remaining on the right side of the statute book. You won't pitch anywhere more remote in Wales than this semi-official site – little more than a couple of paddocks behind Cwm Bychan lake, where fees are placed into a donations box. What makes it special is its location encircled by the Rhinogs, arguably the last true wilderness in Snowdonia. You're more likely to see feral goats than people.

That facilities are as minimal as you'd expect of a lonely walkers' base at the end of the road will deter some campers – portable toilets and a quietly trickling stream for water and a wash if you're brave. Dinas Farm (☎01341 241585, Ⓦwww.dinas-farm.co.uk; adults £5) two miles earlier has basic facilities and permits campfires on a pretty two-field site site. For others, getting back to basics is half the reason to visit.

Practicalities

Cwm Bychan Farm, Cwm Bychal, Llanbedr, Gwynedd, LL45 2PH (OS map ref: SH 644 315), no tel

Pitches & price Grass pitches, no set number. £5 per pitch.

Facilities Minimal: 2 portable toilets and you can wash in the stream. Basic facilties available at Dinas Farm down the road.

Restrictions No dogs, no campfires.

Open Year round.

Getting there Head to Llanbedr, which is situated north of Barmouth and south of Harlech on the A496 coastal road. Turn east in Llanbedr at the *Victoria Inn* and follow signs for Cwm Bychan. Go through Pentre Gwynfryn and at a fork by a bridge beyond the village turn left towards Cwm Bychan. Keep going for 5 miles to the end of the road and you'll arrive at *Cwm Bychan Farm.*

Graig Wen

Natural magic in south Snowdonia

It could be a rainbow propped across the valley, perhaps a badger snuffling in the ferns behind a campfire at dusk. It could just be an hour spent watching a languid flood tide melt golden sandbanks into a shimmering skin of silver. However it happens, there comes a point during your stay at *Graig Wen* when you'll stop and wonder why so few people visit south Snowdonia. Popular perception has it that it lacks the high mountain peaks and giddying gulfs further north. In fact, Cadair Idris, twenty minutes from the site, and proper proud market towns like Dolgellau or Machynlleth trump any of the poster-destinations north. And what the south lacks in tourist brochure images it makes up for in something more intangible – integrity, escap-

ism, magic. For first-timers the area is a revelation. Call it the Eureka moment.

Sarah and John had one in 2007 when the Brighton-based couple saw this site six miles west of Dolgellau. Inspired by eight months' campervanning around Europe and seeking a lifestyle change, they were smitten. Since then their ramshackle purchase has morphed into a place of pinch-me perfection. At the top, adjacent to a stylish B&B created from a former slate-cutting headquarters – all slate floors, raw wood, traditional Welsh blankets and understated interior design – an upper site is undergoing a transformation from touring park to small natural campsite. Leviathan conifers have been removed and native trees replanted. The views are knockout, too, from a communal space above the Mawddach estuary; a natural terrace to sit at sunset and gaze over those golden sandbanks – not hyperbole but real specks in the sand that create the brilliantly white gold used in the wedding rings of British royalty. Thinning out a pretty silver birch woodland behind the area has cleared glades for two yurts – a spacious family-sized number and a romantic Hobbity structure for two, both made snug by wood-burning stoves, rugs and sheepskins on raised wood floors. If there are more relaxed mornings than a breakfast hamper of local produce on their decks they're keeping them quiet.

But what makes this site so special lies downhill. You emerge from the woods into two paddocks that swoop down to the estuary floodplain. In the 43 acres there are just 25 tents pitched among trees and bracken-fern froth. With all facilities except the "Treebog" composting toilet half a mile back uphill, civilization feels fairly distant down here, especially in a car-free lower field. When late-afternoon sunshine rakes across the wooded hills ahead and the estuary winks from behind a lattice of oaks, it feels an exhilaratingly wild place to be – less a campsite than a remote, forgotten corner of the world where time slows to a magical stillness. "Sublime", Wordsworth said of the area over a century ago, and he's still right.

The Romantic poet delivered his eulogy after walking the Mawddach estuary trail beneath the site. Stroll for an hour (or cycle for ten minutes) and a pint and decent pub-grub await

Practicalities

Graig Wen, Arthog, Dolgellau, Gwynedd, LL39 1BQ
☎*01341 250482,* Ⓦ*www.graigwen.co.uk*

Pitches & price Top site: 10 grass pitches and 8 hard-standing pitches with hook-up; lower site 25 grass pitches. 2 yurts for 5 and 2, 1 bell tent for 4. Camping: adults £7–10, children (5–16) £3–5, reduced rates for bikers/backpackers. Small yurt £60–75 per night, £325/week low season, £425 July–Aug; large yurt £85–100 per night, £450/week low season, £550/week high season. Bell tent £60 per night (minimum 2 nights).

Facilities On upper site: amenities block with toilets and basins, shower area with dishwashing area, basic store. On lower site: composting toilet. Wi-fi in B&B.

Restrictions No campfires at top site (communal fire available); campfires permitted on lower site. Dogs allowed on leads. No stag/hen parties. No children under 10 in B&B.

Open Upper site: March–early Jan; lower site: currently July–Aug (possibly June–Aug from 2010); yurts and bell tent: end March–Oct.

Getting there Take the A493 towards Tywyn from the A470 west of Dolgellau. The site is on the left 5 miles from the turn-off. Buses from Aberystwyth/Machynlleth and Dolgellau stop outside on request. Pick-ups available from Morfa Mawddach station a mile away.

you on an idyllic river terrace at the *George III*; *Mawddach* restaurant, ten minutes' drive away, is the choice for sophisticated modern Welsh cuisine. As you return on the path later, drifting back towards *Graig Wen*'s parallel world, you'll see car headlights on the other side of the estuary racing silently north. Why the hurry? Eureka.

◀ En route to revelation at tranquil *Graig Wen* ▶ Yurts don't get much more comfy than this; a sheltered spot beneath the trees

Hafod y Llan
A walkers' secret in Snowdon

Throw another log onto the campfire for Sir Anthony Hopkins. The Welsh actor dipped into his pocket to the tune of £1 million to help the National Trust find £3.65 million for this historic Snowdonia sheep farm, the largest and arguably most impressive of nearly two thousand farms in its care. Just don't call *Hafod y Llan* a museum piece. Rather it is a super-sized experiment to prove the profitability of extensive environmentally friendly farming. Because the flock has been halved to two thousand and native Welsh Black cattle introduced to churn the soil, and because the farm now pursues low-impact organic practices, biodiversity has returned to the 4370-acre estate, which stretches in a wedge to the summit of Snowdon. That's good news for everyone: farmer, conservationist and walker alike.

The trust declared itself "overwhelmed" by the public response to its "Save Snowdonia" appeal in 1998. Purists will reach for the

▼ Tent up? Tick. Cup of tea? Tick. Pure nature? Tick

same adjective because *Hafod y Llan* is a gem. For years an ad hoc hikers' secret at the start of the Watkin path that claws up Snowdon's east flank, this intimate place retains the sort of purity to tweak the guy ropes of any camping connoisseur. With visitor numbers limited by a small car park beneath, nature rules on its well-drained site nestled into the mountain. Sheltered in a natural amphitheatre – all proud bluffs and pine trees – a stream burbling at your side as a campfire crackles in the pit, it's not hard to feel deep in the wilds here, even though a simple, spotless amenities block lies just beneath your pitch. You can almost sympathize with the hikers who protested when the trust installed hot showers in 2008. Almost.

Actually, you're not as remote as appearances suggest – pubs in Beddgelert are a few miles away and at the end of the lane, *Café Gwynant* (Wed–Mon 8am–6pm) rustles up the tastiest, freshest food in the area, plus takeaway lunch boxes. But perhaps the real reason to favour *Hafod y Llan* over other sites hereabouts is that all proceeds from the campsite go to the farm management, which in turn means the preservation of scenery to inspire poetry. A campsite with feel-good factor? Sir Anthony would be proud.

Practicalities

Hafod y Llan Farm Campsite, Nantgwynant, Beddgelert, Caernarfon, Gwynedd, LL55 4NQ ☎01766 510129
Pitches & price 25 tent pitches. Adults £5, children under 16 £2.50, fires (including firewood) £6.50.
Facilities Amenities block with showers, toilets and basins, dishwashing area.
Restrictions No music. Single-sex groups of over 4 people and groups of over 8 by arrangement only. Campfires permitted in fire-pits. Dogs welcome but must be kept on a lead. No cars on site.
Open Easter–Oct.
Getting there The site entrance is beside *Café Gwynant*, around 3 miles north of Beddgelert on the A498. The #S4 bus links Beddgelert to Caernarfon.

Llyn Gwynant

An activities base with scenery to spare

There's a layby halfway along the road east of Snowdon. Pull over and you are rewarded with views of mountain scenery as spectacular as any in North Wales; muscular slopes crowned by a tiara of sharp ridges and the blue waters of Llyn Gwynant glinting in the green of one of the region's most beautiful valleys. It's on the flat meadows behind the lake, cupped in the valley beneath fat knuckles of rock, that you'll find this relaxed campsite. There are many scenic sites in North Wales. Few, though, immerse you as completely into scenery of the very high, very grand variety like *Llyn Gwynant*. Cosy *Pen y Gwryd* hotel two miles up the road served as the training base for Edmund Hillary's pioneering team to Everest in 1953: that's the sort of grandeur hereabouts.

Large by local standards, the site spreads over four well-trimmed fields: popular Pen Helen behind the lake (pitches at the front can be boggy after heavy rain), with copses for windbreaks; spacious, family-friendly meadows Dôl Fawr and Dôl Fach; and the car-free getaway Bridge Field at the back, with pitches beside a shallow river and those heaving slopes almost within touching distance. In all fields you can thwart the midges with a campfire in free fireboxes provided – on conservation grounds, wood must be bought on site – and can pitch where you please. Brownie points to the owners, too, for an outer field in which late arrivals can pitch until morning; good for them, better for on-site campers.

A location at Snowdon's backdoor has long made *Llyn Gwynant* the base camp for hiker and scout groups. Yet it's not all muddy boots and grid references. Canoes and kayaks available for hire in summer are a godsend for family holidays, and in 2009 the young outdoorsy management launched an on-site activities base, Great Adventure UK. Enquire at reception and you can sign on to a guided ascent of Snowdon, rock climbing on crags around the lake or a day-trip to go coasteering.

Adrenalin junkies, take note. Parents, breathe a sigh of relief.

▼ *Llyn Gwynant* from the air

Practicalities

Llyn Gwynant, Hafod Lwyfog, Nantgwynant, Gwynedd, LL55 4NW Ⓦ*www.gwynant.com, no tel*

Pitches & price 450 grass pitches, 10 caravan pitches. Adults £6 or £8 summer and bank holidays, children (5–15) £3, caravans £10, firewood £4, noise bond £20 per person for young groups.

Facilities Large simple amenities block with showers, toilets and basins, disabled toilet with baby-changing facilities, dishwashing area, camping barns for groups.

Restrictions No stereos, radios or bongos. Dogs welcome but must be kept on a lead. Campfires permitted in fireboxes. Main site gates closed nightly by 10pm, or 11pm in summer.

Open Mid-March to mid-Nov.

Getting there The site entrance is signed off the A498 at the north end of Llyn Gwynant, on the left if driving from Beddgelert.

Shell Island
Escape to Europe's biggest campsite

Look among the standard site rules at *Shell Island* and you'll find one very revealing regulation. National law dictates that pitches on UK campsites are at least six metres apart. Here they make it twenty, because *Shell Island* is big. Very big. Two and a half miles long and half a mile wide to be precise, making it the largest site in Europe. This, then, is not your average camping destination. Nor is it an island, to be truly accurate, as it's really a sandy hook cast from the northern end of Cardigan Bay, but there's a touch of *Treasure Island* about the place nevertheless. Like the pirate yarn, Shell Island provides a magical sense of being cast adrift.

The adventure starts in the getting there. Although Shell Island is tethered to the coast by the sands that sweep up the Cambrian coast, it is only accessible by road between low to mid-tide – for around three hours a day campers are marooned. Castaways have never had it so good. Many sites claim to be all-rounders, but few succeed in being both a family resort and a wild camp.

Space is one reason. Diversity of scenery is another. The north of the island is quietest, its neat, well-trimmed fields appealing to motor-homers and families. It also affords picture-postcard views across the bay to nearby Harlech Castle in front of the blue-grey peaks of Snowdonia National Park – North Wales in a nutshell. Young groups and adventurous campers pitch in the wilder south, wagon-circling tents beneath sand dunes or settling down in copses on the landward side, where you get views to the Rhinog Mountains and an all-tide footpath to the "mainland". Between the two, on the west coast, is a sunset strip where lovely snug fields are scalloped into the foreshore behind the beach.

Of course, size has its downsides. It's been a long time since *Shell Island* was a secret, and in school holidays, when half of Manchester and Liverpool seems to migrate west, facilities can struggle. Similarly, the south can feel less of a campsite than an ad hoc festival during holidays. Yet with space to spare, for every

Practicalities

Shell Island, Llanbedr, Gwynedd, LL45 2PJ ☎01341 241453, Ⓦwww.shellisland.co.uk

Pitches & price 800 grass pitches. Adults £6/7 per night (by season), children (3–15) £2.50/3.

Facilities Central amenities/shower blocks with toilets and handbasins. Also disabled cubicle with shower, toilet and basin. Portable toilets throughout site. Dishwashing area, launderette, bar with off-licence, snack bar with ATM, pub, games room, supermarket, camping/outdoors shop.

Restrictions Arrivals by 8pm weekdays, 9pm weekends. Entrance gates closed midnight–8am. No caravans. No sleeping in cars or vans (except campervans). Campfires permitted (in fire grates). Dogs permitted.

Open Mid-March to Oct.

Getting there The turning to Shell Island is by the bridge in Llanbedr, on the A496 south of Harlech. Llanbedr train station is a mile from the entrance; buses from Harlech and Barmouth pass through Llanbedr.

noisy group with a stereo there's a kid crabbing on the causeway and for every boozy night there's a lung-punching dawn with the chance of spotting dolphins or seals from the northern cliffs.

At times *Shell Island* feels less like a mere campsite than a self-contained world. It has its own myths of drunken giants and ghosts that haunt the old farmhouse, its own history of ship-wrecks – former ships' timbers beam the restaurant – and smugglers' tunnels. It's probably also the only site in Britain with a fan website (Ⓦwww.shellislandcampers.co.uk). More than anything *Shell Island* is an unparalleled escape; a getaway with gorgeous vistas of sea and mountains on all sides, where the everyday is suspended and where time seems to warp. And isn't that what camping is all about?

◀ Space is never in short supply on Shell Island ▶ Catching crabs on the causeway; a swan on patrol

Cae Gwyn

Hikers and bikers are well represented at *Cae Gwyn* ("White Field"), across the valley from the Rhinog Mountains. Each pitch comes with a leaflet of walks and the site's friendly owners urge you to roam around their two-hundred-acre organic sheep farm or hook a trout supper in the half-mile section of Afon Eden for which they own fishing rights. Just across the road are the world-class mountain-bike trails of Coed y Brenin (Ⓦwww.mbwales.com; bike rental available from Beics Brenin at visitor centre). "The Beast", 23 miles of heart-pumping, adrenalin-fuelled single-track fun, is as good as it gets in the UK.

Actually, any outdoorsy type who shudders at sterile billiard-table sites will appreciate *Cae Gwyn*. A chilled-out vibe from the ban on children has something to do with it. Mostly it's because you unzip your tent to a panorama of the pass between Rhinog Fawr and Fach, spotlit in the early morning sunshine when the Welsh weather gods smile. Some sites spread their scenery before you like a canvas. *Cae Gwyn*, winner of the Most Beautiful Farm in West Wales 2008, puts you in the painting.

Practicalities

Cae Gwyn, Bronaber, Trawsfynydd, Gwynedd, LL41 4YE
Ⓣ01766 540245, Ⓦwww.caegwynfarm.co.uk
Pitches & price Approximately 80 tent pitches. £7.50 per person.
Facilities Amenities block with showers, basins and toilets, plus dishwashing area with fridge, freezer and microwave. Free wi-fi and bike storage available. Accommodation in camping barn & B&B also offered.
Restrictions No children under 14. No stag or hen parties. No campfires or dogs allowed. Late arrivals by arrangement only.
Open Year round.
Getting there The campsite is signposted right off the A470, approximately 10 miles north of Dolgellau and a mile south of Bronaber. Bronaber is on major bus routes north and south from Dolgellau and Betws-y-Coed respectively.

Bwch yn Uchaf

Remember *The Railway Children*? There's something of the book's yesteryear innocence about this small family-friendly site at the south end of Llyn Tegid. When other sites on Wales's water-sports wonderland teeter on midsummer madness, *Bwch yn Uchaf* is rule-free, relaxed and immaculately maintained, thanks to its unflaggingly helpful manager Gareth Jones, who prioritizes space over squeezing in tents. Of course, the Bala Lake Railway adds to the charm. Pitch on the spacious top field and the children can watch steam trains whistle into a vintage station directly behind. Opt for the smaller lower fields and they can paddle or swim in a shallow stream. Either way, they'll get beautiful views of the great outdoors peeling into the distance.

You're not short of options to get here. Little kids will love steam train rides to Bala (April–Oct; Ⓦwww.bala-lake-railway.co.uk), which has a wealth of eating options – in Llanuwchllyn village there's good pub grub in the *Eagle Inn* – and water-sports rental. For big kids there's white-water rafting at the Canolfan Trywewyn National White Water Centre (Ⓣ01678 521083, Ⓦwww.ukrafting.co.uk) in Frongoch.

Practicalities

Bwch yn Uchaf, Llanuwchllyn, Bala, Gwynedd, LL23 7DD
Ⓣ01978 812179, Ⓦwww.bwch-yn-uchaf.co.uk
Pitches & price 40 grass pitches plus caravans area (6 hard-standing pitches, 15 hook-ups). 1-person tent £7–8, 2-person tent/caravans £11–13. Additional adult £4.50, child £3.40.
Facilities Amenities block with showers, basins and toilets; disabled-access shower; portable toilets; washing-up area; shared freezer.
Restrictions Dogs permitted, campfires only allowed in fire-pits provided.
Open Year round.
Getting there Head to Llanuwchllyn village. just off the A494. Follow signs to Bala Lake Railway and *Bwch yn Uchaf* campsite is right next to the station. The #X94 Barmouth–Wrexham bus stops in Llanuwchllyn via Dolgellau.

Retreat Campsite
Fall for Wales at Pistyll Rhaeadr

Many day-trippers visit Pistyll Rhaeadr, the highest waterfall in Wales. They come by the carful in summer to see a cascade that plumes over 230ft in a single drop, to have afternoon tea in a café among luxuriant woodland or to ascend on a footpath to the head of the falls. Only those who linger here sense that there is more to it than meets the eye. In legend, Pistyll Rhaeadr is the gateway between the living in the pastoral valley downstream and the dead in the Berwyn mountains, known in Welsh as the Rhos y Beddau or "moor of graves", whose thrillingly empty hills ripple back behind the falls. The original Celtic King Arthur is said to have (war)lorded it over their haunting, bleak uplands – perhaps erecting some of the stone circles reached on little-known trails. Another tale relates that the valley head beneath the waterfall was a sacred space for druids, and it's here, cupped within green slopes, that you'll find one of the most magical sites in Wales.

Whether it's the millennia steeped in myth or scenery like a film-set from an Arthurian blockbuster that provoke your wonder, this site has a meditative stillness and a sense of detachment that persists even while day-trippers potter about the waterfall in their hundreds.

Pitches are dotted throughout a gently undulating field, the most appealing sited on terraces beside the Rhaedar River. A "meditation in landscape" as Phill Facey, the site custodian, calls it. Phill reduced capacity from 130 pitches to 28 to preserve the area's stillness, and he also hosts spiritual workshops in the "Druids' Bowl" lower field, a haunting spot at dusk. Because this is camping as retreat from everyday life, alcohol is only tolerated on site in small volumes, which is as good an excuse as any to visit three excellent pubs four miles away in Llanrhaeadr.

Minimal facilities and compulsory membership may annoy some: the midges in summer certainly will. Yet while the former guarantees campers who respect the site's calm spirituality, the latter is as good an excuse as any invented for a campfire.

▼ *Retreat Campsite*: a meditation in landscape

Practicalities

Retreat Campsite, Pistyll Rhaeadr, Tan-y-Pistyll, Waterfall Lane, Llanrhaeadr ym Mochnant, Powys, SY10 0BZ
☏*01691 780392,* Ⓦ*www.pistyllrhaeadr.co.uk*
Pitches & price 28 grass pitches. £5.50 per person (under-3s free, families maximum £16). Annual membership £25 (available on site or in advance); on bank holidays call before arrival to ensure space.
Facilities Public toilet with disabled access and baby-changing facilities in café car park. Standpipe and dishwashing area at site entrance.
Restrictions Dogs on leads. Campfires permitted. Only small volumes of alcohol permitted. No young groups.
Open Year round.
Getting there Follow signs to "Waterfall" beside Greatorex Village Store in Llanrhaeadr. The waterfall is at the end of the road 3 miles away, while the site is behind the café/B&B, which doubles as reception.

Cae Du (Beddgelert)
Comfy camping in the hills

Snowdonia isn't all about muddy boots and toughing it out beneath a mountain. What about rabbits, good showers and an evening pint within strolling distance? *Cae Du* feels a million miles away from the nearby sites beloved by trail junkies, but is only twenty minutes' drive from Pen-y-pass, the gateway for ascents of Snowdon, while good road links from Beddgelert village – home to those pubs, best of which is the *Tanronnen Inn* by the bridge – put much of North Wales within day-trip distance. Climbed every mountain? Caenarfon Castle is only twenty minutes' drive away.

If the location appeals to the head, this thirty-acre site's appeal to the heart is its ability to show off the natural assets of the Gwynant Valley and still provide you with all you'll need. Take the variety of pitches. Campers are spoilt for choice. Nearly a third of the site is comprised of spacious well-drained paddocks, so you can peg down in an upper field for views of the mountains or go beside a river to watch the birds flit between branches.

Motorhomers and caravanners get a separate area with hard-standing pitches and hook-ups, while The Paddock, a pretty field enclosed by a stone wall to corral the kids, is tailor-made for families. Then there is the pastoral charm of a site with

Practicalities

Cae Du Campsite, Beddgelert, Caernarfon, Gwynedd, LL55 4NE ☏*01766 890345,* Ⓦ*www.caeducampsite.co.uk*

Pitches & price 85 grass pitches (40 hook-ups), 25 caravan pitches (15 hard-standing, all with hook-up). 1-person tent £10, 2-person tent and caravans £16, additional adult £6, child (3–13) £4. £10 deposit for site entrance road barrier.

Facilities Amenities block (7am–10pm) with disabled-access showers, toilets, basins and hair dryers, dishwashing area, communal freezer, laundry. Store selling basic provisions at reception.

Restrictions No campfires. No music. No young groups (under-17s only with an adult). Dogs welcome but must be kept on a lead. Last entry by 10pm; car barrier locked 10pm–7am.

Open March–Oct.

Getting there The *Cae Du* site is located just north of Beddgelert on the A498; if arriving from the south, turn right once across the river bridge towards Capel Curig. The #S4 bus to Beddgelert departs every couple of hours from Caernarfon.

dry-stone walls, copses and verges of long meadow grass. Basic facilities these are not, however – shared amenities at the centre are cleaned twice a day and have free hot showers and laundry facilities to put a smile on the face of the grubby.

Indeed, there's much about *Cae Du* to make you smile. Perhaps because of the site's space or its natural charm, possibly just because its managers go out of their way to help, *Cae Du* feels more relaxed and smaller than the 110-pitch quota suggests. Small wonder families and walkers alike settle in for two weeks and don't let on to the hardcore hikers.

◀ Pen-y-pass is twenty minutes from *Cae Du* ▶ The campsite sits in the Gwynant Valley, a view from the ramparts of Caernarfon Castle

Adventure sports

Twenty feet doesn't sound impressive. But it can make you giddy when clinging to a cliff. With only raw fear between you and the sea swirling beneath, twenty feet becomes a leap of faith. Every instinct screams don't jump – but coasteering is as much a test of mental strength as physical.

Pioneered in Pembrokeshire then promoted in the late-1980s by St David's-based eco-activities operator TYF Adventure, coasteering may well be the best liquid refreshment in the country. It's an all-in-one sea-swimming, coast-scrambling, rock-climbing, cliff-jumping, stomach-churning, utterly exhilarating activity – and it can be as easy or as hardcore as your group wants. Fitness helps, but so does the skill to ride ocean swell onto a ledge or to exploit waves that whirl around outcrops.

Trust the Welsh to invent a sport which treats their treacherous coast as a supersized playground. Toughened by traditions of mining, quarrying, fishing and farming, Wales has the outdoors hardwired into its national psyche, a connection deeper than the wacky World Bog Snorkelling Championship in Llanwrtyd Wells. Choose any Welsh town or city and adventure awaits on its outskirts, whether in mist-wreathed mountains or on pounding surf beaches, in steep wooded valleys or wide-open moorland – and camping can put you right in its midst.

Take walking – as relaxing a pastime as you could ask for, right? Well, yes, although you might not agree when halfway along Crib Goch, a precipitous knife-edge arête that forms a tough alternative route to the summit of Snowdon (3560ft). Nearby Tryfan (3002ft) is less well known but as extreme, thanks to the boulder-strewn scrambles to its summit. Both it and the Llanberis Pass road beneath Snowdon provide some of the most challenging rock climbing in Britain – it's no coincidence that "cragging" derives from the Welsh word for cliff, *craig*. Rock-huggers in the south of the country, meanwhile, are spoilt for choice, with routes on the sea cliffs of the Gower and around Bosherston in Pembrokeshire. The former are a friendly place for novices, while the latter offers around 35 challenging routes.

Yet it's latter-day adrenalin fixes like coasteering around St David's and the Gower and surfing which have revitalized Wales's reputation for the PlayStation generation. The surprise is that it took so long. Surfing is a simple enough equation: ragged coastline littered with reefs and beaches and washed by Atlantic swells equals wave-riding paradise. Yet it's only recently that British surfers have caught on to a scene that is neither as hyped nor as aggressive as that in Cornwall, even if discretion is the better part of valour at Langland Bay, the best break in the most consistent surf area, the Gower. Beginners should stick to places

with board rental: Llangennith Beach on the Gower and Newgale or Whitesands in Pembrokeshire. Wind can mess up breaks, although this is as good an excuse as any to go kite-surfing instead. This younger sibling of windsurfing is hugely popular in west Anglesey, the Llyn Peninsula and Pembrokeshire.

Underwater, divers have started to realize the potential of the crisp seas off Wales. With its drift dives and drop-offs, dive partners like seals and conger eels in the shallows and the wreck of the *Lucy*, a 168-foot Dutch coaster, in the gloom 130ft down, Skomer Island marine reserve ranks in most top tens of British dive sites.

On dry land a growing number of bushcraft courses help release the inner Ray Mears of city-dwellers. Bikers have cast an eye over former coal valleys and managed forests to discover some of the best pedalling in Europe: places like Coed y Brenin in North Wales, whose black-grade single-track riding engages your mind as much as your muscles, or Cwmcarn Forest in the south, where even world champions come a cropper on an insane downhill toboggan run.

Such reinterpretation of an ancient landscape is what distinguishes contemporary Wales and its campsites. Camping and the Welsh outdoors were always well suited. But whereas once a campsite was just that, a new breed of sites see themselves as activities centres too; check out *fforestcamp* (see p.164) near Cardigan, *Llyn Gwynant* (see p.189) on the skirts of Snowdon or Anglesey's *Outdoor Alternative* (see p.199). So, is it goodbye to the old Wales of suburban-styled holiday parks, hello to Britain's emergent adventure playground? Here's hoping.

FIVE GREAT ADVENTUROUS SITES

 Cae Gwyn Friendly sheep farm that's bordered by the thrilling mountain-bike trails of Coed y Brenin. See p.192.

 Gwern Gôf Uchaf Popular with hikers and climbers, who pitch in Tryfan's shadow. See p.198.

 Hafod y Llan This simple, intimate site is ideally located for ascents of Snowdon. See p.188.

 Hillend Laid-back surfie place behind the Gower's most consistent break. See p.163.

 Trefalen Farm South Pembrokeshire's best climbing and surf are within minutes of this secluded site. See p.156.

◀ Coasteering near St David's, Pembrokeshire

Gwern Gôf Isaf & Gwern Gôf Uchaf

Wilderness without the wild

Tourists head to Snowdon, Sir Ranulph Fiennes wannabes point their compass towards Tryfan. Unlike its big sister with a railway to the summit, Tryfan's triple-peaked spur is a mountaineers' mountain – famously, it's the only hill in Wales that you can't climb without using your hands. Where Snowdon has well-trodden trails, this stone fin is ascended by a splendid scramble up its steep, fractured north face. Instead of a café at the top, you'll find Adam and Eve, two lava columns which, by tradition, every climber must leap between (and most intend to until faced with the almost sheer drop that plunges down one side of the summit).

That the mountain looms on one side and the rolling Carnedds, with summits of their own to bag, rise on the other is one reason why hikers head to these hill farms within a mile of each other in the Ogwen Valley. Another is that both are proper campers' sites that are as raw and elemental as their surroundings. Where you go depends on your taste. Larger *Gwern Gôf Isaf* to the east has parking beside tents and possibilities of hook-ups. It also has more facilities than its neighbour – five hot showers (buy tokens when you arrive), a communal drying

▼ *Gwern Gôf Isaf*, the larger of the two sites

room, two bunkhouses and a passable toilet quota, even if some require a torch at night – as well as charm and fresh eggs from the chickens that strut beneath the farmhouse.

Gwern Gôf Uchaf, snugged directly beneath Tryfan's chaotic jumble of rock, is the favourite of hardcore hikers and rock-huggers. For a start, it's superbly sited – the summit trail starts behind the farmhouse. Then there are facilities that take the wild out of wilderness: free showers, though fewer in number, are more modern than those of its neighbour, as is an excellent bunkhouse with a good kitchen. Wherever you go, you'll need a decent tent when the wind whips through the valley.

Such scenery begs you to lace up your hiking boots. Should you need encouragement, Plas-y-Brenin (The National Mountain Centre) leads outdoor activities, including rock climbing and canoeing. You'll find it, as well as the nearest pubs and supplies, in Capel Curig.

Practicalities

Gwern Gôf Isaf/Gwern Gôf Uchaf, Capel Curig, Betws-y-Coed, Conwy, LL24 0EU. Gwern Gôf Isaf: ☎*01690 720276,* Ⓦ*www.gwerngofisaf.co.uk. Gwern Gôf Uchaf:* ☎*01690 720294,* Ⓦ*www.tryfanwales.co.uk*

Pitches & price Both sites have around 50 grass pitches; *Gwern Gôf Isaf* has hook-ups available on request. Both £4 per adult (children 3–15 £3 at *Gwern Gôf Uchaf*); *Gwern Gôf Isaf* caravans £10.

Facilities Both have amenities blocks with showers and basins, toilets, washing-up area, drying/storage area, bunkhouse accommodation.

Restrictions Neither site allows dogs. Groups over 10 by arrangement.

Open Both sites: year round.

Getting there *Gwern Gôf Isaf* and *Gwern Gôf Uchaf* are both on the A5, 3 and 4 miles west of Capel Curig respectively. The Sherpa bus (#S6) from Caernafon via Bangor to Betws-y-Coed stops outside.

Outdoor Alternative

When outdoor enthusiasts in North Wales want to drop off the radar, they head to this laudably low-key site sited on the south tip of Holy Island. Though linked to Anglesey by a short bridge, it feels a world apart – the remote offshore island of a remote off-shore island, closer in looks to the west of Ireland than mainland Wales. This perhaps explains why it's a well-kept secret for sea kayaking, or climbing an intricate rocky coastline that ranks as the finest yet least visited scenery in the area. But with the circular Isle of Anglesey Coastal Path on its doorstep and sandcastles on lovely Borthwen Beach just a headland away, *Outdoor Alternative* is just as much a secret getaway for weekend walkers and families.

In the 25 years since Ian Wright set up his small, friendly site-cum-activities base located 100 yards from a pretty cove, his passion for this Area of Outstanding Natural Beauty remains, as do the site's eco-credentials and an intimacy that makes you feel like a guest of the family. Yet the facilities have moved on: sailing, climbing and orienteering are now on offer as well as the original kayaking lessons and rental, and Rhoscolyn's *White Eagle* (a twenty-minute walk) has gone from rural boozer to swanky gastropub.

Practicalities

Outdoor Alternative, Cerrig yr Adar, Rhoscolyn, Holyhead, Anglesey, LL65 2NQ ⓣ*0845 126 0609,* ⓦ*www.outdooralternative.co.uk*
Pitches & price 50 tent pitches. Adults in small tents or campervans £5 (£6 on bank holidays), children £2.50. Family tents £16–18 (£17–20). Caravans by request only £15 (£17).
Facilities Toilets with basins, showers, washing-up area.
Restrictions No campfires (though permitted in cove 200yds away) or stereos. Dogs permitted on leads.
Open Year round.
Getting there Turn off the A5 near Holyhead into Valley (Y Fali) and head towards Trearddur Bay. Once on Holy Island, go left towards Rhoscolyn. Take the first left signposted towards "Silver Bay", then take the right-hand track. The entrance is 200yds on the left. Bus #25 (Mon–Sat) goes to Rhoscolyn from Holyhead.

Conwy

North Wales isn't all OS maps and mountain pitches. Conwy's picturebook castle and Llandudno's seaside Victoriana help make *Conwy Touring Park* a family favourite – and one that couldn't be more different from the static-caravan suburbia that blights much of the north coast. Within walking distance of Conwy – a pretty stroll of a mile or so with views over a river estuary – its intimate leafy fields nudged into a hillside belie an eighty-acre resort-style commercial park. Rugged outdoor-types would probably hate it, but efficient management, generous pitches, heated amenities blocks with free showers and a launderette allow parents to have a holiday as much as their children, who are treated to two playgrounds, including an evening playbarn thoughtfully placed beside the site pub. No faulting the river valley views from the hill-top, either.

While the lack of an on-site shop niggles, Conwy is under two miles away, or a ten-minute drive south there's modern Welsh cuisine in the lovely *Groes Inn*. Keep going for twenty minutes and you'll reach Betws-y-Coed, Snowdonia's premier tourist resort – you don't want to be too far from the mountains, after all.

Practicalities

Conwy Touring Park, Trefriw Road, Conwy, LL32 8UX ⓣ*01492 592856,* ⓦ*www.conwytouringpark.co.uk*
Pitches & price 400 pitches (grass and hard-standing). Hook-ups available. All pitches £10–19 according to season; £2 supplement bank holidays and Fri/Sat in peak season.
Facilities Several amenities blocks with showers, toilets and basins, disabled facilities, dishwashing areas, laundrette and drying rooms. Playbarn and on-site bar.
Restrictions No single-sex groups. No young groups. No campfires. Dogs allowed on leads.
Open Easter–Sept.
Getting there Head to Conwy and turn left at Conwy Castle onto the B5106 towards Llanrwst. Continue 1.5 miles and the entrance is marked by a sign on the left. Bus #19 from Betws-y-Coed to Conwy passes the campsite entrance.

Northwest England

The Northwest may not have the obvious tourist appeal of its neighbours, bordered as it is by the mountains of Wales, the Peak District, the Yorkshire Dales and the Lakeland Fells, but that has its upside: those in the know can enjoy areas of outstanding scenery and cultural interest in relative peace and quiet.

South of Manchester, much of Cheshire is a vast plain fringed with hills, criss-crossed with canals and dotted with historic towns and old-fashioned country pubs. Further north, the historic urban landscape of the Lancashire weaving towns gives way to some of England's finest countryside, notably the green hills and dark moors of the Forest of Bowland and stunning, wild Morecambe Bay.

Locals will tell you, with some justification, that the landscape of the Isle of Man is a microcosm of Britain, from the wild mountains in the north to the relaxed sandy beaches of the south. Its late Victorian heyday has long passed, so visit outside late May, when the island is crammed with motorbike fanatics here for the TT races, and you're likely to get an entire campsite to yourself, even on a bank holiday weekend.

For campers, the region's charm is generally in the quiet, hilly areas, which will tempt walkers, cyclists and anyone who likes to sit and absorb the variety of the British countryside. Our selection takes in pub campsites, family-friendly farms, eighteenth-century camping barns and simple, secluded hill-top gems. Facilities tend to be good quality, and thanks to the proximity of some of Britain's biggest cities, getting around is easy.

Isle of Man inset:

A10
Ramsey
A3
Kirk Michael
Cronk Aashen
A14
ISLE OF MAN
A4
A18
A2
Peel
A3
Ballacottier
A1
Onchan
Douglas
A3
A5
Port Erin
A25
Castletown

Main map labels:

Gibraltar Farm
B5282
A6070
A6
A65
A687
B6480
LAKE DISTRICT
NATIONAL PARK
Morecambe
A5105
A683
Lancaster
Dolphinholme
B6478
A65
A59
Crawshaw Farm
A682
A588
B5272
Garstang
Highgate Barn
Edisford Bridge Farm
A59
Clitheroe
Colne
Keighley
A584
A586
A6
B6243
Wyreside Farm
M6
Middle Beardshaw
A6068
Blackpool
A585
M55
L A N C A S H I R E
M65
Bradfo
A583
Burnley
A59
A584
Preston
A675
Blackburn
Accrington
Halifax
A6177
A646
Leyland
A674
A675
A666
A681
Huddersf
Southport
A565
A581
Charity Farm
Chorley
A676
A58
B5250
A49
Rochdale
Ormskirk
A570
A59
A5209
M6
Bolton
Bury
M66
M62
Formby
Skelmersdale
Wigan
M61
Oldham
A565
Crosby
M58
A570
A571
Leigh
A580
A62
Ashton-
under-Lyne
A628
Kirkby
A580
A573
Salford
PEAK DIST
Bootle
M57
St Helens
M60
NATIONAL P
Wallasey
A57
A6144
Manchester
A553
Liverpool
M62
Warrington
Altrincham
Stockport
Birkenhead
A561
Widnes
A56
M56
A561
Runcorn
M6
Wilmslow
A523
M53
A559
A537
A6
B5470
A5004
Ellesmere
Port
A533
Northwich
A34
Macclesfield
*Common
Barn Farm*
Buxton
M56
A56
A49
A536
A54
A50
A54
Chester
A54
Middlewich
Wild Boar Inn
A53
Birch Bank Farm
A533
Congleton
A34
A523
A55
C H E S H I R E
A534
A523
The Shady Oak
A51
A530
A534
Crewe
A534
Nantwich
Stoke-
on-Trent
The Cotton Arms
A41
A49
A530
A51
Newcastle-
under-Lyme
A525
A529

Northwest England

	PAGE	(walking)	(cycling)	(sailing)	(drink)	(mountains)	(family)	(groups)	(caravan)	(coach)	(accessible)
Ballacottier	215								✓		
Birch Bank Farm	205						✓		✓		
Charity Farm	207				✓				✓		
Common Barn Farm	206	✓	✓			✓			✓		
The Cotton Arms	204						✓		✓	✓	
Crawshaw Farm	211	✓	✓			✓					
Cronk Aashen	216	✓		✓			✓		✓		
Dolphinholme	214					✓	✓				
Edisford Bridge Farm	210						✓		✓	✓	✓
Gibraltar Farm	212							✓		✓	
Highgate Barn	215					✓			✓		
Middle Beardshaw	208	✓				✓		✓			
The Shady Oak	204	✓					✓		✓		
Wild Boar Inn	207	✓			✓				✓		
Wyreside Farm	210					✓			✓	✓	

See front flap for key to symbols

The Cotton Arms

There's no big rule book at this laid-back place, just behind a village pub in the heart of Cheshire's historic salt-mining region. It's popular with families and dog-owners and makes a decent weekend getaway or stop-over on a longer trip. There's a large camping field and a rally field, which is regularly used by caravan and bike clubs and can get a bit busy in the summer, but as long as you're not looking for peace and quiet, this is all part of the fun. You'll see bikers, caravanners and campers socializing in the pub, kids shouting and larking about in dinghies on the Llangollen canal, which runs along the edge of the site, and parents trying their hand on the bowling green.

The friendly pub itself sells simple, fresh food all day at reasonable prices, including a good selection of vegetarian meals. The area is pleasant for outdoor activities: canal boats can be rented just round the corner from *The Cotton Arms*, and the southern end of the Sandstone Trail starts nearby. For a more leisurely weekend stroll, there's lots of easy walking along footpaths or by the canal.

Practicalities

The Cotton Arms, Cholmondeley Road, Wrenbury, Cheshire, CW5 8HG ☎01270 780377, Ⓦwww.cottonarms.co.uk

Pitches & price 60-plus tent pitches, 15 caravan pitches with hook-ups, some of which are hard-standing. £8 per small tent, £10 per large tent, £14 per caravan with hook-up.

Facilities 1 shower and outside toilet, pub toilets available during day. Outside washing-up sink. Wi-fi available in pub.

Restrictions Dogs welcome (free). No campfires or barbecues permitted.

Open Year round.

Getting there The pub is on the main road just beyond Wrenbury, which is signposted from the A530. There's a train station just over a mile away in Wrenbury itself, but note that it's a request stop.

The Shady Oak

The area around *The Shady Oak* is prime walking country, and this pub campsite is conveniently located right in the middle of the Sandstone Trail, a two-day hike through some of Cheshire's most beautiful stretches that takes in dramatic escarpments, ancient woodland and historic villages. Guests camp in a field that slopes gently down to the Shropshire Union Canal. From the lower end of the field, there's an excellent view of Beeston Castle, a ruined medieval stronghold used in campaigns against the Welsh that sits, precariously balanced, on a sandstone crag.

The easy six-hour trip along the Sandstone Trail to the castle and back makes a great day out; while there's no café, it's a great spot for picnics. Less active visitors have the option of sitting outside the pub, sipping a local ale, and eating some of the fairly ordinary but reasonably priced pub food, while kids will enjoy the bouncy castle that the owners set up during the summer. *The Shady Oak* is a family-friendly place, but this is a pub: at weekends, the merriment can continue until late, and there's no particular curfew time.

Practicalities

The Shady Oak, Bate's Mill Lane, Tiverton, Tarporley, Cheshire, CW6 9UE ☎01829 730718, Ⓦwww.shadyoak.co.uk

Pitches & price Space for 12 tents (£8 per pitch) and 12 caravans (£12). 10 pitches are hard-standing, and there are 20 hook-ups (£2 extra).

Facilities 1 basic but clean shower block with 2 toilets and 1 shower. Sandpit, swings and slide.

Restrictions Dogs (free) allowed on leads. Fires must be raised off the ground.

Open Year round. Campers should arrive/depart by 8pm.

Getting there Look for the turning for Tiverton off the A49. The pub is on Bate's Mill Lane, the first proper left after the village. The nearest train station is in Chester, 11 miles away; you'll need to take a taxi from there.

Birch Bank Farm
Urban and rural adventure near Chester

A quiet, tree-lined country road winds its way up to this mellow site, which is part of a small working cattle farm. The grassy, flat camping field is surrounded by trees, with a tidy outdoor washing-up area and a clean toilet block converted from an old outhouse. Overlooking the field, the traditional red-brick Cheshire farmhouse has been in the family since it was built in the mid-nineteenth century, and the owner enjoys chatting about the area. *Birch Bank* is perfect for kids – it's safe, rural and relaxed, but is only three miles from the fascinating city of Chester, which has a good number of interesting, independent shops and was one of the most important settlements in Roman Britain.

The Dewa Roman Experience (Ⓦwww.dewaromanexperience. co.uk), near the remarkably intact medieval city wall, is aimed at children; the patrol around the town in the company of a soldier is a lot of fun. Adults who want a more in-depth look at Chester's history will enjoy the small, quirky Grosvenor Museum (Ⓦwww.

grosvenormuseum.co.uk) just up the road. Exhibits range from a fascinating collection of Roman tombstones to an old-fashioned natural history display of slightly tatty Victorian taxidermy.

There's plenty of good walking in all directions from the farm along footpaths and tranquil country lanes. The "Roman Bridge" near Tarvin is a popular local beauty spot, good for picnics and paddling. The village of Christleton, about fifteen minutes' walk away, has a large pond, a canal, an interesting old church and two pubs which both serve good food.

For rainy days, a popular family trip near the farm is the Cheshire Candle Workshop, in the village of Burwardsley, but if there's one thing kids will remember, it's the Crocky Trail adventure playground (Ⓦwww.crockytrail.co.uk), a few miles east of Chester. There's a cafe for wary parents to sit and watch, although you might be tempted try the gloriously madcap contraptions: look out for the Titanic, a huge platform that appears designed specifically to throw happily squealing victims into the mud.

Practicalities

Birch Bank Farm Caravan & Campsite, Stamford Lane, Chrisleton, Chester, Cheshire, CH3 7QD ☎*01244 335233,* Ⓦ*www.birchbankfarm.co.uk*

Pitches & price 14 pitches, 8 of which have hook-ups. No hard-standing pitches. £5 per pitch (£2.50 for small tents), plus £3 per person.

Facilities Toilet block with 1 shower and toilet each for men and women. Hot water can run out at busy times.

Restrictions Dogs welcome (free). No campfires.

Open Mid–April to mid–Oct. Arrival and departure preferred around midday during busy periods.

Getting there From M53/A55 junction follow the A51 towards Nantwich. Take the second right into Stamford Lane, turn into the second farm on the left. Via public transport, take a train or bus to Chester then a taxi, though you can walk in 40min along the canal. If visiting Chester, use the park-and-ride at the A41/A5115 junction – city-centre parking fees are extortionate.

▼ *Birch Bank* is a working farm

Common Barn Farm

A peaceful panorama above the Cheshire Plain

There's plenty of activities within close reach of this working sheep farm, but you're likely to spend much of your time quietly gazing at the view. If you pitch your tent high in the field above the farmhouse, and look down 1200ft across green pastures to the Cheshire plain, you can see Jodrell Bank's massive white radio telescope gleaming in the sun and the hazy Welsh mountains on the horizon. You might also bump into the radio hams who make use of the farm's elevated position and friendly welcome to erect an 80ft aerial which they use in international morse-code competitions.

Most people, though, come here for the outdoor activities.

▼ The view from Shining Tor, Cheshire's highest point

There's lots of hiking: an energetic ten-mile round trip will take you up to Shining Tor, the highest point in Cheshire. The quiet, hilly roads provide a fun challenge for cyclists, and Chester is a full day's ride away via the nearby Cheshire Cycle Way. There's also a sailing club and fly fishing at nearby Errwood Reservoir – site owner Rona Cooper can arrange day membership.

If, after a day's activity, you fancy a pint or are tired of baked beans on a stove, you might want to try dishes like the beautifully presented Buxton monkfish with herb ricotta gnocchi at *The Highwayman*, less than twenty minutes' walk from the site. If cheap but decent pub grub is more your scene, *The Rising Sun* is another excellent nearby choice.

The site is primarily a rural B&B, and the camping facilities are as basic as they come: cold water, and a field or two to pitch in. Campers are given access to the toilet in a small café, where Cooper serves home-cooked cafe food (including delicious fried breakfasts), and can sometimes supply eggs and milk. You're given pretty much a free run of the farm to pick a pitch, but the atmosphere is tidy and quiet, and most guests keep it that way.

Practicalities

Common Barn Farm, Smith Lane, Rainow, Macclesfield, Cheshire, SK10 5XJ ☎01625 574878, Ⓦwww.cottages-with-a-view.co.uk

Pitches & price 5 tent or caravan pitches in field, 3 hard-standing pitches in yard (with no view). £3.50 per person per night, £5 deposit. B&B from £65 per night.

Facilities Cold-water tap, toilet in café.

Restrictions No dogs. Campfires must be raised.

Open Year round. Arrive before 8pm.

Getting there On the B5470 from Macclesfield, take the second right after Rainow village down Smith Lane. The farm is signposted from here. The nearest train station is Macclesfield, 5 miles away, from where you can get a taxi or a bus – the latter run twice a day to Whaley Bridge, just past the farm.

Wild Boar Inn

The routine at the *Wild Boar Inn* is well established with its many regulars: pitch your tent on Saturday morning, go for a gentle ramble in the hills, return for a nut-brown pint of ale and fresh home-made food in the evening, watch a local band while sinking a few more, stumble to your tent at midnight, and wake up the following morning to a fabulous landscape of green hills unfolding to the horizon. It's crowded during peak season, so if you want to reserve a spot with a view, arrive early.

Among the hills and reservoirs of the Peak District are plenty of places to tour by car, including the towns of Buxton and Bakewell and stately Chatsworth House. There's also good angling in the area and, every other Sunday, supervised clay-pigeon shooting across the road, which the owners can help arrange. The moorland provides a valuable habitat for all kinds of wildlife; at The Roaches, a nearby ridge popular with climbers, you might see peregrine falcons, and if you're lucky, a descendant of the five wallabies released from a nearby private zoo in the 1930s.

Practicalities

The Wild Boar Inn, Wincle, nr Macclesfield, Cheshire, SK11 0QL ☎01260 227219, Ⓦwww.thewildboar.co.uk
Pitches & price 23 tent pitches, 5 caravan pitches, of which 4 are hard-standing with hook-ups. £5 per adult, £2.50 per child. £1 surcharge per person in high season (Jun–Aug).
Facilities Simple but well-kept shower block with 2 showers (£1 coin needed), 4 toilets (only 1 for men!).
Restrictions Dogs allowed (£1). No campfires (raised barbecues permitted).
Open Year round. Pub open Mon–Fri evenings-only, Sun & Sun all day.
Getting there Travelling on the A54, it's the whitewashed building on the right (from Buxton) or left (from Congleton) – it's about 9 miles from each. The nearest train station is in Macclesfield; the pub's well known to taxis, and the fare should be about £12.

Charity Farm

This former dairy farm is in a beautiful, little-known corner of rural Lancashire, not far from Wigan. It's now an expansive campsite, with a well-provisioned caravan area and several large camping fields, all neatly laid out with numbered pitches. The site is centred around three landscaped fishing ponds that cascade down the hillside. They're stocked with several varieties of carp, bream, tench and roach, attracting anglers keen to spend lazy days in picturesque surroundings. For non-anglers, the main attraction is the tangle of footpaths and lanes that meander through meadows and hedgerows, past a variety of friendly country pubs that offer quality food – ask at reception for a rambler's map of the area (£2).

The Mulberry Tree in Wrightington has a particularly inventive menu that showcases local food, including a delicious twice-baked Lancashire cheese soufflé. Martin Mere (Ⓦwww.wwt.org.uk), twenty minutes' drive to the west, is an internationally important wetlands centre. If you're here in autumn, try to pay a visit – you might be lucky enough to witness the awesome sight of 10,000-odd pink-footed geese flying in at dusk.

Practicalities

Charity Farm Caravanning & Camping, Toogood Lane, Wrightington, Lancashire, WN6 9PP ☎01257 451326, Ⓦwww.charityfarm.co.uk
Pitches & price 60 tent pitches, 38 pitches with hook-ups (mostly hard-standing). £10 per 2-person tent, £15 per caravan.
Facilities Reasonable shower block with 8 toilets, wash basins. Canteen with microwave and washing-up area. Disabled toilet with baby-changing. Fishing £6 per day.
Restrictions Dogs allowed on leads (free). No fires.
Open Year round.
Getting there From M6 junction 27, take the A5209 to Ormskirk. Take the second right into Moss Lane just after the church, then first right into Courage Low Land. The farm is on the left after 2 right turns. By public transport, take a train to Appley Bridge from Manchester, then a taxi (01257 401548).

Middle Beardshaw Head
History and culture in the South Pennines

This restored period farmhouse, a mile outside Trawden village in the heart of Brontë country, is a happy blend of campsite, B&B and camping barn. The small camping field has views across the narrow valley, four flat spaces for tents and a rocky outcrop at its top corner where you can build a fire.

It's a decent spot, but what makes *Middle Beardshaw Head* shine is its atmospheric eighteenth-century barn, set just below the camping field. It's been lovingly restored, with a medieval-style gallery, whitewashed stone walls and a wood-burning stove. The attached conservatory has darts and table tennis, and dotted around the building are quirky details including a gargoyle, a stag's head and a Romanesque bust that reflect the owner's interest in historical and architectural detail. If you want

to see more, ask to look inside the B&B, whose dining room is home to a full suit of armour and an assortment of old weapons. In the evening, you can relax by the fire and chat to other guests over pots of pasta before pulling out the barn's foam mattresses at bedtime.

The site overlooks a small valley, with a footpath down to the village of Trawden, fifteen minutes' away, where you'll find two pubs and a post office that sells a very small selection of groceries. The surrounding moorland – a sea of green, brown and golden grassland with lumpy islands of dark millstone grit – offers great walking and is the perfect breeding ground for upland birds such as red grouse, twite and golden plover. It's possible to walk part of the Brontë Way to the village of

Practicalities

Middle Beardshaw Head Farm, Burnley Road, Trawden, Colne, Lancashire, BB8 8PP ☎01282 865257

Pitches & price Normally 5 tent pitches, although the site can accommodate up to 20 on request (£5–£7.50 per tent depending on size). The barn sleeps over 20 people at £7.50 per person. It's often rented to groups; phone ahead to check if there's space.

Facilities 2 toilets, 2 showers. Kitchen with microwave, gas, 2 fridges. Pizza oven in garden (wood available).

Restrictions Dogs allowed on leads (phone ahead to check; free). Quiet after 11pm. Campfires permitted (check with owner).

Open Year round.

Getting there From the A6068, just northeast of Burnley, take the B6250 to Trawden. Pass the church on your left, and continue uphill along the narrow lane (Burnley Rd). *Middle Beardshaw Head* is on the right shortly after a sharp right turn near the top of the hill. By public transport, take a train to Colne, then catch a taxi (£5), or take a bus to Trawden and walk 10min up the hill.

Haworth and back in a day, and visit the vicarage where the famous siblings spent their childhood.

A less well-known but equally absorbing Brontë connection can be found just down the road in the tiny conservation village of Wycoller, where you will find a ruined (and, of course, haunted) hall said to be the basis for Ferndean Manor in *Jane Eyre*. There's also a visitor centre in an ancient wooden framed barn, and a unique sequence of foot bridges across the stream – the oldest is at least a thousand years old.

◀ *Middle Beardshaw Head* has good views and history aplenty ▶ One of Wycoller's ancient bridges; the idiosyncratic B&B interior

Edisford Bridge Farm

Edisford Bridge Farm has perhaps the nicest showers of any campsite in the Northwest. Indeed, the whole place is well-designed and carefully maintained, its pristine, well drained field set on a raised site above the Ribble, with fine views of the surrounding hills, including the mysterious, hunched profile of Pendle Hill (1827ft), which has links to both the Quakers and witchcraft.

The bridge itself is a three-minute walk, past the (average) *Edisford Bridge* pub and down a steep hill. The riverside is a popular picnic spot for families in the summer: the waters are shallow and glassy, and there's a small play park where a miniature steam railway runs in the summer months.

There's plenty more to do in the area, with lots of historic interest. The market town of Clitheroe is ten minutes' walk away (just past a spa and swimming pool), and a lovely stroll downriver will take you to the medieval church at Great Mitton. The gentle countryside is great for a wander in any direction, and is said to have been the inspiration for Tolkien's Middle-earth.

Practicalities

Edisford Bridge Farm, Clitheroe, Lancashire, BB7 3LJ
℡*01200 427868,*
Ⓦ*www.edisfordbridgecaravanandcamping.co.uk*
Pitches & price 6–10 tent pitches, from £10 per 2-person tent. 20 caravan pitches (13 of them hard-standing), £12 with hook-ups
Facilities Marvellous heated toilet block with 6 showers. Disabled toilet, good access to pitches.
Restrictions Dogs allowed on leads. No campfires. No noise after 11pm.
Open March–Jan.
Getting there From Clitheroe, follow signs to B6243 (signposted Longridge). Just outside Clitheroe, the road crosses a bridge and climbs the other bank. The campsite is just off the first road right after the pub. By public transport, take a train to Clitheroe; you'll pay about £3 for a taxi to the site.

Wyreside Farm

This neat campsite, next to an old, thatched farmhouse near the Lancashire town of Garstang, has an English-country-garden atmosphere. Chickens scuttle hopefully after guests and butterflies float between wild and cultivated flowers, while you'll see bats at dusk. There's some patches of old woodland around the camping field, and just through a gate are the banks of the River Wyre, where children love to splash around and build sandcastles.

Most people come to enjoy a relaxing, rural atmosphere in a location conveniently near Blackpool, Preston and the M6. The owner has local Ordnance Survey maps you can borrow – there are charming walks along the river in both directions – and a pile of leaflets covering all the local attractions. Football fanatics will want to visit the National Football Museum in Preston, which displays the 1966 Jules Rimet trophy and the ball from the first World Cup. If you don't fancy eating on site at *Wyreside Farm*, there's a decent bistro, *The Weird Fish*, just up the road.

Practicalities

Wyreside Farm Park, St Michael's-On-Wyre, Garstang, Lancashire, PR3 0TZ ℡*01995 679797,*
Ⓔ*penny.wyresidefarm@freenet.co.uk*
Pitches & price 1 camping field, with statics at one end. 10 caravan and tent pitches, with hook-ups available. 2 people with one tent or caravan £16, £5 per extra adult.
Facilities Shower block with 2 toilets and 2 showers, plug socket. No dish-washing facilities; hot water and bowl available on request.
Restrictions Dogs £1 per night (check first). Phone ahead for security gate code if arriving late.
Open March–Oct.
Getting there St Michael's is on the A586. Look out for a small lane on the river side of the road, with a large street sign announcing Allotment Lane. There are buses direct to St Michael's from Preston or Lancaster.

Crawshaw Farm

Back to basics at Britain's centre

Crawshaw Farm is camping at its simplest: one slightly lumpy field, two taps and a toilet, set in glorious isolation on a hillside above the quiet, wooded Hodder Valley. But with surroundings like this, doing the laundry or playing pool are likely to be low on your agenda. There's room for just five tents or caravans, and you might have trouble finding a flat pitch (the best spot is on the near right as you enter, by the stile). The dark heather moorland of the Bowland Fells looms dramatically above, and a network of fields, coppices and dry-stone walls connects the stone-built farms and villages strung along the valley bottom.

Most people come to walk the grandeur of the hill-tops, but the area has some equally good road cycling: the winding lanes, enclosed by mossy walls and woods, reward you with frequent, unexpected panoramas. This is the only campsite in Dunsop Bridge, declared by the Ordnance Survey as the geographical centre of Great Britain, which makes it a popular stop-over with people making the journey from John O'Groats to Land's End – the spot is marked by a plaque and a commemorative phone box.

The fells all around offer some moderately challenging hiking, and host a wide variety of bird species, from grouse to short-eared owls; ninety percent of the English breeding population of peregrine falcons live in this area. Lower down the slopes, the hour-long circular ramble to Slaidburn is also rewarding. It's a charming village of old, golden-grey cottages, huddled intimately over cobbled pavements. There's an excellent café by the River Hodder that overlooks the village green, and a decent pub for those more inclined to a pint of ale. The nearest pub to the camp-site, the *Parkers Arms* in Newton, is a better (if pricier) bet for food: the menu is a gastronomic tour of the area, with classics like Bowland sausages and Lancashire hotpot.

▼ *Crawshaw Farm* is right on the edge of the Bowland Fells

Practicalities

Crawshaw Farm Caravan & Campsite, Back Lane, Newton-in-Bowland, Clitheroe, Lancashire, BB7 3EE
☎*01200 446638*

Pitches & price 5 pitches (no hook-ups). £5 per tent.
Facilities No showers, 1 toilet. Spring-fed cold-water taps for washing.
Restrictions Dogs welcome (free) but must be kept on leads. No campfires. No young groups unless DofE.
Open Year round.
Getting there Newton village is on the B6478, 7 miles north of Clitheroe. The farm is about a mile up a steep lane signposted "Quiet Lane" just at the west edge of the village. There is a Camping & Caravanning Club sign outside the entrance; satnav takes you to a neighbouring farm. By public transport, take a train to Settle or Clitheroe and jump on the B10 bus which travels between them, getting off at the village of Newton. Walk the final 0.5 miles up the hill.

Gibraltar Farm
Spectacular sunsets and unique wildlife

A working dairy farm presides over this substantial, friendly camping and caravan site, which unfolds across several fields all the way down to the sea and boasts wide views across the sands of Morecambe Bay. The gentle hills and tree-fringed wetlands are an official Area of Natural Beauty, and the geology – a limestone pavement covered with thin soil – provides a unique habitat for an assortment of rare wildflowers and butterflies.

Keen spotters might see dropwort or rock roses, but will be lucky to find the rarest flower in Britain, the lady's slipper orchid, which flowers in several secret spots in the area; one publicly advertised lady's slipper location attracted around a thousand visitors a year until it was stolen by professional flower thieves in 2004. There are also huge areas of reed beds in the region which attract birders keen to spot marsh-dwellers such as bitterns and ospreys. Leighton Moss RSPB, equipped with hides and a good visitor centre, is within walking distance.

Yet much of this natural beauty can be found right outside your tent. The site has room for caravans higher up the hill, and a flat, well-mown camping field nearer the shore. One side is bordered by ancient woodland, dotted with small limestone outcrops, and draped with wild garlic during the spring. Children love playing here, climbing on the rocks and hiding in small caves. A glade surrounded by trees and rocks is rented out by private groups, including regular pagan visitors who hold ceremonies here. Diligent explorers might find a small stone circle, built a few years ago by the warden under the watchful supervision of a pagan high priest.

Morecambe Bay itself can be accessed through the wood, but you shouldn't set foot on the dangerous sands without careful research into tides and safety. A better idea is to stroll along the cliff-tops – going south takes you through a nature reserve to a viewpoint called Giant's Seat, and the route north will take you between boulders and hawthorn to Silverdale village, where there are a couple of average pubs.

A good choice for lunch is the *Wolfhouse Gallery* (ⓦwww.wolfhouse-gallery.co.uk), opposite the farm, where you can eat excellent café food and browse through a fine collection of local craftwork. Wherever you go for the day, time your return so you can watch the vast sky slowly turn red and orange, reflected in a

Practicalities

Gibraltar Farm Caravan & Campsite, Silverdale, Lancashire, LA5 0UA ☎01524 701736, Ⓦwww.gibraltarfarm.co.uk

Pitches & price 80 tent pitches in dedicated camping field, £5–£15 based on size. 50 caravan pitches, £14 with hook-ups. Wooded area for private parties from £100. Separate meadow for rallies.

Facilities 1 basic shower block with toilets, hot water, 3 showers (2 of them for women). Outside dish-washing area. Disabled toilet.

Restrictions Dogs allowed on leads (free). No campfires. Music off and noise down after 11pm. No bookings accepted from under-21s. Groups welcome.

Open April–Oct.

Getting there From the A6 at Carnforth, follow signs up the B5282 to Silverdale and Armside. Hollins Lane is on the left, after a level crossing and a sharp left bend, before the village of Silverdale – the campsite is signposted. Trains to Silverdale connect via Lancaster, Manchester, Liverpool and Barrow, and are met by a shuttle bus Mon–Sat that goes right past the campsite.

flat expanse of sand and water, in one of the most extraordinary sunsets in the country. All around, you'll see trees that have been bent almost double by the fierce wind that blows over the Irish Sea – so when you pitch your tent, choose a sheltered spot and carefully guy it out.

The place is deservedly popular with families and groups – not just pagans, but bikers, young DofE expeditioners and caravan rallies – so it's a shame there's only one shower and toilet block. Still, the showers are free, and there's plenty of hot water all day, so you can always plan your washing time around the morning rush.

◀ The rare lady's slipper orchid ▶ Sunset over Morecambe Bay; bird-watchers scan the marshes at Leighton Moss RSPB

Dolphinholme
Straw castles and goat-milking in a farmyard paradise

This luxury camping environment, in a working goat farm, is the perfect outdoors getaway for families. Grown-ups will love acting out a rustic idyll in one of the farmhouse-styled pre-erected Wendy houses – large, wooden-floored, metal-framed tents, containing a living area, two bedrooms and a quirky sleep-in cupboard. They're full of carefully chosen details: a wood-burning stove, chipped enamel cooking pots, old tea caddies, paraffin lighting and a candelabra hanging over a handmade table.

It's for children that this Lancashire outpost of the Featherdown Farms empire really shines, though. ("This is the greatest holiday ever," says one excited entry in the guest book, "and I want to work here when I'm older.") The seven tents overlook a large field that's good for running around or messing about with a football, and a small river at the bottom is suitable for swimming.

The owners have taken care to provide lots of other entertainment, including a play barn decked out with a straw-bale castle, a slide and a tractor-tyre swing. Little ones are encouraged to play with goat kids, and can watch goats being milked, while inquisitive chickens race around a large pen – children enjoy getting up early to try to collect their free quota of three eggs per day.

Outside the farm, there's excellent walking in the Forest of Bowland. Bikes are available to rent – the nearest village, Scorton, is a pleasant day-trip. For dinner, there's little reason to leave the site. A well-stocked honesty shop (open 24 hours a day) provides locally sourced food, including cheese from the farm. If you can't be bothered preparing dinner yourself, there's also a small selection of fresh, gourmet ready-meals from nearby Bashall Barn in the freezer. If dinner cooked on a wood-burning stove under candlelight doesn't appeal, the nearest pub, *The Fleece*, is a mile away and serves good food and cask ales.

▼ Children can play with the farm's goat kids

Practicalities

Dolphinholme House Farm, Wagon Road, Dolphinholme, Lancaster, Lancashire, LA2 9DJ ☎01524 791469, Ⓦwww.featherdownfarm.co.uk

Pitches & price 7 tents sleeping 5 (6 at a push). Weekend price £245–£545 depending on season.
Facilities Decent block with 3 showers. Washing machine. Each tent has mains water (cold only), flushing toilet, cooking equipment and cutlery, 3 "bedrooms" (1 double, 1 bunk bed, 1 small children's double), dining table and chairs, cold box. Laundry & towels provided.
Restrictions Tidy fires allowed. Dogs welcome (free).
Open Easter–Oct (June's the quietest summer month).
Getting there From M6 junction 33, take the A6 signposted Garstang, and immediately take the next left onto Hampson Lane. Take the first right, then left at the second crossroads to Dolphinholme. Turn left into Dolphinholme and then right down the hill – the farm is on the left up the other side of the valley. The nearest train station is Lancaster – a taxi is about £12.

Highgate Barn

Drive into an orchard of young pine trees on a hot summer's day, pitch your tent on the immaculate grass, open a bottle of wine, and you could be in a grove in the Med. In fact, Highgate Barn is in a lowland area north of Blackpool called Over Wyre that was once notorious as a "swampy bog". In the 1800s the area was reclaimed, and now the landscape around the pretty local village of Pilling looks remarkably like a Dutch polder, complete with windmill.

The marshes are a magnet for birders, but when the weather's good, most visitors choose to enjoy the atmosphere (and the trampoline, climbing frame and picnic tables) on site, or fish in the small, well-stocked pond. Many stay in the orchard in the evening and barbecue local sausages from the butcher's in nearby Hambleton; otherwise, there are a couple of reasonable pubs within walking distance. There's less local appeal when it's raining, though lively Blackpool, with its rollercoasters, aquarium (Ⓦwww.sealifeeurope.com) and slot machines, is only half-an-hour's drive away.

Practicalities

Highgate Barn, Highgate Lane, Stalmine, Poulton-le-Fylde, Lancashire, FY6 0JF Ⓣ*01253 702510,* Ⓔ*webster@stalmine.net*

Pitches & price 5 tent pitches among the trees, £12 for a family of 4. 9 caravan pitches (6 hard-standing) with hook-ups, £15 per unit.

Facilities Excellent shower block with 2 loos, 2 showers, free hot water. Fishing pond (free).

Restrictions Strictly quiet after 10pm. No large groups. Dogs (free) welcome on leads. Raised fires allowed.

Open All year.

Getting there Take A585 from junction 3 of the M55. Before Blackpool, turn right onto the A588, signposted Pilling. Go through Hambleton and take the second left after the *Sunset Park* caravan site onto Staynall Lane. Highgate Lane is the first right. The nearest train station is Poulton; buses to Highgate Lane run from here.

Ballacottier

As you make your way up the drive to the stately, crumbling, nineteenth-century farmhouse at *Ballacottier*, you'll be greeted by a clucking crowd of chickens. Owners Hilary and Bob Kewley have no idea how many there are in the flock: they went feral years ago and now roost in the trees that surround the camping field. If you're lucky, you might find an egg in the bushes. Such low-key eccentricity is typical of this fun site, located amongst reservoirs and woodland in the foothills of the Manx highlands. The facilities have seen better days, but the welcome here is genuine: the Kewleys love chatting to folk, and will go out of their way to help.

Ballacotier is a good base for exploring the atmospheric upland interior of the island, and is only three miles outside the capital, Douglas. The Manx Museum, on Kingswood Grove near the town centre, gives you a great overview of the island's varied history and proudly independent culture. Outside, a curious collection of Victorian attractions, including the world's oldest surviving horse-tram service and the Great Union Camera Obscura, serve as a reminder of Douglas's past glories as a major tourist destination.

Practicalities

Ballacottier Campsite, Ballacottier Road, Onchan, Isle of Man, IM4 5BQ Ⓣ*01624 675 687,* Ⓔ*ballacottiercampsite@manx.net*

Pitches & price 100 tent pitches (only busy during the TT races), 5 small caravan pitches. No hook-ups, but a cable can be run from the house. £4.50 per person.

Facilities Oldish, clean shower/toilet block with 5 showers, 8 toilets, utility room. Owners can arrange lifts, laundry etc.

Restrictions Dogs (free) and groups welcome. Safe fires allowed – ask at the farmhouse.

Open Year round.

Getting there Take the A18 out of Douglas. Ballacottier Road is the first right after leaving Onchan. The entrance to the farm is 0.5 miles further on the left, in some trees – ignore satnav instructions. Phone ahead to get a taxi to meet you off the ferry/plane.

Cronk Aashen
Coastal Manx culture near Sunset City

The Isle of Man's unique identity and intriguing history have been shaped by its position in the middle of the Irish Sea, which both tempted and held back the English, Irish, Scots and Vikings. The sea also guarantees wonderful views from most points on the island, and *Cronk Aashen*, a short drive inland from the west coast, is one of the best campsites from which to enjoy them. The hills of the Mull of Galloway in Scotland are clearly visible on the horizon across the sea, and on a sufficiently clear day, the sun sets in truly spectacular fashion. The locals are justly proud of the wonderful skies: they have christened Peel, seven miles away, "Sunset City".

Glynne Shearman, the owner of this small site, takes pride in

maintaining her former farm as a quiet, family-friendly place. It's laid out across a hillside that includes a private, wooded glen, and the pitches are spread all over the property. The best views are from a platform at the top of the farm, with six hard-standings. There's a tree-lined camping paddock down the hill, which is on a slight slope – the flattest spots are around the edges of the field. The fantastic facilities are in a small converted outhouse near the farmhouse. There's a big gas hob, two fridges, a microwave, a toaster, and various cooking dishes and utensils. There's even an eating area, equipped with books and leaflets, which makes for a snug hideaway on a rainy evening.

The coastline nearby is endlessly fascinating, with cliff-top paths that wind up and down between sandy beaches and rock pools. In the towns at the far south end of the island, you can find scuba diving, basking shark trips, coasteering and sea kay-aking – check out Ⓦwww.isleofman.com/tourism and Ⓦwww.gov.im/tourism. There's wonderful walking in every direc-tion, and because the sea is never more than seven miles away, it's hard to get lost. There's a particularly attractive stretch of coastline around Nyabil, south of Peel, where you can find a row of picturesque thatched fishing cottages tucked into a tiny cove. For more vigorous walkers, a coastal path stretches right around the island and is well worth the week's trek. You can camp all the way around, with the exception of the stretch north of *Cronk Aashen* – and Shearman is happy to pick hikers up after a day's walk and drop them off in the same place the next morning.

There's also plenty of culture and history in the area. A thirty-minute walk downhill from *Cronk Aashen*, the church in Kirk Michael (also home to the nearest pub, and an expensive con-venience store) has the best collection of Norse crosses on the island. They're an intriguing legacy of the island's Viking past, covered in intricate Celtic designs and scenes of Jesus sharing the stage with a variety of pagan deities.

Peel, one of the most interesting towns on the island, has a decent museum, and St Patrick's Isle, across a short causeway, is home to a clutch of ruined buildings including the old cathe-dral. It's also a good place to sample the seafood-focused Manx cuisine. Look out for queenies (scallops) and crab sandwiches

Practicalities

Cronk Aashen Farm Campsite, Barregarroo Crossroads, Kirk Michael, Isle of Man, IM6 IHQ ☎01624 878305, Ⓦwww.cronkaashen.co.uk

Pitches & price 25 standard pitches plus 9 hard-standings (6 with hook-ups), £6 per person, £3 per child. Cottages to rent at £250–£450 per week.

Facilities Well-equipped, converted barn with 3 showers and 3 toilets, kitchen area with cooking facilities, eating area.

Restrictions Dogs allowed – there are also free DIY kennelling facilities. No campfires, although raised barbecues are permitted. Small groups only.

Open All year. Arrange in advance by phone or email.

Getting here Take the A3 from Kirk Michael. *Cronk Aashen* is signposted on the left at a crossroads about 1.5 miles up the hill. Regular buses take a circular route around the coast, but the island is best experienced with a car – there are hire companies in Douglas.

on the promenade, or visit the kipper factory, where you can buy an absurdly cheap kipper bap, washed down with a massive cup of tea.

For perhaps the most quirky experience on the island, head to Jurby Junk, about five miles north of *Cronk Aashen*. It's an aircraft hangar divided into two sections: on one side, a huge store of books, and on the other, a mixture of buttons, teapots, wigs, stag heads, plates and records. There's evidence of occasional attempts to marshal the books into some kind of order, but it's the glorious jumble that makes it so much fun.

◀ The churchyard at Kirk Michael, a thirty-minute walk from *Cronk Aashen* ▶ Books at Jurby Junk; Contrary Head, near Peel

Yorkshire

Yorkshire's identity may be firmly fixed in the minds of both locals and visitors, but the images of wild moorlands and straight-talking villagers that accompany England's biggest shire are far from the full picture.

Sure, the moors are often windswept and wild, but the purple heather plateaus of the North York Moors, the bone-white limestone escarpments of the Dales and the cloud-scudded grouse moors of West Yorkshire all exude very different characters. In between these expanses of high country are narrow valleys with rivers interspersed by hissing waterfalls, undulating agricultural plains and one of the most attractive coastlines in Britain.

And cast aside fears of encountering stereotypical gruff Yorkshire folk – the bluff front usually hides a friendly welcome that will soon see you advised of the best walks, the best views and the best pint in the area, whether you asked for it or not.

This combination of scenery and community makes Yorkshire prime territory for just about anyone who enjoys life under canvas. Admittedly, there are a few too many monolithic, caravan-orientated sites, especially along the coast. But as well as these amenity-packed behemoths, you'll find many simple places with little more than a shower block but views to die for, as well as funky little spots with tipis or old-fashioned caravans. And whether you want to hike a long-distance footpath, stroll along a beach, bike across the moors, surf a chilly North Sea wave or just amble along to the nearest pub for a pint of foaming Yorkshire ale, you'll be sure to find a campsite to suit.

Middlesbrough

Darlington

A171

A66

A172

A19

A167

Park Lodge

B6259

Usha Gap

B6270

A6108

A684

NORTH YORK MOORS NATIONAL P

La Rosa

B1257

Rosedale

A684

A170

A684

Hawes

Bainbridge Ings

YORKSHIRE DALES NATIONAL PARK

A6108

A167

A167

A1

Thirsk

Helmsley Pickering

Golden Square

B6255

B6479

B6160

Studfold Farm

A6108

A168

B1257

Malton

B6480

A687

A65

Pateley
Bridge

Ripon

A19

B1363

N

Dalesbridge

B6265

Y

O

R

K

S

H

I

R

A64

Knight Stainforth

Gordale Scar

Grassington

Malham

Church Farm

A61

A6055

A168

A59

A1237

A64

A16

B6478

Threaplands

B6160

B6265

Masons

B6265

B6165

A1237

York

A10

A682

A65

A59

A59

Harrogate

A661

A11(M)

B1224

Riverside

B6478

Skipton

A65

A658

Wetherby

A659

Wighill Manor

A19

A682

A56

A6068

A650

A61

A58

Tadcaster

B1223

Major Bridge Park

V

M65

A646

A629

A65

A64

A162

B1222

A163

B1228

A614

Keighley

Pennine Camping

A6033

Leeds

Bradford

M621

A642

A656

Castleford

A63

A63

Jerusalem Farm

Batley

Burnley

A646

Halifax

Dewsbury Wakefield

Pontefract

A645

A161

M62

M18

Rochdale

A58

M62

Huddersfield

A642

A638

A19

M180

M62

A62

A629

A636

A628

A1

Holme Valley

A635

A6024

A616

Barnsley

A635

Doncaster

A614

Manchester

A628

M1

A6023

PEAK DISTRICT
NATIONAL PARK

A430

M18

A1(M)

Rotherham

A631

A57

Sheffield

A57

A625

A6135

A621

A61

itby

Hook's House Farm

A171

Pinewood — Scarborough

A64 · A165 · B1253

Bridlington

nture Inn

A614 · A165

Driffield · B1249

Mill Farm

A164 · B1212

614 · B1248

A1035

Beverley

B1230 · A165 · B1238

Hull

A63 · A1033

Sunk Island

cunthorpe · Grimsby

Yorkshire

	PAGE	🚶	🚴	⛵	🍷	🎣	👪	👨‍👩‍👧‍👦	🚐	🚌	♿
Bainbridge Ings	232	✓	✓				✓		✓		
Church Farm	235		✓		✓		✓		✓		
Dalesbridge	228	✓						✓	✓		
Golden Square	241						✓		✓		✓
Gordale Scar	226	✓	✓			✓			✓		
Holme Valley	222						✓		✓		
Hook's House Farm	245		✓	✓			✓		✓		
Jerusalem Farm	225	✓				✓	✓				
Knight Stainforth	225	✓	✓				✓		✓		✓
La Rosa	242					✓		✓			
Major Bridge Park	239		✓			✓			✓		
Masons	236	✓	✓				✓		✓		
Mill Farm	239			✓					✓		
Park Lodge	230	✓	✓			✓					
Pennine Camping	224	✓	✓		✓	✓					
Pinewood	244			✓			✓		✓	✓	
Riverside	238			✓			✓			✓	
Rosedale	245	✓	✓				✓		✓		
Studfold Farm	229	✓	✓				✓		✓		✓
Sunk Island	240					✓	✓		✓		
Threaplands	234	✓	✓		✓						
Usha Gap	228	✓	✓						✓		
Venture Inn	241							✓	✓	✓	
Wighill Manor	234					✓			✓		

See front flap for key to symbols

Holme Valley

Holme from home on the edge of the Peak District

Holme Valley is in the heart of *Last of the Summer Wine* country – indeed quite a few scenes from the series have been shot in the campsite – but the area is about far more than just the BBC's amiable comedy. Enthusiastic and welcoming owners Philip and Hazel Peaker took over the site of a former woollen mill

in the mid-1980s and what was once a scene of dereliction is now a shady, wooded campsite with the River Holme marking the eastern boundary and a quack-filled duck pond as the centrepiece. This is a friendly, family-oriented spot with people passing to and fro all day long between the river, the duck pond and ball games in the "overflow" field, or just sitting outside the shop with a coffee and chewing the fat.

Philip is a trained ecologist and has seen *Holme Valley* receive the prestigious David Bellamy Gold Conservation Award for his commitment to preserving and enhancing the natural environment around the once working mill. The site has been skilfully landscaped so that shady trees and open fields now occupy what were formerly dispatch yards and storage areas, while the old and previously polluted mill pond also provides fishing for carp, bream and perch. Trout and grayling can be caught in the River Holme, which runs past the site, and a labyrinth of footpaths runs from *Holme Valley* through the surrounding woodlands, alongside the river and up onto the nearby hills.

The valley sits tight beneath the eastern flanks of the Pennines on the edge of the Peak District National Park and has that novel West Yorkshire mix of industrialized and urbanized valleys, upon which steep woodland and wild and windswept moorlands constantly encroach. It's possible for walkers and mountain bikers to cover miles of hilly trails midweek and not see a soul, while the roads that snake across the Pennines make for superb cycling, albeit with some challenging climbs.

Not everyone will appreciate the sometimes rough-and-ready urban landscape (Holmfirth itself is very twee but that's not always the case with the towns and villages around it), but this region was at the heart of the Industrial Revolution and for anyone interested in this period, there's plenty to keep you occupied.

Related visitor attractions are numerous and include the Standedge Tunnel Visitor Centre (⑩www.standedge.co.uk) near Marsden, where daily boat rides travel into a tunnel beneath the Pennnines, and the National Coal Mining Museum for England (⑩www.ncm.org.uk; free), where you can descend over four hundred feet into a working coal mine.

In quaint Holmfirth you can also follow in the footsteps of

Practicalities

Holme Valley Camping and Caravan Park, Thongsbridge, Holmfirth, West Yorkshire, HD9 7TD ☎01484 665819, Ⓦwww.holmevalleycamping.com

Pitches & price 62 hard-standing caravan pitches with hook-ups. 75 tent pitches in separate field (gentle slope). Additional rally field. From £5 per person (tent and no car) to £17 (tent, car and up to 3 people).

Facilities Excellent heated shower block with full disabled facilities. Laundry room and separate washing-up area. Well-stocked shop with reasonable prices and off-licence – *Last of the Summer Wine* wine is available for purchase. Good range of information available on local attractions.

Restrictions Dogs allowed (separate dog-walking area). No campfires or single sex-groups.

Open Year round.

Getting there From Holmfirth, to the south, take the A6024 1 mile to Thongsbridge post office (on your right). The campsite entrance is signposted 300yds on the right. From Honley, to the north, take the A6024 through woodland and past the sign for Oldfield, then look out for the entrance 400yds further on the left. Note that, despite its claims to the contrary, satnav will not take you to the site.

Last of the Summer Wine's Nora Batty and co., either under your own steam or on a minibus tour of the series' various filming locations. At day's end there are a couple of decent pubs within easy reach, of which the best is the *Rock Inn* (5min walk away), serving good pub food and a fine range of beers.

◀ Picture-perfect Holmfirth ▶ The rolling hills of the Pennines; exploring the National Coal Mining Museum for England

Pennine Camping
Nowt modern on the edge of the moors

Pennine Camping is as simple and straightforward as a campsite gets – as the owner proudly points out, "Owt modern, we haven't got it". But if you're looking for secluded camping, atmospheric landscapes and pubs within walking distance you'll love it here. The site attracts outdoor types who're looking to explore the wild and woolly Pennine hills and have a few pints of fine ale at day's end, and there's a convivial atmosphere amongst campers and caravanners here.

Set above the steeply wooded valley of Hardcastle Crags and on the very edge of the moors, the slightly sloping pitches will appeal to hardy campers more than beginners. This corner of West Yorkshire is great walking country, and if the weather's wet and windy, dive down into the Crags for sheltered hikes through the glorious woodland beside bubbling Hebden Water.

If conditions are better, the wild moors are the place to head for – the Pennine Way is within easy walking distance and there are some marvellous circular routes over Widdop Moor a mile away; you can make a pit stop at the *Packhorse Inn* (☎01422 842803) en route. Known locally as "t Ridge", it's famous for excellent Yorkshire ales (Thwaites and Black Sheep), a magnificent selection of malt whiskies and a feisty landlord who proudly

serves the kind of home-cooked food that's perfect after a day on the hills – try the steak sandwich.

This part of the Pennines is also renowned for its mountain biking, with some tremendous cross-country trails which offer challenging climbing, rip-roaring descents and magnificent views while generally remaining rideable year round despite the wet climate.

It doesn't have to be non-stop outdoor action here though – Hebden Bridge, the quirky old mill town a couple of miles away down in the valley, has one of the best selections of independent shops of any small town in England, from boutiques to bikes, outdoor gear to pork pies and gifts to obscure CDs, along with a good selection of coffee shops, restaurants and pubs. There's also a surprisingly good gig venue, the small and intimate *Trades Club* (Ⓦwww.tradesclub.info), where you can see everything from indie through blues to stand-up comedy.

▼ The Rochdale Canal, Hebden Bridge

Practicalities

Pennine Camping & Caravan Site, High Greenwood House, Hardcastle Crags, Heptonstall, Hebden Bridge, West Yorkshire, HX7 7AZ ☎01422 842287

Pitches & price 20 standard pitches. Tents £5 per person, caravans from £9.

Facilities 1 shower (no hot water). Fresh water. Male and female toilets.

Restrictions Dogs permitted (free, but maximum 2 per group). Campfires forbidden. Groups other than DofE discouraged.

Open April–Oct.

Getting there Follow signs to Heptonstall from Hebden Bridge and on towards Colden. Take the right-hand fork at Slack onto the minor signposted road to Widdop. The campsite is on the right after about a mile – look out for small signpost. There is a train station in Hebden Bridge; buses run from here at weekends only and stop within easy walking distance of the site.

Jerusalem Farm

Flat, leafy pitches, a brook and wood within spitting distance and all in the heart of a nature reserve – *Jerusalem Farm* is back-to-basics camping at its finest. In the heart of the Calder Valley's relatively unknown rural landscape, the wild moors and deep valleys of the area are dotted with fascinating remnants from the birth of the Industrial Revolution, including old stone weavers' cottages and burly Millstone Grit mills.

If you can drag the kids away from the on-site adventure playground, there is some fine walking to be had on the surrounding moors. Otherwise, take them to the award-winning Eureka! National Children's Museum in Halifax (⬤www.eureka.org.uk) and let someone else entertain them for an hour or two.

Watch out for the midges as dusk descends – you'll need the finest insect repellent money can buy. Alternatively, you could take refuge at the nearby *Cat-I'th-Well* pub, which sells one of Britain's finest ales, Timothy Taylor's Landlord Bitter, brewed in nearby Keighley.

Practicalities

Jerusalem Farm Campsite, Jerusalem Lane, Booth, Halifax, West Yorkshire, HX2 6XB ☎01422 883246

Pitches & price 30 standard tent pitches. £5 per adult, £3 per child under 15, under-5s free. No bookings taken – pitches are allocated on a first come, first served basis.

Facilities Shower block, toilets and taps for fresh water.

Restrictions Dogs allowed (1 per party). No campfires or single-sex groups.

Open Year round. Gates close at 8pm.

Getting there From the A646 at Luddenden Foot turn north up Luddenden Lane. After 1.5 miles turn right to Booth and go down the steep hill through the village to Jerusalem Lane, on the left: *Jerusalem Farm* campsite is the next property on the right. There are bus services to Booth village, from where it's a 10min walk to the site.

Knight Stainforth

If you're seeking a traditional, secluded camping experience then *Knight Stainforth* is not for you; if on the other hand you're looking for a site with all mod cons and over eighty years' experience of providing for campers' needs, then you're in business. The on-site facilities are numerous and include a cosy games and TV room, an outdoor play area and a dedicated space for ball games, so kids will have no shortage of things to do here. The verdant fields are lined by rows of traditional dry-stone walls and caravans, and the peat-tinted waters of the River Ribble flow nearby – indeed, it even has its own modest waterfall, Stainforth Force, a popular picnic spot.

The site is ideally located for exploring Yorkshire's limestone country – huge caverns, limestone pavements, stalactites and stalagmites are part and parcel of the bizarre scenery in this part of the world. The walking is also superb – the Ribble Way passes the site, the Yorkshire Three Peaks are within easy reach (see p.232) – and for mountain bikers and cyclists the surrounding fells offer an inspiring range of riding.

Practicalities

Knight Stainforth Hall Caravan and Camping Park, Little Stainforth, Settle, North Yorkshire, BD24 0DP ☎01729 822200, ⬤www.knightstainforth.co.uk

Pitches & price 100 pitches for tents and caravans, including 75 hook-ups. From £12 (including 2 people and car). Backpackers (no car) £4.50 per person.

Facilities Excellent shower/toilet block. Laundry and baby changing facilities. Wi-fi. Shop sells basic supplies, camping accessories and gas refills. Fishing available for licence holders. Swipe-card-operated security barriers.

Restrictions Dogs and DofE groups (by prior booking) permitted. No single-sex groups or campfires.

Open March–Oct.

Getting there Take the B6469 from Settle towards Giggleswick and turn right onto Stackhouse Lane. After 2 miles the site is signposted at a crossroads. Buses run from Settle to Little Stainforth, a short walk away.

Gordale Scar

Geological delights in limestone country

The campsite at *Gordale Scar* is totally in keeping with its location – basic and a bit rough-and-ready – and you wouldn't want it any other way. The site's pitches have a modicum of tree cover and sit by the clear waters of Gordale Beck, which settle here after tumbling down and through the rent in the landscape that is Gordale Scar, a few hundred yards upstream.

The scar is actually a huge limestone chasm, created when the roof of a massive cavern collapsed, and it attracts everyone from sightseers to hard-core climbers tackling the precipitous walls of the ravine. At busy times, a steady flow of people passes though en route to or from the scar, but when they leave for the day you can fully appreciate the drama of this upland terrain, immersing yourself in one of the Dales' wildest and finest landscapes.

From your tent door you can enjoy a marvellous half-day walk through terrain that has put generations of geography teachers in raptures. First head up to the scar where the waters of Gordale Beck bounce down contorted limestone outcrops within the ravine, and scramble up the side of its small waterfalls (you'll need to be relatively nimble) to emerge eventually onto open moorland.About two miles north is Malham Tarn, a modestly sized, steel-grey lake that is an internationally important nature reserve and home to a multitude of wildfowl and waders; from here it's an easy three-mile hike south to the huge natural amphitheatre of Malham Cove. At the end of the Ice Age a waterfall would have cascaded over the three-hundred-foot drop, but today climbers tackle its overhanging faces. Watch your footing on the surreal limestone pavement that sits atop the cove – the gaps known as "grikes" are easy to turn an ankle in, as well as being the habitat of various rare sub-alpine plants. From here it's an airy half-hour walk across sheep-cropped moorland to the campsite, where you can enjoy a relaxing cuppa beside your tent.

Mountain bikers will find themselves in the heart of a marvellous network of bridleways and green lanes, and the moorland roads hereabouts are perfect for cyclists as long as it's not too windy (the campsite can be pretty exposed in bad weather). A trip underground, meanwhile, offers an interesting chance

Practicalities

Gordale Scar Campsite, Gordale Farm, Malham, North Yorkshire, BD23 4DL ☎01729 830333

Pitches & price 60 standard pitches for tents and caravans (3 hook-ups available). £3 per tent, £3 per person, £3 per car.

Facilities Toilet blocks with sinks and fresh water and 1 hot shower on a timer. Washing-up area and power points. All facilities are pretty basic and can suffer under weight of use at busy times.

Restrictions Dogs welcome. No campfires or groups.

Open Year round.

Getting there From Malham follow signs for Malham Tarn; at the fork take the road to Gordale and you can't fail to spot the campsite. There's a regular bus service from Skipton to Malham, from where it's a 2-mile walk to the site (there aren't any taxis).

to see this limestone landscape in the making. Various show caves are to be found in the area, such as White Scar Caves near Ingleton (🌐www.whitescarcave.co.uk) where you can marvel at caverns up to 300ft long and 100ft high, stalactites, stalagmites and underground waterfalls. A guided tour is a fascinating experience and well worth the price.

All this action is bound to develop your appetite, but you'll be restricted to campsite cooking at *Gordale Scar* unless you make the two-mile trip into Malham, where the famed *Buck Inn* has served plain but filling grub to hikers for decades. The snug and attractive village houses a useful National Park Information Centre (☎01969 652380) and is something of a hub for outdoor types year round.

◀ A climber ascends the sheer walls of Gordale Scar ▶ A tour around White Scar Caves; the Dales from Malham Cove

Dalesbridge

Made up of lush, green hedge-lined fields, *Dalesbridge* attracts many campers looking to explore the surrounding Yorkshire Dales landscape and offers inspiring views across the local countryside. There's a busy, friendly feel to the ten-acre site so it's not ideal if you're looking for solitude, but if you feel that the camping experience is more about mixing and meeting with fellow campers you'll be in your element. An on-site bar opens most Friday and Saturday nights in summer and the *Gamecock* in Austwick (a twenty-minute walk away) does good food, including takeaway pizza.

This part of the Dales is prime caving and walking territory, and you can mix both with the short one-mile hike from nearby Clapham to Ingleborough Cave (mid-Feb to Oct daily; Ⓦwww.ingleboroughcave.co.uk), discovered in 1837 and the Pennines' oldest show cave. Continue for another 1.5 miles and you come to the mountain of Ingleborough (2373ft) and on its flanks, the 365-foot deep Gaping Gill, which is Britain's biggest underground chamber.

Practicalities

Dalesbridge, Austwick, nr Settle, North Yorkshire, LA2 8AZ Ⓣ01524 251021, Ⓦwww.dalesbridge.co.uk
Pitches & price 120 for tents and caravans, 28 of them with hook–ups. From £2 per tent, plus £4 per adult and £3.50 per child (aged 5–11). Caravans £10 (including 2 people). Hook-ups £5. Bunkhouses also available from £11 and B&B from £29.
Facilities Excellent shower/toilet block. Washing-up area with power points. Drying room. Disabled facilities. Shop selling basic groceries and outdoor gear.
Restrictions No campfires; raised BBQs permitted. Dogs (£1) allowed.
Open Year round.
Getting there The site is signposted off the A65, midway between Settle and Ingleton (don't follow satnav). There is a bus service to Austwick and trains run to Settle and Giggleswick, both a bus or taxi journey away.

Usha Gap

Delightfully located at the top end of Swaledale, *Usha Gap* is a cosy site between the waters of Straw Beck and the quiet B6270, popular with the outdoor types this area attracts. Soaring, cloud-shadowed fells rise on all sides, while the evocatively named Butter Tubs Pass rises several hundred feet to the southwest. Walkers are spoilt for choice here – the Pennine Way and Coast to Coast trails pass within easy reach and there are also less demanding options alongside the nearby River Swale. Follow the river as it tumbles down past the stone cottages and stout village church in quaint Muker and on towards the pretty villages of Gunnerside and Reeth.

Swaledale and Arkengarthdale to the north offer riding *par excellence* for mountain bikers – Butter Tubs Pass is a great challenge and old mining tracks meander and undulate across the fells for miles, remaining well-drained in even the worst weather. Thirsty riders can enjoy a delectable pint of Black Sheep ale at the *Farmer's Arms* in Muker (a two-minute ride or five-minute walk away), where they serve a very passable Yorkshire pudding and Cumberland sausage combo amongst other hearty dishes.

Practicalities

Usha Gap Caravans & Camping, Muker-in-Swaledale, North Yorkshire, DL11 6DW Ⓣ01748 886214, Ⓦwww.ushagap.btinternet.co.uk
Pitches & price 20 standard pitches. Adult campers £5, children (aged 5–15) £2. Caravans from £10. Car £2 extra. Holiday cottage available to rent (call for rates).
Facilities Shower block with hot water, toilets and washbasins. Clothes-drying facilities. Separate washing-up area. Small village shop in Muker.
Restrictions Dogs allowed. No campfires or single-sex groups. No noise after 11pm.
Open Year round.
Getting there From the M6, turn off at Tebay, a few miles north of Kendal, and follow the A685 for about 10 miles. At Kirkby Stephen, turn right onto the B6270; the site is between the villages of Thwaite and Muker, just after Usha Bridge.

Studfold Farm
Dalehead delight

Set in leafy grassland at the dramatic head of Nidderdale, the Dales' easternmost and least-known valley, *Studfold Farm*'s location is simply superb. Shadowed by big, rolling hills, it's a great springboard for exploring on foot or bike, while kids can enjoy the children's nature trail and the chance to see a farm at work – lambing time is particularly popular.

It's not perfect, though. Weekend campers, children from the attached activity centre and holidaymakers using the massed rows of static caravans in a rather regimented nearby field can make the place too bustling in high season. Visit in quieter times and you're more likely to have a relaxed stay.

You don't need to go very far to see the drama of *Studfold*'s Dales' landscape up close – just a few hundred yards upstream of the campsite is How Stean Gorge (Ⓦwww.howstean.co.uk), an ice-gouged ravine of waterfalls, pools and hidden caves through which there's a trail. Although somewhat commercial-ized, with a restaurant and bike rental, it's still an impressive spot – you can also camp here amongst very basic facilities (toilet, one shower; £4.50 per adult, £2.50 per child Ⓣ01423 755666) if *Studfold* is too busy or developed for your tastes.

Footpaths and trails run through or from the site, including the Nidderdale Way, a 53-mile circular walk which starts and finishes in Pateley Bridge – parts of this are also accessible to mountain bikers and link into bridleways which provide a fine tour, passing remote Scar House Reservoir and taking you around the upper reaches of Nidderdale.

The pretty hamlet of Lofthouse is a few minutes' walk away – the *Crown Hotel*, which has a good range of local ales and decent pub food, is a good bet for eating out here.

▼ Mountain biking the Nidderdale Way

Practicalities

Studfold Farm Caravan & Camping Park, Studfold Farm, Lofthouse, Harrogate, North Yorkshire, HG3 5SG Ⓣ01423 755084, Ⓦwww.studfoldfarm.co.uk

Pitches & price 40 multi-use pitches with hook-ups. From £12 for a 2-person tent. Hook-ups £3 extra. Also one self-catering cottage for 4 (from £260 per week).

Facilities Smart new shower/toilet block with hot water. Baby-changing. Disabled access. Small on-site shop with basic supplies including camping gas.

Restrictions Dogs (free) allowed on lead at all times. No campfires. No groups.

Open April–Oct.

Getting there From Ripon, take the B6265 to Pateley Bridge, then the minor road past Gouthwaite Reservoir and Ramsgill to Lofthouse, at the head of Nidderdale. Take the left fork at Lofthouse and *Studfold Farm* is about 0.5 miles past the village on the left bank of How Stean Beck.

Park Lodge
Feel the foss

Keld derives its name from the Old Norse for "running water", and this appealing North Yorkshire hamlet is defined by its pools and waterfalls. It sits above the infant River Swale, which is interrupted by numerous colourfully named cataracts – a couple of hundred yards upstream of *Park Lodge* are the modest falls of Catrake Force, where whisky-brown water muscles its way towards the distant North Sea, while a short walk downstream is the more dramatic Kisdon Force, where the river transforms into a thundering mass and plunges into a deep foaming pool beneath.

In warm weather, swimming in the clear, cool pools beside the campsite and between the falls is an absolute must. That said, you'll need to be wary of getting too close to the larger falls, especially after heavy rain, when the term "force" (actually from "foss", meaning waterfall) becomes very apt and the low rumble and hiss of spray mark the powerful flow.

At busy periods competition for the prime camping spots beside the river is keen – this is low-key camping at its best, with no fancy amenities or patrolling wardens, just shady wooded banks, burbling waters and opportunity to light campfires, all making for as good a location as you'll find to pitch your tent. The site's other camping areas, a field above the river and an additional field about four hundred yards to the south, are still splendidly located, however, with fine views up to the hills above Swaledale.

You could come to Keld and sit in the sun beside your tent, read a book, splash in the river and do little else, and there's nothing wrong with that, but this really is prime territory for active types. The Pennine Way and the Coast to Coast Walk bisect each other in Keld, so if you're hiking either this is a potentially useful overnighter, and there are stacks of long walks over the breezy fells which soar above Swaledale; a good local option is Great Shunner Fell (2349ft) to the south, which makes a fine day-walk from the site – the route follows the Pennine Way, so it's also easy to navigate. From the summit you'll enjoy magnificent views across much of the northern Dales and west to the Howgill Fells and the Lake District.

The countryside is festooned with dirt tracks that lead to and from the numerous lead mines that were worked here in the eighteenth and nineteenth century. Well drained in pretty much any weather conditions and easy to follow, they're great for mountain biking. Sure, it can be a bit of a slog up to the higher trails, but once up on top of the fells the tracks often stay high for miles before swooping back down to the valley in rip-roaring descents, and make for a great way to explore Swaledale. For an idea of the riding here, check out ⓦwww.tinyurl.com/mmhoug.

Perhaps the one downside to camping in Keld is the lack of a

Practicalities

Park Lodge, Keld, Richmond, North Yorkshire, DL11 6LJ
℡*01748 886274,* Ⓦ*www.rukins-keld.co.uk*

Pitches & price 30–40 tent pitches, including a limited number of riverside pitches on a first-come-first-served basis. Additional pitches in separate field at south end of hamlet. £5 per adult, £4 per backpacker (without car), £2 per child.

Facilities Block with clean but basic showers, toilets and dish-washing facilities. Small licensed on-site shop, also serving breakfasts, tea and coffee.

Restrictions Dogs allowed (free). Campfires are permitted by the river, otherwise a limited number of fireboxes are available (firewood £4 per bag). No young-adult groups.

Open Easter–Oct.

Getting there Keld is on the narrow B6270, and signs for the campsite are visible in the hamlet. Note that the site can get muddy in wet weather and cars may slip and slide. Keld is the terminus of a daily bus service from Richmond.

local pub, although this does give you a good excuse to head to nearby *Tan Hill Inn*, which at an altitude of 1732ft is the highest (and probably the windiest) pub in England – exposed beams, stone-flagged floors, a roaring fire and a fine selection of ales and food make this a classic moorland stop. It's about three miles away, and a nice bike ride along Stonesdale road, or you can walk along the Pennine Way.

The other dining option, of course, is equally appealing and the first choice of many campers at *Park Lodge*: an open campfire, simple fare and the river just a stone's throw away.

◄ Camping on the banks of the River Swale ▶ Swaledale sheep roam the purple-heathered moors; Dale wildflowers; sign to nearby village

Bainbridge Ings

Say "cheese" in stunning Wensleydale

Located in the bucolic Yorkshire Dales National Park, *Bainbridge Ings* is nestled between lofty, rugged fells and surrounded by a wide vista of lush meadows and handsome dry-stone walls. The attractive market town of Hawes is only ten minutes' walk away, and you're in the heart of famous Wensleydale, peppered with waterfalls and traditionally built farms. Given its surroundings, it's no surprise that this friendly, family-focused campsite is particularly popular with walkers and cyclists.

There are four fields and all of the pitches are situated around the perimeter, leaving plenty of space for kids to run around and for adults to enjoy views up to the moody, open fells. The owners have an admirable policy of making sure things don't become overcrowded, and the space here is a reflection of the broad acres for which Wenselydale is famed – this is prime hiking territory with great walking to be had straight from the campsite, and Hawes itself is on the Pennine Way trail. The three-to-four-hour circuit over Wether Fell (1968ft) is relatively easy to walk and provides inspiring views of the surrounding fells, Wensleydale and secluded Raydale and Semer Water.

If you really want to push it, the Yorkshire Three Peaks Challenge is easily accessible from Hawes, with the start point at Horton-in-Ribblesdale just a short drive away. The "peaks" in question are Pen-y-ghent (2273ft), Ingleborough (2373ft) and Whenside (2416ft and Yorkshire's highest point) – although relatively modest in altitude the ascent of all three in one day involves 25 miles of walking and should be done in 12 hours to "officially" complete the task, which is no mean feat. For something considerably more relaxing, head a few miles east along the A684 to the ever-popular Aysgarth Falls, where a well-signposted nature trail runs alongside the attractive Upper, Middle and Lower Falls.

This is top country for mountain biking, with a great selection of bridleways along which to explore the fells, while road cyclists will also find a number of marvellous routes (although the climbs between valleys can be pretty stiff work). If you're cycling, try to visit mid-week as the roads are busy at weekends, when the occupants of cars, coaches and motorbikes all jostyle to get a peek of the airy fell-top views.

Practicalities

Bainbridge Ings Caravan & Campsite, Hawes, Wensleydale, North Yorkshire, DL8 3NU ☎01969 667354, ⓦwww.bainbridge-ings.co.uk

Pitches & price 40 pitches for tents and 30 for caravans: 24 have hook-ups and 8 are hard-standing. Hikers and cyclists without a car £5 per person (never turned away). Tent, 2 adults and car £13. Caravan and 2 adults from £13. Booking is not possible for stays under 6 days. Two static caravans available from £210 per week.

Facilities Toilets, washbasins, showers, washing machine and tumble dryer. Gas, milk and eggs are sold on site.

Restrictions Dogs must be on a lead at all times (dog-sitting service available). No campfires or young adult groups. 11pm curfew.

Open April–Oct.

Getting there The campsite is signposted off Old Gayle Lane, accessed from the A684 0.5 miles east of Hawes. There are regular daily bus services to Hawes.

Hawes is Wensleydale's main town, a focal point for locals as well as visitors; thanks in part to Wallace and Gromit, the local crumbly white cheese is its most famous export. The Wensleydale Creamery (ⓦwww.wensleydale.co.uk), just out of town on Gayle Lane, is officially the only maker of "real" Wensleydale in the world and you can watch the cheese being produced here – phone ahead to confirm cheese-making times. The Yorkshire Dales National Park Centre is a useful source of tourist information (☎01969 666210) and sits alongside the Dales Countryside Museum. There's a pretty decent selection of pubs, cafés and tea rooms, standouts of which include *The Crown* for good pub food and the *Wensleydale Pantry* and *Chaste Restaurant* for dining out.

◀ Sheep roam the lush fields that surround *Bainbridge Ings*
▶ Mountain biking in the Yorkshire Dales; Wensleydale Creamery

Threaplands

This friendly, unpretentious site is well placed for accessing the southern Dales. It's a good all-rounder, set in lovely countryside on a slight slope – though the pitches are mainly flat. There's fine mountain biking and cycling on the local bridleways and lanes and plenty of less challenging fell walking – not everyone wants to slog their way round the Three Peaks (see p.232) after all. You're also within easy reach of Skipton and Grassington, two of the area's most lively towns, the latter a pleasant two-mile walk away.

If you enjoy eating out as part of your camping experience, meanwhile, *Threaplands* makes a great base. Two miles to the north in Linton is the *Fountaine Inn* (ⓦwww.thefountaineinnatlinton.co.uk), a favourite with local foodies for its daily specials, which include fresh fish, local meat and good veggie options, while in Hetton, two miles to the south, you'll find one of the area's outstanding gastropubs, the *Angel Inn* (ⓦwww.angelhetton.co.uk) – book in advance.

Practicalities

Threaplands House Farm, Cracoe, nr Skipton, North Yorkshire, BD23 6LD ☎01756 730248

Pitches & price 30 pitches, with limited hard-standing. £9.50 per tent or caravan including 2 adults and 2 children. Hook-ups £2 extra.

Facilities Basic, with a shower/toilet block and a small on-site shop with basic groceries including freshly baked bread.

Restrictions No dogs. No campfires.

Open March–Oct.

Getting there From Skipton, 20 miles northwest of Bradford, take the B6265 towards Grassington. After about 6 miles, you'll reach the village of Cracoe. Fork right at the outskirts of the village onto the country lane. The site is on the left after about 200yds. The regular buses between Skipton and Grassington pass through Cracoe.

Wighill Manor

Surrounded by rich farmland and little else, *Wighill Manor* is the perfect place to sit in the sun with a cold drink and a book or three, with only the occasional bleat of a sheep to bother you. The site is part of a working arable farm, and a small field has been set aside and given over to very basic and secluded camping. Tents are welcome but facilities are minimal in the extreme; there aren't any toilets, which means the place tends to be more popular with caravanners. At the time of writing there wasn't a village pub or shop in Wighill, so you really do need to be fully self-contained to enjoy camping here.

The activity options in this part of the world are seriously mellow. In the centre of the site sits a small, tranquil lake, overhung by trees and ideal for angling and watching life drift by. There are also plenty of easy ambles through the surrounding farmland and lots of sweat-free cycle rides along the flat country lanes. The fascinating, if slightly busy, streets of historic York are about a 10-mile ride away – there's no better way of getting around the city than on a bike.

Practicalities

Wighill Manor Caravan Site, Wighill, Tadcaster, North Yorkshire, LS24 8BT ☎01937 833688, ⓦwww.wighillcaravansite.co.uk

Pitches & price 9 standard pitches, 4 hard-standing pitches with hook-ups. £6 per pitch. Hook-up £2 extra.

Facilities Water tap. Local dairy produce and bottled water available for purchase on the farm. Coarse fishing at on-site lake £5 per day.

Restrictions Dogs allowed. No campfires or single-sex groups.

Open Year round.

Getting there Follow signs from Tadcaster to Wighill village (approximately 2.5 miles) and continue through the Wighill Manor estate gate for 50yds. The second turning on the left takes you to the farm. There are bus services from York and Tadcaster to Wighill, an hour's walk from the site.

Church Farm

The best of Yorkshire on your doorstep

Church Farm is splendidly located in the centre of Yorkshire, right between the Dales and the North York Moors. Nestled in the midst of quiet farmland and close to the attractive market town of Ripon, the site allows ready access to these national parks, as well as the historic urban centres of York and Harrogate, both less than an hour's drive away. The landscape provides cyclists with a great range of options, from quiet and relatively flat country lanes to more demanding "out and back" rides to the Dales and Moors.

Or you could chill out at the flat, well-manicured campsite, where thick hedgerows provide good shelter should rain sweep in from the moors. If the kids get itchy feet (ball games are not permitted on site) then take a gentle stroll into the classic English village of Bishop Monkton; the posse of ducks who waddle possessively alongside the small village beck will delight younger children. Parents won't feel too left out either since the walk passes two fine pubs en route – the *Lamb and Flag* has some tasty local beers and the *Mason's Arms* is renowned for its food.

The obvious day-trip from *Church Farm* is Ripon, an appealing market town with a lovely cathedral dating back to the seventh century and a busy Market Place (market day is Thursday) with a ninety-foot obelisk. Ripon is a pleasant place to wander around, with independent shops, a relatively traffic-free centre and sights including the Prison and Police Museum, an 1830s courthouse and the old town workhouse (combined ticket £6; ⓦwww.riponmuseums.co.uk).

▼ Ripon Cathedral's eastern facade

Practicalities

Church Farm Caravan Park, Knaresborough Road, Bishop Monkton, North Yorkshire, HG3 3QQ ☏*01756 677668,* ⓦ*www.churchfarmcaravanpark.co.uk*

Pitches & price 44 pitches for tents and caravans, 20 of them hard-standing with hook-ups. Tents from £9, caravans from £10, or £12 with hook-up. Three static caravans from £275 per week.

Facilities Good facilities include power showers, shaving points, baby-changing and laundry room. Disabled facilities in shower room.

Restrictions Dogs allowed on a lead. No campfires or young groups. 11pm curfew.

Open Mid-March to Oct.

Getting there From the A1 take the A6055 signposted Minskip/Knaresborough then turn right at the sign for Bishop Monkton. *Church Farm* is opposite the village church. There are bus services from Ripon and Harrogate, although they are not terribly regular.

Masons

Tales of the riverbank

There's a busy, friendly buzz to this lovely pastoral site on the banks of the River Wharfe, where children dash to and from the river with fishing nets and skimming stones, dogs leap for balls in the shallows, hikers amble past on the Dales Way and cyclists regularly swoop by on the road above the site. The site's young owners Grant and Georgie Hinchliffe are enthusiastic campers themselves and seem to spend most of their time wandering about the camping fields and ensuring everything is hunky-dory with guests. They're also a good source of information on what there is to do locally, of which there is plenty.

On a warm, sunny day the attractions of the river can easily keep you on site. But you can also follow its course, taking the easy riverside hike a few miles downstream to the village of Bolton Abbey, where the remains of a John Ruskin-endorsed twelfth-century priory stand. You can swim in a large, deep meander of the river here, while en route you'll pass the infamous Strid, where the river funnels through a narrow cleft in the rocks.

It's particularly impressive after heavy rains – do not fall in!

Head upstream for an hour or so and you'll reach pleasant little Grassington, which has a good range of pubs, cafés and souvenir shops around its Georgian centre. The town hosts an eclectic annual summer festival (Ⓦwww.grassington-festival.org.uk) every June featuring everything from international musicians and comedians to dry-stone walling and beer tasting.

More challenging hikes over the fells abound, while climbers can head for nearby Kilnsey Crag – parts of the crag feature a massive and very challenging overhang. For cyclists, the Yorkshire Dales provide some of the finest riding in northern England, although the roads can get busy, especially at weekends. Scores of enjoyable circuits follow the narrow lanes and open roads of the fells – try the loop up the B6160, across the moors to Hawes, south to Ribble Head and Stainforth then back over the moors via Malham and Grassington to Appletreewick. There's also some excellent mountain biking in the area, with the bridle-

Practicalities

Masons Campsite, Ainhams, Appletreewick, North Yorkshire, BD23 6DD ☎*01756 720275,* Ⓦ*www.masonscampsite.co.uk*

Pitches & price Up to 80 pitches for tents and caravans, 30 with hook-ups. £16 per night for up to 2 people, unit and car. £6 per person if you arrive under your own steam: backpackers never turned away.

Facilities Shower block with hot water, toilets and dish-washing facilities. Baby-changing facilities, clothes washing and kit drying. Disabled facilities. A mobile shop visits the site daily. Fully-equipped tents are available to rent from £15 per adult and £9 per child. Self-catering flat also available.

Restrictions Dogs allowed. Campfires only allowed in fire boxes. No young adult groups other than DofE.

Open April–Oct.

Getting there The campsite is just west of the village of Appletreewick (or "Aptrick") on a minor road accessed either from the B6160 Bolton Abbey–Burnsall or the B6265 Grassington–Pateley Bridge. Buses run every 2hr between Ilkley and Grassington.

way over to Rylstone a decent taster.

Masons is only a twenty-minute drive from the reasonably attractive market town of Skipton (markets Mon, Wed, Fri & Sat), which, with its well-preserved Norman castle, makes a fine option for rainy days. If you want to head out at night there are a couple of good options within a few hundred yards of the campsite – the superbly refurbished *Craven Arms* has pub grub and a mouth-watering selection of local and guest ales, and the *New Inn* offers a good range of European beers, well-priced food and regular "pie nights".

◀ Young campers enjoy the River Wharfe ▶ The waters of the Strid gorge, downstream from Masons; Bolton Abbey's ruined priory

Riverside

Vikings, cathedrals and camping on the Ouse

If you visit only one city in Yorkshire it has to be York, and *Riverside* is a great base from which to explore this historic location. It's situated just two miles from the city centre, which you can reach via a leafy footpath along the left bank of the River Ouse, watching pleasure craft, rowing boats and flotillas of ducks heading up- and downstream en route.

You can also access the city by bike along dead-flat roads or by bus – and if you have your own boat you can even launch from the site's slipway (there's a marine service yard alongside) and sail up or down the Ouse. Boats can be rented next to *Riverside Camping* if you don't own one.

The site's riverside location is reasonably secluded, although it gets busy at weekends and the height of the holidays, especially as many visitors are content to stay on site and relax beside their tent or caravan. Other than the engines of passing boats the loudest thing you're likely to hear from the tree-shaded pitches is quacking ducks or barking dogs at what is a very dog-friendly site. There are good facilities close by in the somewhat bland suburban setting of Bishopthorpe, with a grocery store 250 yards

▼ York Minster, Britain's largest Gothic building

away and three decent pubs within five minutes' walk – *Ebor House* has home-cooked food and decent ale.

York's highlights need little introduction: the magnificent York Minster (ⓦwww.yorkminster.org) houses the world's largest single stained glass window, the Jorvik Viking Centre (ⓦwww.vikingjorvik.com) lets you travel in "time capsules" through tenth-century York, while the National Railway Museum (ⓦwww.nrm.org.uk) is as good a free day out as you'll find anywhere – exhibits include the 126mph *Mallard*, the world's fastest-ever steam engine. If you need some refreshments after all this sightseeing you won't do better than *Betty's* on St. Helen's Square, the quintessential Yorkshire tea and cake shop – afternoon tea here is a great opportunity to people-watch as well as refuelling for the return walk or ride back to the campsite.

Practicalities

Riverside Camping & Caravan Park, Ferry Lane, Bishopthorpe, York, YO23 2SB ☎01904 705812, ⓦwww.yorkmarine.co.uk

Pitches & price Around 25 pitches for tents and caravans, 10 of them with hook-ups. No hard-standings. 2-person tent with car £17, caravan with 2 people from £22. Backpackers (without a car) from £9.

Facilities Flush toilets, showers, children's play area. Washing-up and laundry facilities. Fishing. Small tuckshop serving tea and coffee.

Restrictions Dogs allowed (£1). No campfires. No groups.

Open April–Oct.

Getting there From the A64 York bypass, take the exit to Bishopthorpe. In Bishopthorpe turn left at the T-junction onto the main street. After 400yds turn right onto Acaster Lane, then after 100yds turn left onto Ferry Lane. The site is at the bottom of the (fairly narrow) lane. There are buses every 30min from the top of Ferry Lane to and from the city.

Major Bridge Park

Nestled in one of Yorkshire's lesser-known corners, *Major Bridge Park* makes a great base for exploring the lovely Yorkshire Wolds or visiting the attractive Old Town of seafaring Hull. Made up of large open fields and well sheltered by trees and hedgerows, the campsite is popular with both carvanners and campers who enjoy its quiet, unassuming location.

There's easy walking to be had along the disused railway line that runs past the site, and the scenic Wolds Way trail runs through nearby Market Weighton, a pleasant market town. If you bring your bike with you the rolling landscape and quiet lanes of the Wolds beg to be explored; a fourteen-mile cycle to the east is the charming old cathedral town of Beverley, whilst the flat terrain around the Humber Estuary, to the south, couldn't be easier to ride. It's worth making the 25-mile trip south to the port of Hull – often overlooked for nearby York – which boasts an interesting selection of attractions, including a very good aquarium (The Deep) and a range of free museums. Come day's end the best bet for eating out is the home-cooked food at the *Red Lion* in Holme-on-Spalding Moor, two miles east of the site.

Practicalities

Major Bridge Park, Selby Road, Holme-on-Spalding Moor, East Yorkshire, YO43 4HB ☎01430 860992, Ⓔ*philbaldry@hotmail.co.uk*
Pitches & price 30 pitches for tents and caravans, 5 of them with hook-ups. £7 per pitch. Hook-ups £1 extra. Hard-standing pitches are available, and lie adjacent to the main site.
Facilities Shower and toilet block. Separate disabled facilities. Nearest pubs, cafés and shops in Holme-on-Spalding Moor.
Restrictions Dogs and groups allowed.
Open Easter–Sept.
Getting there *Major Bridge Park* is located 20 miles southeast of York on the A163, approximately midway between Holme-on-Spalding Moor and Foggathorpe. Bus services run along the A163 from Hull, Beverley and Selby.

Mill Farm

Just a short walk from *Mill Farm* is Skipsea beach – and some of the most impressive coastal erosion in Britain. The North Sea eats away persistently at the soft boulder-clay cliffs of the area, leaving roads and buildings hanging dramatically in mid-air. Despite groynes that punctuate the coastline, several more yards of low cliff fall into the brown, silty water every year. The beach itself stretches for miles and kids can enjoy a splash in the sea in calmer conditions, while bigger waves attract keen surfers; wetsuits are recommended for the chilly water.

Despite its claims to be a "Country Park", *Mill Farm* is a relatively small and quiet site with well-drained pitches, thick sheltering hedgerows and plenty of space for kids to play ball games. There's a nice communal feel to the place, and although caravanners are generally more numerous than tent dwellers, all are very welcome. Skipsea has few pretensions to being anything other than a cheap and cheerful little seaside town – fish and chips (try *Crossways* on Mill Lane) and a quick bash on the slot machines in one of the town's amusement arcades may not appeal to all, but it does have a melancholy charm of sorts.

Practicalities

Mill Farm Country Park, Mill Lane, Skipsea, East Yorkshire, YO25 8SS ☎01262 468211
Pitches & price 56 for tents and caravans, almost all with hook-ups. From £12 for tent, 2 people and car, or caravan with 2 people. Hook-ups £2.50 extra.
Facilities Toilet, shower block and power points. Disabled access and toilet. Dish-washing facilities. A pub (*The Board Inn*) and shops are a 2min walk away in Skipsea.
Restrictions Dogs and raised BBQs permitted. No campfires.
Open March–Sept.
Getting there Skipsea is just off the A165 from Hull. From Main Street in Skipsea turn left onto Cross Street, then straight on to Mill Lane – the site is 100yds on your right. There are regular bus services to Skipsea from Bridlington, Driffield and Hull.

Sunk Island

Simplicity and solitude at Yorkshire's eastern tip

Located beside Stone Creek, a few miles outside the village of Thorngumbald, *Sunk Island*'s location can hardly fail to evoke childhood adventures, when all you needed for a top weekend was a tent over your head and a place to explore – and to be honest that's all you will get here. But if you're happy with that, then the tranquil atmosphere and distant horizons of *Sunk Island* may well appeal.

You'd never guess you were in Yorkshire – the pancake-flat fields, ruler-straight dykes and mudflats of the mighty Humber Estuary are more reminiscent of Norfolk. The area lends itself to bird-watching, and you might see wagtails, corn buntings, partridges, skylarks and a wide variety of wildfowl.

More active options include cycling along the quiet country lanes and walking in the company of Monty, the resident border collie. Or you can just idle atop a levée and watch the boats and tankers glide in and out of Immingham and Hull across the Humber Estuary.

The North Sea coast is only ten miles away to the north and east, and offers everything from bathing and surfing at Withernsea to tours of deep underground bunkers at RAF Holmpton

(⬤www.rafholmpton.com), built sixty years ago to defend against nuclear attack. But Spurn Head, about fifteen miles to the south-east, is perhaps the area's most remarkable feature. This wind-swept three-mile-long spit stretches out like a crooked fingernail at the end of the Yorkshire coast, pointing into the mouth of the Humber. Composed of sand and shingle deposited by sea currents, it's just a few feet above sea level at its highest point and is only fifty yards wide in places, yet is an internationally important nature reserve, the habitat for a wide variety of migrant birds and waders as well as occasional more exotic species – a black-browed albatross, rarely sighted outside the southern oceans, was spotted here once. Other species include deer and various lizards, and there are good pickings for fossil hunters.

You'll need to travel if you want to dine out come evening time – the *Burns Head Inn* in Patrington (three miles away) is your best option, offering a winning combination of pub food, decent ales and regular live music. Staying on site offers simpler pleasures: just fire up the stove, crack open a beer and enjoy the silence.

▼ Mudflats on the edge of the Humber Estuary

Practicalities

Sunk Island Campsite, Stone Creek House, Cherry Cob Sands Road, Stone Creek, East Yorkshire, HU12 9JX
☏*01964 630801*

Pitches & price 20 standard pitches. £5 per caravan, £2.50 per tent.

Facilities Chemical toilet disposal point and fresh water. No showers.

Restrictions Very dog-friendly (dogs are free). Campfires permitted.

Open Year round.

Getting there From Thorngumbald turn right into Church Lane and follow the sign for Stone Creek for 6 miles, then onto Cherry Cob Sands Road. Ignore "No Through Road" sign and follow the road until 300ft before the sharp left turn by the creek; the campsite is on your right.

Venture Inn

The rolling hills and farmland of the Yorkshire Wolds are relatively unvisited compared to the better-known areas of Yorkshire, despite enjoying the blessing of local resident David Hockney. Sat in the heart of the Wolds, the *Venture Inn* is spacious too, its grassy fields big enough to allow plenty of room between pitches. They sit most conveniently behind the inn itself, a no-frills pub where an evening pint or four and some good honest pub grub is a popular way for campers to see out the day.

The quiet, undulating lanes and attractive towns like Beverley are ideal for exploring under pedal power. Although the site is close to the busy A166, road noise isn't really an issue here and it does make for easy access. Unfortunately, nearby Driffield doesn't have much to offer other than places to stock up on basics, but you're well located for a trip to the east coast, where the choices vary between bustling Bridlington and the secluded and atmospheric beaches to the south, such as Skipsea and Hornsea. To the west is York, which is always worth a visit – especially when you have to travel through the delightfully monikered Wetwang en route.

Practicalities

Venture Inn, Main Street, Garton-on-the-Wolds, Driffield, East Yorkshire, YO25 3EU ☏01377 253242

Pitches & price 50 tent pitches, 5 caravan pitches. There are more pitches for tent or caravan rallies, but call first. £4 per person.

Facilities Toilets, fresh water.

Restrictions Dogs (free) and groups allowed. No campfires.

Open Year round.

Getting there *Venture Inn* campsite is 3 miles west of Driffield on the A166, directly behind the *Venture Inn* pub. The A166 runs straight from York; if you're driving from Hull you'll need to follow the A164, joining the A166 at Driffield. Regular bus services run along the A166 and stop close to the campsite. Trains run direct to Driffield station from Sheffield and Hull.

Golden Square

For campers and caravanners who like their luxuries when away from home, or who have kids in need of non-stop entertainment, *Golden Square* is a great option. The extensive on-site facilities (indoor and outdoor play area, crazy golf and cycle rental) make it easily possible to spend an entire holiday amongst the open fields and woodland that make up this bucolic corner of Yorkshire, but that would be to miss out on the array of interesting attractions nearby. These include the lofty escarpment of Sutton Bank just a few miles west, where on sunny days, you'll see squadrons of paragliders and hanggliders enjoying the superb views across the Vale of York; the A-road that winds up to the bank itself is claimed to be Britain's steepest.

The area is also home to an impressive array of ancient piles including the atmospheric remains of Rievaulx, Byland and Fountains abbeys, and magnificent Castle Howard, which, along with its equally grand grounds, is easily one of England's finest stately homes.

Practicalities

Golden Square Caravan Parks, Oswaldkirk, North Yorkshire, YO62 5YQ ☏01439 788269, Ⓦwww.goldensquarecaravanpark.com

Pitches & price 100 standard pitches plus 20 hardstanding with hook-ups. Cyclists and hikers (no car) £5.50 per person. From £14 per pitch with car or caravan.

Facilities 2 excellent heated shower and toilet blocks. Baby-changing facilities. Disabled access and facilities. Washing-up sinks. Laundrette and well-stocked shop.

Restrictions Dogs allowed (£1 per night; separate dog exercise area). No campfires or single-sex groups.

Open March–Oct. Gates close at 8pm.

Getting there Take the A170 south of Helmsley then turn off on the B1257 for Ampleforth. The site is on the right-hand side of the road. Bus services run from Helmsley, Thirsk and York to within 0.5 miles of the site.

La Rosa
Caravans fit for Gypsy kings

La Rosa is not your average regimented caravan site; in fact, this intriguing spot looks more like a kaleidoscopic travelling circus. Rather than bring your own vehicle, you stay in one of their charming period pieces, which include an authentic chromed Roma caravan full of etched glass, an Elvis-themed van, a tinker's trailer and snug green tourers from the Sixties that many will remember from childhood days. To describe the interiors of the vans as kitsch doesn't come close. To describe

them as cosy and welcoming does.

There is no electricity so lighting is provided by candles and torches, and some of the vans are heated by wood-burning stoves – if it rains what could be better than to curl up beside the fire with an absorbing book and good company, to listen to the raindrops on the roof and the birds in the trees? The laid-back atmosphere of the site is nicely illustrated by the dinky "sweet shop caravan", lined with glass jars full of your favourite childhood sweets – payment is made via an honesty box.

Located in a quiet woodland dell, the wildlife here is confident enough to wander about freely, so don't be too surprised to find deer or badgers, as well as the occasional walker, using the footpaths through the site. The nearest thing you'll get to modernity at *La Rosa* are the toots of the trains on the scenic North Yorkshire Moors steam railway in the valley below, which is well worth a ride (see p.245). In the evening it's possible to dine in style on board the railway's trains, although you're expected to dress appropriately – fear not, *La Rosa* has a massive "dressing up" box to kit you out à la Orient Express.

If you can't resist exploring further afield, then the walks above the site and across the rugged, purple-heathered North York Moors will blow away the most stubborn of cobwebs. Or you might amble through the woods and over tinkling streams for a beer at the atmospheric and award-winning *Birch Hall Inn* (☏01947 896245) in Beck Hole, which has an outstanding range of Yorkshire beers and superb locally made pies and "butties".

About ten miles northeast is the seaside town of Whitby and its dramatic ruined Gothic abbey, which gained fame as one of the settings in Bram Stoker's *Dracula* and has since become something of a magnet for brooding goths. The owners of *La Rosa* have an equally eclectic hotel here (see website) that's right in keeping with the Victorian and Gothic chic upon which the town focuses these days – the themed bedrooms take in Angela Carter, Lewis Carroll and cowgirls. Legend and myth abound in this former whaling port, which has also seen Captain Cook and famous whaler William Scoresby amongst its residents.

Practicalities

La Rosa, Murk Esk Cottage, Goathland, Whitby, North Yorkshire, YO22 5AS ☎01947 606981, ⓦwww.larosa.co.uk

Pitches & price 9 themed caravans, £28 per person including bedding, gas, candles and firewood, under-5s are free. There is a 2-night minimum stay in July and Aug.

Facilities Toilets, washbasins and spacious "open-plan" shower set in a converted byre. Striped big top tent for evening get-togethers.

Restrictions Dogs and campfires not allowed. Arrival after dark is discouraged due to difficult access.

Open April–Sept.

Getting there Tricky! From Goathland take the Egton Bridge/Roman Road turn-off near the *Mallyan Spout Hotel* and look out for a dirt track on the right-hand side, 2.7 miles from this point. There was no sign at the time of writing but you'll see a small bunch of artificial red flowers on a gate post by the turn-off. Watch your suspension if you have a low-slung car. There are buses from Whitby to Goathland and Egton, and the atmospheric steam trains of the North Yorkshire Moors Railway (ⓦwww.nymr.co.uk) run from Pickering to nearby Grosmont. Arriving by bus or train means walking the final part of the journey through woodland – the owners recommend calling for directions.

But the charms of *La Rosa* are such that there is no need to wander far: you could very easily spend the whole of the weekend tucked away here with a group of good friends – which is essentially what this eclectic little site is all about.

◄ A Sixties tourer caravan – look familiar? ▶ Cosy but kitsch interiors define groovy *La Rosa*; the campsite's shower is a converted byre

Pinewood

Tipi-tastic on the Yorkshire coast

The owners of *Pinewood* are sound as a pound, running their site with an admirable green focus and refusing to charge a high-season premium. They believe camping should be fun – you can even enjoy Christmas in one of their tipis, complete with Christmas tree and decorations. The tipis are deceptively spacious and comfy, sleeping up to six people with luxuries such as wood-burning stoves and futons on raised sleeping platforms. The site's well-manicured grassy pitches are sheltered by trees and hedges and elevated enough to provide lovely views across the rolling farmland of the Yorkshire Wolds, making this a good spot for people who bring their own tents as well as tipi-dwellers.

The ethos here isn't to cram in as many people as possible, but to provide plenty of space for visitors to do their own thing, whether that's watching the clouds roll across the hills that un-dulate their way down to the North Sea coast, or wandering into

▼ Pinewood's spacious tipis sleep up to six

Scarborough, England's oldest seaside resort.

And this is a site where you really don't need a vehicle to make the most of what's available. It's only a mile and a half to the centre of bright and breezy Scarborough, and there's a quiet path that takes you all the way there. Here you can enjoy fish and chips above the town's two fine sandy beaches, surf the waves or head out in a boat for a spot of sea fishing; incredible as it may seem, Scarborough was a world centre for big-game tuna fishing in the early twentieth century – these days your haul will invariably be a far more modestly-sized codling or whiting. Fishing trips with Queensferry Cruises (Ⓦwww.queensferrycruises.com), based in Scarborough Harbour, cost £5 per person per hour.

If the fish aren't biting you might console yourself with the good pub food at the *Dennison Arms* in East Ayton, just a mile away from *Pinewood* and also a small selection of local shops in the dinky suburb of Falsgrave, a similar distance away.

Practicalities

Pinewood Holiday Park, Racecourse Road, Scarborough, North Yorkshire, YO12 5TG Ⓣ*01723 367278,* Ⓦ*www.pinewood-holiday-park.co.uk*

Pitches & price 17 hard-standing caravan pitches, 10 of them "adult-only". 20 tents in separate field, 12 tipis in third field. From £10 per caravan or tent and 2 people. Tipis from £25 for 2 people (children free).

Facilities Flush toilets and hot showers. Disabled access. Washing-up facilities.

Restrictions Campfires, well-behaved groups and dogs (free) permitted. Arrival after 7pm must be organized in advance.

Open Year round.

Getting there The site is 1.5 miles inland from Scarborough on the A170. The nearest train station is in Scarborough and there are regular bus services from the town to a bus stop a few hundred yards from the site.

Rosedale

It may describe itself as a "caravan park", but campers are very welcome at this impeccable site, located betwixt the tumbledown ruins of Rosedale Abbey and the River Severn, at the heart of the North York Moors National Park. Although it is fairly large and bustling, *Rosedale* is ideally located for exploring the rolling moors and the nearby cliffs, beaches and resorts of the Yorkshire coast. It's easy to escape the village crowds up on the surrounding purple-heathered moors, where trails for walking and mountain biking run for miles. Marvellous B-roads also spider their way over the hills and bikes can be rented in the village from Abbey Bike Hire (Ⓦwww.abbeybikehire.co.uk), just a hundred yards from the site.

Another popular local attraction is the North Yorkshire Moors Railway (Ⓦwww.nymr.co.uk), the second longest steam line in Britain. It has a wide selection of steam and diesel trains, and features regularly on TV and in films, including the *Harry Potter* movies. A Family Day Rover Ticket allows two adults and up to four kids to ride the line all day long between Pickering at the southern end and Whitby, on the coast, for only £45.

Practicalities

Rosedale Country Caravan Park, Rosedale, nr Pickering, North Yorkshire, YO18 8SA Ⓣ*01751 417272,* Ⓦ*www.flowerofmay.com*

Pitches & price 160 tent pitches and 53 caravan pitches: 28 hard-standing and 14 with hook-ups. From £18 per pitch with hook-up and £14 without.

Facilities Shower/toilet block with baby changing. Disabled access and facilities. Clothes-washing facilities. On-site shop sells basics and camping spares. 2 pubs in the village serving good meals.

Restrictions Dogs allowed (1 per group). No campfires or single-sex groups.

Open March–Nov. Gates close at 8pm, later in high season – call to arrange late arrival.

Getting there Located in the centre of Rosedale, the site is accessible via minor roads from the A170 or A169. There is a limited bus services from Pickering.

Hook's House Farm

On a sunny day the views from *Hook's House Farm* are inspirational; the cliffs of the bay sweep south above the twinkling green North Sea, and seagulls soar above. Right below is Robin Hood's Bay and village, all narrow, tumbling alleyways and warm-red tiled roofs, straight out of a pirate novel. Every turn reveals another souvenir or bookshop, and the coastline has some of the best reef breaks in England for competent surfers. Eating and drinking options include pub fare at *The Laurel* and *Ye Dolphin*, contemporary cuisine at *Swells* or sea views and coffee at *Candy's*.

The Coast to Coast long-distance walking trail finishes in the village and is intersected by the Cleveland Way, which undulates between some of England's highest sea cliffs and prettiest coastal villages – the trails crisscross in front of the popular *Bay Inn*. More excellent walking and mountain biking can be had a couple of miles away on the North York Moors, whilst Whitby Harbour and its imposing ruined abbey are less than five miles away.

The only downside is that pitches are slightly sloped and there is some road noise at times – otherwise this is a well priced base from which to explore the area.

Practicalities

Hook's House Farm, Whitby Road, Robin Hood's Bay, North Yorkshire, YO22 4PE Ⓣ*01947 880283,* Ⓦ*www.hookshousefarm.co.uk*

Pitches & price 75 tent pitches and 25 caravan pitches, 5 of them hard-standing. Adults from £5, children £2.50. Hook-ups £3 extra.

Facilities Basic shower block with disabled facilities. Washing-up area.

Restrictions Dogs allowed. No campfires or single-sex groups.

Open All year.

Getting there *Hook's House Farm* is 5 miles south of Whitby. Take the B1447, signposted Robin Hood's Bay, off the A171 Whitby–Scarborough road. *Hook's House Farm* is on the right, just under a mile before Robin Hood's Bay.

Cumbria and the Lakes

Forever associated with Wordsworth and the Romantic poets, the jagged mountains, sylvan valleys and deep waters of the Lake District are unforgettably beautiful. The Lake District National Park is enclosed within Cumbria: the county also includes a stretch of coastline and a strip of towns and villages to the east, but really there's little here to lure campers beyond the sublime park itself.

What brings visitors to the Lakes is, of course, the great outdoors. Scafell Pike is England's highest mountain, and Windermere its largest lake. There are umpteen opportunities for hiking, climbing, abseiling, mountain biking, sailing, windsurfing, canoeing – even wild swimming in the rivers and tarns if you're feeling brave.

And campsites are a great way to immerse yourself in the region. They range from the utterly basic to relatively luxurious, with farm shops, weather-proof camping pods and yurts. What the sites listed in this chapter have in common are spectacular views and walks to remember. The area has been on the tourist map since Wordsworth's time, and the consequence is that it's wonderfully set up with walkers' inns, tearooms in rugged stone farmhouses and – increasingly – gastro pubs and Michelin-starred restaurants.

One thing to bear in mind is that this is justifiably one of the most popular areas of the country for visitors, and that campsites will be packed out at bank holidays and during the school holidays. If the more celebrated sites, such as the National Trust ones, are full, you could always make do with a tap-and-field site for a night.

NORTHUMBERLAND
NATIONAL PARK

A6071

A7

A689 A689

B5307

A69

Carlisle

B6413

B5302 A596

B5300

B5301 B5299

A595

M6

B5305

A6

C U M B R I A

A594

B5288

A596

Cockermouth

A66 A591

Penrith

A66

B5320

Appleby-in-
Westmorland

Workington

A66

Gill Head Farm

**The
Quiet Site**

A6091

A6

A686

A595

Keswick

A66

A592

Waterside House

A5086

Whinfell Hall

B5292

Castlerigg Hall
Castlerigg Farm

Whitehaven

B5289

**Hollows
Farm**

Gillside

Side Farm

B6260

A66

Syke Farm

Seatoller Farm

Sykeside

B5345

Chapel House Farm

Seathwaite Farm

Egremont

LAKE DISTRICT NATIONAL PARK

A591

A592

A685

Wasdale **Barn Door**

Full Circle

A6

Wasdale Yurt Holiday

Great Langdale

B5343

Ambleside

A685

A683

B6259

B5344

Bays Brown Farm

B5286

Low Wray

The Old Post Office

Fisherground

**Hawkshead
Hall Farm**

Windermere

A591

B6251

Sedbergh

Ravenglass

Coniston

B5285

Hawkshead

B5284

A684

A595

Turner Hall Farm

A5084

A593

Kendal

A684

PEAK DISTRIC
NATIONAL PA

Broughton-
in-Furness

A5074

A591

M6

A683

Park Cliffe

A65

A684

A595

A5084

A5093

A5092

A590

A592

A590

A6

A65

A6070

B6254

Kirkby
Lonsdale

B6255

Ulverston

B5278

A595

A590

Grange-
over-Sands

B5282

B6254

Barrow-in-
Furness

A5087

Cumbria and the Lakes

	PAGE	🥾	🚴	⛵	🎣	⛰️	👪	👨‍👩‍👧‍👦	🚐	🚌	♿
Barn Door	266	✓	✓			✓					
Bays Brown Farm	256	✓	✓			✓					
Castlerigg Farm	274	✓							✓	✓	
Castlerigg Hall	274	✓			✓		✓		✓	✓	✓
Chapel House Farm	276					✓			✓	✓	
Fisherground	260		✓				✓			✓	
Full Circle	254								✓		
Gill Head Farm	276	✓					✓		✓		
Gillside	275	✓		✓				✓	✓	✓	
Great Langdale	258	✓				✓		✓		✓	
Hawkshead Hall Farm	252					✓			✓	✓	
Hollows Farm	272	✓		✓		✓		✓		✓	
Low Wray	250			✓				✓		✓	
The Old Post Office	264						✓		✓		✓
Park Cliffe	253			✓			✓	✓	✓	✓	
The Quiet Site	278	✓		✓	✓		✓	✓	✓		
Seathwaite Farm	267	✓						✓			
Seatoller Farm	271					✓					
Side Farm	277			✓						✓	
Syke Farm	270				✓					✓	
Sykeside	281	✓								✓	
Turner Hall Farm	257	✓				✓				✓	
Wasdale	268	✓	✓			✓					✓
Wasdale Yurt Holiday	265	✓									
Waterside House	280			✓			✓			✓	
Whinfell Hall	271								✓		

See front flap for key to symbols

Low Wray

Swallows and Amazons

A cluster of beautiful stone buildings stands at the northwestern edge of Lake Windermere, marking *Low Wray*'s entrance and housing its reception and basic store alongside cottages and a working farm. A lane winds down from here to the lakeside and the three main areas where you can pitch your tent – a pretty field, a woodland area which gives more of a wild camping feel and "Ransoms" – named after Arthur of *Swallows and Amazons* fame, who spent his childhood holidays in nearby Coniston. Ransoms is right on the shoreline and termed a "premium" site, costing an extra £7.50 per night – worth it if you can manage, as there are wonderful views right across the lake.

With less of a hearty hiking feel than the other National Trust-owned properties in the Lakes, *Low Wray* is more geared to water sports, swimming and also to doing not a lot – the idyllic setting and snoozy atmosphere are very conducive to relaxation. The lakeside location makes it great for gazing at sunsets and swinging in a hammock. If you want to rent a canoe, kayak or mountain bike, head to Grizedale Mountain Bikes in Hawkshead (℡01229 860369, Ⓦwww.grizedalemountainbikes.co.uk. Windermere is also ideal for fishing; just buy a licence from a post office or tourist information centre, and see Ⓦwww.lakedistrictfishing. net for more information. The camp shop sells leaflets (£2) on hiking and mountain-biking routes from the site. There's a wonderful day-long circular walk via Wray Castle, a Gothic Revival baronial mansion owned by the National Trust, to Beatrix Potter's seventeenth-century farmhouse home Hill Top in the village of

Practicalities

Low Wray, nr Ambleside, Cumbria, LA22 0JA ☎*01539 463862,* Ⓦ*www.nationaltrust.org.uk*

Pitches & price Tents and campervans £10.50 high season (1 person & 1 vehicle); additional adults £4.50, children £2. Wooden weatherproof camping pods are currently being trialled, and cost from £30. Hook-ups available. £6 charge for sailboats and motorboats. £3 discount if you arrive by public transport.

Facilities Laundry, washing-up facilities and disabled toilet/shower. Kids' playground. On-site shop.

Restrictions Campervans but no caravans. Dogs (£1) to be kept on a lead. No campfires, just raised BBQs.

Open Easter–Oct.

Getting there Take the A593 from Ambleside and turn left at Clappersgate onto the B5286. Turn left at the sign for Wray. *Low Wray* is less than a mile on the left. Bus service #505/506, the Coniston Rambler from Ambleside or Windermere, can drop you within a mile of the site (call Traveline on ☎0871 200 2233 or visit Ⓦwww.traveline.org.uk).

Near Sawrey (also NT). You return to the campsite along the lake.

A gentle mile-and-a-half walk away is the eighteenth-century *Outgate Inn* in Outgate village, serving real ales and cider on tap; it's a similar distance to the posher *Drunken Duck*, recommended for modern British food. If you want to buy provisions, the best place is nearby Ambleside which has small supermarkets, plus the legendary Lucy's deli. Ambleside is a good place for inclement-weather distractions, including the Armitt Collection dedicated to Lakes' writers and artists, a George Gilbert Scott church plus Zeffirelli's, a terrific four-screen cinema.

◀ *Low Wray* is an ideal site for water-sports fans ▶ Stone buildings at *Low Wray*'s entrance; the National Trust's Wray Castle

Hawkshead Hall Farm

Poetry and Peter Rabbit in a whitewashed village

This is a basic site on a working farm comprising an open field, lovely fell views and a simple toilet block. It's quiet here, which appeals to families, with the only soundtrack being animal noises and tractors buzzing around in the morning. There aren't really any standout features, other than a great location on the edge of Hawkshead village, and a footpath to get you there.

Cars have been banned from the centre of Hawkshead, maximizing the charm of this little walker-friendly village with its intriguing alleyways and whitewashed cottages. It's a must-see destination for anyone interested in Wordsworth's life – he went to the humble little grammar school here, and you can still see his name carved into one of the desks. Fifteenth-century St

Michael's sits above the school, and you might also want to take kids to the Beatrix Potter Gallery which, rather tangentially, was Potter's lawyer husband's office. You can see some of Potter's original illustrations of Peter Rabbit and the gang, plus an exhibit on her life.

Otherwise, the main port of call for campers is the excellent whitewashed *King's Arms* on Market Square, which serves posher-than-average pub food. And a couple of miles south of Hawkshead is Grizedale Forest, home of the high-octane Go Ape assault course (ⓦwww.goape.co.uk), with rope swings, ladders and zip slides propelling adventurous visitors through the trees.

▼ The exterior of Hawkshead grammar school

Practicalities

Hawkshead Hall Farm, Hawskhead, nr Ambleside, Cumbria, LA22 0NN ☎*01539 436221,* ⓦ*www.hawksheadhall-campsite.com*

Pitches & price 55 pitches. £14 for 2 adults & car; same price for caravans and motor homes, though it's £17 plus hook-up. Children 5–15 £2, under-5s free.

Facilities Portacabin toilet block, clean and well-kept. Daily visit from the milkman.

Restrictions No noise between 11pm and 7am. No open campfires. Dogs must be kept on a lead.

Open March–Oct. Check in at the nearby farmhouse.

Getting there Hawkshead is south of Ambleside on the B5286; exit Ambleside on the A593 towards Langdale, and turn left at Clappersgate onto the B road. There's an alternative very attractive route through Bowness, via the regular car ferry which crosses Windermere: the B5285 from the west bank of Windermere on to Hawkshead takes you past Beatrix Potter's home at Hill Top. For public transport, you can take the "Coniston Rambler" bus service (#505), which runs between Windermere, Ambleside and Coniston. There's also a handy shuttle bus to Hawkshead from the Bowness ferry.

Park Cliffe

Pretty parkland on the shores of Lake Windermere

Large, friendly and well-organized, *Park Cliffe* features a beautiful parkland setting and dramatic mountain views. Sprawling across 25 acres near Bowness-on-Windermere, the site is divided into two areas: sheltered Ghyll Side, with allocated pitches and hook-ups; and cheaper Fell Side, which is more exposed to the elements and looks towards the Langdale Pikes and the Old Man of Coniston – here you can pitch where you like. It isn't a site for those who like roughing it, but others will appreciate the heated shower blocks, spacious caravan pitches and on-site restaurant and bar. Kids are well provided for, with an adventure play area, a small games room and a stream to paddle in. If you're up early or late, you're likely to spot some woodland wildlife, which includes foxes and roe and red deer. Bowness itself isn't the most characterful Lakes town: it gets swamped with visitors and has more of a coach tour than outdoorsy vibe. But this campsite definitely has its plus points – there are walks from the doorstep, and of course you're right by Windermere itself, with good opportunities for all kinds of water sports (try Low Wood Watersports in Windermere ☎01539 439441, ⓦwww.elh.co.uk) and lake cruises (ⓦwww.windermere-lakecruises.co.uk). A little car ferry makes the short hop from Bowness across the lake, landing near Beatrix Potter's home at Hill Top. If you want to bring your own sailing boat, launching is available at Ferry Nab (☎01539 442753).

▼ Rowing boats for hire on Lake Windermere

Practicalities

Park Cliffe Camping & Caravan Estate, Birks Road, Windermere, Cumbria, LA23 3PG ☎*01539 531344,* ⓦ*www.parkcliffe.co.uk*
Pitches & price 100 tent pitches: from £18.75 for 2 people plus a car; backpacker/cyclist rate £9.50. 60 hard-standing pitches from £23.50. Hook-ups available. Currently trialling wooden camping pods, £35 per night.
Facilities Good shower block with underfloor heating plus individual family bathroom; private bathrooms available to rent. Laundry. Play park. Restaurant, bar (with wi-fi) and shop selling essentials.
Restrictions Dogs welcome but must be kept on a lead. No campfires, just raised BBQs.
Open Mid-March to mid-Nov.
Getting there Leave the M6 at Junction 36, take the A590 to Newby Bridge, and turn right onto the A592. After 3.5 miles, turn right; the site is signposted after a third of a mile on the right. Caravans and motor homes need to approach *Park Cliffe* from Newby Bridge. For public transport, take the train to Windermere, then bus #618 from Bowness to the campsite.

Full Circle

And oft when in my yurt I lie…

In the grounds of handsome Rydal Hall, this picturesque site on a steep field, punctuated with stately sweet chestnut and redwood trees and tumbling rocks, features luxury Mongolian yurts. These are the real Mongolian deal – they are made of felt, have brightly painted wooden doors, and are equipped with wooden stoves which create a snug refuge in wintery conditions – the structures are designed to withstand Mongolian temperatures of -50 degrees. Indeed the owners are keen to stress the yurts as a practical and romantic cold-weather option as the site has become so popular in the warmer months; the white tents with their colourful embroidery and paintwork look wonderful in the snow.

Part of the pleasure of *Full Circle* is experiencing life in one of these imposing structures – the doors, decorated with folk motifs, represent the earth, the rafters the sky, and a crown on the ceiling the sun. Each yurt contains a double bed and two singles, plus two sleeping mats. There is also an outside decking area with a barbecue, a hammock, books, games, handy cooking utensils, wind-up torches and candles.

The field itself is leased from Rydal Hall, a Neoclassical stately home owned by the diocese of Carlisle that's now a Christian centre; below the yurts are tents belonging to the hall's own site, which often accommodates youth groups. Adjoining the tents is a decent tearoom serving Fairtrade coffee, soup and afternoon teas, and the grounds are cut through by a rocky chasm, with a tumbling stream and a mini waterfall. But the real attraction here is Rydal Mount, just across the road – home to William Wordsworth and his family for 37 years, and you can even see the immortal low leather couch which he stretched out on to recall the daffodils: "For oft when on my couch I lie, in vacant or in pensive mood…"

Full Circle is on the Coffin Trail between Grasmere and Ambleside, named for medieval coffin-bearers en route to St Oswald's church in Grasmere – despite this grim association,

Practicalities

Full Circle, Rydal Hall, Ambleside, Cumbria, LA22 9LX
☎*07975 671928,* Ⓦ*www.lake-district-yurts.co.uk*

Pitches & price Prices vary according to the time of year; in peak season you'll pay £285 for a weekend, £440 for the week. Each of the site's 4 yurts sleeps up to 6 with 2 sleeping on mats (mats are provided, but bring bedding). Arrive by public transport and the owners will give you a 10 percent discount.

Facilities Shower and toilet block; stove; oven; BBQ; fresh water; free firewood.

Restrictions Dogs allowed on a lead. No open campfires but you can light the brazier.

Open Year round.

Getting there Rydal is between Ambleside and Grasmere. Once in the village, follow signs for Rydal Mount – Rydal Hall is just downhill from here. For public transport, catch the train to Windermere station and then the #555 bus to Keswick which leaves around every half-hour on week days. It takes about 25 minutes to reach Rydal.

it's perfect for gentle low-level rambles. Otherwise, follow Wordsworth's example and head up Fairfield, Loughrigg, Red Screes or Wansfell, or take the valley route round Rydal Water, Grasmere Lake and the River Rothay.

Rydal itself is blink-and-you'll-miss-it small, but the honeypot village of Grasmere is a lovely destination, with more Wordsworth associations (including the family graves), as well as beautiful and challenging walks – up to Easedale Tarn for example. It's also the best nearby option for eating: try the *Jumble Room* on Langdale Road which has an eclectic international menu, or the deli on Red Lion Square in the centre of the village.

◀ Big trees surround *Full Circle*'s Mongolian yurts ▶ The yurts, built to handle cold winters; the Neoclassical symmetry of Rydal Hall

Bays Brown Farm
Staggering views in Great Langdale

In the heart of spectacular Great Langdale, *Bays Brown* has a wonderful aspect in the wide, wild open space of this beautiful glacial valley; the approach along a narrow track and over a stone packhorse bridge gives it a fantastically remote Shangri-La feel. This is a good option if the more home-knitted National Trust Great Langdale site (see p.258) is full, and it enjoys the same excellent walking opportunities – take the paths across the valley to Dungeon Ghyll, which itself is a stepping stone for more challenging and steeper hikes. The flat valley floor is also great for cycling.

The welcome here can be less than effusive, but once you've been to the farm and paid your fee, you can pitch in the spacious field and soak in some of the best views you'll ever see, of the lush valley floor with its stands of trees, and up to the imposing fells and mountains. On a practical note, the facilities are limited for such a large site, and you may have a long walk to the loos. If you encounter bad weather, it's just a short drive or bus journey to the restaurants, bars and cinema in Ambleside or there's a good café, *Brambles*, in Chapel Stile itself. There's also a great pub here, the

Wainwright Inn, with a flagstone floor, open fires and substantial pub grub. Or walk to the whitewashed *Britannia Inn* in idyllic lakeside Elterwater – passing *Wainwright Inn*, you take the bridleway on the right, cross the bridge and continue to Elterwater.

Practicalities

Bays Brown Farm, Chapel Stile, Great Langdale, Ambleside, Cumbria, LA22 9JZ ☎*01539 437150*

Pitches & price Around 80 pitches. £4 per adult, £2 per child (5–16), £2 per vehicle.

Facilities Decent toilet block and a washing-up area.

Restrictions No noise after 10.30pm. No single-sex groups. No campfires. Dogs welcome.

Open March–Oct.

Getting there From Ambleside, take the A593. At Skelwith Bridge, turn right onto the B5343 to Chapel Stile. The site is signposted on the left. For public transport, catch the Langdale Rambler from Ambleside (daily service #516, reduced in winter; Traveline ☎0870 608 2608 or visit ⓦwww.traveline.org.uk).

▼ *Bays Brown*'s spacious field is ringed by impressive hills

Turner Hall Farm
Remote pitches and historic pubs

Hidden away in the rocky and wonderfully wild Duddon Valley – immortalized for its beauty in a famous sequence of sonnets by Wordsworth – *Turner Hall Farm* enjoys remarkable views. Reached on narrow twisty lanes – the most stunning approach is from the north, via the Wrysnose Pass – the area has an enduring remote wilderness feel.

A gravel track winds through the grounds of this site, which is punctuated by hillocks and little crags, meaning you can find a distinctive, sheltered spot for your tent – you can even pitch in the lee of a ruined cottage on the edge of the field. It's a basic campsite with no frills, but well kept and with a friendly welcome from the owners. All around are spectacular fells, and the main attraction is – of course – walking. Close to the site is the Walna Scar route, which leads to the iconic Coniston peak, the Old Man (2634ft). Another popular, and much easier, hike from Seathwaite is to Wallabarrow Gorge.

Handily, there's a fine-looking pub – the *Newfield Inn* – just down the road in the village. Visited by none other than Mr Wordsworth himself, it features open fires and flagstone floors and serves food of the solidly filling variety – Yorkshire puds, pies and so on for around £12. Otherwise, walk to the marvellous old *Blacksmiths Arms* at Broughton Mills – the building dates back to 1577, and there's been an inn here since at least 1748.

▼ Pitch in a remote spot at *Turner Hall Farm*

Practicalities

Turner Hall Farm, Seathwaite, Broughton-in-Furness, Cumbria, LA20 6EE ☎*01229 716420,* ✉*turnerhall@ktdinternet.com*

Pitches & price Around 40 pitches: £6 per adult, £1 per child, £1 per car, £2 per campervan.

Facilities Loos are in a simple converted shed, with showers in the tall barn building.

Restrictions No caravans. No campfires. Dogs allowed (£1).

Open April–Oct.

Getting there From Ambleside, take the A593 west to Broughton Mills. From here, take the Duddon Valley road to the T-junction and go right to Seathwaite. The campsite is through the village, up the hill on the right. Alternatively, the site can be accessed from the north by the scenic but steep Wrynose Pass, from Great Langdale. Unless you have a very small car, take the signed detour left of the entrance rather than driving through the farm buildings, as it's a tight squeeze.

Great Langdale
Majestic pikes, crags and tarns

Campers flock to this National Trust-owned site, not for fancy facilities or a party atmosphere but for classic Lakes scenery on an epic scale. *Great Langdale* sits in the expansive Langdale Valley: green, lush, studded with stands of mature trees and with meadows scattered with wild flowers. Ringing the valley are iconic mountains such as Bowfell (2949ft), Crinkle Crags (2818ft) and the Langdale Pikes, landmarks in themselves as well as in the history of climbing in this area. Their lower slopes delineated with the lines of dry stone walls and their peaks often hidden in cloud, these mountains have an imposing, sometimes forbidding aspect, which is irresistible to the hordes of walkers and climbers who come here. It's an impressive place, and one with a long history of human habitation – large numbers of Stone Age axes, hewn out of hard volcanic rock, have been found in the upper valley.

Simplicity is the keynote at the campsite itself, which pretty much consists of open fields with simple but clean toilet blocks. Cars are kept away from the pitches in parking areas, keeping the noise down. Indeed, with a policy of no noise between 11pm and 7am, the snoring of exhausted walkers is the only sound likely to disturb your slumbers here – that and a deafening dawn chorus. There's a shop selling some foodstuffs including bread, milk and eggs, plus snacks including the NT's own Kendal mint cake, and they also sell a handy leaflet (£2.50) detailing walks from the site. For more supplies, you'll need to go to the Coop in Chapel Stile, the nearest village in the Ambleside direction.

Most campers wander up the lane to eat at *Old Dungeon Ghyll Hotel*, where the rugged timber-framed and flagstoned *Hiker's Bar* is hugely popular. They serve real ale and dish up generous portions of lamb curry, Cumberland pie and so on for under a tenner, plus puddings for around £4. (You can also eat in the hotel restaurant, but must reserve in advance.) From behind the hotel, challenging walks lead to the steep rocky face of Pavey Ark and on to a series of peaks (or "pikes"). A less difficult option runs from the neighbouring *New Dungeon Ghyll Hotel* to Dungeon Ghyll Force, a sixty-foot waterfall in a deep ravine ("dungeon" in the name refers to a natural cave). From here you can continue up to Stickle Tarn.

Practicalities

Great Langdale Campsite, Great Langdale, nr Ambleside, Cumbria, LA22 9JU ☎01539 437668, ⓦwww.national trust.org.uk

Pitches & price 220 pitches. Tents and campervans £10.50 high season for 1 person & 1 vehicle; additional adults £4.50, children £2. Discount (£3) if you arrive by public transport. Wooden weather-proof camping pods from £30. Hook-ups available.

Facilities Washing-up facilities, disabled toilet and shower. Laundry. Kids' playground. Small on-site shop selling basics.

Restrictions Dogs (£1) welcome but must be kept on a lead at all times. No campfires.

Open Year round.

Getting there From Ambleside, follow the A593 road. At Skelwith Bridge, turn right onto the B5343. The campsite is lies 6 miles down this road on the left-hand side just before you reach the *Old Dungeon Ghyll Hotel*. For public transport, catch the Langdale Rambler from Ambleside (daily service #516, reduced in winter; Traveline ☎0870 608 2608 or visit ⓦwww. traveline.org.uk).

Great Langdale is a good option if you're not a driver, as it's the endpoint for the trusty "Langdale Rambler" bus (more prosaically known as the #516), which starts at Ambleside – the campsite gives a £3 reduction if you arrive on foot or by bus. If there's even a glimmer of sunshine, this site is packed at weekends, so make your reservation well in advance. And if the weather turns, this is the kind of country where you can see the rain coming – tighten up your guyropes, put on your cagoule and make a beeline for the *Hiker's Bar*.

◀ Surrounded by epic Lakes scenery at *Great Langdale* ▶ The bar at the *Old Dungeon Ghyll* is a hikers' favourite; Dungeon Ghyll Force

Fisherground

Kid heaven: a steam train, an adventure playground and open fires

Verdant Eskdale, one of the Lakes' most scenic valleys, is an area where you're never far from a great view and a great pub, as well as walking and cycling for all abilities. *Fisherground* spreads out from a striking stone crag with tall oak trees, and is otherwise flat – perfect for pitching on as well as for games and general running about. Particularly guaranteed to find a place in the hearts of children, the standout feature here is an adventure play area, accessed via a plank bridge over a stream. Like a mini assault course, it has a Tarzan-style swing, tree huts and rope climbing. If this isn't enough, the site has its own request stop on the irresistible Ravenglass and Eskdale steam line. The sight and sound of the gleaming little train, its steam rising through the tall trees backing the campsite, makes this a really memorable place. And dotted throughout the site are bowls for open fires: from the vantage point of the rock outcrop, watching fires being lit as it grows dark is truly magical.

The valley of Eskdale extends for twelve miles, terminating at its western end at the magnificently located Hardknott Roman Fort. The fort was built during the reign of Hadrian and, as well as having a defensive function, featured bathhouses and granaries. Low walls are all that remain, but you can still get a sense of its scale, and of the loneliness the troops must have felt in this far-flung outpost of the Roman Empire. This is just one of the excursions you can make from the site – and you're spoilt for choice for walks here. Amongst a myriad of options, there are the hikes to Dalegarth Force (waterfall) and the Esk Falls or – if you're feeling particularly brave – you could attempt the tough high-level Woolpack Walk. (The loo block in the campsite has a good array of tourist information about the area, including a handy description of local walks.)

Fisherground is well provided for on the pub front – the sixteenth-century *King George IV* is a stroll away – turn right as you exit the site. It's a traditional Lakes boozer, with cask ales and over two hundred malt whiskies. In the other direction is

Practicalities

Fisherground Campsite, Fellside Cottage, Eskdale, Cumbria, CA19 1TF ☎*01946 723349,* Ⓦ*www.fishergroundcampsite.co.uk*

Pitches & price 215 pitches. Adults £5.50, children £2.50, cars £2.50, hook-ups £3.

Facilities Good toilet block. Laundry facilities and hair dryers available.

Restrictions No caravans but motor homes allowed. Fires allowed in the places provided. No noise after 10.30pm. No single sex groups except DofE. Dogs (£1) to be kept on a lead.

Open March–Oct.

Getting there From the south, leave the M6 at junction 36 for Kendal/Lakes and follow signs for Barrow. Before you reach Barrow, turn right to Workington (A5092) 3 miles beyond Newby Bridge. Follow this road for about 10 miles. Beyond Broughton-in-Furness turn right at the traffic lights towards Ulpha. After 4 miles turn left in Ulpha village to the steep hill signposted Eskdale. Follow the fell road to *King George IV* pub (6 miles). Turn right, and *Fisherground* is 200yds on the left. This is a brilliant option for public transport – take the train to coastal Ravenglass from Barrow-in-Furness, and then make the rest of your journey (40min) on the miniature steam train.

the *Woolpack Inn*, which has its own brewery – try a pint of Woolpacker. Otherwise, the café at Dalegarth, the end station of the steam train (reached by turning left out of the campground), provides rather solid scones and cakes plus cuppas and soft drinks. Eskdale Green has a good grocery, Eskdale Stores, where you can stock up with local, Fairtrade and organic fodder.

◀ The miniature Ravenglass and Eskdale steam line ▶ The remains of Hardknott Roman Fort; kids will love *Fisherground*'s play area

Campsite cuisine

There's something hugely satisfying about cooking and eating in the fresh air. Even a humble cuppa somehow tastes better when prepared just outside your tent, and with today's campsites offering a huge range of foodie treats on site you'll rarely have to worry about bringing much more than a healthy appetite.

Campsite cuisine can rival anything you can cook at home: instead of burnt sausages think baked fish and succulent joints of meat infused with wood-smoked flavours, all served with fluffy potatoes plucked from the coals. Everyone can get involved in gathering and preparing ingredients – kids can stuff bananas with chocolate and melt marshmallows on sticks, anglers can go fishing for dinner and even the most reluctant camper will find something tasty to cook at a local **farm shop** or market (see below for some recommendations).

Many campsites are connected to farms, in which case there's an excellent chance of picking up locally reared meats, freshly laid eggs and delicious vegetables, all mercifully free of preservatives and packaging. Other sites provide freshly baked bread delivered to your tent, while on the Isles of Scilly you can sample home-made ice cream from the local herd. Buying local not only saves food miles, the environment and the rural economy, but when you opt for farm shops, pick-your-owns and roadside stalls you keep in touch with the seasons and guarantee the finest, freshest taste of the area.

When it comes down to **cooking equipment**, forking out on a few choice essentials will save burning your best saucepans and breaking your favourite crockery. Kit up with stainless steel plates and bowls, a camping kettle that whistles at tea-time and thermos mugs (get a cafetière version for fresh coffee). Lightweight aluminium pans are ideal for expedition camping, but if you're not limited by space and weight, any old saucepans will do – just make sure any used on open fires have metal handles and will stand up to a good bit of scrubbing.

The most commonly used **camping stoves** are gas-fuelled, ranging from compact, one-ring stoves big enough to boil a small kettle to double-burners complete with a grill. What type you choose will depend on how many people you are cooking for, how many pans you use and how far you have to carry your gear. Hikers favour pocket-sized versions, families will benefit from multiple burners, while any camper in Britain would be well advised to select a model with a wind guard. Gas refills are sometimes available at campsites, but it pays to pack a spare if there's room. For the lightweight camper one of the best options on the market is a Trangia (pots, pans and a methylated spirits burner all packed together like Russian dolls), and for greenies there are now eco-stoves fuelled by resealable cartridges of non-explosive, non-toxic gel.

While gas is efficient and convenient, cooking over an **open fire** offers a far richer experience: campfires bring people together, warm you up and infuse foods with a delicious smoky aroma. But don't expect the speed and convenience of your fan oven – campfire cuisine takes patience. The only way to avoid charred food is to wait for the flames to subside and the wood or coals to turn white before cooking. You can purchase a steel camp grill (with a mesh top and foldaway legs) to sit over the fire or support pans with damp logs. Many campsites don't allow open fires (we note such restrictions in our Practicalities boxes), in which case a **barbecue** is the next best option: a decent portable one is worth the investment for a regular camper, otherwise a disposable will do.

Finally, for every good camping feast you need a few basic **ingredients** in your stock cupboard. Pack tinned tomatoes, stock cubes, mixed herbs, tomato paste, honey, mustard, onions, garlic, soy sauce, rice and pasta. Don't forget a salt and pepper mill, olive oil, tea and fresh coffee and a bottle of your favourite tipple. A couple of lighters or a box of waterproof matches is another essential – while it can be fun to indulge your inner caveman and make fire with a couple of sticks, it's probably best left to the likes of Ray Mears.

FIVE GREAT FARM SHOPS

Abbey Home Farm, Cotswolds (see p.62) Award-winning organic produce as supplied to one of Britain's most lauded farm cafés.

Dernwood Farm, Sussex (see p.92) Carnivore-heaven: free-range beef, pork and lamb reared on the farm next to the campsite.

Gear Farm Shop, Cornwall (see p.19) Organic vegetables, handmade pasties plus fresh crab and Cornish meats.

Knowes Farm Shop, near Lochhouses Farm, East Lothian (see p.318) Everything from venison burgers and game pie to tasty jams and chutneys, plus free-range eggs.

Stokeley Farm Shop, near Old Cotmore Farm, Devon (see p.35) Pick your own fruit and veg, plus fresh fish, local ice cream and locally reared meats.

◀ Wake up and smell the fresh coffee: campsite cookery has moved on from burnt sausages and lukewarm instant noodles

The Old Post Office

An orderly riverside site and a pub full of liars

Located in the village of Santon Bridge, at the start of the road to Nether Wasdale and spectacular Wasdale Head (see p.266), this neat and attractive site has a domestic feel rather than being exposed to the great outdoors. *The Old Post Office* grounds are grassy and spacious with a good enclosed play area and goalposts – perfect for kids. Groups are discouraged here and there's an early noise curfew, giving the place a definite family atmosphere. The wide river Irt, which runs right alongside the site, has sea and brown trout and salmon – ask the owner about renting rods – and provides good outdoor entertainment.

A stile leads up onto the bridge where the *Bridge Inn* can be found; the inn is the location of the famous and idiosyncratic Biggest Liar in the World competition, which has been held here each November since the late nineteenth century. Other attractions in the area include the wonderful walks that radiate out from Wasdale Head, including the climb up Scafell Pike (3209ft).

And you don't need to stock up with lots of supplies before you arrive – if you want to cook on site, you can buy food from the Santon Bridge farm shop just up the road. Otherwise, hole up in the snug *Bridge Inn*, where you can spend the evening eating, drinking – and lying? – to your heart's content.

Practicalities

The Old Post Office Campsite, Santon Bridge, Holmrook, Cumbria, CA19 1UY ☏*01946 726286,* Ⓦ*www. theoldpostofficecampsite.co.uk*

Pitches & price 35 pitches. £6 per adult, £2 per child (5–15). 2-person tent free, large tent £2. Motor homes & cars £2. Hook-ups £3. Caravans £17, including 2 adults, a car and hook-up.

Facilities Good toilet block, disabled toilet and shower. Laundry and play area.

Restrictions No groups, apart from DofE. No noise after 10.30pm and no campfires – just raised BBQs. Dogs (£1) to be kept on a lead.

Open March–Sept.

Getting there From the south, turn off the M6 at J36 and follow the A590 west to Broughton-in-Furness, passing through Newby Bridge. Follow the A595 through Bootle, Muncaster to Holmrook. At the approach to Holmrook turn right for Santon Bridge, and follow the road to the end, passing Irton Hall and the Wasdale Craft Shop (both on your left); at the junction turn left. The site is at the bottom of the hill near the river. From the north, take the M6 to J40 (west), joining the A595 west to Cockermouth. At Cockermouth join the A66 Keswick road; at the Sheep & Wool Centre roundabout take the A5086 Egremont turning. Turn left at Egremont following the A595 signs for Barrow-in-Furness. Through the village of Holmrook over the bridge, take the first turning left past the petrol station for Santon Bridge.

▼ Relaxing at the campsite in the evening

Wasdale Yurt Holiday
Two attractive yurts, one friendly farm

Set in the heart of wild Lakeland walking country, Rainors Farm is at the western edge of the Wasdale Valley, near Gosforth village. There are two yurts in the grounds of the handsome Georgian farmhouse – one has sweeping views of Scafell Pike (3209ft), while the other, more secluded yurt is surrounded by reeds and wild flowers. Both have their own loo facilities – the lower yurt has a wet room in the farm buildings, and the upper yurt has its own loos and showers in a very neatly converted stone shed. All in all, everything has been done here to guarantee a comfortable and enjoyable stay. The yurts themselves are beautiful circular structures, made with steam-bent ash, lined with felt and decked out with appropriately hippyish and attractive rugs, cushions and throws. They have wooden stoves so are very cosy in winter, and the upper one has a barbecue and terrace. The yurts have electricity, which will appeal to some, but if you want a more natural yurt experience you might be happier at *Full Circle* (see p.254).

The farm also operates as a B&B, and the lovely owners give yurt guests traditional English or vegetarian breakfast in their dining room as part of the deal. For other meals, head east towards Wast Water to the traditional whitewashed *Screes Inn* in Nether Wasdale, where there's bar food, a restaurant, real ales and occasional live music. Push on a little further to the eastern edge of Wast Water, and you come to the legendary *Wasdale Head Inn* (see p.266).

Practicalities

Wasdale Yurt Holiday, Rainors Farm Yurts, Wasdale Road, Gosforth, Cumbria, CA20 1ER ☎*01946 725934,* Ⓦ*www.rainorsfarm.co.uk*

Pitches & price 2 yurts, each sleeps 5 people max. £595 per week high season (plus breakfast), weekends £385.
Facilities Excellent: each yurt has its own bathroom and shower. Both have electricity and a wood-burning stove.
Restrictions Dogs allowed. No campfires.
Open Year round.
Getting there The farm is between Gosforth and Nether Wasdale on the Wasdale Road. It's 1hr 30min from junction 36 of the M6 heading north on the A595, and an hour's drive south from Carlisle on the A595.

▼ The lower yurt, backed by reeds

Barn Door
Dramatic peaks and soaring scree slopes

Barn Door is the most basic of sites in the remotest of settings. The approach road grows narrower as you pass Wast Water, England's deepest lake, and at the end sits the imposing *Wasdale Head Inn*, encircled by peaks including Scafell. Backed by these forbidding scree-covered slopes, the site itself is accessed by a wooden squeeze gate opposite the inn. It's just a field, with minimal facilities, but you'll find compensation in the form of jaw-dropping mountains views when you unzip your tent in the morning, and terrific walking and moutain biking. This iconic Lakes location

▼ The famous *Wasdale Head Inn* lies across the road from the site

has been warming the cockles of visitors since climbing was invented as a leisure occupation – indeed the inn claims to be the birthplace of the sport.

This is a truly wild spot, where you're exposed to the wind and rain that sweeps in over the mountains. If it all gets too much, hole up in snug *Ritson's Bar* in the *Wasdale Head Inn*, with its flagstone floor and wood-burning stove, and enjoy one of the impressive range of ales created in the on-site Great Gable Brewery. The food – goulash, lasagne, chilli and steaks and filling sticky toffee pudding – is perfect after a strenuous day on the fells. The bar was named for Alfred Ritson, a nineteenth-century publican who lived in the valley, and who originated the World's Biggest Liar competition, now held at the *Bridge Inn* at Santon Bridge (see p.264). Nearby is tiny St Olaf's church, whose graveyard, said to be the smallest in the country, bears testimony to the dangers faced by earlier generations of explorers in the area.

Practicalities

Barn Door Campsite, Wasdale Head, Cumbria, CA20 1EX
℡ *01946 726384*, Ⓦ *www.barndoorshop.co.uk*
Pitches & price Around 30 pitches. £2.50 per person – pay at the Barn Door Shop across the way. If it's closed when you arrive, pay the next morning.
Facilities Minimal. Just a simple toilet block. The Barn Door Shop is well stocked with climbing and walking gear, including boots, waterproofs and ice axes, as well as walking guides and a range of camping equipment.
Restrictions No BBQs or open fires. No noise after 10pm. Dogs allowed.
Open Year round.
Getting there Wasdale Head is reached from the main A595. From the south, turn right at Holmrook for Santon Bridge and follow signs up to Wasdale Head. From the north, turn left at Gosforth. *Barn Door* campsite is at the end of the road, opposite the *Wasdale Head Inn.*

Seathwaite Farm

A wild valley at the foot of Scafell Pike

Enjoying a fantastically picturesque spot – backed by a wall of hills and a tumbling waterfall – spacious *Seathwaite Farm* rivals even Wasdale Head for beauty. A side track leaves the Borrowdale road at Seatoller, ending at the rough-hewn buildings of the farm. From here, steep peaks rear up in all directions, their lower slopes dense with grass and ferns and patterned with the wiggly lines of stone walls, the higher slopes bare and forbidding.

This is, needless to say, hugely popular walking territory, as the number of cars parked around the farm will testify. The major ascents here are of Scafell Pike (3209ft), triangular Great Gable (2949ft) and Green Gable (2628ft) – just go through the gate at the end of the farmyard and you're on your way. The classic Scafell Pike route is to go up Styhead Tarn, and then up the Corridor Route (which involves some scrambling), making your descent via Esk Hause – all in all it's a tough eight-mile circuit. There's a wealth of other outdoor options available too, including rock climbing, abseiling, navigation training and ghyll scrambling – contact Keswick Mountain Adventures for more details (Ⓦwww.keswickmountainadventures.co.uk).

Seathwaite is very much a working farm, and campers share the field with sheep. Adjacent to the farm buildings is a café,

only open at weekends; another option is the *Yew Tree* café at Seatoller, though this is only open during the day. This really is a remote spot – the nearest pub is the *Royal Oak* at Rosthwaite – so it's best to come prepared with a stove and supplies for evening meals. Given that Seathwaite is cited by many as being the wettest place in England, you might want to forego your tent and sleep in the simple bunk barn, which has its own kitchen and an area with benches and tables. Campers use the National Trust loo block, and there's a separate unit with showers. There are no luxuries here, but it's truly a magnificent location, and if you want stretching hikes and a memorable dose of the great outdoors, this is a great option.

▼ Borrowdale's dampest corner, Seathwaite is a fine spot for hikers

Practicalities

Seathwaite Farm Campsite and Camping Barn, Seathwaite, Borrowdale, Cumbria, CA12 5XJ Ⓣ*01768 777394*

Pitches & price 100 pitches: £5 per person. Bunk barn (sleeps up to 18): £6 per person.

Facilities Shower block (coin-op) and toilets.

Restrictions No dogs. No loud music after 10pm. No campfires.

Open Year round.

Getting there From Keswick, follow signs for Borrowdale and the B5289; continue on this road through Grange and Rosthwaite. At Seatoller, turn left onto the minor road to Seathwaite. *Seathwaite Farm* is at the road end.

Wasdale

River deep, mountain high, church small

Famously, Wasdale is a place of superlatives, ringed by mighty mountains, including Scafell Pike, the highest in England, and pyramidal Great Gable. *Wasdale* sits just beyond the eastern edge of the valley's lake, Wast Water – the country's deepest lake, and certainly one of its scariest looking, with the barren scree-covered slope of Illgill Head rising steeply above. The valley is also home to St Olaf's, England's smallest church, which has the graves of several local climbing pioneers who met their end here. The gentle tearooms and pastoral charms of the Lakes seem very far away – this is serious hiking country.

If you're of a frivolous disposition, be aware that you'll be surrounded by earnest walking types at this campsite – it's pretty much early nights and early starts here, with strict rules regarding noise. And you won't be regaling your friends with hiking yarns around the barbecue, as they're not permitted. What you will find, in abundance, is natural beauty. The site makes the most of this, keeping cars off the fields, and letting you camp where you like amongst the trees. Wherever you pitch, you can peek out of your tent in the morning and have the stunning sight of high fells all around. Camping pods are being trialled at the site and cost around £30 each per night; if you're coming by public transport and don't want to lug a tent with you, this is a good option (plus they're rainproof, always a good thing in the Lakes).

Wasdale is one of the best places in Britain for outdoor pursuits: climbing, hiking, abseiling, canoeing on Wast Water, fell running, fishing and mountainbiking. A good source of information is Ⓦwww.wasdaleweb.co.uk. (Bear in mind though that there's nowhere to rent boats or canoes in the immediate vicinity, so you'll have to bring your own.) Arrive well equipped for even short hikes as the weather is massively changeable, and the terrain tough – this is not a place for beginners. Classic Wasdale hikes include the Mosedale Horseshoe, a twelve-mile route which starts at Overbeck Bridge and goes via pikes, fells

Practicalities

Wasdale Campsite, Wasdale Head, Seascale, Cumbria, CA20 1EX ☎*01946 726220,* Ⓦ*www.nationaltrust.org.uk*

Pitches & price 120 pitches. Tents and campervans: £10.50 high season for 1 person & 1 vehicle; additional adults £4.50, children £2. Discount (£3) if you arrive on foot or bicycle.

Facilities Good toilet block with washing up area, disabled toilet/shower. Laundry. Small on-site shop.

Restrictions Noise to be kept to a minimum at all times, and no noise after 11pm. No fires or BBQs. Dogs (£1) to be kept on a lead at all times. No vehicles on the pitching area.

Open Year round.

Getting there *Wasdale Head* is reached from the main A595. From the south, turn right at Holmrook for Santon Bridge and follow signs up to *Wasdale Head*. From the north, turn left at Gosforth. Although a green travel discount of £3 is given, arriving by public transport isn't easy: the site is a 4-mile mountain walk from Irton and Dalegarth stations on the Ravenglass and Eskdale Railway.

and the Mosedale packhorse trail to land you up at *Wasdale Head Inn*. And of course Scafell Pike and Scafell, England's highest and second highest mountains respectively, have huge appeal for walkers.

A small shop on site sells canned food but nothing fancy. For more filling grub you're best off at *Ritson's Bar* in the famous *Wasdale Head Inn* down the road. They do stews, pies and sticky toffee pudding – not gourmet, but perfect post-hike fodder. The Great Gable Brewery in the Inn provides traditional ales.

◀ Wasdale valley in winter ▶ Evening at the campsite; you can hike to the summit of Scafell Pike, England's highest mountain, from *Wasdale*

Syke Farm
Footbridge over Lakes waters

This wonderfully pretty site is located in one of the Lake District's most attractive villages: Buttermere. Tucked between two lakes, Crummock Water and Buttermere, there's not much more to the village than the campsite, a couple of great pubs, a church and a scattering of stone-built houses. You park your car by the stream, and then cross the water over a little wooden footbridge, which gives the campsite a nice air of being fortified. There's no reception (pay your fees at Syke Farm itself, uphill in the vil-

▼ Crossing the footbridge to the site

lage), so apart from a toilet block there's nothing to distract from the sylvan charms of the field itself. The ground is hilly, broken up with rocky outcrops and trees, but with just about enough flat ground for a game of badminton or a kickabout. Great views – and footpaths – stretch in all directions. There's the streamside path right by the site, which takes you to the shores of Buttermere, and any number of pikes and crags to explore. One iconic walk from here is the eight-mile hike to Haystacks (1958ft), which was Alfred Wainwright's favourite peak, via Red Pike (2476ft), High Stile (2648ft) and High Crag (2441ft).

The village itself has a quaint, almost alpine air. Amongst its attractions are the *Walkers' Bar* at the venerable *Bridge Hotel*, where you can have a pint of Black Sheep and Cumbrian grub, and the *Fish Hotel*, which also serves real ales and good pub food. At Syke Farm itself, where you pay your camping fees, there's a little café where they dish up home-made ice cream created with milk from their own Ayrshire cows. Amongst the more challenging flavours, such as bubble gum and liquorice, try the excellent lemon meringue pie ice cream dotted with crunchy meringue. There's no shop in Buttermere village, so remember to pick up supplies in Keswick before you head out here.

Practicalities

Syke Farm, Buttermere, Cockermouth, Cumbria, CA13 9XA ☎01768 770222
Pitches & price 40 tent pitches: £7 per adult including a car, £3 for kids.
Facilities Minimal loo block with coin-op showers.
Restrictions No campfires and no noise after 11pm. Dogs allowed on a lead.
Open Year round.
Getting there From Keswick, take the B5289 to Buttermere. The campsite car park is beyond the main village car park. From Keswick, take bus # 77 or # 77a – the Honister Rambler – to Buttermere (April–Oct, 8 daily).

Whinfell Hall

Occupying a quiet spot in the lush Vale of Lorton, this part of the northwestern fells is incredibly peaceful. Rather than being dominated by high crags, this is a rolling rural landscape, and the village of Lorton, despite its twelfth-century church, is not a place to make a huge beeline for.

You are, however, guaranteed to escape the crowds here, and *Whinfell Hall* is close to Cockermouth, birthplace of Wordsworth – beautifully restored Wordsworth House is well worth a visit, and holds imaginative reenactments of eighteenth-century household activities.

You're also within striking distance of the coastline and the Georgian harbour town of Whitehaven, which enjoyed a boom in the eighteenth century as a result of the slave trade. Back in Lorton, the campsite itself is spacious, comprising four gently sloping grassy fields enclosed by beech hedges. The loos are simple but fine, the farmyard pretty and you're within easy strolling distance of the *Wheatsheaf Inn*, which serves Jennings Ales and has a good beer garden.

Practicalities

Whinfell Hall Campsite, Low Lorton, Cockermouth, Cumbria, CA13 0RQ ☏01900 85260

Pitches & price 60 pitches. Tent & 1 person £6; 2/3-person tent & 2 people £12. Caravan & 2 people £12. Extra adults £5; children (4–15) £2.50.

Facilities Decent toilet block with showers and washing-up facilities.

Restrictions Dogs to be kept on a lead. No campfires.

Open Year round.

Getting there From Keswick, you need to take the A66 west out of town, and then turn left onto the B5292 heading towards Cockermouth. *Whinfell Hall* campsite is indicated by a generic camping sign (not by name). As far as public transport goes, Lorton is on the #77 and #77A Honister Rambler bus route which departs from Keswick and makes a circuit through Buttermere.

Seatoller Farm

With sublime hill views in beauteous Borrowdale, this nice, simple little site is just a stroll away from the village of Seatoller. Here, at white-washed sixteenth-century *Seatoller Farm*, you pay the camping fees before pitching your tent. It's worth having a good explore of the site before you decide where to pitch – it's extremely pretty and quiet, with several lovely secluded spots and the River Derwent flowing past. This is lush pastureland, ringed around with traditional rugged stone walls and mature trees. The facilities are pretty simple – just a shed-like stone building with loos and sinks; you need to walk to the farm to get a shower. From the site, a wooden footbridge crosses the Derwent and takes you across country to Seathwaite (see p.267), a starting point for ascents of Scafell Pike and Great and Green Gable. Also close by are the Cumbria Way, which runs from Carlisle in the north of the region to Ulverston in the south. Otherwise you might want to give the Coast to Coast Path or the Allerdale Ramble a go – ask the campsite owners for more details. The village has a nice daytime café, the *Yew Tree*.

Practicalities

Seatoller Farm Camping, Borrowdale, Keswick, Cumbria, CA12 5XN ☏017687 77232, Ⓦwww.seatollerfarm.co.uk

Pitches & price 70 pitches. £6 per adult, £3 per child (5–15).

Facilities Simple toilet block; you'll need to walk to the farm for showers.

Restrictions Campfires not permitted. Dogs allowed on a lead.

Open Easter–Oct.

Getting there From Keswick, follow the signs for Borrowdale and the B5289; continue on this road through Grange and Rosthwaite. Seatoller is located a mile beyond Rosthwaite, just before the road goes over the Honister Pass. Public transport is fairly straightforward – just take the Borrowdale Rambler bus (#79) which departs from Keswick (every 30min–1hr; 30min).

Hollows Farm
Blissed out in Borrowdale

Capitalizing on the spectacular natural setting of the Borrowdale valley, which has an almost primeval feel, with magnificent stretches of mature forest, craggy fells rising above the treeline, huge ferns and tall foxgloves, *Hollows Farm* is a prime spot for camping. Pay fees at the picturesque farm 200 yards uphill from the site and head down the lane to the tents. First you'll come to a pretty meadow, designated for groups, which has a stone wall snaking down one side and tall trees down the other, with tantalizing glimpses of the fells. And further down the lane, at the section for individual campers, things get even more idyllic. It's a wonderfully secluded gently sloping field – park your car and then cross a footbridge over a rushing stream to pitch your tent.

This is neither a rule-bound site nor a quirky one, but it's a truly beautiful spot, and as long as you're not overburdened with kit, it's also a fairly easy place to get to by bus – the Borrowdale Rambler drops you off at the nearby hamlet of Grange-in-Borrowdale.

Rising above are the rocky masses of Goat Crag and Nitting Haws, which provide some terrific walks right on the doorstep. But paths lead in all directions – there are some caves nearby up the hill, and there's also a short path to the wide (but reassuringly shallow, if you have kids) River Derwent, where you can paddle or sit on the shingle strand. Keep your eyes peeled for red squirrels in the woods, and in the evening you might also spot deer. Just south of Grange on the Borrowdale road is a turn-off for the Bowder Stone – a gigantic lump of rock which you can climb via a wooden ladder. On the opposite side of the road from the Stone sits Castle Crag (951ft), said to be the site of an ancient fort, with fine views down into a gorge. And a couple of miles north is Derwent Water, with great opportunities for kayaking, canoeing, windsurfing and sailing (try Ⓦwww.derwentwatermarina.co.uk). One option for exploring Derwent Water without a car is to take the footpath from Grange, and then use the Keswick Launch ferry

Practicalities

Hollows Farm, Grange-in-Borrowdale, Cumbria, CA12 5UQ
ⓣ*01768 777298,* Ⓦ*www.hollowsfarm.co.uk*

Pitches & price 90 pitches: £6 per adult, children (5–15 years) £3.

Facilities The site features a simple breeze-block and timber toilet block with washing-up facilities; showers are located at the farm – a lovely walk in good weather, but otherwise make sure you have rainproof gear.

Restrictions Campervans allowed, but no caravans. No campfires permitted. Well-behaved dogs welcome.

Open March–Oct.

Getting there From Keswick take the B5289 to Borrowdale and after 3 miles turn right for Grange village at the double-humpbacked bridge. After going over the bridge, follow the road for 200yds, going past a couple of cafés on your left. Immediately after the second café turn left down the lane, signposted "Hollows Farm" for half a mile. For public transport, take the Borrowdale Rambler bus (#79) from Keswick (every 30min–1hr; 25min).

to stop off at various points around the lake, with its wooded islands and tall surrounding crags.

While you can feel deep in the heart of nowhere at *Hollows Farm*, the presence of nearby Grange means you'll never be too far from a comforting cuppa and scones. There are two tearooms in the village, with *Grange Bridge Cottage* enjoying a particularly pretty location – its gardens look right onto the old stone bridge. Unusually for a Lake District village there is no pub in Grange – instead head two miles south to Rosthwaite to the hikers' favourite, the eighteenth-century *Royal Oak*. You're best off buying food and other supplies in Keswick.

◄ Grange-in-Borrowdale's stone bridge ▶ The Bowder Stone is thirty feet high and fify feet across; looking down to *Hollows Farm*'s fields

Castlerigg Farm

From its high vantage point, this simple but pleasant site enjoys big views of the brooding profile of Walla Crag (1234ft). Downhill is Derwent Water, whose scattered islets were an early Christian pilgrimage destination – St Cuthbert preached the Gospel here in the middle of the seventh century. Beyond lies Bassenthwaite Lake, the only lake (as opposed to "Water" or "Mere") in the region. You'll be greeted at the campsite reception with a pretty long list of rules about noise and groups, but this should ensure a decent night's sleep, and an early rise for some great walking – you can be out of your tent and on a footpath in a couple of minutes. Walla Crag itself is just a mile away and doesn't get overrun with visitors, as can be the case at nearby Cat Bells (1480ft) – try the route over the crag to Ashness Bridge, with its ancient packhorse bridge, and then down to Derwent Water. Facilities on site are simple but fine, with decent loos and a small shop, and there's the added attraction of the cute *Hayloft Café* located, unsurprisingly, in a tall converted hayloft. They serve breakfast, and mains such as steak, sausage, haddock and lamb for under £10.

Practicalities

Castlerigg Farm Camping and Caravan Site, Keswick, Cumbria, CA12 4TE ☎*01768 772479,* Ⓦ*www.castleriggfarm.com*

Pitches & price 70 tent pitches: adults £4.90, children £2.80, vehicles £1.60. 18 caravan/motor home pitches: £16 with hook-up plus 2 people. Extra people £2.75.

Facilities Good shower block, laundry, café, small shop.

Restrictions Complete quiet between 10.30pm and 7am. No loud music or single-sex groups. Small raised BBQs allowed but no campfires. Dogs allowed.

Open March–Nov (Remembrance Sunday).

Getting there Follow the signs for Keswick. Don't enter the town but take the A591 towards Windermere. After a mile, turn right up the lane signposted "Castlerigg Campsite"; Castlerigg Hall (see below) is on the other side of the road. There's an hourly bus service (#555) from Keswick to the end of the lane.

Castlerigg Hall

It seems churlish to suggest that immaculate *Castlerigg Hall* will be too well organized for some campers. The site is admirably spick and span, but despite the fantastic location – near the Castlerigg Stone Circle, tucked in the shadow of Walla Crag and with views down to Derwent Water – there's no sense of wilderness here. Each visiting bird species is given its own sign for identification purposes, fingerposts point you to every facility (of which there are many), and there's rather kitsch heraldic signage. Amongst the plethora of attractions is a tourist information point with wi-fi; a classy camping store; a farm shop selling good local sausages and cheeses plus other grocery fodder and newspapers; an off-licence; Jigger's Restaurant, which serves breakfast and dinners such as scampi, pizza and pasta for under a tenner; and rain-proof camping pods. Unusually, serious thought has been given to disabled campers – there are two designated toilet/shower rooms, and ramps to the reception, shop, restaurant and loos. It's a great site for families and people who are on a first camping trip and want home comforts close at hand. If you want to walk on the wild side though, go elsewhere.

Practicalities

Castlerigg Hall Caravan & Camping Site, Keswick, Cumbria, CA12 4TE ☎*01768 774499,* Ⓦ*www.castlerigg.co.uk*

Pitches & price 100 tent pitches: £5.50 per adult, £2.50 per child, £2.50 per car. 58 caravan pitches: £20 (2 people & a car); hook-ups £18; additional people £2.50. Camping pods (2 adults & 2 children) from £32.

Facilities Good shower block plus two disabled toilet/shower rooms. Campers' kitchen, laundry, tourist info, camping store, restaurant, shop and off-licence.

Restrictions No groups. Dogs (£2.50) welcome, but they must be kept on a lead. No campfires.

Open March–Oct.

Getting there Follow the signs for Keswick. Don't enter the town but take the A591 towards Windermere. After 1 mile, turn right up the lane signposted "Castlerigg Campsite". There's an hourly bus service (#555) from Keswick to the end of the lane.

Gillside

Striding up Helvellyn

Perched above Glenridding, the working farm of *Gillside* has been in the same family for more than forty years and has all the required ingredients for great Lakes camping: a friendly welcome; a stream rushing by; exhilarating mountain views; and a verdant field to pitch in, studded with mature oaks. Its location on the route up Helvellyn (3117ft) means you really have to get your walking boots on here, whether you tackle the infamous Striding Edge route up the mountain or the more forgiving Swirral Edge path. Pitches at this lovely site fan out from the rambling stone farm buildings, making *Gillside* a fun place for kids to observe some farm life. The bunkhouse, with two rooms sleeping seven and thirteen, has been converted from a stone and slate building and is a sociable option for groups, though you can book individual bunks.

Glenridding itself, built to house miners from the lead ore mine at Greenside, sits on the edge of tranquil Ullswater. It's a great little village with a good pub (the whitewashed *Traveller's Rest*), a camping shop and some endearingly old-style groceries handy for stocking up with food. Head to St Patrick's Boat Landings in the village (℡01768 482393, Ⓦwww.stpatricksboat-landings.co.uk) to rent rowing boats, fishing boats or mountain bikes. You can sail, windsurf or canoe on the lake (rent equipment from *Waterside House* campsite in Pooley Bridge on the north shore of the lake; see p.280), or take to the water in a more sedate fashion on the red-funnelled nineteenth-century Ullswater Steamers (Ⓦwww.ullswater-steamers.co.uk), which ply the lake up to Howton and on to Pooley Bridge.

▼ A tent with a view

Practicalities

Gillside Caravan and Camping, Gillside Farm, Glenridding, Penrith, Cumbria, CA11 0QQ ℡*01768 482346,* Ⓦ*www.gillsidecaravanandcampingsite.co.uk*

Pitches & price Tent pitches: £6 per adult, £3 per child, £1 per tent, £1 per vehicle. Caravans: £6 per adult, £3 per child, hook-ups £4.50, awning £1. Bunkhouse (sleeps 20) £140 or £10 per individual bunk.

Facilities Decent toilet block and washing-up sinks. Fresh milk and eggs from the farmhouse.

Restrictions Dogs allowed (no charge). No campfires, only raised BBQs.

Open March–Nov.

Getting there Take the A592 to Glenridding. Once in the village, take the Greenside road on the opposite side from the lake, and follow the signs to *Gillside*. For public transport, catch the #108 bus which runs from Penrith to Patterdale (Ⓦwww.stagecoachbus.com).

Chapel House Farm

This site is about as simple as camping gets. It's a field, tucked behind a farm and a line of oak trees, with spectacular fells rising all around. Just pitch your tent where you like, and your fees will be collected the next morning. The loos and showers are in need of TLC, and will be too basic for many, but if you want great views and you're not in need of any luxury, this is a good option (though you might want to bring along earplugs to block out the baaing of the farm's sheep, which are in quite close proximity). Just beyond the farmyard is the little white-washed church of St Andrew in Borrowdale, consecrated in 1687; look out for the grave of fell-runner Bob Graham, which records his impressive running achievements. The hamlet of Rosthwaite is just fifteen minutes' walk away – there's a little shop and two good pubs here: the *Royal Oak* with its stone-flagged bar and filling dinners, and posher *Scafell*. You'll find that one absolute essential if you're walking here is to take a decent torch, both to guide you back from the pub, and because the campsite loos have no lights and are hard to locate in the dark.

Practicalities

Chapel House Farm Campsite, nr Rosthwaite, Borrowdale, Cumbria, CA12 5XG ☎01768 777602

Pitches & price Around 40 pitches. Camping fees are collected in the morning: £6 per adult, £3 per child, £3 per caravan.

Facilities Just a simple toilet block with showers.

Restrictions No fires. Dogs to be kept on a lead. No noise after 11.30pm.

Open March–Oct.

Getting there From Keswick, you will need to take the B5289 south to Borrowdale, passing the turn-offs to the Bowder Stone and then to Rosthwaite. *Chapel House Farm* is located on the left-hand side of the road, and is well signposted. As far as public transport goes, just hop on board the Borrowdale Rambler bus (#79) which departs from Keswick (every 30min–1hr; 25min).

Gill Head Farm

Comprising long whitewashed buildings tucked in a dip, *Gill Head* is a working hill farm surrounded by the great open spaces of Blencathra (2848ft) and the northern fells. The camping fields are open, with sweeping vistas of this rather daunting landscape – the names of a couple of Blencathra's Ridges – Sharp Edge and Foule Crag – hint at the challenge that the mountains present to hikers.

Gentler charms can be found at the nearby town of Keswick, which features a sixteenth-century church, the more-interesting-than-it-sounds Pencil Museum and the marvellously atmospheric Castlerigg Stone Circle. The site itself consists of a couple of open fields, with big skies a notable characteristic. While the setting is more domestic and less wild than many other Lakes campsites, you'll emerge from your tent in the morning and get a real blast of the outdoors. An asset if you have small kids in tow is the sturdy outdoor play area and trampoline. If it's raining – let's face it, a distinct possibility in these parts – you can retreat to the log cabin, which has a handy TV lounge as well as a covered barbecue area.

Practicalities

Gill Head Farm, Troutbeck, Penrith, Cumbria, CA11 0ST ☎01768 779652, ⊛www.gillheadfarm.co.uk

Pitches & price 25 tent pitches: £7 per person. 20 caravan/motor home pitches from £18.

Facilities Good clean shower block. Dog-walking area; playground for kids; log cabin with TV lounge, microwave and covered BBQ area. Small shop selling milk, bread, farm eggs, tinned soup and chocolate. Takeaway breakfast available.

Restrictions No campfires; raised BBQ only. Dogs welcome, but must be kept on a lead. Noise to be kept to a minimum after 10pm.

Open Easter–Nov.

Getting there Leave the M6 motorway at junction 40 and take the A66 to Keswick. At the *Troutbeck Hotel* T-junction, take the A5091 signposted Ullswater. After 100yds turn right for *Gill Head Farm*.

Side Farm

Rustic relaxation on the edge of Ullswater

Sitting on a slope above the southern shore of Ullswater, wonderfully sited *Side Farm* has a peaceful atmosphere and warm-hearted welcome. Owned by the National Trust, this is still very much a family-run working farm, with 380 lambing ewes (mainly Swaledales) and a smaller herd of cattle; the owners emphasize respect for the livestock – plus there's a very cute shaggy pony which you may see grazing the verge on the track to the campsite.

The farmyard tearoom, housed in old stables, provides a warm reception to *Side Farm*. You can have a reviving cuppa and a cake in the rustic setting of the farmyard; to the left coming out of the tearoom is an impressive eighteenth-century "bank" barn. Beyond the farm, a rugged track leads to the gently sloping field where the campsite is situated, on the southeastern shore of Ullswater. In the corner of the field, a crow-stepped stone barn has been sympathetically converted into a toilet block. There's a rope swing hanging from a huge oak tree, but that's about it as far as organized activities go – it's just you, the lake and the surrounding hills. You can't book in advance so if you're hoping to camp at *Side Farm* on a bank holiday weekend, try to arrive early.

This is a great place for canoes and small boats, and there's a tracery of paths, including to Patterdale and Glenridding; from Glenridding you can take the attractive steamer up the lake to Howton and on to Pooley Bridge on the north shore, or make an ascent of Helvellyn (3117ft). For pubs, Patterdale has the *White Lion* and Glenridding the *Traveller's Rest* – both do good food and serve local ales. If you want to fish from the site (there are perch and trout in the lake), go to the post office or the garage for a licence – the garage also sells bait. You can hire row boats and bikes from St Patrick's Boat Landings in Glenridding (☎01768 482393). Most people sail their boats from Glenridding on the opposite shore across to moor at the campsite, rather than taking boats on site by road.

▼ The view over Ullswater

Practicalities

Side Farm, Patterdale, Ullswater, Cumbria, CA11 0NP
☎*01768 482337*
Pitches & price 140 pitches: adults £4, children £3, cars £2.
Facilities Shower block, laundry, tearoom.
Restrictions Medium-sized campervans, but no caravans. No campfires but raised BBQs allowed. No large or single-sex groups unless agreed. Dogs allowed on a lead.
Open Easter to end Oct.
Getting there Take the A592 to Patterdale, and turn towards the lake roughly opposite the church. For public transport, take the #108 bus which runs from Penrith to Patterdale; the stop is at the *Patterdale Hotel* (Ⓦwww.stagecoachbus.com).

The Quiet Site

Fell walking and one of Britain's quirkiest bars

The name of this site, combined with its manicured look and the number of static caravans, might suggest it's a staid option. But under the surface this is an engaging and slightly eccentric place. The first clue is the cartoonish wooden dog heads hung on the loo doors, and the camping-themed weathervane spinning overhead. But the standout feature of this friendly and impeccably run campsite is the dark yet inviting bar – a fantastic refuge in wet or wintry weather. Converted from an ancient barn in the 1950s, it's decorated with Gothic flourishes including stuffed animals and antlers, and has two galleries – one with a pool table overhung with a low beam. The chairs are made from old barrels, and there's antique glass and animal traps on either side of the open fire. They even serve bottles of tailor-made Quiet Pint.

Enter *The Quiet Site* by the rugged bar and the adjoining whitewashed office and shop, which resembles an old-fashioned village store – the owner reckons you can make three meals from the supplies on offer here. Beyond this you walk up the gently sloping grassy site, loosely divided into caravan and tent pitches. The field has a sheltered aspect, meaning it doesn't have the spectacular views of other Lakes campsites, though it's less dramatic in wild weather. Indeed, everything has been done here to help families deal with the torrents of rain that can be a feature in the Lakes. Board games are stacked on the bar, there's an indoor play area for small kids, and teenage boys will be kept entertained by table football and the TV lounge. Parents of small children will welcome the spacious individual bathrooms – with bath – that make washing toddlers and babies easier. The wooden camping pods are a popular option – made locally, these little structures are very simple, comprising just a tent-shaped space and a deck – and they're reliably weather-proof. They sleep two adults and two children. And if it's sunny, kids can climb on the rustic wooden playground, or play football or cricket on the open lawn.

At the office you'll be handed the campsite's very own terrific leaflet on four walks you can do in the area – the leaflet is complete with reliable directions and fun hand-drawn maps. The four-hour hike to seventy-foot Aira Force waterfall is particu-

Practicalities

The Quiet Site, Ullswater, Cumbria, CA11 0LS ☎07768 727016, ⓦwww.thequietsite.co.uk

Pitches & price Tent £20 high season (includes car, tent and two adults; extra for hook-up); caravan £24 high season (includes car, 2 adults, awning and hook-up). Camping pods, sleeping 2 adults & 2 children, £40 high season (bring your own bedding).

Facilities Family bathrooms plus blocks; laundry room; dishwashing sinks. TV and games rooms; shop; adventure playground; bar.

Restrictions Dogs allowed (£1) but must be kept on lead. No campfires.

Open Year round.

Getting there Travelling from M6 Junction 40, take the A66 signposted Keswick for a mile and then the A592 signposted Ullswater for 4 miles. Turn right when you see the lake in front of you, still on the A592, signposted Windermere. After a mile you'll see the *Brackenrigg Inn* on the right-hand side; there's a road to the right directly after the Inn. Drive up here for 0.5 miles. *The Quiet Site* is on the right-hand side.

larly recommended – it's especially awe-inspiring and thunderous after heavy rain. Another fine option is to take in Lowther Castle, designed by Sir Robert Smirke of British Museum fame, on the walk from Helton to Ashkam. Serene Ullswater is close by, either for sailing, for a trip on the jaunty Victorian steamer or for visits to the bustling waterside villages of Glenridding and Pooley Bridge. At both villages you can rent any gear you might require for water sports. All this plus you're in a red squirrel hotspot, so keep your eyes peeled.

◀ One of the site's locally made wooden camping pods ▶ The village-style reception and store; Aira Force in full flow

Waterside House
Water sports by an ancient bridge

Tucked at the far northeastern end of Ullswater, Pooley Bridge is an ancient Lakes settlement whose narrow streets are flooded with visitors in high summer. Away from the bustle, *Waterside House*, as its name suggests, sits right on the shores of the lake. It's a brilliant option if you're into water sports: canoes, rowing boats and even sea cycles are available to rent from the campsite. But despite all this aquatic excitement, the neat, well equipped the site itself is on the sedate side. It's on a working farm, comprising handsome seventeenth-century buildings, and kids will enjoy watching the sheep-related action: dipping, shearing,

▼ The shores of Ullswater

lambing and sheepdogs at work. There's also an adventure play area to keep the nippers happy.

Waterside House has a decent shop on site, but the best resource if you're self-catering is the farmers' market in Pooley Bridge (April to September, last Sunday of the month), with local meat, fish, fruit, veg and cakes on offer. The village has a very old market tradition – its market charter was given by King John in the thirteenth century. It's undeniably pretty, with a substantial sixteenth-century bridge, but there are no formal sights – most visitors are content to simply mosy about the place. The best of the village pubs is the eighteenth-century *Sun Inn* near the main square.

Practicalities

Waterside House Campsite, Howtown Road, Pooley Bridge, Cumbria, CA10 2NA ☏*01768 486332,* Ⓦ*www.watersidefarm-campsite.co.uk*
Pitches & price 120 pitches. Tent with 2 adults and car £12; motor home £12; extra adults £3; extra kids £1.50. Hook-ups £2.50.
Facilities Good shower and loo facilities. Laundry. Kids' adventure area. Boat launch and boat storage. Volleyball and table tennis. On-site shop.
Restrictions Dogs (£1) to be kept on a lead. Quiet from 11pm to 8am. No campfires.
Open March–Oct.
Getting there From junction 40 of the M6, take the A66 signposted Keswick. After a mile turn left onto the A592 for Ullswater and Pooley Bridge. Turn left at the lake, continue straight on and then over the river into Pooley Bridge. Go through the village and take the first right to Howtown. Continue along this road for a mile; *Waterside House* is the second campsite on the right. If you're walking, there's a lakeshore footpath from Pooley Bridge to the campsite. Bus #108 runs between Penrith and Patterdale, stopping at Pooley Bridge.

Sykeside

Massive mountain views and greedy badgers

Enclosed by dry-stone walls, this friendly, well-run site has about the best setting of any Lakes campsite – and that's saying quite a bit. In a valley just south of tiny Brotherswater lake and its ancient oak woodland, *Sykeside* is ringed by impressive mountains, some pyramidal and green, others more rugged and high. Part of the pleasure of being here is following the progress of cloud shadows across the hillsides, or watching the diminutive forms of hikers toiling up the steep side of High Hartsop Dodd (1702ft).

It's a perfect site for those who like fairly basic camping with a good dash of the outdoors. The owners are careful to maintain the stunning natural appeal of the site, which comprises a wide grassy field with glorious 360-degree views of the surrounding crags. If you don't fancy spending the night under canvas, there are nine rugged bunkhouses and the handsome tipis at the edge of the site are operated by Tomahawk Tipis (☎01524 854851, Ⓦwww.tomahawk-tipis.co.uk; from £95 for 2 nights). *Sykeside*'s pub, *Barn End Bar*, dishes up Yorkshire pud, pies and burgers for under a tenner, or there's a famous hikers' bar, the *Brotherswater Inn*, just a stone's throw away on the B592. Tinned food, snacks and some camping equipment are available at the camping shop; signs here warn of badgers who have a penchant for getting into tents and eating your supplies.

A path leads from the far side of the camping field to five-hundred-year-old working farm Hartsop Hall and from here several trails fan out to the area's most popular walks, including the Fairfield Horseshoe, which takes in Dove Crag (2598ft) and Hart Crag (2696ft).

Practicalities

Sykeside Camping Park, Brotherswater, Patterdale, Cumbria, CA11 0NZ ☎*01768 482239,* Ⓦ*www.sykeside.co.uk*

Pitches & price Tents £9 high season, adults £3, children over 5 £2. 19 hook-ups. Motor homes £11 (includes hook-up but not occupants). 9 bunkrooms (sleeping 2–6, toilets and wash basin, showers shared with the campsite; from £14 per night).
Facilities Well-maintained toilet block with showers. Laundry/drying and dish-washing areas. On-site shop and pub.
Restrictions No campfires. Dogs (£2) allowed on a lead. No stag or hen parties, no groups of more than 6 adults.
Open Year round.
Getting there The campsite is on the precipitous A592, north of the Kirkstone Pass. Leave the A592 at the *Brotherswater Inn* – turn into the pub car park, then drive through for the campsite. The Kirkstone Rambler (#517) runs between Bowness and Glenridding, stopping at Brotherswater. It also stops at Windermere, where you can connect with the train from Oxenholme.

▼ The tents at *Sykeside* are encircled by high peaks

Northeast England

With its glorious golden beaches, quaint market towns, extensive Roman remains, buzzing city centres and factory-packed flatlands, the Northeast is one of England's unheralded highlights. County Durham is most famous for its picturesque university city, while Tyne and Wear is home to thundering High Force waterfall and the vibrant metropolis of Newcastle. A short distance northwards is remote, stunning Northumberland – without doubt the best place to pitch your tent. Forming the bulk of the border between Scotland and England, this area was heavily garrisoned under the Romans and is today littered with remarkable ruins of forts, battlements and most famously, the cherished Hadrian's Wall. Dotted amongst these are some imposing medieval castles, such as Alnwick, Dunstanburgh and Bamburgh.

Quality campsites are thin on the ground in County Durham and Tyne and Wear but Northumberland is England's least populated patch of land so, whether you're pitching up beside a racecourse, on a working farm, overlooking a windswept beach or next to a Roman wall, you're in the right place if you're after a bit of peace and solitude. Walkers, cyclists and horse-riders will be enthralled by the rolling countryside, miles upon miles of unadulterated scenery and dazzling views over the coastline. Those clutching their bucket and spade won't be disappointed either – the rugged Northumbrian coastline is frequently interrupted by immense, sandy beaches, particularly around the ancient pilgrimage site of Holy Island. It's also the a fine spot for avid anglers and bird-watchers.

Berwick-upon-Tweed

Beachcomber

Holy Island
(Lindisfarne)

A698
B6354
B6353
B6396
B6352
B6625
B6352
B6351
B6349

Budle Bay
Bamburgh

B1340
Seahouses
Beadnell Bay
Beadnell

A1

B6346

Embleton
Dunstan Hill
B1340
Craster
Proctor's Stead

A697
B6341
B1339

Alnwick

A68
A6088

NORTHUMBERLAND
NATIONAL PARK

B6341

B6357

Kielder

B6342

A696

A1
A1068

N O R T H U M B R I A
B6343
Morpeth

Ashington

Demesne Farm
Bellingham
B6320

Blyth
A193

B6318

A68
B6342

A6079

B6309

A1

Hadrian's Wall
A69
B6318
B6321

A69
B6309

Newcastle-
upon-Tyne
Tynemouth

South
Shields

Haltwhistle
A686

Hexham

A695

Gateshead

B6305
**Hexham
Racecourse**
B6306

B6309
A692

Washington

Sunderland

A689

B6303

Consett

A693
Chester-
le-Street

A691

A68

Durham

A689

B6278

D U R H A M

A690
A688
A162
A177

Petertee

A19

A689
Hartlepool

B6277

B6282

Bishop
Auckland

Newton
Aycliffe

A1 (M)

A177

Stockton-
on-Tees

Highside Farm
B6276
B6277

Barnard Castle
Barnard
Castle

A688
A67

A68
A66

Redcar

Middlesbrough

A66
A66

Darlington

A171

Northeast England

	PAGE	🚶	🚲	⛵	🍷	⛰	👪	👫	🚐	🚌	♿
Barnard Castle	288	✓	✓			✓	✓		✓	✓	
Beachcomber	299	✓	✓						✓		
Beadnell Bay	297			✓						✓	
Bellingham	293	✓	✓				✓		✓	✓	✓
Budle Bay	298						✓		✓	✓	
Demesne Farm	293	✓	✓	✓			✓		✓	✓	
Dunstan Hill	296				✓		✓		✓	✓	✓
Hadrian's Wall	290	✓				✓			✓	✓	✓
Haltwhistle	289					✓			✓		
Hexham Racecourse	289								✓		
Highside Farm	286				✓	✓					
Kielder	292	✓	✓	✓		✓			✓		
Proctor's Stead	294				✓				✓	✓	

See front flap for key to symbols

Highside Farm

Rare sheep, fresh sausages and flapping lapwings

The green, rolling uplands of Teesdale – part of the North Pennines designated Area of Outstanding Natural Beauty – stretch for miles in every direction around *Highside Farm*. Nestling on the side of Lunedale valley and sheltered from the bleakest of the weather that can suddenly sweep over the tops, spacious pitches are arranged on neatly manicured grass. Gentle isolation is guaranteed; the nearest pub is two miles away in Mickleton and only eight campers can stay and enjoy the solitude at any one time. The vibe among the families, walkers, cyclists and birdwatchers here is relaxed and sociable. Many are drawn by the spectacular countryside, while the farm's special brand of gastro-hospitality is also in high demand, with exquisite, home-produced meat available to buy and cook on site, or to take home and relish later.

Highside is a small working stock farm specializing in rare breeds such as Teeswater sheep and Shorthorn cattle. Owners Richard and Stephanie Proud took over the site twelve years ago to promote ethical food production and are evangelical about the preservation of native breeds and the natural landscape. They'll happily share their experiences of creating the farm with campers. As well as being devoted to their cause, they're exceptionally attentive hosts, welcoming new arrivals with cups of tea and biscuits, as well as offers of home-cooked breakfasts made – according to season – using their own sausages, eggs and bacon.

The farm's delicious produce makes cooking on site a real treat. As well as free-range eggs, there's mouthwatering lamb – butchered locally and raised on herb-rich pastures – in spring. And get ready for succulent beef in June and July – hung for a month, it makes spectacular burgers and steaks, or joints to take home in the cool box. Pork is also on offer in summer, while August and September are the months to enjoy rich, flavoursome mutton. Make sure you give plenty of notice if you want to buy meat as it's all frozen and needs time to defrost before it hits your barbecue. If you've developed a taste for local produce, try *Café 1618* in Middleton or the *Three Tuns* in Eggleston – and don't forget to pick up some creamy Cotherstone cheese at the local farmer's market, held on the first Saturday of each month.

There's plenty to see and do on the farm itself – especially if you fancy helping out with the cattle, chickens, pigs, sheep and

Practicalities

Highside Farm, Bowbank, Middleton-in-Teesdale, DL12 0NT
☎*01833 640135,* Ⓦ*www.highsidefarm.co.uk*

Pitches & price 8 people max staying on site. £7.50 per person; under-3s £3.75. 2 hook-ups.

Facilities Basic, clean male/female amenities block with one shower and loo in each. Washing up area. Seasonal farm produce, including wool, sold on site. Breakfasts should be booked in advance.

Restrictions No arrivals before 1pm. Depart by midday. No visitors. No campfires. Dogs welcome but must be kept under control on the farm.

Open Easter–end Sept.

Getting there From Middleton-in-Teesdale, head south for 0.5 miles before turning right onto the B6276; the campsite is on the left after 2 miles.

horses – but venturing further afield takes in a timeless, unspoilt landscape that combines rugged Pennine moorland with lush river valleys and some of England's most beautiful waterfalls. Head west over the tops on the B6276 towards Alston and explore around Lunedale's Grassholme and Selset reservoirs, with their disarmingly pretty and diverse bird populations, including snipe, oystercatchers and lapwings, flapping overhead. A trail following the Tees upstream from Middleton, two miles from the campsite, is an easy stroll that becomes more dramatic in wet weather when the river is at its most ferocious. After three miles you'll reach the impressive Low Force rapids and a mile further upstream, the full power of the river crashes down at the spectacular 70ft High Force waterfall. Cauldron Snout – a 200ft cascade below Cow Green reservoir – is also well worth a visit. In late spring, keep your eyes peeled for rare spring gentians, whose brilliant blue flowers stud the area's unique grasslands.

◀ Solitude at *Highside Farm* ▶ The site marries neat pitches with a farm shop and wild surroundings; nearby High Force waterfall

Barnard Castle
Peace and rambling the Pennine Way

The bleak uplands and gentler valleys of Weardale and Teesdale make this quiet, well-sheltered campsite, two miles west of the historic market town of Barnard Castle, a hotspot for cyclists and walkers. Helpful staff, spacious pitches and super-clean facilities add up to a reliable weekend base for the families and hiking groups that often camp here.

The stunning spectacle of High Force waterfall (see p.287) can be incorporated into several nearby hikes, including a section of the Pennine Way. The campsite managers have a useful folder of local walks for rambling campers to consult. For mountain bikers, five-thousand-acre Hamsterley Forest, ten miles north of the campsite, is a major draw. Rental bikes are available from Wood N Wheels (☎01388 488222) opposite the Forest Visitor Centre, or make for Hoppyland Trekking Centre (☎01388 488196), on the road from Hamsterley village to Bedburn, to arrange pony trekking. Four graded cycle routes, from gentle family paths to a severe black route for the more reckless, snake through the forest alongside walking and horseriding trails.

Art-obsessed campers shouldn't miss the nearby Bowes Museum (ⓦwww.thebowesmuseum.org.uk), Barnard Castle's grand, treasure-filled French-style château, commissioned in the nineteenth century by a Parisian actress and her English industrialist husband to bring art and enlightenment to Teesdale. As well as browsing the hugely impressive collection of European art, including Goyas and an El Greco, make sure you're around at 2pm when the life-size clockwork silver swan gives its daily forty-second performance.

Bustling Barnard Castle town, overlooked by its ruined twelfth-century castle, is a good place to stock up on supplies for dinner at the campsite. Local cheeses are on sale at the Wednesday market, while the award-winning farmers' market, held on the first Saturday of each month, is your best bet for quality local produce. For indoor culinary treats, try the *Fox & Hounds* at Cotherstone – a mile beyond the campsite towards Middleton-in-Teesdale on the B6227.

▼ The Bowes Museum houses a fine European art collection

Practicalities

Barnard Castle Camping & Caravanning Club Site, Dockenflatts Lane, Lartington, Barnard Castle, County Durham, DL12 9DG ☎01833 630228, ⓦwww.siteseeker.co.uk

Pitches & price 90 pitches (68 with hook-ups). From around £6–8.50 per person, plus £6.50 per pitch for non-members of the Camping & Caravanning Club.

Facilities Excellent, clean, separate amenities blocks. Disabled shower and toilet. Laundry. Children's play area. Basic shop and information point on site.

Restrictions No campfires. Raised BBQs permitted. No vehicle entry after 11pm.

Open April–Nov.

Getting there Take the B6227 from Barnard Castle towards Middleton-in-Teesdale for 2 miles; the campsite is down a lane on the left, signposted. The #95 and #96 Barnard Castle–Middleton buses stop at the end of the lane.

Haltwhistle

Set in the National Trust's Bellister Wood – carpeted with fragrant bluebells bursting with colour each year in late spring – peaceful, grassy *Haltwhistle* campsite is bordered by the broad South Tyne River. Free fishing, with the chance of catching salmon or sea trout to smoke on the barbecue for dinner, is available for those campers who turn up with a rod licence. The welcoming managers here make a point of finding a pitch for everyone, no matter how crowded the site becomes.

Most places in these parts exist in the shadow of the Roman fortifications of Hadrian's Wall, which snakes across the bleak hills between Carlisle and South Shields. Haltwhistle is no exception and a visit or two to the wall will most likely form the backbone of any enthusiastic historian's visit here (see p.290). The friendly *Wallace Arms* pub at Rowfoot, a thirty-minute walk through the fields, serves hearty pub grub, or try the nearby Herding Hill Farm shop for locally reared rare-breed beef, perfect to cook on site.

Practicalities

Haltwhistle Camping & Caravanning Club Site, Burnfoot Park Village, Haltwhistle, Northumberland, NE49 0JP
T01434 320106, W www.siteseeker.co.uk
Pitches & price 50 pitches (12 with hook-ups). From £4–6.50 per person, plus £6.50 per pitch for non-members of the Camping & Caravanning Club.
Facilities Excellent, clean, separate male and female amenities blocks. Laundry. On-site shop selling basic supplies. Free river-fishing permits for campers.
Restrictions Dogs welcome, free. No campfires. Raised BBQs permitted. No vehicle entry after 11pm.
Open April–Nov.
Getting there From Haltwhistle, take the minor road signposted Alston, south off the A69. After 2 miles, turn right towards Kellah. The campsite is on the right after 100yds. Or catch the #681 bus from Haltwhistle, which stops at the Kellah turning.

Hexham Racecourse

With far-reaching views across the gently undulating grass tracks, scattered with brush fences and lined with bright white railings, Hexham Racecourse is one of the loveliest in England. It's also home to a small campsite, which is situated in a flat field to the right of the main stand. Tents and caravans are pitched close to the track, and on race days, campers get ringside views – they certainly won't need binoculars to watch their favoured horses gallop to victory. For those who want to join in the energetic throng of punters, though, it's reduced admission (£7). Facilities on site are basic but clean; there's a children's play area with swings, and a large games room with a TV, table football, pool and ping-pong. Historic Hexham, with its imposing sand-coloured castle and higgledy-piggledy streets is just two miles away. A short way down the A69 towards Newcastle, outside Corbridge, is Brocksbushes Farm Shop (W www.brocksbushes.co.uk), with its inviting tearooms, pick-your-own fruit fields (strawberries, raspberries and asparagus) and farm shop selling organic fruit and veg, jams and cakes.

Practicalities

Hexham Racecourse Caravan and Camping site, High Yarridge, Hexham, Northumberland, NE46 2JP
T01434 606847 or 07951 054216, W www.hexham-racecourse.co.uk/caravan_site.htm
Pitches & price 10 tent areas, £4 per adult (£2 per child 3–14 years old), 4 hook-ups (£3 extra per night); 40 caravans with hook-ups, £15 each.
Facilities Clean, heated male/female amenities block, laundry, baby-changing. Children's play area.
Restrictions Dogs welcome (free) but to be kept on leads. No campfires (disposable BBQs on bricks only).
Open May–Sept; reception 9am–6pm.
Getting there Following the signs to the racecourse from Hexham will take you up a steep hill, Dipton Mill Road. Turn right at the brow of the hill and the racecourse is on the left after 0.5 miles. On race days, there's a free bus from the train and bus stations.

Hadrian's Wall
Camp with the Romans

One of the greatest testimonies to the power of their mighty Empire, Hadrian's Wall, begun in AD122, was raised in an impressively speedy six years by Roman legions; acting broadly as a border customs control, it kept an eye on the population flow between the north and south of Britain, and provided a fearsome obstacle to marauding Pictish tribes from Scotland. Today, in its rather piecemeal state, the UNESCO-graded structure is the top tourist attraction in the northeast of Eng-

land, a bucolic playground for day-trippers, hikers and Roman history buffs.

Less than half a mile from some of the best-preserved sections of the wall near Haltwhistle village is *Hadrian's Wall*, a quiet campsite nestled in a valley of rolling green hills, which are dotted with fluffy white sheep and the occasional, energetic walker. Run by an enthusiastic team of two, the site is family- and animal-friendly – in fact, it's a little working farm, complete with cats, ducks, chickens and a small pond filled with fish. There's a relaxed atmosphere here that focuses on the natural side of life: tents can be pitched on levels named after mountains – Annapurna, Everest or K2, for example; low-energy, solar lighting ensures that the stars shine brilliantly at night; and recycling is encouraged, with food waste often going to the chickens.

Campers are predominantly hikers who, having traipsed the length and breadth of the wall and its glorious surrounding countryside, use the site as a restful nightly base. And for those who don't want to walk laden with a large backpack, the site can arrange transport to and from your starting/finishing point, as well as advise you on the best areas to see. A number of archeologists – budding and experienced – also stop by, wielding their trowels in readiness for a dig at the nearby Roman site of Vindolanda, occupied by the Roman army c.85 AD; coins, boots, jewellery and fragments of writing tablets are just some of the items unearthed here.

After a long day in the fresh air, campers can put their feet up in front of a roaring fire and tuck into hearty meals at a couple of the nearby country pubs; within a few minutes' walk of the site are the snug *Milecastle Inn* (Ⓦwww.milecastle-inn.co.uk), which serves delicious home-made pies, and the homely *Twice Brewed Inn* (Ⓦwww.twicebrewedinn.co.uk).

Northumberland may be unbeatably beautiful in the sunshine, but this is northern England and it can have its fair share of bad weather. For inclement conditions, the site has an undercover cookhouse, complete with running water and gas ring, for those adamant in continuing their outdoor experience (groceries – and takeaways – are available in Haltwhistle

Practicalities

Hadrian's Wall Camping and Caravan Site, Melkridge Tilery, nr Haltwhistle, Northumberland, NE49 9PG

☎*01434 320495,* 🅦*www.romanwallcamping.co.uk*

Pitches & price 35 pitches for tents and caravans; £6 per tent, £10 per caravan. 24 hook-ups, £2.50. £2 charge to use all facilities. Self-catering Bunk Barn for up to 12 people available by the bunk or as a whole for longer periods, £10 per person per night.

Facilities Separate male/female heated amenities block with 6 loos and 6 showers, sauna, hair dryers, laundry (washing machines and tumble dryer), small library. 1 disabled toilet. Electric pumps available for air beds. Hot running water all day. Horse livery available. Full English breakfast on request.

Restrictions No campfires. Dogs welcome, free.

Open Year round.

Getting there From the B6318 Military Road, take the turning to Melkridge and the campsite is about 300yds down the hill on the left. Or, leave the A69 at Melkridge village, where's there's a staggered crossroads by the green. Go straight on, up the hill, and the site is in a valley 2 miles further along this road. The campsite offers free pick-ups from Haltwhistle train station. In summer, the hourly Hadrian's Wall bus can drop you off at *Milecastle Inn* along the B6318, within easy walking distance (see 🅦www.hadrians-wall. org for bus timetables and routes).

village). Those who are unwilling to brave rain-splattered tarpaulin can stay in the cosy, centrally heated, on-site Bunk Barn, which sleeps up to twelve people.

◀ A well-preserved section of the second-century Hadrian's Wall
▶ Rest up in lush surroundings at *Hadrian's Wall* after walking the wall; The great length of Hadrian's wall lies entirely in Northern England

Kielder

Star-spotting in a faraway forest

Mountain bikers and water-sports fanatics flock to Kielder during summer, drawn by its sheer isolation and its location in the heart of England's largest forest. If you're made of stern stuff and can tolerate the ever-present midges, this riverside campsite, just three miles from the Scottish border, has plenty to offer. Graded walks, cycle trails and horseriding tracks abound in the 155,000 acres of sprawling woodland, while sailing, waterskiing and canoeing are all at hand on the vast expanse of Kielder Water, northern Europe's biggest man-made lake. The site is a social enterprise, run by the Kielder community since 2004, and profits are spent on improving facilities at the campsite and in the village.

Overlooking Kielder village, a ten-minute walk from the campsite, Kielder Castle is a useful first port of call. Once the hunting lodge of the Duke of Northumberland, it's now a tourist centre (daily 10am–4pm), with exhibitions about forestry and a tearoom. It's also the start point for several mountain-bike and walking

trails. For rentals, try The Bike Place (☎01434 250457).

Some come here hoping to catch a glimpse of a red squirrel as this is where England's largest – but nevertheless notoriously elusive – colony lives. Wildlife-loving campers may also spy roe deer, otters and nesting ospreys. Kielder Observatory (ⓦwww.kielderobservatory.org), built high above Kielder Water to capitalize on the remote area's pristine night skies and exceptional lack of light pollution, has attracted a new breed of astro-tourists, drawn by the excellent star-spotting opportunities. Its annual star camps, where enthusiasts descend on *Kielder* to gaze into the dark night skies, have become legendary among amateur astronomers from across the UK and beyond.

For food and drink, the *Angler's Arms* in Kielder village serves up reasonably priced pub grub, but cooking on site is also a good option, with freestanding barbecues provided. The village store is an emporium of useful stuff including meat from a local butcher, ales and, tellingly, a comprehensive array of midge repellents.

▼ Mountain biking in Kielder Forest

Practicalities

Kielder Campsite, Kielder Village, Hexham, Northumberland, NE48 1EJ ☎*01434 250291,* ⓦ*www.kieldervillage.com*

Pitches & price 70 pitches, 32 hook-ups. £8–10 per 2-person tent, £15–18 per 6-person tent, £15–20 per caravan. Backpackers and cyclists £6. 4-berth basic camping pod £30.

Facilities Basic male/female amenities block; separate disabled bathroom. Indoor washing-up area. Laundry room. On-site shop. Children's play area.

Restrictions No campfires; raised BBQs permitted No noise after 10.30pm. Dogs allowed on a lead.

Open March–Oct.

Getting there Take the B6320 to Bellingham (the nearest spot for petrol, so check your tank) and follow the C200 road to Kielder for 19 miles. The campsite is on the right, 500yds beyond Kielder village.

Bellingham

Families, hikers and cyclists alike love *Bellingham* for its location – close to Hadrian's Wall and Kielder Forest, and within easy reach of the Northumberland coast. The Pennine Way passes through here, making this secluded, wooded refuge a welcome rest point for foot-sore hikers. The site is also perfect for cyclists pedalling the coast-to-coast Reivers route from Whitehaven to Tynemouth, as well as those on the gruelling Pennine Cycleway.

The languid North Tyne River, running close to Bellingham, boasts one of the country's top salmon-fishing spots. Day permits cost £35 from nearby *Riverdale Hall Hotel* (ⓦwww.riverdalehall-hotel.co.uk). The hotel also serves tasty food using local produce – try the Kielder venison or North Tyne salmon – at around £20 for three courses. If it's tipping it down, take shelter at their indoor swimming pool, free if you eat at the restaurant.

Bellingham's three village pubs all dish out fairly standard food, making a barbecue or dinner cooked on your stove back at the campsite a tempting option. Stock up on supplies at Kielder Organic Meats farm shop, a mile west of the village at Dunterley, or at Bellingham's more prosaic Co-op.

Practicalities

Bellingham Camping & Caravanning Club Site, Brownrigg, Bellingham, Hexham, Northumberland, NE48 2JY ⓣ*01434 220175,* ⓦ*www.siteseeker.co.uk*

Pitches & price 64 pitches with hook-ups. £7–8.50 per person, plus £6.50 per pitch for non-members of the Camping & Caravanning Club. 4 camping pods (for up to 2 adults and 2 children), with electric lighting, heating and 2 camp beds, £37.

Facilities Spotless, separate male and female amenities blocks. Well-equipped disabled bathroom. Laundry. Children's play area. On-site shop selling basic supplies.

Restrictions No campfires. No large groups. Dogs welcome, free.

Open March–Nov.

Getting there Heading north on the B6320, the site is on the left just before Bellingham village. The #37 Hexham–Bellingham bus stops at the entrance.

Demesne Farm

Starting out as a welcoming haven for weary Pennine Way hikers back in 1972, *Demesne Farm* has since established itself as a popular campsite, which caters to a more diverse range of visitors. For families, the thrill of being able to stay on a working farm – where kids often have the chance to help the owner with tending to his cows, sheep and chickens – entices regulars back time after time. From the site's amenities blocks – redeveloped in traditional outbuildings and set around a characterful cobbled courtyard – to the pot-bellied wood-burning stove that warms the drying room, this place exudes rustic charm. The on-site bunkhouse offers year round accommodation.

A well-known stop-off for cyclists on the Reivers coast-to-coast route and popular with mountain bikers heading for the trails in nearby Kielder Forest, *Demesne Farm* is also a softer option for Kielder Water's canoeists, waterskiers and sailors who can't face the midges that rampage through the closer campsite (see opposite).

Practicalities

Demesne Farm, Bellingham, Hexham, Northumberland, NE48 2BS ⓣ*01434 220258,* ⓦ*www.demesnefarm campsite.co.uk*

Pitches & price 24 pitches for tents, 6 for caravans; 10 with hook-ups. £3. Around £5 per adult; children 11–15 £3, 3–10 £2, under-3s free. 3-bedroom bunkhouse (sleeps 8, 4 and 3) available by the bunk or as a whole, £15 per adult, under-18s £12.

Facilities Basic, clean separate amenities blocks.

Restrictions Dogs welcome but must be kept under control. No campfires. No more than 2 family groups staying together. No loud music.

Open Campsite: May–Oct. Bunkhouse: year round. Arrive by 9pm or, if later, by arrangement.

Getting there Take the B6320 to Bellingham village or catch the #37 bus from Hexham. Turn right at Lloyds TSB bank and the site is on the right after 50yds.

Proctor's Stead

Castles in the air and smoky kippers for tea

This sheltered spot, fronted by emerald-green fields dotted with yellow gorse shrubs, looks out to the glinting North Sea and crumbling fourteenth-century Dunstanburgh Castle, which towers majestically over the coastline. Turn your back to the sea and you're presented with leafy, cow-strewn fields laced with numerous footpaths and bridleways. These are the spectacular views east and west from *Proctor's Stead*, a quiet three-acre campsite in the small village of Dunstan.

If you like your campsites neat and tidy, this is the place for you. The amenities block, painted a pleasing racing green, is immaculate; lavatories, showers, laundry rooms, dishwashing and recycling areas are spotless. The campsite itself, part of a working farm (hence the adjacent cows), is sheltered and perfectly maintained – lumps and bumps in the ground are

few and far between, and the grass is kept neatly trimmed. So, after an energetic day outside with your bucket and spade on Embleton's lovely beach (one mile away), playing golf on one of the numerous surrounding golf courses, walking the rugged coastline or scrutinizing the nooks and crannies of stately Alnwick Castle (a 10min drive), the ground will feel like silk.

Proctor's Stead is about a mile from Craster, a small fishing village, complete with diminutive harbour, that's best known for its kippers. L. Robson & Sons Ltd (ⓦwww.kipper.co.uk) have turned out oak-smoked kippers and salmon here for four generations, and still produce the famous fish in original smokehouses, which are over 130 years old. Stop by and pick up some of the delicious cured seafood from their shop. Craster also features on the Northumberland coastal path; you can walk ten miles along the

Practicalities

Proctor's Stead, Craster, Alnwick, Northumberland, NE66 3TF ☎01665 576613, ⓦwww.proctorsstead.co.uk

Pitches & price 70 pitches; 25 tents, 45 caravans. From £10 for a 2-person tent, from £12 for a 2-person caravan. Additional adults £2.50. Hook-ups £2.

Facilities Very clean mixed male/female amenities block. Laundry. Bikes can be housed. On-site shop selling basics; operates with an honesty box system.

Restrictions Dogs welcome (50p) but must be kept on leads in the camping area. Quiet after 11pm. No campfires, ball games or large single sex groups unless at the owner's discretion.

Open Late March–late Oct. Pitches available from 1pm on day of arrival; on day of departure you must leave by 11am.

Getting there Leave the A1 trunk road at Denwick, signposted for Alnwick Gardens. Take the B1340 for 2.5 miles then follow signposts for Craster until you reach *Proctor's Stead*. The nearest railway is Alnmouth; bus #501 drops you off in Dunstan; see ⓦwww. travelinenortheast.co.uk for timetables.

coast from here to the village of Seahouses, passing by the mighty Dunstanburgh Castle, the golden sands of Embleton Bay and the bustling village of Beadnell (see p.297).

If kippers aren't for you, there are plenty of pubs nearby serving other food. Best of the bunch is the cosy *Cottage Inn* (ⓦwww.cottageinnhotel.co.uk), a couple of minutes' walk from the campsite, in Dunstan village, which serves up a hearty Sunday roast, washed down with real ale. Or stock up on some burgers and sausages and make a barbecue by your tent using the site's bricks.

◀ The mighty ruins of Dunstanburgh Castle ▶ Ripples in the sand at Embleton Bay; *Proctor's Stead* is comfortable and neatly trimmed

Dunstan Hill

Sand and solitude among the dunes

The perfect beachside campsite is an elusive concept too often marred by the irritating realities of a tent-defying onshore breeze, relentless hordes of midges or fellow campers partying on when you want to sleep. Here at *Dunstan Hill*, though, a sheltered, tree-lined site tucked away a mile inland from the coastal village of Embleton, there's a quiet sense of a seaside paradise found among campers, many of them families, who come back to this tranquil place again and again.

The major draw of this location becomes clear when you follow the wooded path out of the grounds towards the sea, skirting an arable field and crossing a golf course to emerge from the dunes onto the vast, often deserted sands of Embleton Bay. From its rock pools and 1930s wooden beach houses to the splendid isolation of fairytale-like Dunstanburgh Castle in the distance, Embleton, like so much of this stretch of the coastline, seems to exist in an ethereal time warp. Following the coastal footpath a mile south takes

you up to the windswept ruins of fourteenth-century Dunstanburgh Castle, once one of the largest and grandest fortifications in northern England. Standing embattled on a rocky headland, the fragmented castle gives a haunting sense of the intense and bloody fighting that took place here during the Wars of the Roses.

Continue on for a mile to the harbour village of Craster, where legendary Craster kippers – splendid on the barbecue – are still smoked over fires of oak sawdust (see p.294). Before the cliff-top trek back to *Dunstan Hill*, slake your hunger over the road at the welcoming *Jolly Fisherman* pub, which has divine kipper pâté, crab soup and crab sandwiches on its reasonably priced menu, and a beer garden with clear views out to sea.

Next door to the pub, stop by the studio/gallery of local artist Mick Oxley. His works – impressionistic watercolour and acrylic local seascapes with evocative titles such as *Dunstanburgh Rain* – capture the changing weather, scudding clouds and thundering seas of this dramatic stretch of the Northumbrian coastline.

▼ Secluded paradise at *Dunstan Hill*

Practicalities

Dunstan Hill Camping & Caravanning Club Site, Dunstan Hill, Dunstan, Alnwick, Northumberland, NE66 3TQ
☏*01665 576310,* Ⓦ*www.siteseeker.co.uk*

Pitches & price 150 pitches (79 with hook-ups). From around £6 to £8.50 per person, plus £6.50 per pitch for non-members of the Camping & Caravanning Club.

Facilities Excellent, clean, separate amenities. Disabled bathroom. Laundry. Children's play area. On-site shop selling basics. Fish-and-chip van calls Wed & Sat teatime.

Restrictions No campfires; raised BBQs permitted. No ball games when busy. No vehicle entry after 11pm.

Open April–Nov.

Getting there Leave the A1 at Alnwick and take the B1340 towards Seahouses. After 7 miles, take the B1339 to Embleton, turn left and the campsite is on the left, a mile beyond Embleton village. The #501 Newcastle–Berwick bus stops at the site entrance.

Beadnell Bay
Dive in the Farnes and peer at puffins

The shipwrecks and coral reefs that punctuate the treacherous rocks of the Farne Islands and the dramatic coastline around Beadnell make this roomy, flat campsite a favoured bolt-hole for divers. It sits a stone's throw from white-gold sand and enticing rock pools, with terrific views across flat fields to the distant Cheviot Hills of the Borders, ensuring divers aren't the only ones to be hooked.

This grassy site is known for being windswept – steel pegs are a staple in the site shop and managers say they've seen many a tent come to grief without them – but in an offshore breeze, prime pitches in the lee of a dry-stone wall give welcome protection from the wind.

Despite the wind, Beadnell is a peaceful spot and an excellent base for exploring the rugged and relatively deserted Northumbrian coast. Boat trips to the Farnes – from the fishing port of Seahouses, two miles north – are a must in the summer when the islands are home to riotous colonies of puffins, guillemots and kittiwakes, as well as languorous grey seals basking on the rocks. If you want to dive, try Farne Island Divers (Ⓦwww.farneislanddivers.co.uk).

Dominating the coastline north of Seahouses is the spectacular sight of much-filmed Bamburgh Castle, sitting on a basalt crag and looking out onto miles of pearly-white beach. The old Anglo-Saxon fortress – substantially rebuilt at the end of the nineteenth century – provides a fantastic backdrop to a picnic, and you can explore its interior from March to October.

For eating and drinking around Beadnell, fish and chips pretty much anywhere in Seahouses is a safe bet. Or for a meal within walking distance there's a chippie in Beadnell village. The *Beadnell Towers Hotel* also serves up locally caught fish, with main courses around £10. Stock up at Seahouses' Co-op if you plan on joining the throngs cooking and barbecuing on the campsite.

▼ Thousands of puffins nest on the Farne Islands each summer

Practicalities

Beadnell Bay Camping & Caravanning Club Site, Beadnell, Chathill, Northumberland, NE67 5BX ☎*01665 720586,* Ⓦ*www.siteseeker.co.uk*

Pitches & price 150 pitches (no hook-ups). From around £3 to £7.50 per person, plus £6.50 per pitch for non-members of the Camping & Caravanning Club.

Facilities Basic, clean separate male and female amenities blocks with showers and loos. Baby-changing cubicle. Separate disabled shower and toilet. Laundry. Shop selling basic supplies and information point on site.

Restrictions No campfires; raised BBQs permitted. Dogs welcome, free. No vehicle entry after 11pm.

Open Late April–late Sept.

Getting there Leave the A1 at Alnwick and follow the B1340 to Beadnell. The campsite is on the left just past the village. The #501 Newcastle–Berwick bus stops at the site entrance.

Budle Bay
Twitching on the mudflats

Nestling among leafy trees, clumps of pampas grass and the odd dovecote, tents and caravans at *Budle Bay* overlook a babbling, freshwater stream bordered by soft, lush banks. Peace and quiet reigns here – except when children, or adults, shriek with delight from the sturdy tree swings. There's also a dinky little log cabin to hire, in case you don't fancy a night under canvas. The campsite

is located in Waren Mill, a charming workaday hamlet in the top northeast corner of Northumberland, which peers over the vast mudflats of Budle Bay itself; the bay is a sanctuary for sea and land birds, from chattering kittiwakes and guillemots to honking brent geese and chestnut-coloured common shelducks – birdwatchers will be transfixed for hours. The loyal camping fan base here is a mix of fishermen, walkers, cyclists, sailors and families, all keen to explore the coastal delights of Northumberland. The imposing eleventh-century castle at Bamburgh (see p.297), just four miles away, and the beautiful tidal island of Holy Island (see p.299) – a quick boat ride from the village of Seahouses (six miles) – are also well worth a visit. At the end of a long day, cosy up with a cup of tea and a slice of fruit loaf at the *Copper Kettle Tearooms* (Ⓦwww.copperkettletearooms.com), or tuck into hearty meals at *Blacketts* in the heart of Bamburgh.

▼ Budle Bay at low tide

Practicalities

Budle Bay Campsite, Waren Mill, Bamburgh, Northumberland, NE70 7EE ☎*01668 214598,* Ⓦ*www.budlebaycampsite.co.uk*
Pitches & price 250 pitches; 170 for tents. 90 hookups, £2.50. Medium-sized tent (sleeps 3) £3, caravan £4. Log cabin (sleeps 2), £7.
Facilities Basic, unheated male/female amenities block with basins, loos and 5 mixed showers. Laundry. On-site café serves snacks and meals at the weekend.
Restrictions Gates locked at 11pm, quiet after 11pm. Dogs welcome (£1) but must be kept on a lead in the camping area. No campfires.
Open March 20–Oct 30.
Getting there The campsite is signposted in Waren Mill, 3 miles east of Belford on the B1342, off the A1 trunk road. Regular buses (#411, #501, #173) stop here, running up and down the coast between Alnwick and Berwick. Check Ⓦwww.arriva.co.uk and Ⓦwww.travelsure.co.uk for current timetables.

Beachcomber

A windy gallop along the sands

A gently sloping, grass-flecked dune and a brisk thirty seconds separate peaceful *Beachcomber* from Goswick Sands, a vast stretch of golden, pancake-flat sand, six miles south of Berwick-upon-Tweed on the Scottish border. Campers here are particularly happy when the tide is out as, whether you're six or sixty, it's hard to restrain yourself from running full-pelt towards the shimmering sea, whooping with joy.

Exposed to the elements and without much shelter, camping at *Beachcomber* definitely requires a thick jumper or two, a few steel tent pegs and a sturdy windbreak. And while facilities are pretty basic, it's the relaxed atmosphere and fantastic location that make this place special. This is the closest camping ground to the revered Holy Island (or Lindisfarne), whose beautiful priory has been pulling in pilgrims for centuries. Connected to the mainland by a causeway from nearby Beal, the island is only accessible when the tide is out: as tides vary significantly daily, make sure you check crossing times (Ⓦwww.northumberlandlife.org/holy-island), or

you might find yourself staying longer than you anticipated.

The focal point of the campsite is its stableyard full of horses, and you can bring your own trusty steed along, or hire one (there are also plenty of ponies for children), and go for an invigorating gallop along the beach. Golfers will be happy, too – a few minutes down the road (you'll have passed it on arrival) is the undulating Goswick Golf Club. Meanwhile, walkers and cyclists can indulge in Northumberland's numerous trails, paths and hills, in particular the 200-mile Newcastle–Edinburgh Coast & Castles cycle route and the 97-mile St Oswald's Way walk, from Holy Island to Heavenfield, near Hadrian's Wall. History-steeped villages – some graced with stupendous castles like Bamburgh (fifteen miles) and Alnwick (25 miles) – aren't far, and are also dotted with cosy, traditional pubs. If you're into locally brewed real ales, try the *Barrels Ale House* in Berwick (Ⓦwww.thebarrels.co.uk).

▼ Lindisfarne Priory

Practicalities

Beachcomber Campsite, Goswick, Berwick-upon-Tweed, Northumberland, TD15 2RW ☎*01289 381217,* Ⓦ*www.beachcomber-campsite.co.uk*

Pitches & price 50 pitches; 45 tents, 5 caravans. Ordinary pitch £5–7 per person (£2–3 per child); serviced pitch (with hook-up) £18.50 for 2 people.

Facilities Basic male/female amenities block. Laundry. Horse livery and riding lessons available (£22 per adult per hour, beach gallop on request). Small on-site shop selling basic groceries. Recycling facilities.

Restrictions Dogs welcome (free) but must be kept on a lead. No campfires. Quiet after 11pm.

Open April–Oct. The best time to call is 6–7pm.

Getting there The campsite is located off the A1 trunk road; follow the signposts to Goswick and Cheswick down a narrow country road, over a level crossing and past Goswick Golf Club.

The Lowlands

Writers and poets have waxed lyrical about the dramatic and rugged Highlands of Scotland for centuries. The Lowlands – grand Edinburgh aside – have often felt neglected by comparison. Thankfully, in recent years the region has come increasingly under the tourist spotlight, and with good reason.

Stretching from the peaceful Solway Firth to the farmland, woods and glens around Stirling, Perth and Dundee, the Lowlands house most of Scotland's people and almost all of its key cities, but still manage to fit in fantastic forest parks, surprisingly wild hill country and spectacular coastlines.

Outdoor enthusiasts will relish the 212-mile, coast-to-coast Southern Upland Way and the famous 7stanes trails, which offer genuinely world-class mountain biking in the Borders and Dumfries and Galloway. If you're here for sights and culture, meanwhile, the campsites listed here offer decent access to Edinburgh, Glasgow and Linlithgow, as well as grand castles, picturesque coastal villages and memorials to Scotland's national poet, Robert Burns.

The Lowlands' proximity to England and Ireland has helped encourage larger campsite operators, and there are numerous big, comfortable and ever-so-slightly bland holiday parks with endless activities and facilities. But you'll find a good number of smaller, more individual sites too, offering a more traditional camping experience. You can camp among rare bird species, enjoy splendid views, rove around a country park or stay in an Iron Age hut.

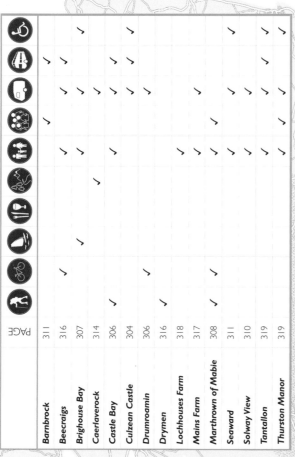

The Lowlands

	PAGE
Barnbrock	311
Beecraigs	316
Brighouse Bay	307
Caerlaverock	314
Castle Bay	306
Culzean Castle	304
Drumroamin	306
Drymen	316
Lochhouses Farm	318
Mains Farm	317
Marthrown of Mabie	308
Seaward	311
Solway View	310
Tantallon	319
Thurston Manor	319

See front flap for key to symbols

Montrose
Arbroath
Forfar
Dundee
Perth

ANGUS
PERTH & KINROSS
LOCH LOMOND & THE TROSSACHS

Culzean Castle

Ayrshire woodland and a fairytale castle

Grand, imposing Culzean Castle is one of Scotland's most famous landmarks – it can currently be seen on the Royal Bank of Scotland's £5 notes. Its turrets, towers and seaside setting form a fine backdrop to this Camping & Caravanning Club Site, located in the castle grounds. On a clear day, campers can gaze across the water to the Isle of Arran, although there's plenty to see closer up – the castle is surrounded by six hundred acres of parkland, and a wide variety of walks through woodland and along the sandy South Ayrshire coast are possible.

If you're staying at the campsite, you get half-price entry to the castle and its grounds (Ⓦwww.culzeanexperience.org; May–Oct; usually £13 per adult, £9 per child) and the building's interior makes for a fascinating day-trip. Much of what you're able to see inside today – highlights include the stunning Oval Staircase, animal-head motifs and a small exhibition on President Eisenhower – still incorporates the Neoclassical designs of the famous eighteenth-century Scottish architect and interior designer Robert Adam.

The magnificent grounds and formal gardens feature a walled Victorian garden, a restored vinery, a swan pond and a children's adventure playground. Outdoor events and guided walks run throughout the year, weather permitting, but there's a great deal of pleasure to be had from just strolling about the place. There are substantial sea caves beneath the castle that may be turned into a museum, but for now they remain closed.

The professional, well-maintained site itself, set near the castle entrance, has hardly a hint of litter or a blade of grass out of place. Most visitors are touring Scotland and are here for the castle, but there's much of interest off site – a car helps if you want to explore. Robert Burns was born in nearby Alloway, and related attractions include the Burns Cottage and Museum, ten miles from Culzean, where you can see Burns's painstakingly restored first family home and assorted exhibits including a lock of his hair, a pistol and the family Bible. For golfing fans, meanwhile, world-famous Turnberry and its fabled Ailsa course is only four miles away.

The quaint and traditional harbour village of Maidens, less than three miles from the site, sits at the southern end of Maid-

Practicalities

Culzean Castle Camping & Caravanning Club Site, Maybole, South Ayrshire, KA19 8JX ☎01655 760627, Ⓦwww.campingandcaravanningclub.co.uk

Pitches & price 30 grass pitches for tents, 7 of which have hook-ups. 30 hard-standing pitches, 26 of which have hook-ups. Non-member pitch fees start at £6.47, plus £5.53 per adult and £2.45 per child.

Facilities Shower and toilet blocks (including disabled facilities with easy-access shower) with laundry facilities.

Restrictions Group bookings welcome. Campfires not permitted. Dogs allowed (free).

Open April–Nov.

Getting there From Glasgow take the M77 signposted for Kilmarnock. This becomes the A77. Stay on it until Maybole then turn right onto the B7023, signposted for Culzean. Both the country park and campsite are clearly signposted. Regular buses run between Ayr (with good rail links to Glasgow) and Girvan, stopping directly outside the site entrance.

enhead Bay, and has a popular hotel-restaurant, *The Wildings* offering tasty, well-priced food including the day's catch. For essential provisions, meanwhile, you can head to the campsite reception's small shop, while the town of Maybole, with a post office, supermarket and pub, is four miles down the road.

Maybole has its own castle, dating back to the sixteenth century and a former residence of the earls of Cassillis, open most weekends during the summer – it's not on a par with the exquisitely designed Culzean, but remains an interesting diversion.

◀ Culzean Castle's grounds are magnificent ▶ Burns Cottage; chipping out of the sand at Turnberry; the tidy campsite itself

Castle Bay

Set high above the picturesque coastal village of Portpatrick – you'll need to brave 129 steep steps on your way back from town – *Castle Bay* is exposed to the wind but blessed by splendid views. Pitched just up from the site's permanent statics and caravan pitches, campers can see across the Irish Sea to the Mountains of Mourne on a clear day. Portpatrick's days as a significant port, ferrying coal and livestock between Scotland and Northern Ireland, have long gone, but its charming surroundings and old-fashioned centre means it remains popular with holiday-makers.

Several paths lead from the site, and the surrounding coastline offers fine walks; for serious hikers the 212-mile Southern Upland Way (Ⓦwww.southernuplandway.gov.uk) begins nearby. Staff at the site shop, which offers essentials including milk and bread, are happy to advise on routes. In Portpatrick, fifteen minutes' walk away, you could easily while away an afternoon by the picturesque harbourfront, having afternoon tea at one of the village cafés or sampling the local fish. The *Crown* and *Waterfront* hotels have specials depending on the catch – the latter has a lovely terrace where you can watch the village's colony of guillemots.

Practicalities

Castle Bay Holiday and Residential Park, Portpatrick, Stranraer, Dumfries & Galloway, DG9 9AA Ⓣ*01776 810462,* Ⓦ*www.castlebayholidaypark.co.uk*

Pitches & price 30 grass pitches for tents or caravans, 8 of which have hook-ups. 1 adult, 1 child and tent £10. £2.50 per additional adult, £3 per hook-up.

Facilities Shower and toilet block with laundry facilities.

Restrictions No campfires. No single-sex groups. Dogs allowed (£1).

Open March–Oct.

Getting there From Stranraer, turn right onto the A77, signposted for Portpatrick. After 8 miles, just before arriving in the village, you'll see *Castle Bay* signposted up a lane on your left. Continue past other caravan parks, until you reach *Castle Bay* on your right. There are regular buses from Stranraer and Ayr to Portpatrick village, a 15min walk from the site.

Drumroamin

This small but well-formed camping and caravan site sits in farmland in the shadow of the Galloway Hills, with views across to Wigtown Bay. It's an idyllic location, and *Drumroamin*'s laid-back atmosphere attracts repeat visits from families escaping the hustle of city life and mountain bikers who want to tackle some of the 7stanes network (Ⓦwww.7stanes.com) – Kirroughtree, with its forest-set trails and singletrack, is fifteen miles away. Enchanting Kilsture Forest lies at the top of the site's entrance lane and has marked trails, while an hour's tramp takes you to Wigtown (with its osprey-viewing room) and Bladnoch (home to a distillery).

The facilities are excellent, with new amenities blocks and a games room with a pool table and DVD player. Kirkinner village, two miles away, offers essential groceries and the *Kirkinner Inn*, which serves traditional pub grub and will keep its kitchen open for late arrivals – ask *Drumroamin* to call ahead. A butcher's van and a fish van visit the site once a week, and a local fresh veg supplier can deliver on request.

Practicalities

Drumroamin Farm Camping & Caravan Site, 1 South Balfern, Kirkinner, Newton Stewart, Dumfries & Galloway, DG8 9DB Ⓣ*01988 840613,* Ⓦ*www.drumroamin.co.uk*

Pitches & price 50 grass pitches for tents and caravans (20 with hook-ups). £6 per pitch (hook-ups £2 extra), plus £3 per adult and £1 per child. £1 discount for cyclists or backpackers without a car.

Facilities Shower and toilet block with hot water. Dish-washing area, washer/dryer.

Restrictions No campfires allowed. Dogs (free) must be kept on the lead.

Open Year round.

Getting there From the A75 Newtown Stewart roundabout, head south on the A714, continuing through Wigtown and Bladnoch until Kirkinner village. Turn left on the B7004 towards Garlieston; *Drumroamin* is the second turning on the left.

Brighouse Bay
Camping with bells on

This substantial holiday park isn't for those looking to avoid the crowds, but if you want a fun-packed family camping experience whatever the weather, *Brighouse Bay* is well worth a visit. Smart facilities and accommodation – on arrival you're greeted by finely groomed pitches and an array of lodges and statics – sit comfortably alongside an old-fashioned, family-run ethos. The main, "pitch-where-you-like" tent areas are in separate fields, giving campers a sense of privacy, safely out of view from the caravanners. Back at reception, the presence of a Gloster Meteor plane dating back to the 1940s only heightens the sense of being on a postwar holiday camp, and the sound of children's laughter fills the air from early morning until late at night.

The Solway Coast location provides spectacular views out over the Irish Sea – the holiday park even has its own private slipway in case you happen to have your boat in tow. If not, an on-site boating pond has mini-kayaks for the kids. The list of outdoor activities available at *Brighouse* is exhaustive: there's everything from an eighteen-hole golf course through lawn bowling to quad biking and pony trekking. You can hire bikes, use the leisure club, explore the wildlife ponds and enjoy direct access to the beach for paddling, swimming and sea-fishing off the rocks, while the staff organize themed seasonal events like Easter egg hunts.

In the unlikely event that you manage to exhaust *Brighouse*'s facilities, there are plenty of day-trips that don't involve too much driving. The Cream O' Galloway Organic Farm has an ice-cream parlour as well as an adventure playground and miles of nature trails and cycle paths (Ⓦwww.creamogalloway.co.uk), while Mabie Farm Park has pedal go-karts, donkey rides, an astro slide and an aerial runway, as well as animal paddocks and a barn area (Ⓦwww.mabiefarmpark.co.uk). Alternatively, pick up the *Nature Walks in and around Brighouse Bay* brochure and do a bit of exploring – the Borgue coast is a Site of Scientific Interest and harbours perennial flax, lizards, adders and kestrels.

Practicalities

Brighouse Bay Holiday Park, Borgue, Dumfries & Galloway, DG6 4TS ☎*1557 870267,* Ⓦ*www.brighouse-bay.co.uk*

Pitches & price 90 grass tent pitches (10 with hook-ups), 120 hard-standing pitches (all with hook-ups). From £14.30 for a 2-person tent or caravan. £2.45 per additional adult, £1.65 per additional child. Hook-ups are £4.10 extra.

Facilities Toilet and shower blocks with hot water, laundry facilities and a well-stocked site shop.

Restrictions No campfires. Dogs permitted (£2.35).

Open Year round.

Getting there From Castle Douglas take the A75 southwest through Twynholm. Veer left onto the A711, which briefly joins the A755 west. Turn left onto the B727 and head south towards the coast, through Borgue, picking up signs for *Brighouse Bay Holiday Park*.

▼ Kids will enjoy camping in the shadow of a World War II plane

Marthrown of Mabie

Relax in the roundhouse and ride the Dark Side

You can camp in the woods or party in an Iron Age hut before biking some of Scotland's best trails at this activity-packed site. *Marthrown* is nestled in Mabie Forest, just south of Dumfries, home to one of the lauded 7stanes mountain-biking areas (Ⓦwww.7stanes.com). Juicy trails run right from its doorstep, with something for all levels, from the beginner's green- and blue-graded tracks to the expert-only Kona Dark Side technical trail – see Ⓦwww.cycle-centre.com/shed.html for rental information.

Non-riders need not despair: Mabie Forest has miles of

excellent marked routes for walkers. The area is home to an extensive range of wildlife, including red squirrels, roe deer, hares and bats, while the appealing woods – a mix of younger spruce and ancient woodland, as well as birch and rowan – are carpeted ankle-deep in bluebells in May.

Two caravan pitches at the entrance aside, *Marthrown*'s camping area is for tents only, with no formal pitches or electric points, and you can pitch amongst the trees for added shelter. Little wooden huts dotted around the site house hot showers and composting loos, blending in with the surrounding forest.

On two elevated sites above the main campsite sit a Mongolian *ger* (complete with pot-bellied stove) and a replica Iron Age roundhouse with a thatched roof, one main room and a wood-burner. The roundhouse is a big draw for groups and the site managers are happy to run an electric cable up to the building on request if guests want to party into the small hours with their own music. The *ger* is a good option for families as it is in a separate, more secluded area, away from any potential stag or hen nights.

There's a bunkhouse below, sleeping 26 across four rooms, and campers can use the bunkhouse kitchen and dining room for £5 per tent if the weather takes a turn for the worse. Full catering options are available year round for groups and hog roast suppers, outdoor spit and all, can also be arranged in advance. Food – hot, hearty and freshly prepared on the premises – is available to individual campers too, who can order a full cooked breakfast, packed lunch or three-course evening meal at the bunkhouse. For a pub meal or to quench your thirst after a day of activities, the *Mabie House Hotel* is a twenty-minute walk from the site, while substantial Dumfries is only three miles away.

The communal chill-out area is popular with weary mountain bikers, wherever they are bedding down at *Marthrown*. Its treats include a Finnish sauna and wood-fuelled open-air hot tub – both at no additional cost. There is also an outdoor barbecue for guests to use and a choice of games when the sun shines, including basketball, badminton and football. High- and low-level rope courses incorporate two forty-foot climbing walls – guests

Practicalities

Marthrown of Mabie, Mabie Forest, Dumfries, DG2 8HB
☏*01387 247900,* Ⓦ*www.marthrown.com*

Pitches & price 20 woodland tent pitches (2 additional pitches can take caravans on request). 2-person tent £12, family tents £20. Roundhouse prices start at £270 (sleeps 16), while the *ger* (comfortably sleeps 4) starts at £50 – weekend and longer stay rates available.

Facilities Hot showers, dry-composting loos, self-catering kitchen in bunkhouse, laundry on request, catering by arrangement, sauna, hot tub and BBQ area.

Restrictions Communal campfire area at the roundhouse. Dogs are permitted (free).

Open Year round.

Getting there From Dumfries take the A710 (Solway Coast Road) for New Abbey. At the village of Islesteps turn right at the signpost for Mabie Forest. At the *Mabie Hotel* bear left, following signs for Marthrown of Mabie Education Centre. Continue past the white stone building on the right and forest ranger's wooden office on the left, up the track and through the gates into the forest. Follow the track for about a mile, going straight over at the crossroads. The hostel and campsite are on your left at the top of the track.

can prearrange (paid) instruction via the site's management.

Because of the range of trails at Mabie, the site is very popular with mountain bikers all year round, and in the evenings they can often be found in the hot tub or sauna, comparing hardtails and discussing traction. But, in a testament to the site's wide appeal, you'll probably see walkers, groups and families waxing lyrical about the wonders of Mabie right alongside them.

◀ Mabie Forest in autumn ▶ A range of mountain-bike trails stretch for miles from the campsite; dry-composting loos, ready and waiting

Solway View
Wicker men and rustic charm

The Solway Firth's sheltered waters reach from Cumbria to Galloway, edged by a stunning coastline of rolling hills and farmland. This landscape formed the backdrop to cult classic *Wicker Man* and, seen from rustic *Solway View*, its gentle contours stretch as far as the eye can see. Once busy with shipping, the Firth was crossed by a railway viaduct in the late 1800s, but the boat traffic petered out, the railway failed, and now the region is a peaceful one.

Solway View only opened in 2005, and while other sites in the area might have flasher facilities, its simple charms make it a fine base. Plenty of open grassland helps the site retain a spacious and rural feel, even when it's busy and, though basic, the facilities are clean, modern and eco-friendly, with a solar-heated shower and toilet block and recycling facilities.

It's a family-orientated place, with traditional activities for the kids ranging from tree-climbing and rope swings to picnicking and woodland walks; there's also direct access to a secluded bay with a sandy beach and numerous rock pools worthy of exploration. Children tend to congregate in the middle in the evenings for a mass game of tag before bedtime while parents relax around the communal campfire.

At the site's reception, campers can purchase free-range eggs and firewood, and a two-mile walk leads down to the general store for supplies and the local pub for refreshments. Kirkcudbright, with further shops, cafés, bars and restaurants, is a twenty-minute drive away.

Should the weather take a turn for the worse, you might want to rent one of three large wooden wigwams, all fully equipped with mattresses, microwave, kettle, fridge and toaster. If the sun does shine, wigwam guests can make use of their own barbecue area, picnic bench and fire-pit.

▼ Knockbrex beach, near Kirkcudbright, on the Solway Firth

Practicalities

Solway View, Balmangan Farm, Ross Bay, Borgue, Kirkcudbright, Dumfries & Galloway, DG6 4TR ☎*01557 870206,* Ⓦ*www.solwayviewholidays.com*

Pitches & price 12 grass tent pitches (4 with hook-ups), 5 hard-standing pitches (all with hook-ups), 3 large wooden wigwams. Pitches start at £9 for a 2-person tent. £2 per additional adult. Wigwams sleep 4–5 and start at £25 based on 2 adults sharing.

Facilities Shower/toilet block, cooking area with covered seating, dish-washing sinks, recycling facilities.

Restrictions No hen or stag parties. Campfires allowed in designated spots. Dogs permitted (free).

Open Year round.

Getting there From Castle Douglas take the A75 southwest through Twynholm. Veer left onto the A711 which briefly joins the A755 west. Turn left onto the B727 and head south towards the coast, through Borgue, before picking up signs for the campsite. A single-track road leads to the farm entrance.

Seaward

The Gillespie family run five camping and caravanning sites in Dumfries and Galloway, but while nearby *Brighouse Bay* (see p.307) is very much a holiday park, *Seaward* is a smaller and more mellow site. That doesn't mean it doesn't offer good facilities – families will certainly enjoy the heated outdoor swimming pool, pitch and putt, outdoor play area and games room – but it does mean you might spend more time exploring the area around than you do being entertained on site. Panoramic views stretch over the River Dee estuary, looking out towards Ross Island lighthouse and beyond to the brooding Irish Sea, and the large sandy beach at Dhoon Bay is only a few minutes' walk away.

The camping field is set apart from the caravans, which gives added privacy and better views, but does mean a slightly longer walk to the facilities. A small bar by the pool is open at weekends during high season, when campers congregate to exchange day-trip recommendations over a beer – numerous jaunts around the Solway Coast are possible. Several nearby towns have good eating options; try the *Selkirk Arms Hotel* at Kirkcudbright, three miles away, or the *Star Hotel* at Twynholm, four miles away.

Practicalities

Seaward Caravan Park, Dhoon Bay, Kirkcudbright, Dumfries & Galloway, DG6 4TJ ☏01557 331079, Ⓦ*www.seaward-park.co.uk*

Pitches & price 15 tent pitches, 9 grass caravan pitches with hook-ups, 18 hard-standing pitches with hook-ups. 2 adults and tent from £12.30. £1.50 per child.

Facilities Shower/toilet block, incorporating 2 family shower rooms and 1 disabled shower and bathroom. Undercover dish-washing area and laundry facilities. On-site shop.

Restrictions No campfires allowed on site. Dogs permitted (£4.35).

Open March–Oct.

Getting there From Dumfries take the A75 southwest towards Castle Douglas. Continue to Kirkcudbright and take the A755, then veer left onto the B727 along the coast. The site entrance is on your right.

Barnbrock

This sleepy and fairly basic site, set in Clyde Muirshiel Regional Park, offers outdoor activities, value-for-money wigwams and – perhaps most importantly – proximity to Glasgow. The city, with its shopping, museums and nightlife is twenty miles away, while Glasgow Airport is only ten miles down the road, making this a useful stop-over for campers heading around west or central Scotland. There's no real entertainment on site, but Clyde Muirshiel offers miles of cycle paths and a network of marked trails – you can also book taster sessions in sailing, canoeing, orienteering and mountain biking via the visitor centre (see Ⓦ*www.clydemuirshiel.co.uk*).

Facilities are simple, with an honesty box but no full-time warden, and the wigwams on offer range from minimal models with a lino floor and a solid wooden roof – you'll need your own mats and sleeping bags – to more upmarket versions with electricity and mattresses. If you need basic supplies, the village of Lochwinnoch is only four miles away and an easy downhill walk from the site, though the journey back up can be more of a struggle: you might want to get a taxi.

Practicalities

Barnbrock Campsite, Barnbrock Farm, nr Lochwinnoch, Renfrewshire, PA10 2PZ ☏01505 614791, Ⓦ*www.clydemuirshiel.co.uk*

Pitches & price 15 tent pitches. £4 per adult, £3 per child. Wigwams available from £20 for a basic model with no facilities. Groups can book the whole site.

Facilities Shower and toilet block. Undercover kitchen and dining area, drying room for kit.

Restrictions No campfires.

Open April–Oct.

Getting there From Glasgow, leave the M8 at junction 28A and merge onto the A737 towards Irvine. After 8.5 miles join the A760 west. Follow the signs for Lochwinnoch, then the brown signs past the village for Clyde Muirshiel Regional Park. There is a train station in Lochwinnoch, 4 miles away, with a regular service to Glasgow Central.

Festivals

Britain's music festivals are the world's best, and camping at them is the definitive way to experience the mud, the music and the glorious hubbub that they bring with them.

You don't have to camp at a festival – you can stay at a B&B at the Brecon Jazz Festival, slumber at a Butlins chalet at All Tomorrow's Parties or stay up all night in Notting Hill. But the modern music festival and the tent are stuck together like glue. Some of the most iconic sights are not this headline act or that lager-sponsored stage, but a mass of tents, a temporary community stretching out into the darkness, lit up by stalls and headtorches and punctuated by flags from half the countries under the sun. Likewise, it's hard to see camping's increasing trendiness, all designer canvas and swish glampsites, without thinking of the companies who started renting pre-erected tents to festival-goers in the early noughties, or the movers and shakers whose most memorable camping experiences came in a big field full of party-goers, wondering if it was time to get up or go to bed.

That doesn't mean today's festivals are just about hedonism. The smaller festivals, especially, can be fun places to stay even when the bands aren't playing. **Green Man** (late Aug; Ⓦwww. thegreenmanfestival.co.uk) has a lovely location on the edge of the Brecon Beacons, a line-up that borrows heavily from folk and quirky indie and a cheerful crowd that's heavy on families but still packs out the dance tents come the early hours. **End of the Road** (mid-Sept; Ⓦwww.endoftheroadfestival.com) mixes a devout affection for post-rock, Americana and recycling with a fine setting in a Dorset country park populated by peacocks and organic-cider-drinking punters.

For a similarly relaxed and pleasantly uncommercial vibe, but less beard-stroking musos, check out ethical freak-fest **Shambala** (late Aug; Ⓦwww.shambalafestival.org) and trustafarian rave-up **Secret Garden Party** (late July; www.secretgardenparty. com), where the bands often draw smaller crowds than ad hoc mud-wrestling and bike stunts, and the lakeside setting feels simply magical.

It's hard to stay distinctive when you house the population of a small town. Of the larger festivals, **Latitude** (mid-July; www. latitudefestival.co.uk) makes a good fist of it, with theatre, literature and comedy stands and a sylvan Suffolk setting. **Bestival** (early Sept; Ⓦwww.bestival.net), meanwhile, has shifted from

a boutique festival to attracting almost forty thousand people, but still just holds onto its alternative status, thanks in large part to its fancy-dress Saturday, which can see you sharing tent-side chats with a Scrabble letter, a mermaid and an alien on stilts. If you fancy a mellower, more family-friendly vibe, try its cousin **Camp Bestival** (late July; Ⓦwww.campbestival.net).

Camping at the biggest festivals, by contrast, is a means to an end rather than a thrill in itself – **T in the Park** (mid-July; Ⓦwww.tinthepark.com) may set its main stage against a backdrop of Scottish hills, but you'll be too busy dodging drunken revellers to notice. It and fellow leviathans **Reading** (late Aug; Ⓦwww.readingfestival.com), **Leeds** (late Aug; Ⓦwww.leedsfestival.com), **V** (mid-Aug; Ⓦwww.vfestival.com) and the **Isle of Wight** (mid-June; Ⓦwww.isleofwightfestival.com) are all about eager crowds, corporate sponsors and big headline acts.

Yet for all their efforts, **Glastonbury** (late June; Ⓦwww. glastonburyfestivals.co.uk) remains the UK's – and probably the world's – definitive music festival. The years of hippies, travellers, free milk and fence-jumpers are now long gone, but despite the fawning TV coverage and enormous crowds (around 130,000 tickets go on sale) it remains rather special, partly because of the array of entertainments on site, but also because enough of the crowd keep faith with the event's utopian ideals to make camping and mingling a huge part of the midsummer fun.

Glastonbury embodies the modern festival's contradictory nature. Avowedly counter-cultural events, festivals are increasingly regulated, sponsored and planned with an accountant's precision. Commentators have worried that Glastonbury crowds are getting too old, that high prices are stopping real fans get in, and that the arrival of chain brands – Pizza Express stands are now visible at some festivals – has put a boot in the face of any concept of the festival as a spontaneous, communal "happening". Yet changes have been good as well as bad – the food stalls are far better than they used to be, offering a vast range of ethnic cuisines and (heavens!) vegetables, and toilets have improved immeasurably, meaning the business of camping for the weekend can be a pleasure rather than a survival mission. And for all the stories you'll read in rock heritage magazines about the joys of getting through a weekend with nothing but a blanket, a beard and two tabs of acid, that's a good thing.

◄ The costumed crowds: Camp Bestival (top) and Latitude (bottom)

Caerlaverock

A bird's-eye view on the Solway Coast

Many campsites in Scotland offer guests the chance to get up close and personal with nature, but *Caerlaverock* is truly special. Just nine miles south of Dumfries, the Wildfowl & Wetlands Trust's only site in Scotland lets campers wander around after hours using marked paths and hides, watching seasonal birds, spending the night on badger watch and waking up to a dawn chorus.

The reserve was opened in the 1960s, but camping here is a relatively new concept. Following a successful trial, campers are now welcome as long as they respect the environment – due to the sensitive nature of the site and the restricted space, booking in advance is essential. The basic facilities can seem something of an afterthought – you essentially get a patch of

grass for tents and an overflow section of the car park for tourers and motor homes – but there are picnic tables, and campers can use the showers in the self-catering farmhouse as long as they ask in advance.

The centre and camping area is open every day, bar Christmas Day, and there are different birds and animals to discover year round. In spring the ospreys begin to arrive, in summer the wildflower meadows are carpeted with butterflies and dragonflies, and in autumn barnacle geese arrive from the Arctic and whooper swans return from Iceland. The winter months may be chilly for campers, but hardy types or those snuggled up in a caravan get to experience the centre at its very best, with thousands of swans, geese and ducks for neighbours. The

Practicalities

WWT Caerlaverock Wetland Centre, Eastpark Farm, Caerlaverock, Dumfries & Galloway, DG1 4RS ☎01387 770200, Ⓦ*www.wwt.org.uk*

Pitches & price 12 grass tent pitches, 12 hard-standing pitches for caravans. No hook-ups available. £5 per adult, £2.50 per child. Non-WWF (Wildfowl & Wetland Trust) members must pay £6.30 per day to enter the nature reserve.

Facilities Toilet block and sinks with hot water. Hot showers available by arrangement. Drying room.

Restrictions No dogs, campfires or BBQs allowed.

Open Year round.

Getting there From Dumfries take the A75 south, then follow the tourist signs for WWT Caerlaverock. The site owners will drop campers at the road head (from where buses run the 10 miles to Dumfries train station) for a small donation, or will head to or from Dumfries for £10.

centre's website advises of guided walks and feeding times.

If the centre's wildlife isn't enough to keep you occupied, you could head to the Solway Coast's lovely beaches, while both Ae and Mabie forests are within easy driving distance for nature trails and mountain biking. Caerlaverock Castle, an eye-catching thirteenth-century construction with a broad moat, is only two miles from the centre.

The reserve's café and gift shop (Mon–Sat 11am–4.30pm) offers sandwiches, paninis, homemade soups and tray bakes, but for groceries you'll need to head the nine miles to Dumfries. The *Nith Hotel* in Glencaple (five miles away) serves bar meals and has a restaurant; steaks feature heavily on the menu.

◀ A mute swan leads the pack at feeding time ▶ Ducks on the water; Caerlaverock Castle, constructed from local red sandstone

Drymen

The West Highland Way stretches from the outskirts of Glasgow to Fort William, taking in drovers' roads, high moors and remote lochs. Hikers breaking their trip in Drymen, twelve miles in, have little choice of where to stay – this is the only campsite in the area. Thankfully, this basic place, run by tree surgeon Gavin Cross and set on his family homestead overlooking the Campsie Fells, is welcoming and relaxed. The pitches are informal, and tents sprout haphazardly amongst the site's wooden wigwams. The main priority is a good night's sleep, although the *Clachan Inn*, two miles away in the village itself, might tempt you to stay out – the pub dates back to the early 1700s and offers home cooking and a wide choice of cask ales. The Crosses will taxi campers to and from the pub by request.

Drymen village has an outdoors store, a café, pubs, a well-stocked village shop and the *Drymen Tandoori*, while if you phone ahead Gavin's mum will serve hearty sit-down meals in the cosy farmhouse. There were plans for expansion as we went to press, with more amenities and wigwams on the cards.

Practicalities

Drymen Camping, Easter Drumquhassle Farm, Gartness Road, Drymen, Stirling, G63 0DN ☎*01360 660597,* Ⓦ*www.drymencamping.co.uk*

Pitches & price Unlimited pitches – the owners will find room on the farm for tents. £5 per person. No hook-ups. 2 simple wigwams (sleeping 6) £32.

Facilities Outdoor tap and sink. Portakabin shower and toilet block. There's a cooking area in the barn.

Restrictions No campfires. Dogs allowed (free).

Open Year round.

Getting there From Stirling, travel along the A811 for 20 miles; from Glasgow, take the A809 until it joins the A811, which you should follow towards Stirling for 2 miles. From the A811, turn off towards the village of Gartness – you will see signs for both Easter Drumquhassle Farm and *Drymen* along the Old Gartness Road.

Beecraigs

Just fifteen minutes' walk from Linlithgow and its historic palace and with good transport links to Edinburgh (20 miles east) and Glasgow (35 miles west), this finely groomed campsite has a splendid location in Scotland's Central Belt. It sits in the middle of Beecraigs Forest Park, 913 acres of upland forest offering stunning views across the Forth estuary. Within the park there's a fly-fishing loch, a deer farm and an outdoor pursuits centre offering archery, canoeing, climbing and kayaking, while a network of walks and mountain bike trails wind their way through the woodland – the popularity of these activities means the site can be very busy during the school holidays.

The park's farm shop sells local produce including venison steaks and freshly caught trout, and there's a reasonable restaurant on site. Linlithgow is full of shops, bars and restaurants and steeped in history – Mary Queen of Scots and James VI of Scotland both lived in the handsome palace. When James moved his court to London in 1603, the palace declined, but the majestic, almost maze-like building still manages to convey its original grandeur despite missing roofs and walls in sections.

Practicalities

Beecraigs Country Park & Campsite, nr Linlithgow, West Lothian, EH49 6PL ☎*01506 844516,* Ⓦ*www.beecraigs.com*

Pitches & price About 15 grass tent pitches, from £7.50 per tent (hook-ups available on request). 26 secluded hard-standing pitches for caravans, all with hook-ups, from around £13.50 per pitch.

Facilities Modern, well-maintained toilets and showers.

Restrictions No campfires, though there is a BBQ area. Dogs permitted (free).

Open Easter–Oct for tents. Year round for caravans.

Getting there From Glasgow, take the M9, leaving at junction 4 for Linlithgow. From Edinburgh, follow the A803 into Linlithgow. *Beecraigs* is clearly signposted from town. Regular buses and trains, and a canal path, run to Linlithgow from both cities, then it's a 15min walk to the site or a 5min taxi journey.

Mains Farm
Cowboys, Indians and Monty Python

With its brightly coloured canvas tipis and wooden wigwams, *Mains Farm* is a child's delight. Its Stirlingshire-countryside location will appeal to adults too, who might recognize the cracked battlements of Doune Castle, four miles east, from *Monty Python and the Holy Grail*, and can take their charges to nearby Bannockburn and Stirling Castle and the appealing walking country of the Trossachs.

The main campsite, which contains the wigwams and tipis (with a separate area for tourers and motor homes), is an orderly place with good facilities and a dining area with bright Wild West murals. There are fire-pits at each wigwam (and logs for sale at the site reception), and each has its own barbecue, filling summer evenings with the sounds and smells of sizzling sausages and burgers, not to mention the cries of little cowboys and Indians. The wigwams and tipis all come equipped with mattresses, kettle,

fridge and electric heater so all you need is a sleeping bag and pillow. There's a child's play area opposite the site, next to a field with grass pitches for campers with their own tents. There are no facilities in the field, although campers can use the main kitchen and toilets, and the main focus of *Mains Farm* is on its tipis and wigwams.

The site is in Thornhill, a small village with a grocery store and two family-friendly pubs, the eighteenth-century *Crown Hotel* and the *Lion and Unicorn*, which has log fires and real ale on tap. And if history and hiking aren't to your taste, there are plenty of options for kids: Blair Drummond Safari & Adventure Park (Ⓦwww.blairdrummond.com) is four miles away and a Go Ape (Ⓦwww.goape.co.uk) high-wire forest obstacle course – with the UK's longest zip-slide – is ten miles away in Aberfoyle.

▼ *Mains Farm* offers tipis and wigwams in rural Stirlingshire

Practicalities

Mains Farm, Thornhill, Stirling, FK8 3QB ☎*01786 850735,* Ⓦ*www.mainsfarmwigwams.com*

Pitches & price 5 wigwams and 5 tipis available from £30. 20 tent pitches and 20 caravan pitches, 12 of which have hook-ups. £5 per pitch plus £2 per adult and £1 per child. £3 extra per hook-up.

Facilities Shower/toilet block, plus camp kitchen with oven, microwave, kettle, pots, pans and crockery. Additional wigwam available with full disabled access. Plans are in place to build a new shower/toilet block and kitchen in the camping field by late 2010.

Restrictions Campfires permitted in fire-pits. Dogs allowed (free). No stag/hen parties.

Open Easter–Oct.

Getting there From Stirling, take the M9 and leave at junction 10. Join the A84 signposted for Callander and, after 6 miles, bear left onto the A873, to Thornhill. Entering the village come to a crossroads. Turn left, signposted for Fintry. The farm is 150yds on your right.

Lochhouses Farm
Five Go Mad in East Lothian

Featherdown Farms' neatly nostalgic network of sites (see p.84) has expanded into France and the Netherlands, but *Lochhouses* is their only Scottish outpost so far. Yet, with private access to the beach and tranquil surroundings, this charming campsite could give any of its English stablemates a run for their money.

This is very much a camping experience to be shared with the kids and completely removes the hassle of having to keep an eye on your brood while pitching your tent in a gale. Instead you'll find a small group of pre-erected tents in a clearing next to the beach on the edge of John Muir Country Park, a few miles up the coast from Dunbar, complete with wooden floors,

▼ Early risers get the eggs at *Lochhouses Farm*

pot-bellied stoves, flushing loos and separate sleeping areas. This may be "camping for cheats", but the comfort doesn't compromise the lovely rural feel and the setting is spectacular, with rolling farmland to one side and golden sand dunes to the other offering plenty of opportunities for exploration.

In the centre of the clearing is a communal area for campfires and a section with chicken coops and pens for newborn lambs, rabbits and geese. The eggs can be collected by campers each morning on a first-come, first-served basis – set your alarm for sunrise to be in with a chance of an omelette.

An old boat on site houses emergency provisions, or you can stock up at Knowes Farm Shop (Wwww.knowesfarmshop.co.uk) in East Linton or the cafés, restaurants and stores of North Berwick, both about five miles away. North Berwick's Scottish Seabird Centre (Wwww.seabird.org) makes an interesting half-day trip, although those in search of adventure might prefer to rent a bike or organize a pony trek through *Lochhouses Farm*, and head out either along the pretty East Lothian coast or into John Muir Park, home to numerous butterfly and bird species.

Practicalities

Lochhouses Farm, Tyninghame, nr Dunbar, East Lothian, EH42 1XP ☎01420 80804, Wwww.featherdownfarm.co.uk

Pitches & price Tents house up to 6 people. Prices start at £195 for a mid-week 3-night break. Check the website for further info.

Facilities Four shared showers (each tent has its own toilet, stove and kitchen). Firewood is free.

Restrictions Campfires permitted in designated spots.

Open Easter–Oct. Check-in 4pm–6pm.

Getting there Take the A1 towards Edinburgh. Just before East Linton, turn right onto the A198 signposted for Tyninghame. Pass through the village and you will see *Lochhouses Farm* signposted on your right.

Tantallon

This large, purpose-built site, twenty minutes' walk from North Berwick, might not immediately appeal to intrepid campers. Look up and around you and its appeal is more obvious. The tent field sits in the distinctive, humped shadow of North Berwick Law, a private path gives campers direct access to a beach that's great for paddling and the views at sunset, looking out across the Firth of Forth to Bass Rock (an impressive 100m high volcanic plug with its own gannet colony) offer a fine way to end your day.

The site's well-ordered nature has its advantages too, with pristine pitches and well-maintained facilities including an outdoor play park, a putting green and a games room with air hockey and a snooker table. Visitors can climb the law (worth it for the panorama), visit the Scottish Seabird Centre (Ⓦwww.seabird.org) or get a tour of Bass Rock from the harbour, while daunting, fourteenth-century Tantallon Castle is only a mile from the campsite. The site shop has only limited supplies but there's a large supermarket in North Berwick as well as a decent range of cafés, bars and restaurants.

Practicalities

Tantallon Caravan & Camping Park, Dunbar Road, North Berwick, East Lothian, EH39 5NJ Ⓣ*01620 893348,* Ⓦ*www.meadowhead.co.uk*

Pitches & price 120 tent pitches (40 with hook-ups), 133 caravan pitches (all with hook-ups). £13.50–£21 for a 2-person tent, depending on season. Hardstandings with electric hook-ups £16–£24.
Facilities 6 toilet and shower blocks (with disabled facilities) and laundry facilities.
Restrictions No campfires. Dogs permitted (£3).
Open March–Oct.
Getting there Take the A1 through Newcastle and Berwick-on-Tweed. After Dunbar there will be a sign for North Berwick. At the sign, turn right onto the A198 and continue past Tantallon Castle. The site entrance is a mile further on, on the right. Regular trains and buses run to Edinburgh.

Thurston Manor

Set within 250 acres of a former Scottish estate at the foot of the wild Lammermuir Hills, *Thurston Manor* almost lives up to its grand name. Its proximity to Edinburgh, just thirty minutes' drive away, makes it very popular with campers wanting to combine their exploration of the Scottish Borders and the dramatic Berwickshire coastline with a trip to Scotland's capital. But you can enjoy your holiday here without ever leaving the site, whose beautifully maintained grounds are crossed by a number of signposted trails, most leading walkers past the site's well-stocked freshwater fishing loch – rods and gear are available to rent if you fancy fly fishing.

With organized activities for kids, an upmarket statics area called "The Glen", a leisure centre complete with pool, sauna, gym, bar and restaurant, and tribute-band-dominated live entertainment, *Thurston Manor* won't be everyone's cup of tea, and it gets chock-a-block with families during the school holidays. But if you're looking for a smart, convenient site with plenty of entertainment it's well worth a visit.

Practicalities

Thurston Manor Holiday Home Park, Innerwick, Dunbar, East Lothian, EH42 1SA Ⓣ*01368 840643,* Ⓦ*www.thurstonmanor.co.uk*

Pitches & price 76 pitches for tents or caravans – all have hook-ups, 15 are hard-standing. From £7 per person in a 2-person tent in low season to £27 for a fully serviced hard-standing pitch in high season.
Facilities Modern, well-maintained facilities, including shower and toilet blocks, dish-washing area and laundry facilities. Separate disabled shower room.
Restrictions No campfires on site. Dogs permitted (£5 per stay).
Open March–Oct.
Getting there From the south, take the A1 towards Edinburgh. After passing Berwick-upon-Tweed, turn right at the signpost for Innerwick and Crowhill. The site, a mile off the A1, is well signposted.

The Highlands

"The Highlands" conjures up shortbread-tin images of heather-clad hills, majestic stags, hairy cows, snow-capped mountains and – thanks to *Braveheart* – several thousand men in tartan rampaging through the glens.

You may not encounter too many rampant clans on your visit – indeed, the Highlands have been sparsely populated since the Clearances of the nineteenth century and the mass emigration that resulted – but the landscape is every bit as spectacular as you'd expect, and an ideal backdrop for embracing the great outdoors.

Thousands of visitors each year are drawn to the area by the West Highland Way, which runs from the outskirts of Glasgow up to the foot of Ben Nevis, taking in 95 miles of the country's finest scenery, including Loch Lomond, Loch Leven and Glen Coe, but all manner of routes are open to hikers and climbers, and outdoor pursuit centres offer a wide range of activities.

For campers keen to immerse themselves in Scottish culture there are historic ruins, Highland Games and whisky tours, while anyone will enjoy the idyllic locations, enchanting lochs and amazing sunsets that are part and parcel of the camping experience here. The downside of visiting, in high season at least, are the dreaded midges, the "scourge of the North"; between June and August insect repellent is essential.

Yet, with hundreds of Munros to bag and miles of countryside and coastline to explore, the Highlands are a splendid destination. Whether you take in the landscape from the top of a hill, the saddle of a bike or the porch of your tent, you're unlikely to forget its impact.

Thurso

Wick

Fraserburgh

Peterhead

Aberdeen

Elgin

Keith

East Grange Farm

Forres

Nairn

MORAY

Inverness

Grantown-on-Spey

Aviemore

Lazy Duck

Rothiemurchus

CAIRNGORMS NATIONAL PARK

ABERDEENSHIRE

ANGUS

Dundee

Ullapool

Ardmair Point

Badrallach

Northern Lights

Clachtoll Beach

HIGHLAND

The Wee Camp Site

Borlum Farm

Fort Augustus

Faichemard Farm

Morvich

Kyle of Lochalsh

Shielbridge

Applecross

Mallaig

Camusdarach

Invercaimbe

▲ Ben Nevis

Fort William

Caolasnacon

Red Squirrel

Invercoe

PERTH & KINROSS

Blair Castle

Glengoulandie

Loch Tay

Comrie Croft

Perth

Strathfillan

Wigwams

LOCH LOMOND & THE TROSSACHS

By the Way

Beinglas Farm

ARGYLL & BUTE

Oban

The Highlands

	PAGE	Accessible	Caravan	Facilities	Dogs	Groups	Fishing	Dining	Campfires	Cycling	Walking
Applecross	350			✓				✓			
Ardmair Point	352		✓	✓						✓	✓
Badrallach	352			✓					✓		✓
Beinglas Farm	324							✓		✓	✓
Blair Castle	337		✓	✓				✓		✓	✓
Borlum Farm	348		✓	✓		✓					
By the Way	330		✓	✓							✓
Camusdarach	346		✓	✓		✓	✓		✓		✓
Caolasnacon	335		✓				✓		✓		✓
Clachtoll Beach	353		✓				✓		✓	✓	✓
Comrie Croft	328	✓	✓	✓		✓	✓	✓		✓	✓
East Grange Farm	342				✓			✓			
Faichemard Farm	337			✓						✓	✓
Glengoulandie	336					✓					✓
Invercaimbe	343		✓	✓			✓		✓		✓
Invercoe	334	✓	✓	✓		✓		✓	✓	✓	✓
Lazy Duck	344				✓		✓		✓	✓	
Loch Tay	327					✓		✓	✓	✓	
Luss	326	✓	✓	✓		✓				✓	✓
Morvich	347	✓		✓		✓					✓
Northern Lights	349		✓	✓			✓				✓
Oban	331			✓					✓		
Red Squirrel	330				✓			✓	✓	✓	
Rothiemurchus	338			✓		✓		✓		✓	✓
Shielbridge	343		✓	✓					✓		✓
Strathfillan Wigwams	332		✓	✓		✓					✓
The Wee Camp Site	349			✓							✓

See front flap for key to symbols

STIRLING · Stirling · Luss · Campbelltown

Beinglas Farm
A walkers' haven on the West Highland Way

Many a weary walker has been tempted to take off their hiking boots and set up camp at *Beinglas Farm*. The challenging West Highland Way runs right through the middle of this attractive rural campsite, located in the village of Inverarnan and nestled at the foot of Ben Glas, the farm's namesake. Outdoor enthusiasts will find other activities to occupy them too; the site is an ideal base for trying water sports at Loch Lomond, just two miles south, or for spotting and photographing wildlife.

The farm has an impressive range of facilities including a bar and restaurant serving wholesome meals (the menu changes seasonally) and a beer garden, which is lovely in the summer sunshine. A purpose-built shelter offers refuge if the weather turns nasty, and houses a kitchen and dining area with laundry facilities. Campers who have suffered the full wrath of the Scottish elements can dry their kit out or unwind by playing a game of pool, and the on-site shop stocks all the walking essentials, from high-energy snacks to first-aid kits.

The site attracts walkers throughout the year, but the summer months are jam-packed. *Beinglas* has over a hundred pitches and the owners guarantee that they will find space for everyone, but it's best to arrive early to guarantee your choice of pitch. Four curious-looking, heated wooden wigwams can accommodate guests wanting slightly more protection from the Scottish elements. A list of rules is displayed around the site, including "No noise after 10.30pm" – a nod to the campers preparing to tackle the next leg of the Way in the morning. Despite the presence of written regulations, the site has a relaxed, communal feel, particularly in the evenings when walkers swap tales of their Highland explorations before bedding down. And though *Beinglas* is busy, it still feels incredibly serene, with fantastic views in all directions. From any of the pitches you can see the spectacular Grey Mare's Tail waterfall tumbling down through the rocks above.

The A82 leading up to the farm is the only real downside of visiting *Beinglas*; it can be very busy so do take care if you decide

Practicalities

Beinglas Farm Campsite, Inverarnan, Loch Lomond, Dunbartonshire, G83 7DX ☎01301 704281, Ⓦwww.beinglascampsite.co.uk

Pitches & price 100 grass pitches for tents with no hook-ups. £6 per adult, £3.50 per child. Call for family rates. Additional charge of £1 per night for cars and vans. 4 heated wooden wigwams, prices starting at £25, depending on number of occupants (maximum 4).

Facilities Bar and restaurant, on-site shop, toilets and showers, communal area with kitchen, laundry, kit-drying space and pool table.

Restrictions No campfires. Dogs allowed (£1).

Open Year round (except Christmas).

Getting there From Glasgow, stay on the A82 past Luss and on to Inverarnan. Around 300yds past the *Drover's Inn*, turn sharp right into the site's entrance. Continue over the wooden bridge and up to the campsite reception. Though most campers arrive here on foot via the Way, there are seasonal bus services from Glasgow to Crainlarich, via Inverarnan.

to walk to the *Drover's Inn*, just over three hundred yards from the site's entrance. The *Inn* is a well-known landmark, crammed with ancient taxidermy, from stag heads to foxes, and bar staff in full Scottish kilt 'n' sporran combo (though most of them seem to be Australian). It's always packed with mud-covered walkers, warming themselves in front of the open fires and tucking into large plates of hearty food from the reasonably priced menu – the rack of sticky ribs will challenge even the hungriest veterans of the West Highland Way. In the summer there is often live music in the evenings when energetic, traditional Scottish musicians distract tired walkers from their blisters and midge bites.

◀ Heated wigwams at the foot of Ben Glas ▶ Hikers descend the flanks of Ben Lomond, on their way to Loch Lomond

Luss

Soap opera sets and loch-side pitches

For those prepared to admit they've watched an episode of *Take the High Road*, the village of Luss may look strangely familiar. From its pilot in 1980 until the series ended in 2003, Luss played the part of Glendarroch, the fictional home to Mrs Mac and her neighbours in the long-running Scottish soap. Though the television crews have long departed, the cobbled streets, ancient church, quaint teahouses and stone pier all remain, adding to the village's irrepressible charm.

Luss, set in a stunning location on the western shores of Loch Lomond, only five minutes' walk from town, can be choc-a-bloc during the summer months, meaning purists in search of tranquillity might be disappointed. Thankfully, the Camping and Caravanning Club, who run the site, have a policy never to turn away backpackers, no matter how busy it might be.

The campsite has a playground and a circular pitching policy for family tents, forming a safe central play area for children – often the starting point for giant games of hide and seek before bedtime. The rest of the campers get the choice of loch-side pitches, away from the caravans and motor homes and with splendid views, from the glassy stillness of the loch's dark waters at dawn to the summer sun glinting off the brightly coloured sailboats and dinghies that traverse the loch in the afternoon.

Luss itself has a number of resources for visitors: speedboat tours of the Loch (£5) leave from Luss pier at regular intervals during the summer, while private boat charters start from £50 (☎ 07973 354 707). A sixteen-mile cycle path runs alongside the Loch from Balloch to Tarbet with Luss as its half-way point, giving you a choice of direction for a day-trip. There is also a well-stocked local store for cooking provisions, while *The Village Rest* serves up an excellent choice of local dishes including salmon, venison and haggis, neeps and tatties. For a bit of craic and some interaction with the locals, try the *Colquhoun Arms* in the evenings.

▼ Loch Lomond, the British mainland's biggest lake

Practicalities

Luss Camping and Caravanning Club Site, Luss, Alexandria, Loch Lomond, Dunbartonshire, G83 8NT
☎ *01436 860658,* Ⓦ *www.siteseeker.co.uk*

Pitches & price 23 grass pitches for tents with hook-ups, 36 without. Non-member tents £6 plus a charge of around £7 per adult per night (children £2.60), depending on season. Non-member backpackers (without a car) pay no tent charge.

Facilities 2 toilet and shower blocks, dish-washing area, laundry room, parent and toddler room with changing facilities and a disabled-access toilet and shower.

Restrictions No campfires. Dogs welcome but must be on a lead.

Open Easter–Oct.

Getting there On the A82 from Stirling, there are 2 turn-offs on the right signposted for Luss. Take the second one and continue past the wooden footbridge. Another right turn followed by a sharp left will take you down a small hill, past the hotel and into Luss campsite.

Loch Tay

Heaven for waterbabies

Set in the heart of the beautiful Perthshire countryside, on the western shores of Loch Tay, this large modern complex makes the most of its position with an outstanding range of activities. The site is made up of privately owned self-catering lodges, a camping area, putting green and a marina that houses a bar, a restaurant and an activities centre – so there's enough to keep both adults and children amused for days.

The small camping area has an elevated and secluded position, which affords it a great position looking over the water. For those that fancy a change from canvas, there are also a number of wooden tipis for rent, which sleep between three and six people and include fridges and TVs, providing a little more luxury (though you still need to bring bedding). There's also one yurt, made cosy by its log-burning stove, and wooden wigwams that sleep up to five and enjoy lovely views of the loch.

The marina here offers a wide range of activities, including sailing, kayaking, high-speed rib boat rides and fishing, or you can head a little further afield for some exhilarating white-water rafting. If you'd rather stay on land, the choices are extensive, from archery and whisky tours to downhill cycling trips. Overlooking the loch, the *Boathouse Restaurant & Bar* serves up a good range of home-cooked meals (including a reasonably priced children's menu), featuring local produce. Barbecues are held on summer weekends when the weather is good, or guests can buy barbecue packs to cook themselves. During the summer months, the sun decks provide the perfect space to soak up the surroundings over a glass of wine.

▼ The Tay river meets Loch Tay at Kenmore

Practicalities

Loch Tay Highland Lodges & Campsite, Milton Morenish Estate, by Killin, Perthshire, FK21 8TY ☎*01567 820323,* Ⓦ*www.lochtay-vacations.co.uk*

Pitches & price 20 grass pitches. £15 per small tent, £18 per large tent. Standard tipis start at £28 for 2 people, £12.50 per additional adult, £6 per additional child. Yurt £40 for 2 people, £15 per additional adult, £7.50 per additional child. Wigwams £32 for 2 people, £16 per additional adult, £8 per additional child.

Facilities All-weather camp kitchen, shower block and toilets; laundry room at marina.

Open Year round – but the camping field is open Easter–Oct only.

Restrictions Groups welcome. Campfires not permitted. Dogs allowed (free).

Getting there Head north on the A84 from Stirling, past Loch Earn and on to Killin. Take the A827 from Killin and 4 miles further on *Loch Tay Highland Lodges* will be signposted on your right.

Comrie Croft

Collective camping in the Perthshire countryside

Set in 230 acres of Perthshire farmland and collectively owned by over fifty people, *Comrie Croft* isn't a traditional Scottish campsite. It was a working farm and hostel until 2008, when five entrepreneurial employees cajoled friends, family and neighbours into helping them buy the farm outright. The enthusiastic team have since expanded the hostel and opened a campsite, bike-rental shop, and built a series of walking paths and mountain bike trails. *Comrie Croft*'s eco credentials come in the tangible form of low-energy lighting, compost toilets, recycling units and solar heating for showers. But more significant is the team's assumption that visitors want to be eco-friendly, so you won't be overwhelmed by Do and Don't signs, just conscious of the site's willingness to guide visitors in an environmentally sound direction.

   Comrie Croft is open 365 days a year and campers willing to brave the dead of a Scottish winter can stay in two large Swedish

kåta tipis, each with platform beds and a pot-belly stove for heat (these are available all year). A romantic notion, but thermals are definitely advisable! Future plans will see more alternative accommodation on site, including the addition of a Mongolian *ger* by 2011. The main camping area is set amidst birch woodland with small clearings scattered among the trees. Every pitch feels wonderfully secluded, enabling campers to enjoy an (almost) wild experience, but with the reassurance of knowing that their neighbours aren't too far away. Unzipping your tent to experience uninterrupted views over the rolling hills of the Perthshire countryside makes an inspiring start to the day. When the weather is milder, campers can forgo the protection of canvas and sleep beneath the stars in hammocks strung between the trees. For those reluctant to pitch in the forest, there's a smaller additional camping field near the site reception.

   Lighting campfires is encouraged and around a dozen wheel rims have been recycled and fashioned into fire braziers with metal arms and hooks for hanging cooking pots over the open flames. With no kitchen facilities on site, a Swallows and Amazons attitude is essential. If the weather prevents you from frying sausages and baking spuds over an open fire, there are plenty of eating options available in the village of Comrie, four miles from the site, including a fantastic fish-and-chip shop on the corner of Main Street, several cafés, a great deli (Thompsons) and the *Royal Hotel*. The town of Crieff, also four miles from the site, has dining choices from Indian to Italian.

   A few nights camping in the forest might make you feel that the outside world is a long way away, but an impressive range of Highland attractions lies within half-an-hour's drive of *Comrie Croft*. The Famous Grouse Experience Distillery, offering campers the chance to sample some fine whiskies, Drummond Castle and its attractive formal gardens, Loch Erne water sports, the beautiful Killin Waterfalls and several excellent golf courses are all easily accessed local highlights.

   Throughout the summer months there are numerous campsite activities on offer, ranging from musical workshops to storytelling circles and camp craft. These are held in a central glade at the heart of the site, which also functions as a general meeting

Practicalities

Comrie Croft Eco Campsite, Crieff, Perthshire, PH7 4JZ
☎*01764 670140,* Ⓦ*www.comriecroft.co.uk*

Pitches & prices 24 grass pitches for tents only (no hook-ups). £6.50 per adult mid-week, £8 per adult at weekends, free for under-5s, half-price for under 16s. 2 Swedish *kåta* tipis, £49 for the first night and £29 for additional nights. A limited number of 4-person tents to rent on request.

Facilities Shower (solar-heated) and toilet block with disabled facilities. Dish-washing area, laundry facilities and recycling units. Firewood for sale from the office.

Restrictions Campfires allowed. Dogs allowed (free). No noise after 11pm.

Open Year round.

Getting there Take the A85 north from Crieff and travel 4 miles; *Comrie Croft* will be signposted on your right. Alternatively there is an excellent bus service from Perth (#15; hourly until midnight), which will drop you at the bottom of the driveway up to the site on request.

place where campers socialize around the evening fire.

Campers seeking more active pastimes can fish for little brown trout in a small pond on site (rods are available to rent at the campsite office) and the newly created walking paths and mountain-bike trails are very popular. The site's Cycle Hire Shop (Ⓦwww.comriecroftbikes.co.uk) caters for all ages and levels of experience and the owners have drawn up a series of route-maps and guides with levels of difficulty ranging from easy to expert. As part of the area's annual autumn walking festival, the Drover's Tryst (Ⓦwww.droverstryst.co.uk), *Comrie Croft* plays host to the wonderfully named Hairy Coo mountain-bike race.

◀ Hammocks strung between the birch trees at *Comrie Croft* ▶ The woodland under a blanket of winter snow; a pheasant on site

By the Way

With the West Highland Way right on its doorstep, and Munros including Ben Lui, Beinn a'Chleibh, Ben Oss and Beinn Dubhcraig within easy striking distance (walks for all four start from the campsite), *By the Way* is a favourite haunt of walkers and climbers. Their bustle and camaraderie defines this small and welcoming campsite between May and August, when it can swell with hikers comparing blisters and swapping stories.

Nestled in the heart of the Loch Lomond and Trossachs National Park, the site is on the outskirts of the former mining village of Tyndrum. If you've a few hours to spare you can try your hand at gold-panning in the nearby river. Access to a car will allow you to experience plenty of outdoor activities nearby, from white-water rafting to mountain biking; Tyndrum Taxi Tours (☎01838 400251) offers trips to historical sites.

In Tyndrum itself, *The Real Food Café* does a great sit-down fish and chips, *Paddy's* has a wide range of hearty bar meals (and live traditional music on Tuesdays during the summer) and the family-run *Green Welly Stop* serves up award-winning home cooking, with a whisky shop and outdoors store attached.

Practicalities

By The Way Hostel & Campsite, Lower Station Road, Tyndrum, Stirlingshire, FK20 8RY ☎*01838 400333,* Ⓦ*www.tyndrumbytheway.com*
Pitches & price 20 pitches, £6 per person. Limited number of caravan pitches with hook-ups. Trekker huts available for £9 per person (own bedding required).
Facilities Kitchen, kit-drying area, laundry room, toilets and hot showers.
Restrictions Dogs permitted. No campfires, although BBQs are allowed.
Open Easter–Oct.
Getting There Located 50yds from Tyndrum train station, with arrivals from Glasgow and Oban 3 times daily. Arriving by car, follow the A82 from Stirling along the west side of Loch Lomond. On entering Tyndrum, take the first road on your left, Lower Station Road; the site is clearly signposted.

Red Squirrel

Lying in the shadow of the breathtaking Glen Coe Munros, *Red Squirrel* offers a luxury that makes it stand out from other sites – space. With no formal layout or pitches, campers can choose to be as far away from one another as they like. Set in over twenty acres of unkempt woodland and meadow, the site exudes a laid-back atmosphere, and guests range from families and large groups to backpackers. This can, of course, lead to some noisy evenings, although the idyllic location goes some way to make up for it.

Less than a mile away from *Red Squirrel* is the legendary *Clachaig Inn*. With 160 malt whiskies on offer, three bars, live music and excellent grub, it's no surprise that the campsite asks that you pay for your stay before visiting the pub. It's also worth heading down there to start your day, alongside the early morning Munro Baggers, with "the whole hog" – a hearty breakfast that includes some energy-providing Stornoway black pudding and wild boar bacon. The site allows small campfires, and it's just a one-and-a-half-mile walk to Glencoe's village shop for basic grocery provisions and barbecue supplies.

Practicalities

Red Squirrel Camp Site, Glencoe, Argyll, PH49 4HX ☎*01855 811256,* Ⓦ*www.redsquirrelcampsite.co.uk*
Pitches & price 400 grass pitches for tents. £7.50 per person, 50p per child. Will permit small campervans on some pitches (price on request).
Facilities Very basic – washing-up troughs with hot water and several toilet and shower blocks – expect queues in high season.
Restrictions Groups welcome. Small campfires allowed between 7am and 11pm. Dogs permitted (free).
Open Year round.
Getting there Take the A82 north to Glencoe; once in the village, turn onto Old Glencoe Road, on the right. Travel over the hump-backed bridge – the site is signposted 1.5 miles further on, on the right. A regular daily bus service from Glasgow to Fort William passes through Glencoe.

Oban

West coast by water

In a gorgeous coastal location, overlooking the tranquil farming island of Kerrera, *Oban* makes an ideal base for exploration. The town itself, just three miles from the campsite, is the central hub for ferry departures to the Western Isles, so this is the perfect place for either a stopover or a longer stay to make the most of the many local attractions.

This is a large campsite, set on fifteen acres and with an additional 350 acres of private land that campers can roam over and explore. Though it lacks the cosiness of smaller sites, the owners are very welcoming, and are only too happy to help campers plan their itinerary for exploring the area. There are two separate camping fields for tents: one has well-groomed pitches with easy access to the amenities, while the other is a lot more rural and secluded. Though the latter does not offer direct access to the facilities, the privacy and fantastic views across the water make it a popular choice.

The site shop is licensed and sells groceries and basic camping gear, and there is also a well-equipped kitchen and laundry room. The games room, which has a pool table, board games and a television, is a welcome diversion in wet weather.

Water sports are the big attraction here – just a short walk from the campsite is the Puffin Dive Centre, which provides tuition for all levels, alongside a number of boat dives for experienced divers. Guided sea-kayaking trips along Oban's spectacular coastline are a fantastic way to see the area, and it's particularly worth joining the sunset paddle to Kerrera with Oban Sea Kayak Guides. Whale- and dolphin-watching trips are also organized in Oban, and though you're not guaranteed to spot a whale or a dolphin, the odds are definitely stacked in your favour, and it's worth it for the breathtaking scenery alone.

The town itself offers lots of choice when it comes to eating out, including the four-star *Manor House Hotel*, where Oban Bay prawns are a house speciality, and *The Barn Country Inn* which has a children's play area and beer garden, and a wide range of local ales on tap.

▼ The coastline by *Oban* is ripe for water sports

Practicalities

Oban Caravan & Camping Park, Gallanachmore Farm, Gallanach Road, Oban, Argyll, PA34 4QH ☏01631 562425, Ⓦ www.obancaravanpark.com

Pitches & price 150 grass pitches. 35 hard-standing. £14 per tent (2 people), £2 per additional adult. £15.50 per campervan (2 people), £2 per additional adult. Hook-ups £2.

Facilities Shower and toilet blocks, laundry facilities, camp kitchen, games room.

Restrictions No single sex groups allowed. Campfires not permitted. Dogs welcome (free).

Open April–Oct.

Getting there From the ferry terminal in Oban, turn right and follow the one-way system, picking up the signs for the campsite. The campsite is 3 miles outside the town centre. Regular bus and train services run to Oban, from where it's a 40min walk or a short bus journey (contact campsite reception for details).

Strathfillan Wigwams

Imaginations run wild in the Trossachs

One of the official campsites of the West Highland Way, *Strathfillan* provides a welcome stop for weary walkers, as well as to families and non-walkers who want to experience the great outdoors in the Scottish Highlands. Its dramatic position between Crianlarich (three miles south) and Tyndrum (two miles north), and its proximity to a scattering of Munros ensures that the

site attracts visitors throughout the year, as does the number of activities located on its doorstep – from canoeing and white-water rafting to canyoning and paint ball.

The views from within the campsite are spectacular – encircled by Munros, every camping pitch and wigwam offers a picture postcard Highlands view. It's hard to resist the childish excitement that comes with staying in a wigwam, especially when each wigwam has its name – such as Raging Bull and Stumbling Bear – carved above the door, helping to further fuel the imagination. The wigwams are heated and have electric lights and fridges, and each has its own picnic bench. There is also one Mongolian yurt, which sleeps five and has a pot-bellied stove that's perfect when you need a little extra warmth and shelter from the elements.

The land is owned by the Scottish Agricultural College, but the campsite is managed by a couple who have pulled out all the stops to make it as family-orientated and child-friendly as possible, while maintaining its appeal to walkers. The grounds are part of a working farm and visitors are encouraged to watch the farm staff at work as they tend to the livestock, and there's also a great "pet's corner" with rabbits, guinea pigs, goats and geese, which is perfect for younger children.

The Trading Post, decked out like a set from *Bonanza*, sells an eclectic range of supplies, including equipment like tomahawks for young cowboys and cowgirls. Crocodile steaks and wild boar sausages are available, and they also have a basic menu offering bacon butties and fresh coffee. Outside every wigwam is a fire-pit so guests can cook over an open flame if they get the urge – firewood is for sale at the Trading Post – while campers can make use of the well-equipped camp kitchen. Within a ten-mile radius there are several good bars and restaurants, including the famous *Drover's Inn* with its hearty portions of fabulous home-cooked meals, which are ideal for famished walkers. Evenings here often involve local musicians playing folk songs, and the roaring fire in the bar is always welcome on more blustery days.

A small burn flows through the farm and guests can fish it without a permit. However, for a more challenging fishing session, permits can be purchased at the shop for the nearby River Tay (children fish for free). The site is also in a prime position

Practicalities

Strathfillan Wigwam Village, Auchtertyre, Tyndrum, Stirlingshire, FK20 8RU ☎*01838 400251,* Ⓦ*www.wigwamholidays.com*

Pitches & price Over 50 grass pitches for tents and campervans: £6 per adult, £3 per child. Hook-up £3. £28 per small wigwam (sleeps 4), £33 per large wigwam (sleeps 5), based on 2 sharing. £10 per additional adult, £8 per additional child. Mongolian yurt (sleeps 5) £55 for 2 people, £10 per additional adult and £8 per child.

Facilities Camp kitchen and dining area, shop, toilet/ shower block, laundry room and drying area, bedding to rent and on-site taxi available to and from local bars and restaurants.

Open Year round.

Getting there From Stirling take the A82 heading north to Crianlarich. 3 miles from Crianlarich there is a sign advertising the site's location in 0.5 miles. At the second sign for the campsite, turn right.

for attempting to bag a few Munros – including Ben Challum (3362ft), one of the easiest in the area, which can be accessed directly from the site. Alternatively, the more challenging Ben Lui (3703ft) is a two-and-a-half-mile walk from the campground. If walking or climbing isn't your thing then there are plenty of other sports to try in the area including white-water rafting on the Orchy (category 5), as well as canoeing, quad biking and mountain biking.

The wealth of outdoor activities on *Strathfillan*'s doorstep, not to mention the West Highland Way running right past its gate, makes this the ideal base for both walkers and families looking to indulge in some Highland pursuits.

◀ The wigwams ▶ The *Trading Post* shop; the West Highland Way and numerous Munros attract hikers; white-water rafting on the Orchy

Invercoe

Home comforts and adrenalin highs

Five-star *Invercoe* ticks all the boxes when it comes to a family camping holiday. Situated five minutes' walk from Glencoe village, the site lies at the heart of the stunningly beautiful valley of Glen Coe. Pitches have breathtaking views over the glassy waters of Loch Leven and the environment is safe and secure, offering parents peace of mind. There is nothing rough and ready about camping at this well-maintained site and the welcoming owners, Iain and Lynn Brown, are always on hand to give advice on places to see and things to do.

The area has Munros in abundance, from the relatively easy Buachaille Etive Beag to more challenging scramble along Aonach Eagach. Glen Coe ski-slopes are also within easy driving distance, although snow cover has been very variable in recent years. Campers who would rather take to the waters of Loch Leven than the slopes can arrange lessons in sailing, adrenalin-fuelled high-speed rib boat trips (a firm favourite with the kids) or charter a yacht. The Lochaber Watersports Centre (Ⓦwww.lochaberwatersports.co.uk) has details of water-based activites. Alternatively, fishing permits for Loch Leven can be purchased from the *Invercoe* shop – the loch covers 3500 acres of predominantly shallow water and is renowned for its brown and rainbow trout. If the weather breaks, then nearby indoor attractions include the Ice Factor (Ⓦwww.ice-factor.co.uk), which boasts ice-and rock-climbing walls.

The site is arranged over several different levels, ensuring many of the grass tent pitches have an uninterrupted view of the loch. Excellent on-site facilities include a children's play area, a licensed shop that sells camping essentials and several anti-midge machines which make the summer months much more pleasant. Glencoe village has a shop for groceries and is also the location of the *Claigh Inn*, renowned for its hospitality, hearty food, traditional live music and extensive choice of over a hundred Scottish malts. If you're looking for a wild camping experience then *Invercoe* is not for you, but if you want to take the kids to a safe, family-run site with a few home comforts, then it's the perfect choice. And they promise never to turn away a tent.

▼ *Invercoe* lies on the shores of Loch Leven

Practicalities

Invercoe Highland Holidays, Glencoe, Argyll, PH49 4HP
Ⓣ*01855 811210,* Ⓦ*www.invercoe.co.uk*
Pitches & price 60 pitches for tents and caravans (50 with hook-ups). From £15 per tent.
Facilities Excellent toilet and shower block with disabled and baby-changing facilities. Laundry room with washer/dryer. Covered picnic area for BBQs and stoves.
Restrictions No coach parties. No campfires. Dogs allowed (free).
Open March–Oct.
Getting there From the south, take the A82 to the Glencoe Crossroads and then the B863 for 500yds to the site entrance. There is a daily bus service from Glasgow to Glencoe.

Caolasnacon
Linger by scenic Loch Leven

Patsy Cameron fell into running *Caolasnacon* by accident. She arrived in Kinlochleven with her husband almost forty years ago when he took up the post of head shepherd for the surrounding farmland. To their surprise, returning from a weekend break, they discovered several occupied caravans in their bottom field. *Caolasnacon* is an incredibly scenic spot and once one caravanner deemed it the perfect place to pitch, others followed. The campsite was, in a sense, self-started.

Located halfway between the villages of Glencoe and Kinlochleven (three miles from each), *Caolasnacon* has a friendly atmosphere and attracts both repeat visitors and first-timers. Despite its proximity to supplies and civilization, the site still feels blissfully remote and offers campers the opportunity to pitch a tent right on the southern shores of Loch Leven. Such is the warm welcome and the draw of the tranquil surroundings that campers have been known to book in for a weekend and stay for a month. Children can run free in the wide open spaces and walkers have their pick of the Glens to explore, while bird-watchers and fishing enthusiasts are spoilt for choice at the loch.

Having "caravan" in the site's name might ring alarm bells for canvas purists, but *Caolasnacon* has much to offer campers staying in both tents and caravans. The site's distinguishing features include first-class opportunities to see local wildlife (birds such as black-throated divers, goosanders and mergansers), lochside pitches, a separate camping area for groups and one of the friendliest owners in the business. Kinlochleven is a five-minute drive away and the local shop stocks essential groceries. The child-friendly restaurant at the *MacDonald Hotel* serves up a good choice of reasonably priced food (mains range from £7.40 for a venison burger to £10.90 for steak in whisky sauce). In the unlikely event that you grow tired of the spectacular views at *Caolasnacon*, Kinlochleven is also home to the Ice Factor with its ice- and rock-climbing walls and high wires (Ⓦwww.ice-factor.co.uk).

Practicalities

Caolasnacon Caravan & Camping Park, Kinlochleven, Argyll, PH50 4RJ ☎01855 831279, Ⓦwww.kinlochlevencaravans.com

Pitches & price 50 pitches (30 with hook-ups). From £10 for a 2-person tent to £15 for a large tent (3-person plus). Weekly rates available. Caravans to rent, prices depend on type and season – contact the site for details.

Facilities 6 showers, 12 toilets and a laundry room with washer and dryer.

Restrictions Dogs allowed (free). Campfires allowed on the beach.

Open April–Oct.

Getting there From the south, take the A82 to Glencoe. In Glencoe, follow the signs to the right for Kinlochleven. 3 miles along this road, *Caolasnacon*'s entrance is on the left. The Fort William to Kinlochleven bus stops at the entrance and connects with both Glasgow and Oban.

▼ *Caolasnacon* offers wide open spaces and easy access to the water

Glengoulandie
Under canvas in deer country

A small, family-run camping park at the foot of misty Schiehal-lion ("Fairy Mountain" in Gaelic), *Glengoulandie* makes an excel-lent base for touring Perthshire. The park is ideal for those who want to get close to nature, with a deer park (free to campers and a big hit with families) that's home to over three hundred red deer, a herd of Highland cattle and a small manmade fishing lochan that is stocked with rainbow and brown trout (permits can be purchased from the site shop). Schiehallion itself can be accessed from the park, and a path leads most of the way up the 3547ft peak, though the final section involves scrabbling over rocks. If you'd rather an easier walk, you'll find yourself spoilt for choice,

▼ Highland cow and calf in Glengoulandie Country Park

whether in the deer park or beyond. Alternatively, it's possible to drive around the deer park in a 4WD provided by the campsite – always a popular option with children. There's also a children's play area on site, and the shop can provide books and games for wet-weather days.

The camping area is divided in two by a small burn, and the policy is to put groups on one side and families on the other – a great help for those camping with young children. There is an additional field next to the coffee shop and reception for privately owned static caravans. Although there aren't any shops or amenities within easy walking distance of *Glengoulandie*, the on-site coffee shop makes up for this by serving home-cooked breakfasts, lunches and very tempting tray bakes. It provides a great chance to try some delicious traditional Scottish dishes – from stovies and haggis clapshot to crannachan – and, if you can face it after visiting the deer park, it's definitely worth trying out the venison burgers. Although groceries aren't stocked in the shop, campers can pre-order newspapers, bread and milk, and bacon and eggs are sometimes available if you fancy a DIY breakfast back at your tent.

Practicalities

Glengoulandie Country Park, Foss, Near Pitlochry, Perthshire, PH16 5NL ☏*01887 830495,* Ⓦ*www.glengoulandie.co.uk*
Pitches & price 20 grass pitches for tents. Hard-standings available on request (no hook-ups). Prices range from £6 to £14 for tents, depending on size.
Facilities Shower and toilet block, dish-washing area, laundry room, café.
Restrictions Walking groups welcome. No campfires. Dogs allowed (free), except in deer park.
Open Easter to mid-Oct.
Getting there Take the A827 to Aberfeldy, turning right at the main crossroads to join the B846. The campsite is 8 miles further on, on your left-hand side.

Blair Castle

Not many caravan parks can claim to be situated in the grounds of a castle, but well-groomed *Blair Castle Caravan Park* lies adjacent to its thirteenth-century namesake. Spectacularly located in the heart of beautiful Perthshire and bordered by the River Tilt, this unusually large site has almost three hundred pitches, but still manages to retain warmth and charm. VisitScotland awarded it five stars, and its comprehensive facilities even include a hair and beauty salon. Well-heeled tourer and motor home owners use the site as a base for exploring central Scotland, and campers in search of peace and quiet are attracted by *Blair Castle*'s picturesque location and plentiful amenities.

Entry to the impressive neighbouring castle and gardens is discounted for campers and the nearby Blair Castle Trekking Centre and Atholl Estate offer a forty-mile network of trails for walkers and cyclists. The pretty village of Blair Atholl, five minutes' walk from the site entrance, is home to the award-winning *Loft Restaurant* (Ⓦwww.theloftrestaurant.co.uk; Ⓣ01796 481377). *Blair Castle* lacks the more informal atmosphere you might find at smaller sites, but its location and impeccably high standards compensate.

Practicalities

Blair Castle Caravan Park, Blair Atholl, Pitlochry, Perthshire, PH18 5SR Ⓣ*01796 481263,* Ⓦ*www.blaircastlecaravanpark.co.uk*

Pitches & price Over 280 hard-standing and grass pitches for caravans, motor homes and tents. From £15 for a 2-person pitch without hook-up, to £30 for a pitch for a family of 5 with a hook-up.

Facilities 5 toilet and shower blocks with disabled facilities. Dish-washing area and laundry room. A shop, internet facilities, pitch and putt, playground and a salon.

Restrictions No single-sex groups. No campfires. Dogs allowed (£1).

Open March–Nov.

Getting there From Edinburgh, take the M90 to Perth, join the A9 north towards Inverness. Bypass Pitlochry and 5 miles on follow signs for Blair Atholl and the site. Trains run from Edinburgh to Blair Atholl village.

Faichemard Farm

Generously spread over ten acres and located at the foot of the Glengarry Mountains, the tranquil setting of *Faichemard Farm* is, remains unbroken by noisy children. This adults-only campsite is perfect if you want a relaxing camping break and is in an ideal location for touring the Highlands – Fort William, Inverness and Skye are all within an hour's drive. There are a number of forestry walks and cycle trails right on the site's doorstep, including direct access to the popular local fishing spot, Loch Lundy. In addition, the Great Glen cycle route is just two miles away so it's no surprise that the site is a firm favourite with cyclists.

The small and historic village of Invergarry is a gentle two-mile walk from the campsite, where you can pick up all the essentials, including bread and milk, at the general store. For a meal out, the *Invergarry Hotel*, with its roaring fires and real ales on tap, does a great range of bar meals from 8am to 9pm every day, making use of local produce. On weekends during the summer, there's also live traditional music at the hotel.

Practicalities

Faichemard Farm Camping Site, Invergarry, Invernesshire, PH35 4HG Ⓣ*01809 501314,* Ⓦ*www.faichemard-caravancamping.co.uk*

Pitches & price 17 grass tent pitches and 14 hard-standing campervans (11 with electric). £12 per pitch (2 people), £3.50 per additional adult. Hook-ups £1.50.

Facilities Large laundry and drying room, 2 toilet and shower blocks.

Restrictions No children. No groups. Campfires not allowed. Dogs permitted (free).

Open Easter–Oct.

Getting there Take the A82 to Invergarry. At Invergarry continue through the village and stay on what becomes the A87, signposted Kyle of Lochalsh for approximately 1 mile. The turn-off to Faichemard is on the right – a small minor road with the farm signposted. *Faichemard Farm* is the fourth turn-off on the right along this road.

Rothiemurchus
Outdoor adventures on a Cairngorm estate

Rothiemurchus Camp & Caravan Park is set in amongst some of the Highland's finest woodland, in the heart of Cairngorms National Park. It's a fantastic location for campers looking to combine rural tranquillity with activities and amenities – the tourist town of Aviemore is less than two miles away.

On arrival, it's hard to gauge exactly what sort of camping experience lies ahead as the current entrance takes guests past consecutive rows of caravans. However, tucked away in a secluded patch of woodland to the rear of the site is a spectacular camping area. The setting is idyllic, hidden amongst towering Caledonian pines and next to the small, fast-flowing Am Beanaidh burn (be extra vigilant if camping with young children). It's easy to be fooled into a sense of isolation once your tent is pitched – but the site's modern facilities are just a stone's threw away.

The campsite is part of the 25,000-acre Rothiemurchus Highland Estate, which has a host of outdoor activities and attractions right on the doorstep. Cycle routes and walking trails for all levels start within the estate – in particular, the popular Lairig Ghru footpath, which cuts through the Cairngorm Plateau with imposing peaks towering above each side. The managers of the park, David and Gill, are incredibly helpful when it comes to organizing any of the activities available, from pony trekking and clay-pigeon shooting to fishing, quad biking and canoeing, and they can also arrange trails and guided walks on request with the local rangers. Whatever your age or interests, you can be guaranteed that there will be something that grabs your attention on the estate.

The campsite is popular throughout the year with visitors who want to make the most of the excellent location, and especially with snowboarders, skiers and ice-climbers during the colder months, as access to the Cairngorm Mountain ski slopes is only six miles away. If you're here during the ski season (Dec–April),

Practicalities

Rothiemurchus Camp & Caravan Park, Coylumbridge, by Aviemore, Invernessshire, PH22 1QU, ☏01479 812800, Ⓦwww.rothiemurchus.net

Pitches & price 22 woodland tent pitches. £8 per person, £2 per child. 17 hard-standings with hook-ups, from £17 for 2-person caravan.

Facilities Large modern block with 6 showers, 11 toilets, dish-washing sinks and laundry room.

Restrictions No group bookings. Campfires not allowed. Dogs not permitted.

Open Mid-Dec to mid-Nov.

Getting there Head north on the A9 from Stirling, then take the B970 into Aviemore. On entering the town, turn right at the roundabout and cross the bridge. You're now in Rothiemurchus and the camping park is clearly signposted. Trains run from London King's Cross and Glasgow Central to Aviemore, and buses run on a daily basis from both Glasgow and Edinburgh. From the town it's a 20min walk to the campsite.

you can rent equipment and arrange tuition on the slopes.

The estate has its own farm shop, café and delicatessen, selling a wide range of local produce at reasonable prices. Aviemore is a twenty-minute walk away and has a good choice of bars and restaurants, including the child-friendly *La Taverna*, which serves a good range of Italian meals, and *Ski Ing Doo Restaurant*, which offers up a great home-made veggie burger and mighty steaks. Just ten minutes' walk from the entrance to the estate is the *Hilton Hotel*, which has a great "fun house" area for children.

It would be easy to stay for a fortnight at *Rothiemurchus* and still not have time to sample everything that's on offer on the estate – which just means you'll have to come back.

◀ The Caledonian pines are home to stoats, pine martens, wildcats and voles ▶ Cycling through *Rothiemurchus*; camping by the burn

Wild camping

Running water comes from streams, pitches lie where nature puts them, and most people don't come here at all. If you want to get away from the crowds, wild camping is the way to do it.

Heading off into the wilds with a tent is the ultimate way to enjoy the great outdoors. You can't beat spending the evening on a grassy ledge, looking up at a starry sky free from light pollution, then waking up to gaze out at the open countryside as bacon sizzles on the camp stove. Though you say goodbye to hot showers and the convenience of traditional campsites, wild camping gives you the luxury of picking where you stay without running the risk of noisy neighbours, generator hum and caravan congestion. And it doesn't cost a penny.

Wild camping is legal in most of Scotland, as long as you pitch well away from dwellings and roads. Inland you can camp in the gentle beauty of the lowland valleys and the dramatic mountainsides of the Highlands, while out on the west coast there are plenty of quiet islands, secluded bays and white-sand beaches where you can spend the evenings staring out to sea, keeping an eye out for seals and dolphins. Midges can be a problem in summer, especially on windless days, so take a midge hat and plenty of repellent.

In England and Wales, the strict letter of the law obliges you to seek permission from the landowner before you camp, but as that is not always practical, low-impact wild camping is often tolerated in more remote areas (rather than near farmland), so long as you are discreet and keep to the following guidelines: camp well away from livestock, dwellings and nesting birds (particularly from March to July), do not build open fires (and avoid fire-prone areas altogether), stay for one night only (ideally pitch late and leave early), and obey the golden rule of the wilderness: leave no trace. If in doubt, seek legal advice.

The best places to wild camp are in dry, well-drained, sheltered sites (a natural windbreak, such as a large boulder, is a good start), and where the ground is firm enough to peg out the tent, but not so bone-hard you'll wake up with a sore back. It's also sensible to be within walking distance of a clean water source – but not right next to it, as water can attract insects and might be prone to flooding. In addition to all the usual camping equipment, including a warm sleeping bag, spare clothes, a waterproof layer and a head torch, take a good insulating mattress, plastic bags to carry out all your rubbish and a trowel to bury human waste at least thirty yards from running water and lakes, and pack water-purifying tables if you going to areas where you're unsure of the water quality. Good preparation is essential, but once you've tasted the freedom, the spontaneity and tranquillity of this kind of back-to-nature camping, the possibilities are endless. Great expanses of wilderness are at your feet.

FIVE GREAT WILD-CAMPING SPOTS

Cairngorms National Park From the Linn of Dee in the beautiful Dee Valley, just west of Braemar, walk for three miles towards Derry lodge and you'll find lots of spots to pitch a tent near the river among ancient Caledonian pine forest, close to Ben Macdui.

Dartmoor National Park Wild camping is expressly permitted in areas of "Common Land" on barren, beautiful Dartmoor. See Wwww.dartmoor-npa.gov.uk/vi-crowmap.pdf.

Knoydart Peninsula Knoydart can only be reached via ferry from Mallaig or by a rough fifteen-mile trek from the end of the road at Kinlochourn. Camp on moorland, in woods and just behind the "long beach", a short stroll from Inverie Bay.

Sandwood Bay A dune-backed, soft sand beach on the far northwest coast of Scotland, with the sea stack of Am Buachaille to the south and the cliffs of Cape Wrath to the north. The bay is a four-mile walk across flat moorland from Blairmore car park.

Summer Isles Sea kayak to the islands of this little-known archipelago and you'll have the turquoise shallows and white-sand beaches to yourself. Camp in the sheltered areas of peat just back from the shore.

Useful websites

Wwww.mcofs.org.uk/advice-and-policies.asp General guidelines, plus specifics on the situation in Scotland.
Wwww.legalisewildcamping.com Information and campaigning in England and Wales.
Wwww.v-g.me.uk/WildCamp/WildCamp.htm Practical tips.
Wwww.nationalparks.gov.uk The wild camping policies of National Park authorities.

◀ Wild camping on Scaraster Beach, Harris, the Outer Hebrides

East Grange Farm
Big breakfasts, bands and biathlons

Home to a live music venue, quad biking, laser tag, fly fishing and the UK's only biathlon centre, *East Grange*, just a few miles from the Moray coast, is not your average working farm. Family-run since the late nineteenth century, the farm is now firmly anchored in the twenty-first century and it's no surprise that it appeals to a wide range of outdoor enthusiasts, as well as to families and hen and stag parties.

Live music at the *Loft* ranges from indie to blues and folk, and it was the popularity of the venue, combined with that of the biathlon centre (where guests can try several varieties of target shooting in international-standard facilities), that led

▾ Exploring the Moray coast near *East Grange*

to a demand for accommodation on site. As a result, there is now a small grassy camping field for tents and two further areas – one for the site's two lodges, which are popular with groups and fully equipped with heating and cooking facilities, and another for the six wigwams, which each sleep five and have electric heating, a kettle and a toaster. Fortunately, everything is within easy walking distance, so after an exhausting day of activities or a night at the *Loft*, you'll be within stumbling distance of your bed.

The proximity of *East Grange* to the coast is reflected in the menu on offer at the *Loft*'s bar and bistro, which features regular seafood specials, plus a hearty all-day breakfast that's ideal for kicking off a busy day of on-site activities. Basic provisions like milk and eggs can be ordered, and the farm also sells barbecue packs, which include charcoal and a choice of local produce like sausages and burgers.

Needless to say, *East Grange Farm* is not your typical campsite. But groups and families – as well as biathlon fans – will find its combination of decent facilities and myriad activities offer than enough to keep them busy.

Practicalities

East Grange Farm, Kinloss, Forres, Moray, IV36 2UD
Ⓣ*01343 850111,* Ⓦ*www.eastgrange.co.uk*
Pitches & price 10 grass tent pitches. £5 per person. Wigwams (sleep 5) £30 for 2 people, £10 per additional adult, £5 per child. Lodges (sleep 5 & 8) £50 for 2 people, £5 per additional adult.
Facilities Kitchen, shower and toilet block, plus bar and restaurant.
Restrictions Groups welcome. Campfires permitted using metal hubs. Dogs allowed (£2.50).
Open Year round.
Getting there From Inverness, take the A96 towards Elgin until you reach Forres. Leaving Forres, you'll see signposts for the *Loft*.

Invercaimbe

Family-run *Invercaimbe*, next to the village of Arisaig on Scotland's northwest coast, is nestled in a sheltered inlet with a beautiful sandy beach on its doorstep. Though the site is basic, the wonderful location compensates and every pitch enjoys a sea view. Protected by the Inner Hebrides and the Gulf Stream, *Invercaimbe* experiences uncharacteristically warm Scottish summers. There is no nicer way to while away a summer's day than paddling in the clear blue sea, hopefully catching sight of a minke whale or dolphin in the distance, before retiring to your tent to watch the sun set over the village.

The atmosphere is relaxed and campers are a mix of repeat visitors, often in tourers and motor homes, and first-timers. *Invercaimbe's* proximity to the beach makes it popular with families as well as kayaking groups. Arisaig, a mile away, has several shops and a couple of bars and restaurants; try the *Old Library Lodge & Restaurant* for good seafood with a harbour view. Arisaig lies on "The Road to the Isles" and you can explore the rolling hills and rugged coastline with the local coastal ranger, who is happy to arrange guided walks for small groups (max 12; ☎01687 462983).

Practicalities

Invercaimbe Caravans & Camping, Arisaig, Invernessshire, PH39 4NT ☎*01687 450375,* ⓦ*www. invercaimbecaravansite.co.uk*

Pitches & price 5 tent pitches, 14 tourer/motor home pitches (all with hook-ups). Tents £8–£12. Caravans £10. Awnings £2, hook-ups £3.

Facilities Toilet/shower block, laundry room, and a washing-up area with a fridge/freezer and a microwave.

Restrictions Kayaking/canoeing groups welcome. Campfires allowed on the beach. Dogs allowed (free).

Open Mid-March to mid-Oct.

Getting there Take the A82 to Fort William then head west on the A830, towards Mallaig. As you pass through Arisaig you'll see signs for *Invercaimbe*. Citylink (ⓦwww.citylink.co.uk) runs a bus service to Arisaig from Edinburgh/Glasgow/Inverness, via Fort William. The campsite is one mile from the village stop.

Shielbridge

A blink of the eye and you'll miss *Shielbridge*, tucked away behind a petrol station and a shop on the A87. It's an inconspicuous and simple little site, consisting of a grassy field and a small toilet and shower block. Located at the base of the imposing Five Sisters of Kintail and with thirty Munros in the wider Ross-shire area, it's no wonder that *Shielbridge* is a big attraction for hill walkers. On-site entertainment is limited, so tents, tourers and motor homes are often deserted during the day as campers head for the hills.

Camping provisions, including maps of the area's walking trails and cycle routes are sold at the petrol station at the site's entrance. The *Kintail Lodge Hotel*, located on the shores of Loch Duich, is within ten minutes' walk of the site and offers a choice of bars with real ales on tap and live music in high season. If you've worked up a serious appetite after a hard day's walking, the hotel's excellent *Conservatory Restaurant*, overlooking the loch, serves local fish and game dishes. With your own transport, you can access attractions further afield; Skye is only seventeen miles away and the very picturesque Eilean Donan Castle – allegedly the most photographed castle in Scotland – is a seven-mile drive.

Practicalities

Shielbridge Caravan Park & Campsite, Shiel Bridge, Glenshiel, Kyle of Lochalsh, Rossshire, IV40 8HW ☎*01599 511221,* ⓦ*www.shielbridgecaravanpark.co.uk*

Pitches & price 75 grass pitches (hook-ups available on request) and 16 hard-standing pitches (all with hook-ups). £5 per adult, £2.50 per child. Family rates available.

Facilities Shower and toilet block with a small drying room for walking kit.

Restrictions Groups welcome. No campfires. Dogs allowed (free).

Open March–Oct.

Getting there From Fort William, take the A82 to Invergarry then the A87 Kyle Road to the village of Shiel Bridge. By public transport, the daily bus services to Skye from Glasgow, Fort William or Inverness will make a stop at Shiel Bridge on request.

Lazy Duck

Pure and simple camping beneath the pines

From its rural setting on the fringe of the peaceful Abernethy Forest to its outdoor solar shower, *Lazy Duck* is all about getting back to nature. Small and perfectly formed, this little Nethy Bridge campsite has just four pitches and is strictly for tents, which helps preserve the peace and beauty of its wonderfully appealing surroundings.

The owners originally opened a hostel on their three-acre homestead (one of Scotland's smallest, with a maximum capacity of just eight people) but received so many requests from campers that they added a small area for tents. In fact, the grounds were originally used as a camping stopover by drovers from Lochaber as they moved their sheep through Strathspey to the Inverness Wool Market in the late 1800s – so it's appropriate that it's been opened up for camping again.

Campers share the garden area with a pond and a small bird reserve that includes Aylesbury, mandarin and Bahamian pintail ducks. A family of red squirrels are also frequent visitors and the area is sheltered by clusters of hundred-year-old Caledonian pine trees. Between the trees is a solitary hammock, perfect for soaking up the atmosphere during the day, and a wood-burning stove for gathering around in the evening.

The only shower is an outdoor bush shower – an experience that requires campers to abandon most of their inhibitions and to brave the sometimes less-than-warm water on offer. It's best to plan in advance – borrow one of the site's solar-panelled water bags and leave it out in direct sunlight for an hour or two before you shower. Although it is outside, there is a screen around the shower, preserving at least a hint of privacy. Though facilities are very basic, there is one luxurious addition only a stone's throw away from the camping area – a two-person wooden shed sauna. Guests need to book the sauna in advance and are asked to make a donation, at their own discretion, towards its upkeep.

For a bit of gentle exercise, there's a private half-hour walk that starts from behind the main house and leads through a coarse moor of heather and juniper. If you're looking for something a little more challenging and are a seasoned walker you might want to tackle mounts Bynack More (3576ft) and Cairn Gorm (4084ft) – both only nine miles away by car. There's also an excellent range of outdoor activities available at the Rothiemurchus Estate (Ⓦwww.rothiemurchus.net; see p.338), which is just a short drive from the site and also has a good farm shop, deli and café.

Practicalities

Lazy Duck Hostel & Campsite, Badanfhuarain, Nethy Bridge, Invernessshire, PH25 3ED

ⓔ*lazyduckhostel@googlemail.com,* Ⓦ*www.lazyduck.co.uk*

Pitches & price 4 grass pitches. £9 per tent (including 1 person), £4 per additional person.

Facilities Very simple: outdoor shower (solar-heated), toilet, washing-up sink, laundry facilities on request and a wet-weather shelter.

Restrictions Small tents only (3-person max). No dogs allowed. Campfires not permitted. Can't accommodate large groups.

Open April–Oct.

Getting there From Perth, take the A9 north to Aviemore. At Aviemore follow the signs to the right for the A95 towards Grantown-on-Spey. Nethy Bridge is 10 miles further on and clearly signposted. At the *Nethy Bridge Hotel*, turn out of the village and follow the signs for *Lazy Duck*. It is located on the right, a mile along this road. Alternatively there are daily bus and train services to Aviemore, from where it's a £15 taxi ride to the campsite.

The village of Nethy Bridge is a fifteen-minute walk from the *Lazy Duck* and has a combined shop and post office for any grocery essentials. If you have children in tow then the village's interpretive room is well worth visiting in order to delve into the history of the area and to see live webcam footage of the area's wildlife.

If you want to avoid the more commercial camping experience and get back to basics (and nature), then the *Lazy Duck* could be just the solution.

◀ Paddling on the pond at *Lazy Duck* ▶ Red squirrels, rare in southern Britain, are regular visitors; *Lazy Duck*'s bucolic surroundings

Camusdarach
Wildflowers, buzzards and golden sands on the west coast

Carefully developed and nurtured by the Simpsons, a husband-and-wife team who are an animal scientist and a horticulturist respectively, *Camusdarach* is a very special place. This sheep farm, cottage and campsite is a haven for wildflowers and birds, including buzzards, pine martins and ravens.

May is a magical time to visit, when the site is carpeted in bluebells, but *Camusdarach*'s permanent highlight is a family-friendly beach that can be reached via a short path from the camping area. With its golden sands and clear blue waters, the beach had a starring role in the award-winning 1983 film, *Local Hero*, and is now referred to as "the *Local Hero* beach" by visitors and locals alike. The campsite is located in a grassy field above the beach, sheltered by mature trees. But despite the surrounding woodland, most pitches have uninterrupted panoramic views across the sea to the small islands dotted along the coastline.

Though *Camusdarach* is within easy reach of the villages of Arisaig (four miles) and Mallaig (six miles), it still feels wonderfully remote thanks to its rural surroundings and coastal location. Arisaig is home to The Land, Sea and Islands Centre – housed

▼ Camusdarach beach: the star of *Local Hero*

in what was once a derelict old smiddy – which explores the social and natural history of the area. During the summer campers of all ages will enjoy the breathtaking views on the steam engine between Mallaig and Fort William (Ⓦwww.steamtrain.info), voted the "Top Railway journey in the World" by *Wanderlust* magazine in 2009.

For explorations further afield, regular ferries operate from Mallaig to Skye and some of the Small Isles (Ⓦwww.calmac.co.uk.). The site's information room has details of other highlights, and you can pick up a copy of the newsletter which lists local activities and on-site "Dos and Don'ts". In keeping with the site's environmental initiatives, which include rearing a small flock of Hebridean sheep and planting reed beds, the Simpsons are also happy to take the time to talk to campers about the area and what can be done to keep it sustainable. The ethos behind *Camusdarach* is to respect your environment and enjoy your surroundings. And there's no finer spot to do either.

Practicalities

Camusdarach, Arisaig, Invernessshire, PH39 4NT
Ⓣ*01687 450221,* Ⓦ*www.road-to-the-isles.org.uk/camusdarach*

Pitches & price 42 standard grass pitches (20 hook-ups), 4 pitches with hook-ups for larger tents. 6 hardstanding pitches for caravans. Walkers with solo tents £8.50. Serviced tent pitches for 2 adults with access to hook-ups £16 (£2 extra for tourers and motor homes).
Facilities New toilet and shower block (key access) and a laundry room with washer and dryer.
Restrictions Small groups welcome. No campfires. Dogs allowed (free).
Open March–Oct.
Getting there Take the A82 to Fort William then head west on the A830, signposted for Mallaig. At Arisaig continue north on the coastal road (B8008) for 4 miles. The entrance is on the left.

Morvich
Munros and magical views

Morvich is located just two miles from Shiel Bridge, en route to Skye, on the valley floor of an much-photographed stretch of the Highlands that's owned by the National Trust and has deservedly been designated a "National Scenic Area". The site feels incredibly rural and tranquil, encircled by spectacular Munros.

Although it is a Caravan Club Site, *Morvich* welcomes non-members and the two tent fields are set away from the tourers so caravans don't have to take centre stage in your view. Club sites pride themselves on their high standards when it comes to facilities and upkeep, and *Morvich* has well-groomed camping areas and spotless shower and toilet blocks. Though it doesn't offer much in the way of children's activities (bar a games room with a television), the location is a big draw for families wanting to get away from it all in the school holidays. The spacious site makes the perfect outdoor playground for children to explore.

Even the keenest of baggers will be satisfied by the plentiful Munros in the area, which include the Five Sisters of Kintail, a classic ridge walk that involves bagging three Munros (though it can only be walked in one direction, starting just off the A87). The Five Sisters is best tackled by more experienced walkers, while the less taxing five-hour return hike from the site's entrance to the Falls of Glomach is a walk that families can enjoy. The dramatic 375-foot falls are among Britain's highest and are at their most impressive on a drizzly day.

Eilean Donan Castle, five miles from *Morvich*, on the banks of Loch Duich (no permit required for fishing), is one of the area's star attractions. There are also several good restaurants, including *The Conservatory* at the *Kintail Lodge Hotel*, and the *Jac-O-Bite*, located just below the Five Sisters, which serves delicious local game dishes. The local Mountain Rescue team organizes sociable charity summer barbecues for campers. Basic camping essentials can be purchased at the site reception, while two miles away at Shiel Bridge there is a shop with a wider range of groceries.

▾ Eilean Donan Castle

Practicalities

Morvich Caravan Club Site, Inverinate, Kyle, Rossshire, IV40 8HQ ☎01599 511354, Ⓦwww.caravanclub.co.uk

Pitches & price 34 grass tent pitches (4 hook-ups), 77 hard-standing pitches (all with hook-ups). From £10.50 for a small tent and 2 adults. Prices change seasonally; check website for details.

Facilities Shower and toilets with disabled access. Covered food-preparation and dish-washing areas. TV lounge. Laundry facilities.

Restrictions Groups welcome. No ball games. No campfires. Dogs allowed (free).

Open March–Nov.

Getting there From Invergarry take the A87 towards Kyle of Lochalsh. Pass through Shiel Bridge and after 1.75 miles follow the signs for *Morvich* and the National Trust. Access to the site is along a single-track road; the entrance is on the left.

Borlum Farm
Here be monsters

Camping in the vicinity of the UK's most mythologized beast might not sound desirable, but *Borlum Farm*, a fantastic campsite located across the road from Loch Ness, has much to offer families and horse-lovers. The four-hundred acre working farm has an on-site Equestrian Centre (BHS Approved) offering tuition and hacks for all levels. Lying in the shadow of horse chestnut, larch, poplar, Scots pine, Douglas fir and beech trees, *Borlum* is also home to an abundance of wildlife. Guests who fancy mucking in or mucking out are invited to help out with farm duties – from grooming the horses to collecting the morning eggs.

There are two camping areas – a level lower field and a

▼ Loch Ness: spot the plesiosaur

sloping top field with fabulous views over Glenurquhart – and the atmosphere is relaxed with pitches assigned on a first-come, first-served basis. While the farm is located on the west shore of murky Loch Ness, it's well worth making the thirty-minute-drive to the small village of Dores on the east shore. The village's famous *Dores Inn*, situated on the banks of the loch, has a pretty beer garden and an extensive menu offering a good range of vegetarian dishes and local produce (Ⓦwww.thedoresinn.co.uk). Steve Feltham, Dores's long-resident monster hunter, is another of the village's attractions. He has patiently camped beside the loch for the last seventeen years, waiting for Nessie to put in an appearance.

Other local highlights include the Loch Ness Exhibition Centre (Ⓦwww.lochness.com) in Drumnadrochit – a good rainy-day refuge less than five minutes' drive from the site. The ruins of Urquhart Castle, half a mile from *Borlum Farm*, provide uninterrupted views across the loch and conjure up images of a bygone era in the Highlands. There's a grocery store a ten-minute walk from the site and the *Loch Ness Inn*, a few minutes further on, serves hearty portions of decent pub grub.

Practicalities

Borlum Farm, Drumnadrochit, Invernessshire, IV63 6XN
Ⓣ*01456 450220,* Ⓦ*www.borlum.co.uk*
Pitches & price 35 tent pitches (no hook-ups). 9 hard-standing pitches (with hook-ups). £5.50 per person, £3 per child. Hook-ups £3 extra.
Facilities Shower and toilet blocks. Laundry facilities and a covered dish-washing area.
Restrictions No campfires. Dogs allowed (free).
Open Year round.
Getting there From Inverness, take the A82 towards Fort Augustus. After 15 miles you'll reach Drumna-drochit. Just past the village, *Borlum Farm* is on your right. There's a regular bus service that runs from Inverness to Drumnadrochit.

The Wee Camp Site

Small but perfectly formed, *The Wee Camp Site* certainly toes the line when it comes to the Trade Descriptions Act. Located above the sleepy village of Lochcarron and arranged over a number of elevated steppes, the panoramic views from the site take in the village below and the dark, steely expanse of Loch Carron. The facilities are basic, but most campers are avid Munro-baggers (there are twelve in the area) and content with a simple place to rest their weary limbs after a long day's walking. Joanna Boldra, the sister of the owner, lives on site and can recommend walks for all abilities, from easy, level paths that leave directly from *The Wee Camp Site* to more challenging trails further afield.

A five-minute stroll brings you to the village of Lochcarron, which has a grocery shop as well as several good options for eating out. Two hotels, *Loch Carron* and *Rock Villa*, serve evening meals but the tastiest option for food is the village's bijou *Bistro*. With only five tables and mouth-wateringly good food, it's best to pre-book in high season (☎01520 722799). The ruins of Strome Castle, which dates back to the fifteenth century, make a pleasant picnic stop just four miles southwest of Lochcarron.

Practicalities

The Wee Camp Site, Dunrovin, Croft Road, Lochcarron, Rossshire, IV54 8YA ☎01520 722898, Ⓦ*www.lochcarron.org.uk*

Pitches & price 40 pitches (6 hook-ups). £4 per adult, children free. Tourers £4 extra, motor homes £2 extra. Hook-ups £1.50 extra.

Facilities A small, basic toilet and shower block. Washing machine. No chemical disposal.

Restrictions Dogs allowed (free). No campfires.

Open Easter–Oct.

Getting there From Inverness continue on the A9 before taking the A835 towards Ullapool, then the A832 towards Gairloch. Follow signs for the A890/A896 to Lochcarron. From the village the campsite is clearly signposted. The nearest train station is Strathcarron (3 miles away). You can take a Lochcarron Taxi (☎07774499767) to bring you to the site.

Northern Lights

Though campers can't be guaranteed sightings of the Lights themselves, which usually appear off-season, *Northern Lights* can promise views to die for. This boutique-sized site, located on a grassy patch of land above Little Loch Broom, has only fourteen pitches and it's worth booking to avoid disappointment. Facilities are basic, but the spectacular views across the loch and Badrallach compensate – on a clear day you can see Skye. The majority of guests are backpackers, walkers and motor-home owners.

There's an extensive range of local hikes, including notorious An Teallach, whose top (3484ft) can be tackled as part of a stunning ridge-walk. The surrounding area is also rich in wildlife; at Gruinard Bay, eight miles from *Northern Lights*, golden eagles are often seen soaring overhead and otters can be spotted by the shoreline. Though the site's rural location feels remote, it's still well-supplied: Dundonnell Stores and Post Office are within easy reach and the *Dundonnell Hotel*, serving reasonably priced local specialities, is four miles away. The hotel also serves beers produced at the nearby An Teallach Micro Brewery, all named after the area's Munros and considered to be top tipples by the locals.

Practicalities

No 9, Northern Lights Campsite, Badcaul, Dundonnell, Rossshire, IV23 2QY ☎07786 274175, Ⓔ*thelarches@hotmail.co.uk*

Pitches & price 12 tent pitches (8 hook-ups). From £5 per camper. 2 hard-standing pitches (1 hook-up).

Facilities Shower and toilet block. Covered dish-washing area where campers can set up their own stoves in adverse weather conditions.

Restrictions Dogs allowed (free). No campfires.

Open The week before Easter to early Sept.

Getting there From Inverness take the A835 towards Ullapool. At the Braemar Junction turn left onto the A832. Continue past the *Dundonnell Hotel*; the entrance is 2 miles further on the right. The Wester Bus Company runs a service from Inverness to Gairloch, which passes the site's entrance on a Mon, Wed and Sat (☎01445 712255 for timetable information).

Applecross
Fun and games on a tranquil peninsula

Spectacularly situated on the Applecross Peninsula, this laid-back site has one of the best locations in Scotland. Nestled above Applecross village, with stunning views across the Inner Sound towards the Western Isles of Raasay and Skye, it is peaceful and tranquil, and remote enough to be outside the reach of mobile phone reception.

The surrounding area remains pleasantly unspoilt, partly

because of the effort it takes to get here. The journey is an experience in itself, requiring drivers to cautiously wind their way along the steepest ascent of any road in Britain. The 2000ft high single-track, known as the Bealach na Ba ("the pass of the cattle"), is not for the fainthearted, but its frequent passing places and viewpoints provide breathtaking opportunities to gaze over the Outer Hebrides and the Kintail Mountains. If your nerves aren't up to the Bealach na Ba, or you're driving a heavier vehicle, there is an alternative low-level coastal route from Shieldaig to the campsite. It's not quite so white-knuckle but still features wonderful views over the west coast and south towards the Torridon Hills.

With over six acres, the site is spacious and allows campers some privacy. There are two main fields, both with wooden wigwams to rent. The first field has hard-standing pitches for tourers and motor homes as well as a grass tent area, while the second grass field is only suitable for tents. Since the BBC's screening of *Monty Hall's Great Escape*, which follows a marine biologist turning his back on modern conveniences to become a beachcomber in Applecross, the world and his wife now regularly descend on the village during school holidays. Fans have travelled from as far as Holland with their campervans, tourers and kids in tow.

Local events such as the Applecross Highland Games in July, create a lively atmosphere on site. Other special events and activities in the area include the annual Applecross Boat Race, the Bike Dash and seasonal guided kayaking and hill walking with the Mountain and Sea Guides (☎01520 744394). There are also a range of easy level walks around charming Applecross village, five minutes from the site. On the shorefront, the *Applecross Inn* oozes character, complemented by award-winning, locally sourced food and occasional live music. Menu highlights include Applecross Bay prawns, local scallops and Applecross Estate venison (mains cost between £8 and £15). The inn also serves up a great range of hearty puddings: try to leave room for the scrumptious homemade raspberry cranachan.

For groceries, there's a local post office next to the inn, which stocks bread, milk and other basics. Back at the campsite, the

Practicalities

Applecross Campsite, Applecross, Strathcarron, Rossshire, IV54 8ND ☎*01520 744268,* Ⓦ*www.applecross.uk.com/campsite*

Pitches & price 55 grass pitches for tents (10 hook-ups). 5 hard-standing pitches with hook-ups (first-come, first-served). £6.50 per adult, 12–16yrs £3, under 12s free. 10 heated camping huts (wigwams) with electric lighting, £26 for 2 adults (additional adults £13, 10-15yrs £7, under 10s free). Huts sleep 4 people and a maximum of 2 dogs allowed per hut (£5 each).

Facilities Recently refurbished shower and toilet block, laundry room with washer/dryer and a kit drying room available on request.

Restrictions Dogs allowed, free on campsite but £5 per night in a wigwam. No campfires.

Open Good Friday–Oct 31.

Getting there Approximately 2hr drive from Inverness. Head northwest through Garve and Lochcarron and follow the signs for the Bealach na Ba and Applecross. An alternative route for heavier vehicles travels via Shieldaig in the North. On reaching Applecross village, the campsite is clearly signposted. The Torridon to Applecross bus service was cancelled in April 2009 making it virtually impossible to reach the village without your own transport.

Flower Tunnel's Café Bar, open in the summer months, serves simple, tasty food. Fish and chips and stone-baked pizzas feature on the menu and the cafe is also licensed. The popularity of Monty's *Great Escape* means that *Applecross* can no longer claim the status of hidden gem, but this relaxed campsite is still definitely worth heading off the beaten track for.

◀ The Applecross Peninsula, popularized by Monty Hall ▶ Camping next to the Inner Sound; sheep on the road to the site

Badrallach

The phrase "the back of beyond" could have been coined for remote *Badrallach* on the northwest coast. Dramatically located at the foot of Beinn Ghobhlach and on the shores of Little Loch Broom, the site is reached via a seven-mile single-track road. A few brave tourer and motor home owners tackle this precarious approach, but the majority of guests – typically walkers and families doing the Highland Loop – stick to camping under canvas.

The owners, Mick Stott, a former architect, and his wife Ali, are passionate about this little corner of Scotland and have spent seventeen years developing the site from scratch. They have renovated the existing outhouses to create alternative accommodation and modern facilities, and in addition to camping pitches there is a well-equipped bothy and a very sexy Airstream trailer to rent. A private path leads to the secluded beach and guests seeking outdoor adventures can rent a range of equipment including kayaks, a sailboat, mountain bikes and fishing rods. The nearest shop for supplies is Dundonnell Stores, eight miles away, though local crofters sell free-range eggs and vegetables on request. For a meal out try the tasty, locally sourced dishes at the *Dundonnell Hotel*.

Practicalities

Badrallach Camping Site, Croft 9, Badrallach, Dundonnell, Rossshire, IV23 2QP ⓣ*01854 633281,* Ⓦ*www.badrallach.com*

Pitches & prices 12 tent pitches and 3 caravan pitches (4 hook-ups, £2). £3 per adult, £1.50 per child. £5 per adult for the bothy. Airstream for hire from 2010.

Facilities Shower and toilets. Communal area and kitchen in bothy (no cooker). Laundry facilities.

Restrictions Dogs allowed (free). Stone circles provided for campfires.

Open Year round.

Getting There From Inverness take the A835 northwest towards Ullapool. At Braemar Junction turn onto the A832 towards Dundonnell and continue for 10 miles. Turn right onto a single-track road signposted for *Badrallach* (7 miles). Owners operate a pick-up service from Ullapool on request.

Ardmair Point

Ben Mhor Coigach ridge, Scotland's very own Table (shaped) Mountain, provides a striking backdrop to *Ardmair Point*. Located on a peninsula with views across to the Summer Isles, many of the pitches overlook an attractive pebbled bay. Lazy summer evenings can be spent watching seals and otters play, or huddling around a campfire as the sun sets. Campers in tourers, motor homes and tents use the site, which is a ten-minute drive from the bustling fishing village of Ullapool, as a base to explore the rugged and rural northwest Highlands.

Ardmair Point's waterside location ensures that there's plenty to entertain campers; the site has several moorings, two public slipways and a private pier for sea fishing. Rods and fishing gear can be purchased in the well-stocked and licensed campsite shop (8am–9pm). *Ardmair* attracts a fairly athletic clientele – many arrive with kayaks and mountain bikes as the coastline is perfect for kayaking and there are several mountain-bike trails a mile from the site. This sociable campsite also offers an adventure playground, and high-season evening entertainment takes the form of giant outdoor cooking sessions undertaken by a local chef.

Practicalities

Ardmair Point Caravan & Camping Park, Ullapool, Rossshire, IV26 2TN ⓣ*01854 612054,* Ⓦ*www.ardmair.com*

Pitches & price 50 grass pitches in tent field (18 with hook-ups). 7 waterfront grass pitches for tents (all with hook-ups), 14 hard-standing pitches (all with hook-ups). From £13 for a 2-person tent.

Facilities Shower and toilet blocks. Dish-washing area and laundry facilities.

Restrictions No single-sex groups allowed. Dogs welcome (free). Campfires allowed on the beach.

Open April–Sept.

Getting there From Inverness take the A835 to Ullapool. Pass through Ullapool, continuing northwest along the coast to Ardmair. The campsite is clearly signposted. Buses from Inverness to Ullapool stop within 100yds of Ardmair Point (Ⓦwww.ullapool.co.uk).

Clachtoll Beach

Sun, sea and scenery in Assynt

Since buying the once run-down *Clachtoll Beach* ten years ago and reopening it in 2001, the Galways have wasted no time in transforming it into one of the northwest Highlands' most popular sites. Campers at the reinvented *Clachtoll Beach* are guaranteed golden beaches, stunning views and a friendly welcome. When the summer sun is shining on the site, it takes on a tropical appearance and many of the pitches have sea views – on a clear day the Outer Hebrides are visible in the distance.

Outdoor enthusiasts make up the typical camping community here, enticed by the superb bird-watching possibilities of the Assynt area, and excellent walking on Suilven – a distinctive mountain that rises powerfully from Inverpolly National Nature Reserve. Climbers tackle the Old Man of Stoer (a 200ft tall sea-stack), sometimes spotting dolphins and whales during their ascent, while sea kayakers explore the dramatic coastline. The award-winning Assynt Visitor's Centre in the fishing village of Lochinver (Wwww.assynt.info) is a useful source of local information.

Campsite entertainment is not usually of the organized variety, though you might experience an impromptu summer ceilidh. As most campers are keen to embrace the Great Outdoors, the site is quiet after 11pm, when guests bed down in preparation for an early start. There's more than enough sun, sea and scenery at *Clachtoll Beach* to keep you entertained on site, but should you need supplies or fancy an evening out, there's a grocery store, a butcher's and a couple of bars and restaurants just five miles away in Lochinver. For the finest dining around, the *Albannach Hotel*'s Michelin-starred restaurant serves local fish and game specialities.

Practicalities

Clachtoll Beach Campsite, 134 Clachtoll, Lochinver, Lairg, Sutherland, IV27 4JD ☎01571 855377, Wwww.clachtollbeachcampsite.co.uk

Pitches & price 42 grass pitches, 12 with hook-ups. 2-person tent £8, family tent £10. Fully serviced pitches £3 extra. Tourers and motor homes from £10.

Facilities Shower and toilet block. Laundry facilities. Dish-washing area.

Restrictions Outdoor activity groups welcome. Dogs allowed (free). No campfires.

Open Easter–Sept.

Getting there From Inverness, head north on the A9. Bear left on the B9176, which becomes the A836. Join the A837 northwest towards Lochinver. Before entering the village take the B869 to Clachtoll. 6 miles on, descend the hill and follow the signposts to the campsite. In the rural northwest Highlands having your own transport is advisable for exploring.

▼ The idyllic sands of Clachtoll Beach

The Scottish Islands

Weather-beaten landscapes, remote locations and stunning beaches define the Scottish Islands. Hundreds of islands, many of them uninhabited, lie off the mainland, harbouring fascinating wildlife (including seals, eagles and skuas), unparallelled natural scenery and the prospect of peace and solitude. The camping options are varied and atmospheric – you can wild camp along an idyllic coastline, stay in a shieling hut or pitch up within putting distance of a golf course.

Indeed, grouping the islands should not obscure their differences. Across from the Ayrshire coast, and within easy reach of Glasgow, Arran's rocky north and lush south have earned it the description of "Scotland in miniature". Skye, perhaps the best-known island, is a hill walker's paradise, home to eleven of the twelve Island

Munros – Mull claims the twelfth. Mull's own star has risen recently thanks to children's TV series *Balamory*, set in a fictionalised version of the island's main town, Tobermory. Further north, low-lying Lewis and dramatic Harris in the Outer Hebrides are steeped in history.

Just a short step from John O'Groats, within sight of the Scottish mainland, the fertile archipelago of Orkney boasts some of the finest Neolithic sites in the country. Far beyond the horizon lies Shetland – closer to the Arctic Circle than it is to London – whose rugged moorland is in complete contrast to Orkney.

Regular ferries connect the islands and the mainland, but these are places to linger, not to rush through; camping here opens up some of Europe's most far-flung – and most magical – corners.

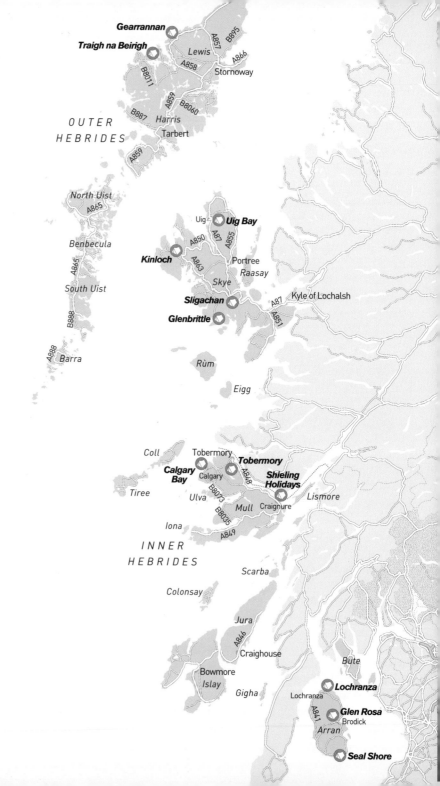

Gearrannan

Traigh na Beirigh

Lewis

A857

B895

A866

A858

Stornoway

B8011

OUTER

HEBRIDES

A859

B8060

B887

Harris

A859

Tarbert

North Uist

A865

Uig

Uig Bay

A850

A87

A855

Benbecula

Kinloch

A863

Portree

Raasay

A865

Skye

South Uist

Sligachan

A87

Kyle of Lochalsh

B888

Glenbrittle

A851

A888

Barra

Rùm

Eigg

Coll

Tobermory

Tobermory

Calgary

Bay

Calgary

A848

Shieling

Holidays

Tiree

Ulva

B8073

Mull

Craignure

Lismore

B8035

Iona

A849

INNER

HEBRIDES

Scarba

Colonsay

Jura

A846

Craighouse

Bute

Bowmore

Islay

Gigha

Lochranza

Lochranza

A841

Glen Rosa

Brodick

Arran

Seal Shore

Fair Isle

Papa
Westray
North
Ronaldsay
The Barn
Ayre's Rock
Westray
Sanday
Rousay
A966
Eday
Stronsay
A986
ORKNEY
A967
Shapinsay
Mainland
Kirkwall
A964
Stromness
A961
Hoy
Hoy
Rackwick
Lyness
South
Ronaldsay

John O'Groats

Unst
A968
Gardiesfauld
A968
A970
Yell
Fetlar
Papa
Stour
SHETLAND
A968
Sandness
Mainland
Whalsay
Foula
Lerwick
Bressay
A970
Levenwick
Levenwick
Fair Isle

The Scottish Islands

	PAGE	🚶	🚲	⛵	🍴	🏔	👨‍👧	👥	🚐	🚌	♿
Ayre's Rock	372						✓		✓	✓	
The Barn	369								✓	✓	
Calgary Bay	361			✓		✓		✓			
Gardiesfauld	373					✓				✓	
Gearrannan	366					✓					
Glenbrittle	364	✓		✓		✓					
Glen Rosa	358	✓						✓		✓	
Kinloch	365				✓				✓	✓	
Levenwick	372					✓			✓	✓	
Lochranza	359	✓							✓	✓	
Rackwick	370	✓				✓				✓	
Seal Shore	360							✓	✓	✓	
Shieling Holidays	360						✓	✓		✓	✓
Sligachan	365	✓						✓	✓	✓	
Tobermory	362	✓					✓	✓	✓		
Traigh na Beirigh	368			✓		✓	✓	✓	✓		
Uig Bay	369								✓	✓	

Glen Rosa
Golden eagles and hill walking in a glacial valley

The Isle of Arran is a hill walker's paradise and *Glen Rosa*, located at the foot of the Arran hills' granite peaks, is perfectly positioned for walking opportunities. Though basic and accessed by a steep single-track lane, the site's proximity to the hills and peaceful setting – the Rosa Burn gently winds its way through the camping field – attracts a steady stream of walkers.

Glen Rosa is a Site of Special Scientific Interest on account of its unusual geology, flora and fauna. The area is one of the best examples of a glacial valley in the UK, and golden eagles, deer and red squirrels are a common sight. Serious walkers and climbers

▼ Tents pitched at the foot of the Arran hills

are spoilt for choice; nearby Goatfell (2866ft) is a popular climb which takes around five hours there-and-back and offers spectacular views across to the mainland.

Groups appreciate the site's informal layout and the space afforded by its 25 acres. Although choosing a pitch within earshot of the gently bubbling burn may be tempting (it's stocked with brown trout and salmon; ask at reception for Arran Estate permits), the lower part of the site can flood so camping on higher ground is advisable. Brodick has a grocery store and several bars and restaurants, while just outside the village, the *Auchrannie Spa Resort's* three restaurants offer a range of eating options: fine dning, a grill and a bistro. Family ceilidhs are a regular occurrence in the village hall and a number of festivals take place on Arran each year – from folk music to wildlife – check Ⓦwww.visitarran.net for details and dates.

Practicalities

Glen Rosa Campsite, Glen Sherraig House, Glen Rosa, Isle of Arran, KA27 8DF ☎*01770 302380,* Ⓦ*www.glenrosa.com*

Pitches & price Unlimited grass pitches on 25 acres. No hook-ups available. £4 per adult, £2 per child.

Facilities Very basic. Toilets and a cold water dishwashing area (no showers or hot water).

Restrictions Groups welcome. Campfires permitted. Dogs allowed (free). The single-lane track is a deterrent for tourers and motor homes.

Open Year round.

Getting there From the ferry terminal, turn right and follow the B880 signposted for Blackwaterfoot. Less than a mile further on follow the signs for *Glen Rosa* (Glen Rosa Road). This becomes a single-track lane and the reception is in the whitewashed cottage on your left at the top of the lane. Buses coincide with ferry arrivals and stop at the Glen Rosa Road, or alternatively it's a 40min walk from the terminal.

Lochranza
Getting into the swing of things

Keen golfers will be in seventh heaven at *Lochranza*, where you can pitch your tent within putting distance of the eighteenth hole. Located at the northern tip of the mountainous Isle of Arran, this small, friendly campsite is also conveniently placed for exploring both the east and west coasts of the island. *Lochranza*'s regulars include international visitors, attracted by Arran's mix of landscapes and the affordable golfing on offer – many campers stay in tourers or motor homes and bring their own clubs with them. The site has sufficient charms to attract non-golfers too, though the stunning views of the island from the course could persuade amateurs to start playing.

Northern Arran has a dramatic volcanic landscape with excellent hill walking that isn't too challenging as long as you're fairly fit. As a result, geologists and hill walkers descend on the site in their droves. Caisteal Abhail (2817ft), the island's most northerly

Corbett (Scottish peaks measuring between 2500ft and 3000ft), is a day's walk, round-trip. Campers who prefer to focus on watching wildlife also have plenty to keep them entertained; red deer are often seen grazing in amongst the pitches, and otters, seals, dolphins and the occasional basking shark can be spotted along the shoreline. On site there is a well-stocked shop for essentials, as well as the *Stags Pavilion Restaurant*, which prides itself on home-cooked meals (8am–9pm in high season). In Lochranza village, options for eating out include the child-friendly *Lochranza Hotel*, which has wonderful panoramic views across the bay.

Arran's other highlights are easily accessible from the campsite. The ruins of Lochranza Castle dominate the shoreline; it dates back to the 1200s and legend has it that in 1306 Robert the Bruce landed here on his return from Ireland to claim the Scottish throne. The Arran Distillery and Visitor's Centre is a great rainy-day option just a short walk from *Lochranza* – tours and tasting sessions run most days (Ⓦwww.arranwhisky.com).

▼ The ruins of Lochranza Castle

Practicalities

Lochranza Golf Caravan & Camping Site, Lochranza, Isle of Arran, KA27 8HL Ⓣ*01770 830273,* Ⓦ*www.lochranzagolf.com*

Pitches & price 40 grass pitches and 8 hard-standing pitches. From £13 for a small 2-person tent. Caravan and 2 adults, £18. £2.50 per child. Hook-ups £3.50.

Facilities Shower and toilet block. Dish-washing area and laundry facilities with washer/dryer.

Restrictions No campfires. Dogs allowed (free).

Open March–Oct.

Getting there From the ferry terminal at Brodick, turn right and head north on the coastal road through Corrie and Sannox. Lochranza is well signposted and on entering the village you will pass the distillery on the left. The site entrance is 100yds further on the right. If you arrive on Arran without a car, local buses at the ferry terminal run in conjunction with ferry times to all of the island's towns and villages (get #324 for Lochranza).

Seal Shore

With a prime beachfront location on the southern tip of the Isle of Arran, and seals often spotted basking along the shore, well-named *Seal Shore* is a firm favourite with repeat visitors. The site's private beach is lapped by the Gulf Stream and on a clear day it offers panoramic views of the flat island of Pladda, Ailsa Craig (a 1114ft uninhabited magma plug), and beyond to Ireland. As pitches are assigned on a first-come, first-served basis, those with a sea view usually disappear quickly.

Maurice Deighton, the site's affable owner, creates a welcoming atmosphere with impromptu barbecues and get-togethers on the terrace. On summer evenings, groups often congregate around campfires on the beach to share tales of their island explorations. The south of the island is usually the driest and sunniest area, but there's an undercover cooking area and a games room should the Scottish weather turn. Campers can also try their luck fishing in Deighton's private loch – tuition is offered and kit can be rented from reception. An on-site shop sells essentials and Kildonan village, only a mile away, is an easy walk for groceries or an evening out at the *Kildonan Hotel*'s lively bar and *Stone Garden* restaurant.

Practicalities

Seal Shore Camping & Touring Site, Kildonan, Isle of Arran, KA27 8SE ☎*01770 820320,* Ⓦ*www.campingarran.com*
Pitches & price 43 grass pitches. 8 hook-ups, £2.50 extra. Adults £6, 6–15yrs £3, under-5s free. Additional charge of £1–4 per tent, depending on size. Essential to book in advance.
Facilities Toilet and shower block. Laundry facilities. Games room, undercover cooking area.
Restrictions Campfires only allowed on the beach. Groups welcome. Dogs allowed (£1).
Open March–Oct.
Getting there From the ferry terminal in Brodick, turn left and continue to the south of the island for about 12 miles. Take a left turn for Kildonan and follow the signs for *Seal Shore* campsite. There are regular daily bus services from Brodick to Kildonan that coincide with ferry arrivals.

Shieling Holidays

As the ferry to Mull approaches Craignure harbour, identical white canvas buildings stand to attention on the hillside, keeping watch over the boats below. At first sight, *Shieling Holidays*, an unusual campsite just a stone's throw from the ferry terminal, is reminiscent of a WWII Field Hospital. But rest assured, this is where the military comparison ends. The thirteen spacious shielings have impressively equipped interiors, including facilities as luxurious as hot showers, toilets, kitchens and gas heaters. Most also offer breathtaking views across the Sound to Ben Nevis. A great alternative to pitching your own, they can withstand even the harshest of Hebridean climates.

Shieling Holidays is a sociable site with a designated communal campfire area and a common room. It's also in an excellent position for exploring the island's attractions. A short distance from the site is a good pub, the *Craignure Inn*, the popular *McGregor's Roadhouse* restaurant and a village shop. Children and rail enthusiasts will love the Isle of Mull Miniature Railway (Ⓦwww.mullrail.co.uk), which runs past the site, and there is direct access to a small and pristine beach – perfect for paddling on a hot day.

Practicalities

Shieling Holidays, Craignure, Isle of Mull, PA65 6AY ☎*01680 812496,* Ⓦ*www.shielingholidays.co.uk*
Pitches & price 60 AstroTurf tent pitches, 10 with hook-ups (car, tent and 2 adults from £14.50) and 13 shielings (from £30 for 2 adults; minimum 2-night stay).
Facilities Shower and toilet block. Disabled and family bathroom facilities; some shielings have disabled access. Laundry facilities, washing-up area, common room.
Restrictions Dogs allowed (£1 per night in tents; £1.50 per night in shielings). Campfires restricted to the designated communal area.
Open Camping: March 13–Nov 1. Shielings: April 3–Oct 12.
Getting there From the ferry terminal at Craignure, turn left, signposted Iona. After 400yds, take the next left, following the signs for the campsite. The reception is on your right.

Calgary Bay
A walk on the wild side

Scotland has always been a favourite for campers seeking a more adventurous experience, away from the well-groomed pitches of traditional caravan parks. Wild camping (see p.340), which involves pitching a tent in informal spots – from ridges to road-sides – is particularly embraced by visitors. The long-established wild-camping area running alongside the silver sands of *Calgary Bay*, on the Isle of Mull, is an excellent option for those keen to get closer to nature and further away from facilities blocks and on-site entertainment.

In recent years *Calgary Bay* has become increasingly popular with campers visiting Mull, so it's no longer the relatively undiscovered gem that it was a decade or two ago, but as long as visitors respect their surroundings and stick to the general wild-camping rules there doesn't seem to be a problem. The atmosphere is friendly and sociable and campers can be found swimming in the bay from dawn until dusk, before someone inevitably reaches for their guitar and the campfire songs begin. Despite being free and "wild", there are public toilets directly across the road from the camping area so it's still possible to have a quick wash (cold water) and to clean dishes. Campfires are allowed, but only in designated areas – not on the protected machair grassland. Though you may be hoping to escape rules and regulations on your wild-camping trip, read the instructions on the camping signpost to ensure you're camping sensitively.

Calgary Bay has the best beach on Mull, which borders on being Caribbean in appearance on a sunny day, although tropical swimming temperatures cannot be guaranteed. The site is five miles from Dervaig, a small, historic village with a post office and long-established pub – *The Bellachroy Inn* (1608), said to be the oldest on the island – which is worth visiting for home-cooked bar meals and live music. Tobermory, the island's main town, lies about twelve miles from *Calgary Bay* and has a wider choice of shops, bars and restaurants, but as much of the road is single-track, the drive can take over half an hour. Within walking distance of the camping area, the *Calgary Hotel* has a splendid tearoom and restaurant – after a free night's camping you can definitely justify treating yourself to their delicious Highland Venison Pie (£14.95).

▼ Sea-view pitches at *Calgary Bay*

Practicalities

Calgary Bay, northwest corner of the Isle of Mull,
Ⓦ*www.calgarybay.co.uk*
Pitches & price Machair grassland next to the beach is suitable for tents, no hook-ups. No fee for camping.
Facilities Toilet block directly opposite camping area with cold running water.
Restrictions No campfires allowed on the protected machair grass.
Open Year round.
Getting there From the Craignure ferry terminal, turn right and follow the signs to the north for Tobermory. At the village roundabout, take the first exit and continue through Dervaig and on to Calgary Bay. Or catch a bus from the ferry terminal to Tobermory and a local taxi (try ☎07760 426351) on to Calgary Bay.

Tobermory
What's the story in Tobermory?

Wouldn't you like to know? This small harbour village on the north coast of Mull is the island's main settlement and lies just over twenty miles from the ferry terminal at Craignure (45min crossing from Oban; ⓦwww.calmac.co.uk). Until 2005, when filming stopped on the children's television phenomenon *Balamory*, the village was home to a BBC Scotland production crew. Despite the cancelling of the programme, repeats are still aired every day on CBeebies, fuelling the imaginations of a new generation of toddlers. The appealing rainbow-coloured houses that dominate the waterfront still have the power to inspire toddlers to scream with delight and sing loud renditions of the programme's theme tune – adults will enjoy wandering about atmospheric streets too.

The relaxed *Tobermory* campsite is a twenty-minute walk from the familiar harbour. Located within a mixture of farm and woodland, it's run by the friendly Williams family. The campsite has two fields, one for short stays and one for longer visits; the long-stay field is a mix of tents, tourers and motor homes. The short-stay field, situated next to a trout burn where guests can fish for their supper at no additional cost (fishing equipment can be borrowed on request or purchased in Tobermory), is reserved for campers sleeping under canvas. Each summer when *Balamory* was at its most popular, the site was inundated by young families on a pilgrimage to find the homes of their favourite characters. Some continue to visit during school holidays, but now most campers use the site as a base to explore Mull and the Islands.

Mull has much to offer enthusiastic walkers, including the opportunity to bag the impressive Ben More (3169ft), the only Island Munro outside Skye. Maps and further information on local walks can be picked up at the Tobermory Tourist Information Centre (ⓦwww.tobermory.co.uk). Many routes finish in and around the village, allowing walkers a well-earned chance to visit the island's only distillery, Ledaig, for a dram or two. Just remember that there's a steep uphill walk back to the campsite before indulging in too many!

There are several good pubs and restaurants in Tobermory, including the popular *Mishnish Hotel* and its *One Up Restaurant*, overlooking the waterfront, where diners can arrive by boat. The *Mishnish* has been owned by several generations of the MacLeod family, the best known being 1950s Scottish accordion player and band leader, Bobby MacLeod. His record sleeves and concert posters still adorn the bar walls. All of the food is locally sourced, including daily fish specials such as the excellent roasted halibut fillet with sauce vierge (£13.75). Downstairs, the *Mishnish* offers more traditional pub grub, and when the sun is shining there is the option of eating in the hotel's pleasant beer garden.

Camping essentials, groceries and an impressive range of Balamory memorabilia can be purchased from the village shops. If you'd like to embrace the open seas, a number of boat

Practicalities

Tobermory Campsite, Newdale Cottage, Dervaig Road, Tobermory, Isle of Mull, PA75 6QF ☎01688 302624, Ⓦwww.tobermory-campsite.co.uk

Pitches & price 25 grass tent pitches. 10 hard-standing pitches (all with hook-ups). £6 per adult, free–£3 per child. Hook-ups £2 extra.

Facilities Toilet and shower block. Covered dishwashing area with gravel floor, suitable for lighting camping stoves in bad weather. Laundry facilities available in the Harbour Association building on Tobermory waterfront.

Restrictions No campfires. Separate camping area for groups. Dogs allowed (free).

Open March–Oct.

Getting there From the Craignure ferry terminal, turn right and follow the signs for Tobermory. The village is at the north of the island, about 23 miles away (much of the road is single track). At the village roundabout, take the first exit towards Dervaig, staying left, and continue uphill for 1.5 miles; *Tobermory* campsite will be signposted on your left. Alternatively, catch a bus from the ferry terminal to Tobermory and walk to the site, or book a local taxi from the terminal directly to the campsite (☎07760 426351).

trips and excursions leave from the harbour in high season. They include sea safaris to spot minke whales and basking sharks – a must for anyone wanting to experience Mull's spectacular coastline and marine life. Trips can be booked via the Explore Mull website or booking line (Ⓦwww.explore-mull.co.uk, ☎01688 302875). Younger campers will enjoy the distraction of playing with animals at the Tobermory Open Farm (Ⓦwww.tobermorychildrensfarm.co.uk), or visiting the aquarium at the village's Sea Life Visitor Centre.

◀ Camping alongside the trout burn ▶ Tobermory harbour

Glenbrittle

Paradise for climbers in the Cuillins

Evenings at *Glenbrittle* campsite can be eerily quiet. Campers staying at this remote site at the base of the Black Cuillin mountains, overlooking Loch Brittle, are usually asleep by 10pm, preserving their energy for some vigorous walking or climbing the following morning. In the warmer weather, kayakers, kitesurfers and windsurfers join the walkers at *Glenbrittle*, attracted by the smooth black sands of the idyllic neighbouring beach.

The on-site shop doubles up as the reception and is usually staffed by the manager, Alex McGregor, who is a mine of information on the best local climbs and walks. As well as stocking essentials such as bread and milk, it sells an impressive range of outdoor kit – from walking sticks and gaiters to inflatable mattresses and torches. You can also buy local maps, including "Walks from Sligachan and Glenbrittle" (£1 goes to the Skye Mountain Rescue Team); a valuable purchase for planning a relatively gentle day on the hills, as none of the walks involve rock-climbing. The Glen Brittle Path (easily accessed from the site) which takes around three hours, offers unrivalled views of the rugged Cuillin mountains.

Having your own transport is essential for getting to and from *Glenbrittle*. It also affords you the freedom to explore the rest of Skye. The island is home to twelve of Scotland's Munros – including Sgurr Dearg (3235ft), topped by the famous Inaccessible Pinnacle – and is heaven for hill walkers and climbers. *The Old Inn at Carbost*, eight miles from the site, has excellent food and its sticky toffee pudding alone justifies the trip! The atmosphere at *The Old Inn* is warm and welcoming and in high season there is usually traditional music played live at the weekends.

▼ Hiking in the Black Cuillin

Practicalities

Glenbrittle Campsite, Glenbrittle, Carbost, Isle of Skye, IV47 8TA ☎01478 640404, ⓦwww.dunvegancastle.com

Pitches & price 65 grass pitches. 8 hard-standing pitches with hook-ups. £8 per adult, £3.50 per child. Hook-ups £3 extra.

Facilities Basic, but there is a toilet and shower block (due for refurbishment in 2010) and an on-site shop.

Restrictions Outdoor groups welcome. No campfires. Dogs allowed (£1).

Open April–Sept.

Getting there Follow the A87 to Sligachan before turning left onto the A863, signposted Dunvegan. 5 miles further on, take the turning for Carbost. After 2 miles, the road becomes a single track leading to *Glenbrittle*.

Sligachan

Skye's famously intense sunsets draw many visitors to the island, and watching the sun sink over the rocky Cuillins from *Sligachan* is a memorable experience. Though the site is very basic, its convenient location makes it one of the most popular on the island. Slap-bang in the middle of the Cuillins, with spectacular views, *Sligachan* is the first main campsite as you drive northwards through Skye. The site is informal, consisting of a large camping field which can get quite boggy in wet weather, and a facilities block. Though *Sligachan* takes tourers and motor homes, it's most popular with tents in high season.

The atmosphere is congenial, with many of the typically active campers swapping tales of their island explorations at the *Sligachan Hotel*, across the road from the site, in the evenings. The hotel has a good range of ales, many brewed on the premises in the Cuillin Brewery, and a staggering 250 malt whiskies to sample. You can also tuck into a hearty dinner at the hotel's *Steakhouse and Grill*. If the hotel's whiskies inspire you to discover more about Scottish malts, the Talisker Distillery lies just eight miles away, in Carbost (call ahead for tours, ☏01478 614308).

Practicalities

Sligachan Campsite, Sligachan, Isle of Skye, IV47 8SW
☏*01478 650204*, Ⓦ*www.sligachan.co.uk*
Pitches & price 80 grass pitches. £4 per adult, £2 per child. 15 hook-ups available. Note that there are no advance bookings.
Facilities Toilet and shower block and a basic laundry room with washer/dryer.
Restrictions Groups welcome. Campfires not permitted. Dogs allowed (free).
Open Easter–Oct.
Getting there From Kyle of Lochalsh, head over the Skye Bridge and follow the A87 directly to Sligachan. There are regular bus services to Skye from Glasgow, Fort William and Inverness, and the site is opposite the *Sligachan Hotel*, on the main road (A87) that runs from the south of the island to the north (Ⓦwww.citylink.co.uk).

Kinloch

Situated at the head of Loch Dunvegan, *Kinloch*'s shoreline pitches enjoy panoramic views across dark, icy waters. Foodies flock to the site, attracted by its proximity to the multiple award-winning *Three Chimneys Restaurant* in Colbost (voted one of the world's fifty best restaurants). Dunvegan Castle and the breathtaking Coral Beaches at Claigan are also within easy reach. *Kinloch* sits on the edge of Dunvegan village, once a thriving nineteenth-century port with daily ferries to Oban, but now a sleepy port of call for throngs of tourists in the summer. The site is family-run with a relaxed atmosphere. Pitches are assigned on a first-come, first-served basis, and the waterfront is usually occupied by a mix of tourers, motor homes and tents.

Dunvegan has a grocery store and the *Dunvegan Hotel*'s *Cellar Bar* buzzes with live music in high season. But the biggest draw for campers at *Kinloch* is definitely the *Three Chimneys*. Well worth the four-mile drive, it's owned by famous local chef and television regular, Shirley Spear, and her husband Eddie. Reservations are essential (☏01470 511258), and a delicious three-course meal costs around £50 per person.

Practicalities

Kinloch Campsite, Dunvegan, Isle of Skye, IV55 8WQ
☏*01470 521531*, Ⓦ*www.kinloch-campsite.co.uk*
Pitches & price 50 grass tent pitches (no hook-ups), 25 hard-standing pitches (all with hook-ups). £5 per person, £1 per child. Hook-ups £3 extra.
Facilities Toilet block with 6 showers. Washing-up area and a laundry room with washer/dryer.
Restrictions No campfires or large group bookings permitted. Dogs allowed.
Open April–Oct.
Getting there From the Skye Bridge follow the A87 to Sligachan, then turn left onto the A863 and continue to Dunvegan. At Dunvegan the campsite is clearly signposted. Citylink Coaches run a service from Glasgow and Edinburgh to Portree on Skye (daily; 6hr 30min). From Portree you can catch a local bus directly to Dunvegan village.

Gearrannan

Stepping back in time

If you like the idea of semi-wild camping – with some compromise on comfort – *Gearrannan* strikes the perfect balance. Situated in Carloway, on the west coast of the windswept Isle of Lewis, this is not technically a campsite, but an elevated grassy clearing adjacent to the conservation village, which campers can use absolutely free of charge. As long as tents are pitched beyond the village perimeter fence, the trust that oversees the running of *Gearrannan* is happy. Unlevelled terrain outside the village

boundaries can make finding a good pitch difficult, so it's advisable to arrive before dusk while the light is still good. Campers who make an effort to find the right spot are rewarded with dramatic views over the Atlantic on one side, while the other end of the clearing overlooks lovingly restored and beautifully thatched stone blackhouses. It's a magical location and a truly evocative stop on any camper's tour of remote Lewis. Sitting on the cliff-top as the untamed waters crash onto the rocks over 200ft below, anyone watching a sunset over Gerrannan will find themselves in the perfect location for some soul searching.

Traditionally a crofting village, where villagers eked a living from the land and sea, Gearrannan Blackhouse Village dates back to the seventeenth century. But post-WWII, village life changed dramatically. Electricity arrived in the 1950s and piped water in the 1960s. Despite the introduction of modern amenities, younger residents left to seek employment elsewhere on the island or in mainland Scotland. Without its younger generation, the village rapidly deteriorated as the crofts, often with only elderly residents remaining, fell into various states of disrepair. By the mid-1970s it was completely deserted as the last villagers had moved into nearby council housing. Sadly, Gearrannan remained that way until the formation of the Gearrannan Trust in 1989.

The trust has made a tremendous effort to raise awareness about the blackhouses and embarked on an intensive period of painstaking restoration. There are now nine fully restored buildings, attracting thousands of visitors each year; some of these are holiday lets, while others contain a shop and a café. The café provides an impressive range of homemade lunches and tempting tray bakes while the shop stocks books on the area and a choice of Harris Tweed souvenirs. A small museum and a crofters' hostel can be found in two of the other restored buildings. Campers are allowed to use the public toilets within the village and the hostel's metered showers and kitchen area – a sign of the good relationship between the trust and its guests. In return campers are asked to respect their surroundings and, of course, any money spent in the village shop or café is always welcome. For the best range of camping supplies, stock up when you arrive off the ferry either at Stornoway or Tarbert, as shops in the more

Practicalities

Gearrannan Blackhouse Village, Carloway, Isle of Lewis, HS2 9AL ☎*01851 643416,* Ⓦ*www.gearrannan.com*

Pitches & price Free, but you must pitch outside the village perimeter fence.

Facilities Campers can use the village toilet block and the hostel's metered showers on request.

Restrictions No dogs or campfires allowed due to the surrounding farmland and close proximity to the conservation village.

Open Year round.

Getting there From Stornoway, head west out of the town following the A858 to Callanish. Bypassing Callanish and the Standing Stones, follow the signs for Gearrannan Blackhouse Village.

remote parts of Lewis are few and far between. Stornoway is a beautiful harbour town with plenty to justify a short stop before setting up camp at *Gearrannan*. It's the largest settlement in the Western Isles and bustling with shops, cafes and bars. For an excellent lunch, try the bright and airy restaurant at An Lanntair (the town's arts centre).

The island is home to some of Scotland's best-known prehistoric monuments. Both the Dun Carloway broch and the Callanish standing stones, only a short drive from the village, are veiled in thousands of years of mystery and intrigue. The broch (stone defensive towers, originally 30ft tall and unique to Scotland – Carloway's has been excellently preserved with over 16ft remaining) is an Iron Age prehistoric site that has borne witness to Viking raids and warring clansmen, while the ancient Callanish stones could date back as far as 3000BC. Lewis is steeped in history, and camping at *Gearrannan* gives you a unique opportunity to immerse yourself in the island's past.

◀ The remains of Dun Carloway broch, believed to predate the birth of Christ ▶ Fields surround *Gearrannan*; traditional village blackhouses

Traigh na Beirigh
The best-kept secret on Lewis

A little-known gem awaits campers who make it to the unspoilt white sands and clear turquoise waters of the west coast of the Isle of Lewis. Here lies (whisper it…) the beautiful and remote *Traigh na Beirigh*. This collectively-owned and -run site belongs to the local villagers at neighbouring Cnip (pronounced "neep"). They formed the Cnip Village Grazing Trust in the 1990s and committed to developing the area into a proper campsite with a modern facilities block. Agnes Maclennan, the site's long-standing and lively caretaker, lives at Croft/Keep 15 on the single-track approach road. Campers can book in with her on arrival or pay their site fees when she does her rounds in the evenings.

The layout is pleasantly informal with owners of tents, tourers and motor homes simply finding a spot they like and staking their claim. Needless to say, the pitches overlooking the beach tend to go first. Its gorgeous bay is relatively sheltered and when the Scottish sun eventually decides to make an appearance it has an almost-tropical feel. Many campers bring their own kit in order to take advantage of the waterside location, and surfers and kayakers are a common sight. The freedom to gather wood and build your own campfire down on the beach is also a draw for large families and groups.

It does take some effort to reach *Traigh na Beirigh*, especially with a tourer hitched behind you. The site is thirty miles from the nearest town, Stornoway, and the last leg of the journey along a narrow single-track can be a challenge – but the spectacular location will reward your efforts.

The much-mythologised Callanish standing stones, around twenty miles inland from the site, make a fascinating day-trip. The prehistoric stones date back to 3000BC and form an unconventional Celtic cross. They look incredible on a sunny day as the rays of sunlight dance a two-step with the stone's shadows. There are also plenty of walks to enjoy in the hills surrounding the campsite and a small, private beach one-and-a-half miles further along the coast.

▼ Camping next to the turquoise sea

Practicalities

Traigh na Beirigh Campsite, 15 Cnip nr Maibhaig, Uig, Isle of Lewis, HS2 9HS ☎01851 672265

Pitches & price All grass pitches (no hook-ups). 20 for tents, 5 for tourers or motor homes, 25 reserved for the Caravan Club. £5 for a 2-person tent, £6 for a 3-person tent and £7 for a 4-person tent or larger.

Facilities Shower and toilet block. Additional sinks for washing-up.

Restrictions Groups welcome. Dogs allowed (free). Campfires permitted on the beach only.

Open May–Oct.

Getting there Leave Stornoway on the A858 heading west. After 13 miles, turn left onto the B8011 to Miabhig. This leads out to the west coast and on to the single-track road to Cnip. Check in at Croft 15 at the junction, and continue up the hill and round the corner to Traigh na Beirigh Bay and the campsite.

Uig Bay

Uig is usually associated with an unremarkable ferry terminal, but it also makes an excellent base for touring Skye's imposing northern headlands. An hour's drive takes you from Kyle of Lochalsh to Uig and on a clear day the view over the Minch and across to Harris is nothing short of spectacular. By the harbour, on the shores of Loch Snizort, is the friendly, family-run *Uig Bay*. The site's close proximity to the terminal makes it an ideal overnight stop before catching an early-morning ferry. But don't dismiss *Uig Bay* as a mere pit stop; this attractive area counts the beautiful double waterfall of the River Rha and the Clach Ard Uige (the last remaining relic of an ancient stone circle) among attractions that might entice you to stay a little longer.

On-site facilities are basic and the toilet and shower blocks are a little dated – a bizarre soundtrack of Eighties hits, interspersed with Scottish pipes, is piped into the loos. But *Uig Bay* is well-maintained with a large gravel area for tourers and motor homes and a separate camping field for tents. Campers can join guests at the owner's B&B for a Scottish breakfast at the bargain price of £4.50; just give half-an-hour's notice as it's freshly cooked.

Practicalities

Uig Bay Campsite, Uig, Isle of Skye, IV51 9XU ☎01470 542714, Ⓦwww.uig-camping-skye.co.uk
Pitches & price 45 grass pitches for tents (10 with hook-ups). 22 hard-standing pitches (20 with hook-ups). £5 per adult, £2 per child. Hook-ups £3 extra.
Facilities Toilet and shower block and a washing-up room with washer/dryer.
Restrictions No large group bookings. Campfires permitted on nearby beach. Dogs allowed (free).
Open Year round.
Getting there From Kyle of Lochalsh, continue over Skye Bridge and along the A87 until you eventually reach Uig Pier. A right turn before the start of the pier will lead you to the campsite. If you're arriving into Uig by ferry, the site is just to the left of the terminal. The National Bus Company has a stop at the terminal.

The Barn

It might be quite a palaver to reach *The Barn*, but few campers make the journey and regret it. For a start, the Westray born-and-bred Harcus family, who run the site, couldn't be more welcoming. And although this is one of Orkney's remote outer isles, you can reach the campsite using public transport. Parking your combie or pitching your tent on the lush mown grass of *The Barn*'s large open camping field is a cinch, and the excellent facilities in the farm outbuildings are a real boon in bad weather.

Outside the campsite, everything's close at hand – you can smell the bakery across the bay in Pierowall and it's a short stroll to the local shops. If you don't fancy cooking, the local pub (aka the *Pierowall Hotel*), serves fantastic fish and chips, fresh off the boats. The sea is a stone's throw away, and there are some lovely dunes just a mile or so to the northwest, not far from the substantial ruins of sixteenth-century Noltland Castle. Further afield, equipped with a good pair of boots (or a rented bike), you can check out seabirds nesting on the dramatic cliffs of Noup Head in the northwest, or the seastack of Castle o'Burrian in the southeast.

Practicalities

The Barn Campsite, Chalmersquoy, Westray, Orkney, KW17 2BZ ☎01857 677214, Ⓦwww.thebarnwestray.co.uk
Pitches & price 25 pitches: £5 per tent, £9 per caravan, plus £1.50 extra per person. 16 hook-ups, £3 extra.
Facilities Toilets and showers, a kitchen/games room, a utility room and a heated drying room.
Restrictions Dogs allowed (free). No campfires.
Open Year round.
Getting there From Kirkwall harbour on the Orkney Mainland there are 2 or 3 ro-ro ferries daily to Westray (1hr 25min). It's 7 miles from the Rapness ferry terminal on Westray to *The Barn* campsite – a minibus meets the ferry and will take you directly there. If you're bringing your own vehicle, book the ferry trip in advance with Orkney Ferries (Ⓦwww.orkneyferries.co.uk).

Rackwick

Angry seabirds and a spectacular location on Orkney

Perhaps the Orkney poet George Mackay Brown put it best: "the beauty of Rackwick struck me like a blow." It certainly is a magical, unforgettable place, but staying here is not for the faint-hearted. This is back-to-basics camping: no warden greets you on arrival, facilities are limited and it's a long way to the nearest shop, let alone the nearest pub. The setting is superb, but it's a beauty tinged with melancholy, for Rackwick was a thriving crofting and fishing village until the mid-twentieth century. The school closed in 1953, and the last fishing boat put out to sea in 1963. These days only a few houses are inhabited all year round.

Rackwick's heyday may be over, but the reason to come and camp here is simple: the location is truly awesome. It's real ends-of-the-earth stuff – a virtually empty village, at the end of a dead-end road, right by the sea, with towering red sandstone cliffs on either side, and the Scottish mainland just visible across the treacherous Pentland Firth. Even the beach has an other-worldly quality – it's made of giant, stripey sandstone pebbles that rumble ominously when waves crash onto them. Nature is writ large here, and you are only a very small part of it.

The village sits in a deserted corner of Hoy, the largest and least typical of Orkney's outer islands. While the rest of Orkney tends to be flat, sandy and fertile, Hoy is a hulking brute of an island, covered in bleak moorland and with some of the highest cliffs in Britain. *Rackwick*'s restored Burnside Bothy sports a lovely heather-thatched roof, and, beside it, a stone-walled camping area of tufty overgrown grass. Inside the bothy, campers, who are usually keen walkers and climbers, swap stories over a driftwood fire that (literally) occupies centre-stage.

Bring your own supplies to *Rackwick*, as there's no local shop, though you will find a post office and a (summer-only) café in Hoy village; you can also arrange for groceries to be brought over from Stromness on the ferry. With your own transport, you can drive down to Lyness, ten or so miles south, where there's the *Hoy Hotel* (which has a bar), a shop and a fascinating museum on the wartime history of the naval base of Scapa Flow. Be warned though, on a warm, windless summer's day the midges on Hoy can be terrible – but fortunately the wind is rarely absent.

Despite Rackwick's geographical isolation, it can get quite busy on a fine summer's day, as walkers pass through on their way to see (or climb) Orkney's most famous sea stack, the 450ft-high Old Man of Hoy. The three-hour walk to the Old Man and back is pretty straightforward, but during the breeding season it's

Practicalities

Rackwick Burnmouth Bothy & Campsite, Hoy, Orkney, KW16 3NJ Currently no telephone.

Pitches & price Space for 12 small tents, but it's rarely full, and it's easy to find another sheltered spot nearby. There's no fee, just a donations box inside the bothy.

Facilities An unusually attractive public toilet block. Campers can use the bothy, with its simple kitchen facilities (no electricity), and driftwood open fire.

Restrictions No restrictions on dogs, though keeping them on a lead is advisable as there are sheep and breeding birds in the area.

Open Year round.

Getting there Take the car ferry from Scrabster, near Thurso, to Stromness on Orkney's Mainland. A small passenger ferry runs from Stromness to Moaness Pier on Hoy, and a minibus will take you to Rackwick. Alternatively, it's an easy and beautiful, 2hr walk through the narrow gully of Berriedale. If you have a vehicle, you'll need to catch the ferry from Houton on Orkney's Mainland to Lyness on Hoy and then drive up the road to Rackwick.

enlivened by the antics of Hoy's "bonxies" – the local name for the aggressive great skuas – which nest on the moors, and dive-bomb anyone attempting to reach the Old Man. Holding a stick over your head is a sensible precaution. Hoy's hills are also home to much cuddlier mountain hares, while the cliffs are packed with nesting seabirds. Other nearby points of interest include the Dwarfie Stane, a unique chambered cairn cut from a solid block of sandstone in 3000BC, and Ward Hill (1577ft), Orkney's highest point, from which – on a clear day – there's an incredible view across the whole archipelago.

◀ On the summit of Cuilags, just north of Ward Hill ▶ The Old Man of Hoy – first climbed in 1966 – stands proud; Rackwick Bay

Ayre's Rock

If there's one thing Sanday isn't short of, it's sand, which makes it the perfect hideaway for campers looking for a beach holiday without the crowds. Like most businesses in Orkney, *Ayre's Rock* – named after the local inlet, the Noust of Ayre, not the Australian monolith – is a family enterprise. And very enterprising the Allan family have been, too, since they moved from Bristol to Sanday in 2006. Not only do they run a cute little campsite, with direct access to its own seal-strewn beach, they also have a handful of hostel rooms and two static caravans to rent, run a craft shop and heritage centre, operate a popular fish and chip business (Tues & Sat 4.30–8pm) and cook meals for lazy campers.

The site itself is grassy and safely enclosed on all sides, yet has a wonderful sandy beach immediately adjacent and a playground on site, making it a popular site for families as well as young couples. Aside from its superb golden beaches and dunes, Sanday also boasts one of Orkney's best-preserved chambered cairns, a wool farm supplied by angora rabbits and a very fetching stripey lighthouse, which occupies its own tidal island.

Practicalities

Ayre's Rock Campsite, Sanday, Orkney, KW17 2AY
☎*01857 600410,* Ⓦ*www.ayres-rock-sanday-orkney.co.uk*
Pitches & price 11 grass pitches for tents (£4–8 depending on size) and caravans (£6–8), with 4 hook-ups (£2.15 extra). 2 static caravans for hire (£25).
Facilities A kitchen, a TV lounge, showers and a washing machine.
Restrictions Dogs allowed (free). No campfires on site, but they're permitted on the adjacent beach.
Open Year round.
Getting there From Kirkwall Harbour on the Orkney Mainland there are 2 ro-ro ferries daily to Sanday (1hr 25min). It's 6 miles from the Loth ferry terminal on Sanday to *Ayre's Rock*; a minibus meets the ferry and will take you there on request. If you're bringing your own vehicle, book the ferry in advance with Orkney Ferries (Ⓦwww.orkneyferries.co.uk).

Levenwick

Levenwick campsite in Shetland is little-known and never full. This is DIY camping: you just need to pitch up and pick a spot, befriend the local ponies and then hunker down. Shetland is almost completely treeless and although the site is relatively sheltered, it can get windy, so be sure to secure your tent. They say the Shetland islands can have all four seasons in a day, but when the weather is fair, the views from Levenwick eastwards across the North Sea, with the dramatic 500ft cliffs of Noss visible to the north, are absolutely stunning.

This simple site is community-run by the nearby village of Levenwick, where you'll find a small shop for supplies. The campsite warden usually comes round to collect the money in the early evening, and will happily stay for a chat. If the warden isn't around, you simply pay in the honesty box. *Levenwick Campsite* is perfectly placed for going on a midnight boat trip to Mousa broch to see the storm petrels, for exploring the superb tombolo at St Ninian's Isle and for checking out the Iron Age dwellings (and the puffins) at Sumburgh.

Practicalities

Levenwick Campsite, Levenwick, Shetland, ZE2 9HX
☎*01950 422207*
Pitches & price 10 grass pitches for tents (£6–8 depending on size). 4 hard-standing pitches for caravans (£10), with hook-ups (£1.50 extra).
Facilities 1 toilet block, and campers can use the new laundry, kitchen and shower block, by the adjacent village hall.
Restrictions Dogs welcome but must be kept on a lead. No campfires.
Open May–Sept.
Getting there The campsite lies on the A970, which runs from Lerwick, where the ferries arrive, to Sumburgh, the location of Sheltland's main airport. There's a regular bus service to *Levenwick* campsite from both Lerwick and Sumburgh (Mon–Sat 6–8 daily; 4 on Sun).

Gardiesfauld
Next stop the North Pole

Closer to the Arctic Circle than to London, *Gardiesfauld* is located on Unst, the northernmost inhabited island in Britain. It's primarily a hostel, but campers are welcome to pitch their tents on the sloping grass that surrounds the house and use the facilities. Though the site is popular with backpackers, it's never full. As there's no resident warden, if no one's about, simply find a sheltered pitch by a bit of drystone wall, or your tent might fall victim to the island's powerful winds. Unst can claim the UK's highest recorded wind speed – 177mph measured by an anemometer on Saxa Vord mountain (936ft) in 1962, before the equipment blew away – so secure your guy ropes!

Campers visiting Unst in June or July will be treated to what the locals refer to as the "simmer dim", when it's almost always light both day and night – like the midnight sun, only with dodgy weather. On the theme of which, there are several wet-weather options on the island, from the Unst Boat Haven, with its beautifully presented collection of historic sailing craft, to Unst's

supremely ugly former RAF base, now home to, among other things, the island brewery and chocolate factory.

If you've made it as far as Unst, you should definitely make the pilgrimage to Hermaness, the peninsula at the tip of the island, partly to view the thousands of nesting seabirds (from gannets to guillemots), but mostly to look across the sea to the wonderfully named Muckle Flugga lighthouse, and Out Stack, the two most northerly bits of Britain. You can reach both points by walking – while trying to avoid being dive-bombed by "bonxies" (or great skuas) – or hold onto your stomach and brave a boat trip.

▼ Bluebell season at *Gardiesfauld*

Practicalities

Gardiesfauld Hostel, Uyeasound, Unst, Shetland, ZE2 9DW ☎01957 755279, Ⓦwww.gardiesfauld.shetland.co.uk

Pitches & price Around 20 pitches. £6–9 per tent, plus works under way to provide hard-standing pitches and hook-ups for 4 caravans.

Facilities Excellent toilet and shower facilities, kitchen, lounge, drying room and washing machine.

Restrictions No dogs. No campfires.

Open April–Sept.

Getting there From Lerwick, Shetland's capital and ferry port, it's about 40 miles north to Unst as the seagull flies. You have to take 2 ferries: one from Toft (mainland) to Ulsta (Yell) and then one from Gutcher (Yell) to Belmont (Unst). *Gardiesfauld* is on the main road from Belmont to Baltasound. A bus will take you from Lerwick all the way to the hostel door.

End matter

Directory

Planning makes perfect, and these websites and forums should help you do just that. We've included user-review sites, official organizations, government bodies and websites that simply offer great advice on camping in the UK and beyond, as well as an assortment of Britain's main outdoors stockists.

Reviews and forums

Ⓦwww.thehappycampers.co.uk Great selection of listings, user reviews and forum topics on this engaging it-never-rains-when-we're-camping website. Also has recipes, tips and ideas for games and activities.

Ⓦwww.campingforums.org.uk or Ⓦwww.thecampingforum.co.uk Not much between these two. The former is more UK-focused, while the latter covers camping in the UK and some other European countries.

Ⓦwww.guardian.co.uk/travel/camping Lots of general camping tips and articles, plus good UK-based information. The *Telegraph* (Ⓦwww.telegraph.co.uk/travel/campingholidays) is also a worthy resource.

Ⓦwww.pitchup.com Slick and extensive. Lists over 5000 UK and Ireland sites, and offers extensive filtering options and a growing number of user-generated reviews.

Ⓦwww.scottishcamping.com Excellent directory, plus user reviews of campsites and caravan parks in Scotland.

Ⓦwww.tripadvisor.com User reviews, often from the grumpier end of the spectrum. The larger sites usually have a few comments.

Ⓦwww.ukcampsite.co.uk Best used for its users' campsite reviews – of which there are a good number – but also includes advice and gear reviews.

Ⓦwww.youcamp.co.uk A bit sparse on content as we went to press, but has videos of sites and gear reviews.

Useful organizations

Ⓦwww.thebmc.co.uk The British Mountaineering Council, with information on England and Wales.

Ⓦwww.campingandcaravanningclub.co.uk Comprehensive guide to camping and caravanning, with over 1400 UK campsite listings. They also run over a hundred sites; members get special rates.

Ⓦwww.caravanclub.co.uk Listings, tips and advice aimed at caravanners. Members get special rates.

Ⓦwww.forestholidays.co.uk The accommodation arm of the UK Forestry Commission, running 24 sites across the UK.

Ⓦwww.mcofs.org.uk The Mountaineering Council of Scotland; advice and discussions on mountain climbing and walks.

Ⓦwww.nationalcaravan.co.uk The National Caravan Council; a good resource for information on caravanning in the UK.

Ⓦwww.nationalparks.gov.uk Check the "Visiting" section for camping-specific information.

Ⓦwww.nationaltrust.org.uk Search for "camping and caravanning" to find out more about staying at any of the National Trust's fifty camping or touring sites. See Ⓦwww.nts.org.uk for the equivalent information in Scotland.

Ⓦwww.outdooraccess-scotland.com Detailed information and guidance on the Scottish Outdoor Access Code, legislation and contacts; useful for wild camping.

Ⓦwww.ramblers.org.uk The UK's largest walking charity, with branches for Scotland and Wales, and an excellent source for walking itineraries; check the "Accommodation" section for campsite listings.

Ⓦwww.undiscoveredscotland.co.uk Excellent resource for finding out more about everything from the smallest of Scottish villages to the largest towns and cities.

Camping lifestyle and advice

Ⓦwww.campingexpert.co.uk Not a bad place to start looking for entry-level advice.

Ⓦwww.the-camping-manual.com Reads slightly like somebody's no-nonsense parents laying down the rules, but very thorough, with tips on everything from choosing a tent to camping games.

Ⓦwww.campr.co.uk Professional site with plenty of information on equipment, camping life and festival camping as well as some campsite reviews.

Ⓦwww.chuckwagondiner.com US-based site with a lengthy list of recipes and cooking methods, suitable for most camping trips.

Ⓦwww.go-camping.org Its advice and tips on everything from sleeping bags to camping with children are sometimes painfully obvious, but sound if you're a first-timer.

Ⓦwww.lovetheoutdoors.com US-focused site, but with plenty of information – tips, tricks, recipes, planning tools – applicable to UK camping.

Ⓦwww.netmums.com/holidays/Camping.646 Everything from camping with children to recipes, equipment tips, checklists and campsite reviews. Ⓦwww.mumsnet.com/travel/camping offers similar information.

Ⓦwww.scoutorama.com/recipe Nearly 500 recipes, all said to be contributed by the global Scouting community.

Festivals

Ⓦwww.efestivals.co.uk A thorough guide to all things festival for the UK; good for line-up rumours.

Ⓦwww.joe-bananas.co.uk A pick-your-camping-gear service for festivals. You collect the goods from a stall on arrival.

Ⓦwww.tangerinefields.co.uk Book pre-pitched tents, yurts, tipis and other equipment, depending on the festival.

Stockists

www.albioncanvas.co.uk Handmade yurts, tipis and geodesic domes, all made from locally sourced and sustainable materials.

www.alpkit.com More into alpine activities than anything, but sells some attractive, well-designed camping gear, and has a neat backstory. Online only.

www.army-surplus.org.uk Offers a slew of decently priced, no-frills camping equipment (but no tents), much of it in that charming shade of olive green.

www.armytents.co.uk A commanding presence once set up – but you're going to need a car to lug any of these heavier canvas tents around. Shop in Bedford, by appointment only.

www.blacks.co.uk Tents, sleeping bags, furniture and more, on a high street near you.

www.camperlands.co.uk Caters mostly to caravan and motor home users, but has a good range of tents, stoves and other accessories. Shop in Manchester.

www.campingworld.co.uk Huge range of camping and caravan equipment. Shop near Farnham.

www.cotswoldoutdoor.com A decent selection of tents, gear, clothes and outdoor kit at this major retailer.

www.decathlon.co.uk This sports superstore offers cheap camping gear, although the range is dominated by their own brand, Quechua. Six UK stores.

www.ellis-brigham.com Mountain-sports specialists since 1933, stocking high-end camping equipment. Seventeen shops across UK.

www.fieldandtrek.com All the usual kit, from this branch of the massive Sports Direct empire.

www.foxsoutdoor.co.uk Started as a "Men's Outfitters", post-Suez crisis. Fifty-odd years later, it's still going, offering a solid range of camping and walking gear. Shop in Amersham.

www.gooutdoors.co.uk All manner of camping and caravanning gear, competitively priced. Sixteen locations in UK.

www.hikebikeandride.com Will appeal mostly to the cyclist who needs to stock up on bike gear. Very comprehensive selection, but online only. Has a service/repair shop and offers weekend biking holidays from shop in Hathersage, Peak District National Park.

www.itchyfeet.com Great range of camping and general outdoor equipment. Shops in London and Bath.

www.littleadventureshop.co.uk Good selection of outdoor and camping gear and clothing – including sleeping bags – all for kids. Online only.

www.lovingoutdoors.co.uk Check the "Outdoors" section of this online-only retailer for camping gear. The big pull? Free postage on every item, regardless of size.

www.millets.co.uk Affordable camping kit without the glitz. Branches on many UK high streets.

www.nevisport.com Rock climbing and mountaineering are a speciality, but its camping equipment is worth a look. Six shops in northern England, seven in Scotland.

www.nomadtravel.co.uk Impressive range of tents and other gear you'd need for any level of camping trip. Shops in London, Bishop's Stortford, Bristol, Southampton and Manchester.

www.outdoorcampingstore.co.uk Huge selection of stock helps keep the prices low at this online-only camping specialist.

www.outdoorkit.co.uk Over 2000 outdoor products, including a great range of tents and other camping accessories. Shop in St Albans.

www.outdoormegastore.co.uk Claims to be the "biggest online camping equipment retailer in the UK". If you can get past the irritating line in alliteration sprinkled through the website, you'll find some very competitively priced gear.

www.outdoorworlddirect.co.uk Camping and water-sports gear from this West Yorkshire-based retailer. Shop in Huddersfield.

www.penroseoutdoors.co.uk Good for tents and sleeping bags; also sells new and used folding campers and trailer tents. Shop in Truro.

www.raymears.com A bit niche for the casual camper, but there's some neat gear on offer here. And who wouldn't trust Ray when it comes to the outdoors?

www.robertsaunders.co.uk Does one thing and does it well: lightweight tents.

www.ryedalerambler.com Extensive selection of camping and general outdoor gear, right on the edge of the North York Moors National Park. Shop in Pickering.

www.simplyhike.co.uk Another one-stop shop for all your camping needs, whether a first-time camper or an old pro. Shop in Whitstable.

www.singersoutdoors.co.uk Lancashire-based outdoor experts with excellent range of tents and other camping equipment. Shops in Preston, Chorley and Wigan.

www.snowandrock.com Skiing and climbing specialists, but with (sometimes pricey) tents, sleeping bags and accessories. Nineteen shops across UK.

www.summits.co.uk Scottish retailer offering camping and outdoors equipment including inflatable kayaks and dinghies. Shops in Paisley, Stirling and Dunfermline.

www.tauntonleisure.com Good selection of tents and camping accessories. Shops in Taunton, Bristol and Exeter.

www.tentipi.co.uk It's a tipi. It's Swedish. It's rather pricey.

www.tiso.com Massive selection from a retailer that's been in the business for nearly fifty years. Eleven shops across Scotland, one each in Newcastle and Belfast.

www.towsure.com A caravan-equipment bonanza; also has a good camping-gear and outdoor-clothing section. Shops in Sheffield, Halesowen and Southampton.

www.webtogs.co.uk Camping and outdoor equipment from an online-only retailer who uses "carbon-neutral delivery".

www.worldoftents.co.uk Does what it says on the tin, plus sells other camping and caravanning equipment.

www.yeomansoutdoors.co.uk Wide selection of tents and camping equipment in over seventy stores across UK. Also operates "camping exhibitions", with up to a hundred tents on display – great for hands-on comparison shopping.

Picture credits

© Kevin Richardson/Photolibrary. p.180 Cae Du Campsite © James Stewart. p.182 Eco Retreats sign © James Stewart. p.183 Eco retreats Tipi © Eco Retreats Campsite. p.184 Owen Tyddyn Farm © James Stewart. p.186 Graig Wen sign © James Stewart. p.187 Yurt © Graig Wen Campsite, Graig Wen Campsite © James Stewart. p.188 Hafod y Llan © James Stewart. p.189 Llyn Gwynant © Llyn Gwynant. p.190 Shell Island campsite © James Stewart. p.191 Crabbing © James Stewart; Shell Island © James Stewart. p.193 Retreat Campsite © James Stewart. p.194 View of Pen Y Pass © Dave Porter/ Photolibrary. p.195 Cae Du campsite © James Stewart; Caernarfon Castle © Diana Jarvis/Rough Guides. p.198 Gwern Gof Isaf © James Stewart

Northwest England
p.200–203 Fairsnap and Totridge Fells © Eli Pascall-Willis/Alamy. p.205 Birch Bank © Seb Bacon. p.206 Cheshire's highest Hill © Fran Halsall/ Photolibrary. p.208 Middle Beardshaw © Seb Bacon. p.209 Wycoller Bridge © Seb Bacon; Dining Hall, Middle Beardshaw © Seb Bacon. p.211 Crawshaw Farm © Seb Bacon; p.212 Ladys Slipper Orchid © Graham Ella/Alamy. p.213 Sunset over Morecambe Bay © Jon Sparks/Alamy; Leighton Moss RSPB © Robin Weaver/ Alamy. p.214 Dolphinholme © Seb Bacon. p.216 Kirk Michael churchyard © Seb Bacon. p.217 Jurby Junk © Seb Bacon; Contrary Head, Peel © Holmes Garden Photos/Alamy

Yorkshire
p.218 Stone Farm building in the Yorkshire Dales © Dave Porter/ Photolibrary. p.222 Holmfirth © Steven Gillis hd9 imaging/Alamy. p.223 View over Holmfirth and Holme Valley © Ian Dagnall/Alamy; National Coal Mining Museum © National Coal Mining Museum. p.224 Hebden Bridge © Andy Stothert/Photolibrary. p.226 Gordale Scar © Alf Alderson. p.227 Straw stalactites in Battlefield Cavern © Robbie Shone/White Scar Caves; Malham Cove © iStock. p.229 Mountain Biking Nidderdale © Tom Broadbent/Alamy. p.230 Park Lodge © Alf Alderson. p.231 Swaledale Sheep walking through purple heather © David Forster/Alamy; Walking in Muker near Swaledale © Christina Bollen/Alamy; Park Lodge © Alf Alderson. p.232 Bainbridge Ings © Alf Alderson. p.233 Mountain biker on the North

Yorkshire Moors © Wig Worland/ Alamy; Wensleydale Creamery © Mike Kipling Photography/Alamy. p.235 Rippon Cathedral © Wojtek Buss/ Photolibrary. p.236 Masons Campsite © Alf Alderson. p.237 The Strid, near Bolton Abbey © Jason Friend/ Alamy; Cows at Bolton Abbey © Mike Kipling Photography/Alamy. p.238 York Minster © Tim Draper/Rough Guides. p.240 Sunk Island © Alf Alderson. p.242 Caravans at La Rosa © Alf Alderson. p.243 Interior at La Rosa © Alf Alderson; La Rosa Campsite © La Rosa Campsite. p.244 Pinewood Tipis © Pinewood Campsite

Cumbria and the Lakes
p.246 Wast Water, Lake District © Joe Cornish/Photolibrary. p.250 Low Wray campsite © Helena Smith. p.251 Low Wray's entrance © Helena Smith; Wray Castle © NDP/Alamy. p.252 Hawkshead School © Tony West/ Photolibrary. p.253 Boats for hire on Windemere © Thierry Bouzac/ Photolibrary. p.254 Full Circle Yurts © Helena Smith. p.255 Interior of Yurt © Full Circle Yurts; Rydal Hall © Helena Smith. p.256 Bays Brown Campsite © Helena Smith. p.257 Turner Hall Campsite © Helena Smith. p.258 Great Langdale Campsite © Helena Smith. p.259 Old Dungeon Ghyll Hotel © Helena Smith; Waterfall near Langdale Fell © Jason Friend/Photolibrary. p.260 Train near Fisherground Campsite © Helena Smith. p.261 Hardknott Roman Fort © Gr. Richardson/ Photolibrary; Fisherground Campsite © Fisherground Campsite. p.264 Old Post Office Campsite © Helena Smith. p.265 Wasdale Yurt Holidays © Helena Smith. p.266 Barn Door Campsite © Helena Smith. p.267 Seathwaite Campsite © Helena Smith. p.268 Wastwater from Greendale © Val Corbett/Photolibrary. p.269 Wasdale Campsite © Helena Smith; Scafell Pike © James Osmond/Photolibrary. p.270 Syke Farm © Helena Smith. p.272 Grange in Autumn © Derek Croucher/Alamy. p.273 Bowder Stone © Simon Whaley/Alamy; Hollows Farm © Helena Smith. p.275 Gillside © Helena Smith. p.277 Side Farm © Helena Smith. p.278 Pod at Quiet Site © Quiet Site. p.279 Quiet Site © Helena Smith, Aira Force © John Prior Images/Alamy. p.280 Ullswater boathouse © Gerry Adcock/Alamy. p.281 Sykeside © Helena Smith

Northeast England
p.282 Hadrian's Wall, Northumbria © Dave Porter/Photolibrary. p.286 Highside Farm toilet block © Highside Farm. p.287 Highside Farm sign © Highside Farm; High Force Waterfall © Highside Farm. p.288 Bowes Museum © Jeff Greenberg/Alamy. p.290 Hadrian's Wall © Tim Draper/ Rough Guides. p.291 Hadrian's Wall Campsite © Hadrians Wall Campsite; Wall view of Hadrian's Wall © iStock. p.292 Bikes at Kielder Forest © Mark Pinder/Kielder castle forest park. p.294 Dunstanburgh Castle © iStock. p.295 Ripples in sand, Embleton Bay © Lesley Jacques/iStock; Proctors Stead Caravan Park © Proctors Stead Caravan Park. p.296 Dunstan Hill Campsite © Dunstan Hill Campsite. p.297 Puffin © Susan Leonard/iStock. p.298 Budle Bay © Graeme Peacock/ Alamy. p.299 Lindisfarne Priory © Roger Coulam/Photolibrary

The Lowlands
p.300 Walkers in Scotland © Aliki image library/Alamy. p.304 Culzean Castle © Rolf Richardson/Alamy. p.305 Burns Cottage © Ian Paterson/ Alamy; Culzean Golf © Paul Bock/ Alamy; Culzean Castle Campsite © Ally Thompson. p.307 Brighouse Bay © Ally Thompson. p.308 Mabie Forest © South West Images Scotland/Alamy. p.309 Mountain biker, Mabie Forest © Jon Sparks/Alamy. Shower and loo blocks © Marthrown Campsite. p.310 Solway Firth © Gary Cook/ Alamy. p.314 Barny Take off © Caerlaverrock Campsite. p.315 Caerlaverrock Wetlands © Ally Thompson; Caerlaverrock Castle © Ally Thompson. p.317 Mains Farm © Ally Thompson. p.318 Lochouses © Ally Thompson

The Highlands
p.320 Buchaille Etive Moor, Glen Coe © Rod Edwards/Photolibrary. p.324 Beinglas Farm © Ally Thompson. p.325 Hiking Loch Lomond © David Chadwick/iStock. p.326 Luss C&CC © Ally Thompson. p.327 View of Kenmore and Loch Tay © BL Images Ltd/Alamy. p.328 Hammocks at Comrie Croft Site © George Sloan. p.329 Comrie Croft in the snow © George Sloan; Pheasant © George Sloan. p.331 Oban Caravan and Camping Park © Andy Stothert/ Photolibrary. p.332 Strathfillan Wigwams © Ally Thompson. p.333 Signpost © Ally Thompson; The Trading Post © Ally Thompson, Splash White

Water Rafting © www.rafting.co.uk. p.334 Invercoe Caravan and Camping © Andy Stothert/Photolibrary. p.335 Caolasnacon © Caolasnacon campsite. p.336 Cow and Calf © Glengoulandie Campsite. p.338 Rothiemurchus © John Macpherson/Alamy. p.339 Mountain biking © Doug Houghton/ Alamy; Camping by the Burn © Ally Thompson. p.342 Morayshire coast © Fergus Mackay/Alamy. p.344 Lazy Duck Pond © David Dean/Lazy Duck Campsite. p.345 Red Squirrel © Matthew Doggett/Alamy; Lazy Duck Campsite © Lazy Duck Campsite. p.346 Camusdarach © Camusdarach campsite. p.347 Morvich © Ally Thompson. p.348 Loch Ness © Chloe Roberts. p.350 Plockton and Loch Carron © Derek Croucher/ Alamy. p.351 Applecross Site © Ally Thompson; Sheep, Applecross © Peter Thompson/Photolibrary. p.353 Clachtoll Beach © Iain Sarjeant/ Photolibrary

Scottish Islands
p.354 Inner Hebrides © Lee Beel/ Photolibrary. p.358 Glen Rosa © Ally Thompson. p.359 Lochranza © Ally Thompson. p.361 Calgary Bay © Ally Thompson. p.362 Tobermory Campsite © Ally Thompson. p.363 Tobermory © Charles Bowman/ Photolibrary. p.364 Glenbrittle © Cody Duncan/Alamy. p.366 Dun Carloway Broch © John Peter Photography/Alamy. p.367 Gearrannan © Ally Thompson; Gearrannan Village © Gearrannan. p.368 Traigh Na Beirigh © Ally Thompson. p.370 Hoy, Orkney Isles © Gareth McCormack/Alamy. p.371 The Rock Tower © Bernard Van Dierendonck/Photolibrary; Rackwick Bay © Doug Houghton/Alamy. p.373 Gaudiesfauld © Gauldiesfauld

Features
p.28 Woman in sleeping bag © Phillip and Karen Smith/Getty; Guy rope detail © Diana Jarvis; Headtorch detail © Diana Jarvis; Boy with kit © Pauline St Denis/Photolibrary. p.84 Barefoot Yurts © Robin Mayes. p.196 Coasteering near St Davids © www.luddingtonmarine.co.uk. p.262 Camping in the Ogwen Valley © Paul Harris/Photolibrary. p.312 Crowds at Camp Bestival © Diana Jarvis/Rough Guides; Couple at Camp Bestival © Diana Jarvis/Rough Guides; Sheep © Diana Jarvis; Festival © Diana Jarvis. p.340 Wild camping on Scaraster beach © Tim Jones/Alamy

Over 100 award-winning camp sites

The Camping and Caravanning Club
The Friendly Club

FROM THE CAMPING AND CARAVANNING CLUB
NEW TO CAMPING

Cannock Club Site

If you love camping as much as we do, you'll love staying on one of The Camping and Caravanning Club's 109 UK Club Sites. Each of our sites are in great locations and are an ideal base for exploring the UK.

There's just one thing: once you've discovered the friendly welcome, the excellent facilities and clean, safe surroundings, you'll probably want to join anyway!

To book your adventure or to join The Club

call **0845 130 7633**

quoting code **2851** or visit

www.thecampingandcaravanningclub.co.uk/info

- More choice of highly maintained, regularly inspected sites
- Friendly sites that are clean and safe, so great for families
- Preferential rates – recoup your membership fee in just 6 nights' stay
- Reduced site fees for 55's and over and special deals for families
- Exclusive Member Services including specialist insurance and advice

CAMPING DESIGNED FOR YOU

WHY COMPROMISE AT THE CAMPSITE?

Discover a tent style that is just right for your family in the new Coleman® tent range.

Fusing practical designs with Coleman® expertise, the range offers a wealth of flexible configurations with podded bedrooms and large living areas that are a perfect fit for today's family camper.

RIVERSIDE™ 9

RIVERSIDE™ 6

The new Riverside™ range offers removable, separate bedrooms and a large living area to provide a more relaxed family break.

The tents are subjected to a rigorous testing programme, ensuring your family's protection from the elements.

WATERFALL™ 5

The new Waterfall™ 5 features a large living area and spacious bedroom offering comfort on any family camping trip.

For further information visit www.coleman.eu

LET'S GO OUTSIDE

Coleman
The Outdoor Company™

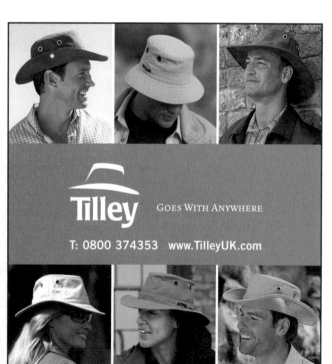

TENT
flask
MALLET
stove JACKET
boots GO

COME OUT AND PLAY

Regatta clothing – great outdoors

It's called the *great* outdoors for a reason – so grab your gear and get out there! Regatta jackets, fleeces, trousers, rucksacks, boots and wellies are exceptional value and will last camping trip after camping trip.

Look out for us in all good outdoor and camping shops or visit regatta.com

DESIGNED
BY
ELITE
MEDICAL
PROFESSIONALS

FOR SURVIVING ADVENTURE

ADVENTURERS, MOUNTAINEERS AND INDEPENDENT
TRAVELLERS WILL REGULARLY FIND THEMSELVES OFF
THE BEATEN TRACK. IF INJURIES ARE SUSTAINED IN THIS
ENVIRONMENT IT IS ESSENTIAL TO HAVE THE SPECIALISED
KIT TO HAND WHICH WON'T LET YOU DOWN.

LIFESYSTEMS FIRST AID KITS ARE DESIGNED BY ELITE
MEDICAL PROFESSIONALS TO PERFORM IN EVERY
ENVIRONMENT. THE FIRST AID KITS ARE EACH INDIVIDUALLY
DESIGNED AND TAILORED TO SUIT YOUR NEEDS. WHETHER
ON AN ARCTIC EXPEDITION, A GAP YEAR OR A SUNDAY
WALK LIFESYSTEMS WILL MAKE SURE YOU ARE
CARRYING THE BEST KIT FOR EVERY SITUATION.

FOR MORE INFORMATION VISIT

WWW.LIFESYSTEMS.CO.UK

Index